DECADES OF DISCONTENT

DECADES OF DISCONTENT

The Women's Movement, 1920–1940

EDITED, WITH AN INTRODUCTION AND

A NEW FOREWORD, BY

LOIS SCHARF and JOAN M. JENSEN

Northeastern University Press • Boston

Northeastern University Press edition 1987

Copyright © 1983 by Lois Scharf and Joan M. Jensen
DECADES OF DISCONTENT: THE WOMEN'S MOVEMENT, 1920–1940
Lois Scharf and Joan M. Jensen, Eds.,
Originally published by Greenwood Press, Inc., Westport, Conn.

Library of Congress Cataloging-in-Publication Data

Decades of discontent

    Bibliography: p.
    Includes index.
    1. Feminism—United States—History—20th century.
2. Women—United States—History—20th century.
3. Women in politics—United States—History—20th
century.   I. Scharf, Lois.   II. Jensen, Joan M.
HQ1426.D39   1987   305.4'2'0973   86-28573
ISBN 1–55553–013–3 (pbk. : alk. paper)

Printed and bound by Edwards Brothers, Inc.,
Lillington, North Carolina. The paper is Warrens
1854, an acid-free sheet.

MANUFACTURED IN THE UNITED STATES OF AMERICA
91 90 89 88 87   5 4 3 2 1

To Victor and to John

Contents

Illustrations

Tables

Preface

From the perspective of twentieth-century feminism, the years covered by this volume were, indeed, decades of discontent. From the vantage point of the historiography of American women, the same description is not inappropriate. Any historian who compiles a bibliography of monographs and articles on women between the wars is immediately struck by the dearth of material.

In 1978, both editors of this volume presented versions of their articles, revised and reprinted herein, at professional conferences. Since they each shared their respective platforms with colleagues whose topics were chronologically related, the outlines of a collection of articles to address the serious scholarly gap became immediately apparent. What follows is a tribute to the growing field of women's history itself, recognition of a rapidly building network of scholars with shared interests, and evidence of the firm friendship and fruitful collaboration which has grown between the coeditors, separated by more than half a continent.

L.S.
J.M.J.

Foreword to the 1987 edition

In the introduction to the first edition of *Decades of Discontent* we asked many questions about the years from 1920 to 1940. Why were these years seemingly a time of great individual achievement, yet a time of great opposition to women in their quest for equality? How could it be that women individually challenged the physical limitations attributed to them, while women collectively suffered inferior health care, physical abuse, and continually diminished value as human beings?

We wondered at the ways in which women found themselves at odds with each other. Sometimes, the same single women moving into new occupations were the ones opposing the right of married women to work outside their homes. Even though a black women's movement emerged in politics, white women seldom championed their causes until the late 1930s. The War Department was able to recruit women, such as the Daughters of the American Revolution, to oppose the feminist pacifists who challenged the war-making powers of men. Women realized that their common identity as women was flawed by racial, ethnic, class, and ideological differences. Even leaders of organized, middle-class white reformers clashed over programs, especially protective legislation for women.

Despite the contradictions, the years between World War I and World War II were ones of great political and economic change for women. More single women worked for a longer part of their lives, while married, middle-income women began to move into wage work. Women used their votes to support peace initiatives, to elect other women campaigning for office, and to expand their political rights after the Supreme Court's narrow interpretation of the nineteenth amendment. Women wrote, organized, and challenged the male-dominated system of politics in new ways. These were years in which not just individual women, but organized women, made a mark on society.

All these contradictory themes have made it difficult for historians to generalize about the years from 1920 to 1940. That task remains almost as difficult today as it did when this book was first published four years ago. Historians have not thoroughly investigated the lives of women to give us an accurate picture of the "new woman." They have not explained why some women fled to Europe to join expatriate communities or how those fared who remained in the "Bohemian" enclaves that existed in most major cities of the United States. There are few studies comparable to those of Winifred Wandersee, Dolores Janiewski, and Rosalinda González to explain how uneven economic development affected women of different regions and classes.

Historians have been unable to develop effective theories and methodologies for the analysis of popular culture, including the images of women. The analysis of popular culture remains difficult owing to inadequate methodological tools. The question, why and how were the aspirations of women to define their own images blocked in various ethnic groups, remains unanswered. How applicable were the male images of women for women? Is it possible that women used images for empowerment in a fashion that baffles historians? What methods can historians utilize to recreate these crucial contexts, since the context of popular culture is so critical?

Our questions have multiplied as research in women's history has broadened and deepened in recent years. New sources, methodologies, and theories applicable to other areas in women's history have opened up opportunities for more studies in this era of history. Yet, these studies have produced few new interpretations about women in the years between the two world wars.

There are indications that the limited research in this period of women's history will soon end. Scholars are now beginning to address questions posed in this book. During the next few years, biographies and assessments of women's influence on politics, parties, and unions will be published. We will know more about radicals like Agnes Smedley, liberals like Eleanor Roosevelt, chicanas in the California labor movement, rural women's struggles, and political organizing of urban middle-class women in the 1920s and 1930s.

We feel this volume will continue to serve scholars and students although new studies will help define the momentous changes in the decades between the wars. It will provide an overview and an introduction to this period—so close and yet so distant—which seems difficult to understand. It will also provide a beginning place for those who wish to expand their knowledge of the individuals who struggled and the movements fueled by women. Although this volume charts only a few of the changes in the interwar period, it provides an introduction to women's first decades as citizens with voting rights, the debates over how to fashion public policy, and the ways that ethnicity, race, and class intersected with gender as women sought identity and change.

This new paperback edition will make the debates over women's history more easily available. It will encourage students to ponder, discuss, and challenge traditional views of the roaring twenties and the destitute thirties. We need to analyze further for whom and to what extent were these the decades of discontent. We therefore invite our readers to join in the search.

DECADES OF DISCONTENT

Introduction

JOAN M. JENSEN AND
_____ LOIS SCHARF _____

Why call the twenty years from 1920 to 1940 decades of discontent?

Certainly not because women as individuals were failures during that time. Never before had so many individual women accomplished so much: Willa Cather, Ellen Glasgow, Zora Neale Hurston, Lillian Hellman, Margaret Mead, Agnes Smedley, and Gertrude Stein as writers; Isadora Duncan, Billie Holiday, and Katharine Hepburn as performers; Georgia O'Keeffe and Dorothea Lange as visual artists; Frances Perkins and Mary McLeod Bethune as administrators; Eleanor Roosevelt as a unique political leader; Amelia Earhart as pilot; Gertrude Ederle as athlete; Margaret Sanger and Jane Addams as international reformers. A list of famous, strong, and achieving women of this period is long and varied. We are, in fact, only now beginning to appreciate the diversity and creativity of American women at this time. Their accomplishments are evidence of the wide range of activities in which women engaged.

American women of these years consciously challenged limits on their physical autonomy as few had done earlier. Margaret Sanger helped expand sexual limits for middle-class women with her continued advocacy of birth control, while women like Gertrude Stein tested the boundaries of their sexuality by living as lesbians and writing about their experiences. Gertrude Ederle swam the English channel. Agnes Smedley became a war correspondent and returned from the Chinese civil war broken in health. Amelia Earhart never returned from her flight in the Pacific.[1]

Besides new challenges to their physical limitations, women also left an unprecedented number of artifacts testifying to their creativity. Katharine Hepburn's film portrayals of independent career women; Billie Holiday's blues records; Dorothea Lange's photographs of farm women; Georgia O'Keeffe's giant flowers on canvas; and Zora Neale Hurston's brilliant record of black life in Florida are all enduring records of women's creativity in this period.[2]

Why, then, call these decades of discontent?

There was discontent because of the great contradictions that clashed in the background of the historical stage upon which these women performed so brilliantly. The purpose of this book is to take a closer look at these conflicts, probing some corners of women's lives, not as individuals but in

groups as they faced contradictions and paradoxes. The economic structure, the political institutions, and the social ideology all made it possible
for individual women to achieve. The same conditions made it difficult for
the women's movement to either maintain its strength or expand as an
organized group committed to social change in opposition to the established
order. These selections attempt to locate patterns that will help explain the
faltering of a movement which had made such impressive gains in the years
before 1920.

The paradoxes that mark these years touched every aspect of the female
experience. While limits on sexuality were challenged, they were also
reinforced. Contraceptive failures increased as expectations rose. The
search for safe abortion became more desperate. Criticism of traditional
sexual abstinence abated, and large numbers of women abandoned single,
celibate lives only to encounter the uncertainty of contraceptive techniques
and the fear of "problem pregnancy."[3] While assured control of sexuality
remained elusive, so did women's freedom to use their bodies in other ways.
The army blocked creation of a Women's Army Corps during the period.
Officials refused to allow women to become military pilots and have just
now recognized those who served during World War II. The Olympics
limited events in which women could compete. Denied physical autonomy
in these ways, women were still encouraged to display their bodies in public
spectacles like the Miss America pageant. The lines between physical or
sexual freedom and exploitation could easily dissolve.[4]

Contrasts and contradictions increased in areas of physical health and
safety as life in rural areas became more remote from social services and
urban living dissolved female support networks. Hunger and malnutrition
stalked the rural poor throughout many of these years. Medical care was
insufficient as states phased out the grannie midwives who had serviced the
rural poor, and doctors remained in the cities. Infant mortality remained
high among poor black, white, and Hispanic peoples because of unsafe
water and inadequate rural public health programs. Women who had
carried, birthed, and nourished infants in poverty saw them slip away
before they reached their first birthdays.[5]

Physical abuse of women privately in families and publicly on streets
continued and perhaps increased, generally defying attempts at quantifica-
tion. Beatings, incest, and rape went officially unnoticed within families
along with more public physical intimidations and sexual harassment. The
fear of physical abuse encircled and restricted the lives of most ordinary
women. Minority women were less safe than white women, but all took
precautions and lived defensively. Women could not dispense with protectors during these years. Brothers, husbands, lovers, and pimps continued to
provide protection. Women could still seldom be alone in public places.[6]
For those women who wanted to become artistically productive, male
protectors were also necessary. Women writers were categorized as
"flowers." They were expected to provide small and fragile works of art but

were criticized if they worked on a small scale. When Georgia O'Keeffe began to paint her large flowers — people would not have paid attention to small ones, she later observed — she transcended the metaphor of the creative woman as "flower" in a way that awed and disturbed many critics.[7]

Women were not only characterized as flowers but also as doves. Yet when they displayed leadership in challenging the hawkishness of some Americans, they encountered furious resistance. The only political difference that social scientists have been able to find between men and women in these years is women's persistent pacifism, yet a total war climaxed the period. The peace movement, while enormously powerful and influential during the interwar years, fluttered to the ground before the onslaught of fascism and the inability of politicians to find alternatives to war. Institutional support for women's concerns seemed to fail at every level. Their equality as public beings found little acceptance in ideology or practice.[8]

As Estelle Freedman points out in her historiographic review of the 1920s, the flapper was the dominant image of the "new woman." The flapper became the symbol of female emancipation, of a new freedom in manners and morals. Yet historians often confused the illusion of reality transmitted through ideology for the reality itself, assuming that the emergence of the image of yet another "new woman" reflected the real lives of women. The concept of the flapper was a confusing one, ideally suited to mistaking liberation in clothes and behavior for political and social power. The flapper began to appear before World War I at both ends of the class spectrum, in the dance craze among young upper-class women and among the working-class women who imitated them and who were already being identified as "flappers." As so often seems to be the case with terms applied to women, the word had come from reference to young birds. A flapper, once defined as a young wild duck or partridge just out of the nest, became in the 1920s a young woman playing at sophistication. She was, most often, a single young working woman whose consumer tastes exceeded her meager income.[9]

The image of this new single woman in the 1920s in the movies was, as Mary Ryan notes, one of physical freedom, lack of parental interference, sexual awareness but not gratification, and escape from routinized work into marriage. While these film images reconciled women to their lot of work, home, and consumer activities, they also depicted young working women free from the obligation to contribute to the family economy. This was perhaps the most important change in the image of young women — that they were depicted working independently outside the home before marriage. Earlier images of women had attempted to contain both married and single women within a larger category of familial responsibility. As the gap between the roles of single and married women widened and became more contradictory, the old monolithic image of women broke into two distinct images — the first a model of public activity for the single woman, the second a model of domesticity for married women. The transition from one role to the other was papered over with an increasingly apocalyptic view of romantic love.[10]

In the nineteenth century, Louisa May Alcott's *Little Women* had responded to an earlier contradiction in familial responsibility of young women brought on by industrialization and the Civil War. Those conflicts were resolved in favor of familial duties and submission to expected roles after a period of extreme personal conflict. For the flapper, familial duties disappeared. There was no conflict with her family before marriage. All potential conflict focused on the heterosexual relationships as single middle-class women, economically free, tested the sexual boundaries. Then the Depression altered priorities.

It is likely that economic collapse had something to do with the popular success of *Little Women* as a movie in 1933. The Depression may have changed the single woman's relation to the family economy, making her obligation to the family rather than to her own freedom once more predominant. Yet the debate over the "right" of segments of the labor force to jobs during the thirties indicated that the different social expectations for married and single women persisted. Public rhetoric explicitly castigated working wives and in some cases legislated them out of employment — not only to make room for deserving men, but also for single women who often verbally attacked their working married colleagues.[11]

As the wide-ranging public furor over working wives indicated, the growing gap between the image and the reality of single and married women's lives was intricately related to questions of women's work — where they worked, what pay they received, what ideology applied to their work, and how that work contributed to the economy. Throughout the period 1920 to 1940, women's work remained split, with approximately three-fourths of women working at home performing nonwage earning labor while one-fourth were gainfully employed. The fact that a majority of women received no wages remains basic to any discussion of politics and ideology. For the majority of American women, primarily married, who worked at home, their relationship to the economy changed drastically during these years. As the majority of the population became urban and food processing became centralized, old rural home industries like butter making and poultry raising ceased to be ways in which women could contribute substantially to the family income. Ways of contributing to urban family incomes, like taking in boarders and home sewing, also disappeared in these years. Whether or not women should follow men out of their workplace in the home to engage in paid work was a major issue of debate.[12]

For married women, the decision was an important one. Some married women had always worked outside the home. By 1920, 9 percent of wives did so, making up about 20 percent of the entire female work worce. These women tended to be from lower socioeconomic classes. Black married women had worked outside their homes in larger numbers than those of any other racial group, particularly in paid household labor, and that tradition continued. Immigrant women and their daughters also worked in large proportions. By the end of the 1920s, however, as Winifred D. Wandersee shows, increasing numbers of married middle-income women were joining working-class women outside the home, but were moving into white-collar jobs. A complex interplay between the changing patterns of occupations, family expenditures, and the desire of some women for standards of living that lay beyond the economic capacity of the conventional one-earner family contributed greatly to this trend. This response to altered trends in employment and consumption patterns which surfaced in the 1920s was reinforced and dramatized by the deprivation of the Depression. Yet when the proportion of married women in the work force jumped to 15 percent in 1940, two-thirds were still blue-collar workers. Moreover, as these married women moved into the work force other women dropped out to return to work at home, thereby almost cancelling out overall increases although increasing the wage-earning experience for women generally.[13]

The growing proportion of women working outside agriculture — married and single — who could be termed white-collar composed an important political group. Almost entirely white and native born, they held the best-paying jobs, and for them the twenties were heady, optimistic times. Feminization of teaching, nursing, librarianship, and social work and a spectacular increase in clerical and sales occupations had altered the social characteristics of the female work force. Organizations sprouted and grew to accommodate specific professional categories, and the National Federation of Business and Professional Women (BPW) was founded to embrace white-collar workers in general. That the majority of professionals were teachers and that most "business women" were secretaries did not dampen the enthusiasm with which the leadership and other advocates of female economic progress expropriated and expounded upon the virtues of the work and success ethics. File clerks would climb the office ladder to become managers; waitresses would become proprietors of their own tearooms and restaurants; real estate sales would bring handsome incomes. Aviation would afford opportunities to women as pilots. Later women would reconcile themselves to work as flight attendants, but in the 1920s Amelia Earhart was not just a national heroine. For proponents of women's inevitable economic progress, she represented an opportunity for women to enter and excel in a new occupational field. By the end of the decade, such optimism had swept over 60,000 members into the BPW.[14]

During the 1920s, a group of articulate professional women and feminists actively encouraged married women to occupy economic space as well. They developed a wideranging rationale contending that homes, families, and society generally would benefit if married women worked outside their homes. Equally important, these advocates of combined work with marriage insisted that women would benefit immeasurably. Outside employment would compensate for the loss of productive domestic functions (to which they believed household technology was a major contributing factor), end women's economic dependency, cure the physical and psychological disorders that plagued bored homemakers, and, ultimately, elevate the women's self-esteem. For women, married as well as single, gainful employment could replace Lydia Pinkham's tonic as the panacea for all female ills.[15]

But, by the end of the 1920s the realization surfaced and spread that earlier expectations had been unrealistic, occupational gains were minimal, and internal structural and personal psychological barriers continued to block women's paths to success in areas of economic endeavor. Then the Depression completely halted progress and set the motion in reverse. By 1940 about 44 percent of working women held white-collar jobs, unchanged from 1930. Even within the white-collar classification, professional employment decreased and clerical work became more specialized, standardized, and occupationally immobile. And the working wife became an object of contempt. The belief in work as liberation, even for white-collar middle-class women, had difficulty surviving the realities of the day-to-day job and conventional social values.[16]

While professional women had attempted the lay a new ideological foundation for female employment, women's magazines brought a different message into the home. Single women could have careers in the public sphere; married women had their careers at home. In the home, as Ruth Schwartz Cowan shows, women could express their artistic creativity through consumerism. They could show a limited range of emotions with guilt and embarrassment and general fears being most acceptable. This new "feminine mystique" offered a functional solution to the demands of the economy. It justified the creation of a separate group of women trained to use the new domestic technology but not to move into the job market as a consequence of it.[17]

Ultimately, this ideology was repressive, as Schwartz Cowan points out. To be accepted, however, an ideology must not be perceived as limiting but as natural. The feminine mystique may have seemed "natural" because few alternatives for married women were available. The negative ideology of married women who worked certainly enhanced these fears. By the 1930s, the limited mystique for married women had triumphed over earlier expansive views of married women's work. In defending married women's right to work, reformers placed them firmly within the familial context, thereby undermining the positive feminist features that advocates had used in the 1920s. Margaret Mitchell's best-selling novel of the 1930s, *Gone With the Wind*, popularized the message still further. To be socially accepted, married women must reject work outside the family unless it was absolutely necessitated by a family economic crisis.

In the course of the triumph of the feminine mystique the "new" political married woman also perished. Volunteerism flourished, but political careers, like other full-time careers, remained socially unacceptable in a period when women might have challenged male political hegemony.[18] The political and ideological debate over married women's position in society remained complex and unresolved. During the nineteenth century the first wave of industrialization and urbanization resulted in an ideology of "true womanhood," which expanded women's roles in public reform while placing firm outer limits on both work and sexuality. First surfacing in New England, these concepts spread throughout the nation as decades passed. By the 1880s, married women in the New South could engage in political activities through the Women's Christian Temperance Union (WCTU), women's clubs, and even suffrage organizations without endangering their place in traditional society. Increasingly, the freedom of married women in America to engage in public roles was legitimized by linking political and social aims to familial responsibilities. The ideology of motherhood, which Joan Jensen points out as justifying the efforts of pacifist feminists, was used widely as a justification of political activity in both domestic and foreign affairs. The amount of space accessible to women in public life remained precarious because of this link to traits supposedly peculiar to women alone. The immediate effect, however, was to legitimize the political activities of women in a period unsympathetic to concepts of equality.[19]

In a collective context, women could still choose between the male-dominated organizations where auxiliary subsidiary status was the rule or women's organizations where female leadership and female-defined issues prevailed. A complex network of organizational activities existed in which interests ran the gamut of issues and positions. The women's peace movement was not only a force that aroused and confronted the War Department; it also clashed ideologically with the female flag-wavers of the Daughters of the American Revolution (DAR) and similar patriotic groups. The WCTU, which in the late nineteenth and early twentieth centuries had unified middle-class married women in a massive, sophisticated political campaign for prohibition that matched, and at times intertwined with, the suffrage movement, encountered well-organized and increasingly visible opposition from the upper-class Women's Organization for National Prohibition Reform as the 1920s ended.[20]

One of the greatest failures of women in this period was their inability to find common ground between the races for political action. Black feminists who had organized and campaigned for suffrage found most organizations formed by middle-class white women either indifferent or actually hostile to their struggles for political freedom. What Alice Walker once called "the flood of whiteness and maleness of the times" engulfed the black woman as she struggled with class, race, and gender oppression. By the end of the period, as Rosalyn Terborg-Penn shows in her analysis, black feminists had turned almost entirely to race issues in their search for change. Combining work at home, in the marketplace, and in movements for social change, these women provided a model for later feminists — black and white. At that time, however, they worked mainly alone within their communities. White leaders were almost never by their side. The granddaughters of these women would carry their work into the larger community of nation and world in the civil rights movement.

Even within organizations, the leadership was not always certain it marched in step with the rank and file. Official League of Women Voters (LWV) defense of embattled working wives during the Depression aroused resentment among some of the league membership. The General Federation of Women's Clubs (GFWC) backed United States membership in the World Court through the interwar period, but its polyglot constituent organizations did not always agree or, at least, were indifferent. And by the mid-thirties, the Jewish and black members of the Women's International League for Peace and Freedom (WILPF) were at loggerheads with the peace organization as well as personally frustrated because their pacifism conflicted with events in Europe and Ethiopia. If the dream of a unified women's vote failed to materialize, blame need not be placed solely on women with the convenient accusation that they voted like their fathers and husbands. Women voted for Republican, Prohibition, Democratic, or Communist candidates because of the same complex assortment of cultural, economic, and social predilections and ideological commitments as their male counterparts.[21]

Nevertheless, instead of expanding their power by breaking new ground economically, politically, and ideologically, women after World War I found themselves refighting many of the old prewar battles. Only 25 percent of all women in the paid labor force were engaged in industrial work; yet, surprisingly, they remained the focus of much of the political conflict during the period. Women employed in industry benefited somewhat from hours regulations imposed by states during the 1920s, but working conditions, especially in large, female labor-intensive sectors of the economy like the garment industry, had always been precariously seasonal. With the onset of the Depression, working conditions deteriorated for those who retained or gained jobs in industry; unemployment became a fact of life for others. Although employment in manufacturing pursuits continued to diminish in importance relative to the female work force as a whole between 1920 and 1940, the conditions of women in industry retained a special significance. These women captured and held the attention of a number of women's organizations, just as the industrial working class, in general, remained the focus of radical political parties and trade union organizations.

By the second decade of the twentieth century, consensus had been reached among a number of organizations that protective legislation was the most efficacious way to improve the working conditions of women. The Oregon statute regulating working hours for women survived the Supreme

Court in 1908, and the movement for maximum-hour legislation swept the states by 1920. At the time, the newly established Women's Bureau and the reconstituted but weakened moderate wing of the suffrage movement, the LWV, joined forces to work for the extension of hours standards as well as legislation establishing minimum wages, regulating work conditions, and prohibiting female employment in some occupational categories. The most prominent and visible women on the political scene, Eleanor Roosevelt and Frances Perkins among them, supported and advocated the extension of protective legislation for women. Only the National Woman's Party (NWP), composed of more militant feminists, equated protection with economic restriction. Because the equal rights amendment proposed by the NWP threatened protective legislation, bitter and widespread conflict developed among women's groups. Susan Becker demonstrates the extent to which the struggle over these conflicting concepts of feminism and female equality in the economic sphere spilled over national borders. The extent to which these disputes completely paralyzed women reformers and feminist activities when discrimination during the Depression menaced women workers is questioned by Lois Scharf. Female reformers continued to form coalitions and to work together in opposition to legislation that they all agreed threatened and undermined women's place in the American economy and society.[22]

During all these battles, the Women's Bureau supplied the data upon which proponents of sex-typed legislation supported their positions. Although many reports surveyed work patterns among immigrant, black, and married women and studied the impact of female employment on family income levels, the predictably dry, lifeless bureau reports overlooked the complex social and cultural environments in which new work roles were assumed by women. In chapter 3, Rosalinda González brings a Marxist perspective to changing patterns of Chicana labor as these women moved from work in Mexican agriculture to new work roles in an industrial milieu, showing the subtle ways in which wage compensation both challenged and reinforced patriarchal values and family structure in Mexican-American communities. A comparative analysis provides the framework in chapter 4 with which Dolores Janiewski explores the same complex interaction among class, race, and sex as white and black women in North Carolina migrated from rural areas to the textile and tobacco factories of company towns, bringing disparate values and life styles to factory labor and union organizing campaigns.[23]

Union organizing campaigns similar to those in North Carolina offered one way women workers could attack problems inherent in their working class conditions. By the end of the 1930s, the victories of industrially structured unions had swelled the ranks of women in unions to 800,000. Where organization endured and collective bargaining became an institutionalized feature of industrial capitalism, women in the organized sector of the economy achieved greater and more permanent economic gains and security than ever before. But contracts also solidified job and wage differentials in a number of industries, and leadership structures duplicated the patriarchal patterns that permeated society. The common concerns of industrial labor — male and female — stopped where the special problems of women or the integration of women into positions of leadership were involved. In industries still dominated by racial and geographical constraints, large numbers of women received no gains from unionization and the negotiated contract. As unions modified economic inequities, they ignored the basic inequalities of race and sex.

Political organizations ideologically committed to basic structural change in American society seemed to do no better than the unions. Both Norma Fain Pratt and Sherna Gluck raise questions concerning the ability of women to find meaningful roles and to reconcile their own personal need to define a female identity with the overall social and economic injustice they saw in society. Radical women were conscious of the continuity of women's subordinate status in the male-dominated radical parties for which they had abandoned their traditional cultural moorings. Tensions and conflicts faced women moving from one economic sphere to another, ethnic heritages and values barely mitigating new demands on their time, energy, and identity. Women who consciously sought working-class utopias through radical policy action faced complex dilemmas. Pratt and Gluck furnish evidence that gender-related consciousness surfaced among radical women only to find little support for its growth and few rewards for its presence as class and ethnicity often came before loyalty to themselves or to other women.[24]

The anticipated freedom and excitement which had once fueled radical women gradually became a distant dream in the political hard times of the decades of discontent. Many radical women had come from immigrant Jewish families, yet their struggles to become *mentchen* (human beings) seemed even more difficult as the Americanization process of the 1920s challenged their roles as keepers of the Yiddish culture. The "new woman" turned out to be a flapper or a housewife and not the *New Woman* (1920) presented by Alexandra Kollontai. Kollontai defined, in coherent form, a working-class woman, usually single but certainly childless, who devoted her life to political and sexual liberation as well as intellectual and spiritual growth. The radical woman emerged from the culturally determined male sphere to serve professions, causes, and ideas and to protest as an equal against universal servitude to "the state, family, and society."[25]

This vision of the new radical women burned out in the trials of women's individual lives. Agnes Smedley's autobiographical *Daughter of Earth*, published in 1929, summed up some of the difficulties in living out this image. Writing her book on the advice of a Freudian analyst, Smedley laid out clearly the trials a new woman would have in surviving the world of the 1920s. She pictured herself abandoning a kinship network, attempting to take control over her own life, and developing her own humaneness in the context of a political cause. Reconciling lifework and sexuality is a major theme in Smedley's book. The risks of attempting to reconcile work and sexuality within a society that was not prepared to provide alternative support structures to the family should not be minimized.[26]

Determination of one's own sexuality and work thus emerge once more as the main areas of conflict for women which the ideology of the period consistently attempted to reconcile. The young woman was free to work but not to control her sexuality. Safe within the sexual confines of marriage she was no longer free to control her work but had to subordinate her desires to the needs of the family, usually defined by the husband.

Popularized Freudian psychology aided this growing divide defined by marital status and hampered attempts to build alternative network systems for women as well. To experience the rights and pleasures of female sexuality women must marry, as they had always been expected to do. But some women had always remained single — for whatever social, demographic, or personal reason — and as long as they led celibate lives, they escaped the status of social pariahs. The maiden aunt, and later the welfare worker, writer, or educator could contribute to the family circle or the new, growing demands of modern society without arousing suspicion over the texture of private life-style. A female activist or career woman could be single, apparently celibate, and still engage in commendable public nurturing, educating, or housekeeping.

By the 1920s, however, spinsterhood and celibacy became suspect. If heterosexual relations were normal and healthy, then women who lacked such experiences became, by inference, deviant. If latent homosexuality lurked in the recesses of all psyches, then the same-sex friendships and networks that had underlain and supported the variegated activities of single women in earlier decades must be suspect. If single women vented their anger against their married working sisters during the Depression, working wives could return the diatribes in kind. Why dismiss teaching wives and mothers, they asked, and turn schools into havens for bitter, sexstarved old maids who were unfamiliar with "normal" life-styles?

These developments exacerbated instead of confronting the ideological contradictions inherent in the dual images of the single and married woman, especially when women engaged in employment and organizations that were increasingly competitive with men rather than in activities that were separate from or tangential to male structures and patriarchal hierarchies. Single, women were suspect; married, they were deprived of the same-sex camaraderie that could soften the discrimination, hostility, or neglect they encountered.[27]

The female community, though continuing to function organizationally, was thus impoverished, limited, and under attack. Society had not established alternative institutions to enable women to survive outside of the family. Women were caught in the contradiction of an idealized home life and the harsh reality of life outside the family-kinship network. Yiddish women seemed to perceive this same dilemma. When Celia Dropkin wrote "I Am a Circus Lady," she caught precisely the precariousness women felt in trying to balance the desired freedom outside the family with the feared consequences and bleak prospects.[28]

In her conclusion to the first article in this collection, Estelle B. Freedman applauds the burgeoning study of women that marks recent historiography. Freedman notes, however, the particular need for more extensive examination of the years between the suffrage victory and World War II. Her survey of historical assessments of women's status, roles, accomplishments, and failures during the 1920s indicates the persistent lack of substantive information and interpretative analysis. In addition, she warns against the tendency to assume that gender can explain all social and demographic variables. The purpose of this volume is to begin to fill in chronological and topical gaps, to examine the diversity of female experience, and to grope toward possible patterns that can embrace that diversity. We focus on social and economic reality as modified by class, ethnicity, geography, individual awareness, collective activity, and ideology.

To begin this task, the contributors have relied upon both traditional and new methodologies and sources. Literary materials, both published and in manuscript form, furnish the basis for most of the articles. As Pratt and González show, however, ethnic variables necessitate foreign language skills so that rich, unutilized written documents can be retrieved. Where the written record is absent, Janiewski and Gluck demonstrate the rewards of oral history and interviewing. González and Wandersee do not employ sophisticated quantitative methods, but they both indicate that the contours of women's experiences can be discovered in gross statistical data. Mary P. Ryan and Julie Boddy give credence to the equation concerning words and pictures.

The results of this research are divided into topical sections, but the reader will quickly discover that these sections are arbitrary in nature and that subject matter overlaps categories. Images in movies and photographs are often closely related to the economic context of women's lives. Unionization among southern textile workers is organizational activity. Household appliances are often part of the changing consumption patterns that motivate middle-income wives to seek gainful employment. Difficulties in categorization highlight the emergence of these interrelated and contradictory new realities for women. Employment in the work place and consumption in the marketplace are additions to, not necessarily alternatives to, more traditional roles; and, furthermore, they were subject to the economic vagaries of the 1920s and 1930s. How the economic limits of these years affected women's political and ideological place in American society is as yet known only imprecisely, but it is hoped that this volume will open up the period we have called decades of discontent to more critical evaluation by scholars and feminists.

Notes

1. See *Notable American Women: The Modern Period*, Barbara Sicherman and Carol Hurd Green, eds. (Cambridge, Mass.: Harvard University Press, 1980) for biographical sketches of many women whose achievements span the 1920s and 1930s. The best discussion of birth control is in Linda Gordon, *Woman's Body, Woman's Right* (New York: Penguin Vintage Press, 1976, 1977), 249-300. See also Margaret Sanger, *Margaret Sanger: An Autobiography* (New York: W. W. Norton, 1937), and *Motherhood in Bondage* (New York: Brentano's, 1928). On lesbianism see Gertrude Stein, *The Autobiography of Alice B. Toklas* (New York: Harcourt, Brace and Co., 1933) and Margaret Anderson, *My Thirty Years War* (New York: Horizon, 1939 reprint of 1930 edition). Anderson founded the literary magazine *Little Review* and published James Joyce's controversial *Ulysses*. For a review of publications see Blanche Wiesen Cook, "'Women Alone Stir My Imagination': Lesbianism and the Cultural Tradition," *Signs*, 4 (Summer 1979), 718-739; for middle-class "closet" lesbianism see Vern Bullough and Bonnie Bullough, "Lesbianism in the 1920's and 1930's: A Newfound Study," *Signs*, 2 (Summer 1977), 895-904. On Ederle and women's sports of the period see Paul Gallico, "Gertrude Ederle," in Stephanie L. Twin, *Out of the Bleachers: Writings on Women and Sport* (Old Westbury and New York: Feminist Press/McGraw-Hill, 1979), 142-154 and Twin's introduction. On Smedley see Jan and Steve MacKinnon, *Portraits of Chinese Women in Revolution* (Old Westbury, N.Y.: Feminist Press, 1976). On Earhart, her *Last Flight* (New York: Harcourt Brace, 1937).

2. See Molly Haskell, *From Reverence to Rape: The Treatment of Women in the Movies* (New York: Penguin, 1974), 42-152, and Garson Kanin, *Tracy and Hepburn: An Intimate Memoir* (New York: Viking, 1970); Billie Holiday and William Duffy, *Lady Sings the Blues* (New York: Doubleday, 1956); Dorothea Lange, *Dorothea Lange Looks at the American Country Woman* (Fort Worth, Tex.: Amon Carter Museum of Western Art, 1967); Georgia O'Keeffe, *Georgia O'Keeffe* (New York: Viking, 1976); Zora Neale Hurston, *Their Eyes Were Watching God* (Urbana, Ill.: University of Illinois Press, 1978 reprint of 1937 edition), her autobiography *Dust Tracks on a Road* (Philadelphia: Lippincott, 1971 reprint of 1942 edition), and Alice Walker, editor, *I Love Myself When I am Laughing: A Zora Neale Hurston Reader* (Old Westbury, N.Y.: Feminist Press, 1979).

3. Gordon, *Woman's Body, Woman's Right*, 301-340; Richard Easterlin, *The American Baby Boom in Historical Perspective* (New York: National Bureau of Economic Research, 1962). In 1910, 27 percent of all women and 37 percent of all urban women had no children. By 1930, only 21 percent had no children. The big decline, however, came between 1950 and 1970, when the number of women with no children declined to 12 percent and then to 8 percent according to Jeanne Mager Stellman, *Women's Work, Women's Health* (New York: Pantheon, 1977), 26.

4. Mattie E. Treadwell, *United States Army in World War II: Special Studies, The Women's Army Corps* (Washington D.C.: Office of the Chief of Military

History, Department of the Army, 1954), 10-155. Eight hundred women served as Women's Airforce Service Pilots ferrying all types of military combat aircraft but were never given full military status. See Martin Binkin and Shirley J. Bach, *Women and the Military* (Washington D.C.: Brookings Institution, 1977), for postwar developments. For film treatment of women pilots see Marjorie Rosen, *Popcorn Venus: Women, Movies and the American Dream* (New York: Avon, 1973), 151. The Olympics are discussed in Nancy Theriot, "Towards a New Sporting Ideal: The Women's Division of the National Amateur Athletic Division," *Frontiers*, 3 (Spring 1978), 5, and Babe Didrikson Zaharias, *This Life I've Led: My Autobiography* (London: Robert Hale, 1956). The Olympics still do not allow women to run the marathon. Henry Pang, "Miss America: An American Ideal, 1921-1969," *Journal of Popular Culture*, 2 (Spring 1969), 687-696, gives details on the contest but no cultural context.

    5. Joan M. Jensen, "Politics and the American Midwife Controversy," *Frontiers*, 1 (Spring 1976), 19-33.

    6. Susan Brownmiller, *Against Our Will: Men, Women and Rape* (New York: Simon and Schuster, 1975), 224-255, 314, 316-322, touches upon some issues of this period: the white woman-black man controversy, the literary romanticization of rape, and Helen Deutch's theory of masochism as an element of feminity, but no one has yet explored the reality of violence in women's lives. Richard A. Cloward and Frances Fox Piven, "Hidden Protest: the Channeling of Female Innovation and Resistance," *Signs*, 4 (1979), 651-669, suggest some fruitful ways of looking at how ideology, social norms, and social organizations affect forms of female and male deviance.

    7. Cynthia Ozick, "Women and Creativity: The Demise of the Dancing Dog," in Vivian Gornick and Barbara K. Moran, eds., *Women in Sexist Society: Studies in Power and Powerlessness* (New York: Basic Books, 1971), 307-322, and Lucy R. Lippard, "Sexual Politics: Art Style," in *From the Center: Feminist Essays on Women's Art* (New York: E. P. Dutton, 1976), 31-35, suggest ways of looking at this issue.

    8. Joan Hoff Wilson,"'Peace is a Woman's Job': The Foreign Policy of Jeanette Rankin," *Montanan Magazine* (January-April 1980).

    9. Ruth Rosen, ed. *The Mamie Papers* (Old Westbury, N.Y.: Feminist Press, 1977).

    10. Kate Millett, *Sexual Politics* (Garden City, N.Y.: Doubleday, 1970), 237-293. D. H. Lawrence was the best-known literary proponent of the apocalyptic sexual act, but other versions can be found in movies and popular literature as well. Michael Gordon, "From an Unfortunate Necessity to a Cult of Mutual Orgasm: Sex in Marital Education, 1830-1940," in James Henslin, ed., *Studies in the Sociology of Sex* (New York: Appleton-Century-Crofts, 1971), 64-76.

    11. Martha Saxton, *Louisa May: A Modern Biography of Louisa May Alcott* (New York: Avon, 1977), 1-8, discusses the ideology of *Little Women*, as does Thomas H. Pauly, "Ragged Dick and Little Women: Idealized Homes and Unwanted Marriages," *Journal of Popular Culture*, 9 (Winter 1975), 583-592. Lois Scharf, *To Work and To Wed: Female Employment, Feminism and the Great Depression* (Westport, Conn., Breenwood Press, 1980), chapter 3.

    12. Joan Jensen, "Cloth, Butter and Boarders: Women's Household Production for the Market," *Review of Radical Political Economics* 12 (Summer 1980): 14-24.

13. D'Ann Campbell, "Women Numbered and Armed: Demography of the Bloodless War," (Paper presented at the Newberry Library Conference on Women's History and Quantitative Methods, July 5-7, 1979). See also Margaret H. Simeral, "Women and the Reserve Army of Labor," *Insurgent Sociologist*, 8 (Fall 1978), 164-179. "Women's Work and Economic Crisis: Some Lessons of the Great Depression," *Review of Radical Political Economics*, 8 (Spring 1976), 73-97, by Ruth Milkman disputes the notion of a reserve army of women workers.

14. Scharf, *To Work and To Wed*, chapters 1 and 5.

15. Frank Stricker, "Cookbooks and Law Books: The Hidden History of Career Women in Twentieth Century America," *Journal of Social History*, 10 (Fall 1976), 1-19, and Margaret W. Rossiter, "Sexual Segregation in the Sciences: Some Data and a Model," *Signs*, 4 (1978), 146-158, both discuss careers in the 1920s and 1930s. Steven J. Diner, "George Herbert Mead's Ideas on Women and Careers: A Letter to His Daughter-in-Law, 1920," *Signs*, 4 (1978), 407-409, is a liberal middle-class male view about the importance of married women working. Dolores Hayden, "Two Utopian Feminists and Their Campaigns for Kitchenless Houses," *Signs*, 7 (1978), 274-290, discusses the continuing issue of household work and who is to do it.

16. Scharf, *To Work and To Wed*, chapter 5.

17. Ruth Schwartz Cowan, "The 'Industrial Revolution' in the Home: Household Technology and Social Change in the 1920s," *Technology and Culture*, 17 (January 1976), 1-23; Joan Vanek, "Time Spent in Housework," *Scientific American*, (November 1974), 116-120, and *Married Women and the Work Day: Time Trends* (Baltimore: Johns Hopkins, 1982).

18. Paula J. Dubeck, "Influential Alliances? Cincinnati Women in the Political Arena, 1920-1945," in *Women and Men: The Consequences of Power* (Cincinnati: University of Cincinnati Office of Women's Studies, 1976), 287-297, and Anne Firor Scott, "After Suffrage: Southern Women in the Twenties," *Journal of Southern History*, 30 (1964), 298-318, both describe the limited political successes of women, as does June Sochen, *Movers and Shakers: American Women Thinkers and Activists, 1900-1970* (New York: Quadrangle Books, 1974).

19. Barbara Welter, "The Cult of True Womanhood: 1820-1860," *American Quarterly*, 18 (Summer 1966), 151-174; Nancy F. Cott, *The Bonds of Womanhood: "Woman's Sphere" in New England, 1780-1835*, (New Haven: Yale University Press, 1977), and "Passionlessness: An Interpretation of Victorian Sexual Ideology, 1790-1850," *Signs*, 4 (1978), 219-236; Anne Firor Scott, "The 'New Woman' in the New South," *South Atlantic Quarterly*, 65 (Autumn 1962), 473-483; Susan M. Strasser, "The Business of Housekeeping: The Ideology of the Household at the Turn of the Twentieth Century," *Insurgent Sociologist*, 8 (Fall 1978), 147-163; and Ronald Schaffer, "The Problem of Consciousness in the Woman Suffrage Movement: A California Perspective," *Pacific Historical Review*, 45 (1976), 469-493, trace this attitude.

20. J. Stanley Lemons describes the attacks of the Women Patriots on social feminists in *The Woman Citizen: Social Feminism in the 1920s* (Urbana, Ill.: University of Illinois Press, 1973). On conflict over Prohibition, see Paul A. Carter, *Another Part of the Twenties* (New York: Columbia University Press, 1977), 96-98.

21. Scharf, *To Work and To Wed*, chapter 3. Jeane Westin, *Making Do: How Women Survived the '30s* (Chicago: Follette, 1976), 289-292.

22. The conflicts among women's organizations are stressed by Lemons, *Woman*

Citizen, chapter 7; William L. O'Neill, *Everyone Was Brave: The Rise and Fall of Feminism in America* (Chicago: Quadrangle, 1969); and William Chafe, *The American Woman: Her Changing Social, Economic and Political Roles, 1920-1970* (New York: Oxford University Press, 1972), chapter 5.

23. See also Julia Kirk Blackwilder, "Women in the Work Force: Atlanta, New Orleans, and San Antonio, 1930-1940," *Journal of Urban History,* 4 (May 1978), pp. 331-58.

24. Robert Shaffer, "Women and the Communist Party," *Socialist Review,* 9 (May-June 1979), 73-118.

25. Alexandra Kollontai, *The Autobiography of a Sexually Emancipated Communist Woman* (New York: Schocken, 1975), 51-102.

26. Agnes Smedley, *Daughter of Earth* (Old Westbury, N.Y.: Feminist Press, 1973 reprint of 1929 edition).

27. On close, personal female relationships in the nineteenth century see Carroll Smith-Rosenberg, "The Female World of Love and Ritual: Relations between Women in Nineteenth-Century America," *Signs,* 4 (Spring 1979), 1-29. The value of female support systems for publicly active women in the early twentieth century is discussed by Blanche Wisen Cook in "Female Support Networks and Political Activism: Lillian Wald, Crystal Eastman, Emma Goldman," *Chrysalis,* 3 (1977, 43-61. Estelle Freedman explores the relationship between fewer separate female public activities, the breakdown of female networks, and the dissipation of feminism after 1920 in "Separatism as Strategy: Female Institution Building and American Feminism, 1870-1930," *Feminist Studies,* 5 (Fall 1979), 512-529.

28. Jane Humphries, "Women: Scapegoats and Safety Valves in the Great Depression," *Review of Radical Political Economics,* 8 (Spring 1976), 98-117.

PART I

The Historical Context

Until recently, most historians and observers writing about the 1920s have focused their attention on the so-called new woman without really examining the realities of or variations in women's life patterns during the decade. But historians, as well as other contemporary critics, are influenced by the times in which they live and by their own expectations or sexual stereotypes. Estelle Freedman reviews historians' changing analyses of women's roles and status.

Why would historians tend to concentrate on the economic opportunities of women during the interwar period? How and why does this differ from the treatment of women by historians in the 1960s? Why was there so much curiosity and concern among social scientists about women's "place" during the 1940s and 1950s?

1

The New Woman:
Changing Views of Women
in the 1920s

_____ ESTELLE B. FREEDMAN _____

In his suggestive article, "What Happened to the Progressive Movement in the 1920s," Arthur S. Link analyzed the legacy of the pre-World War I "progressive coalition" of businessmen, farm groups, labor unions, and "advocates of social justice."[1] However, he neglected to mention the fate of the feminists, either those women active in the suffrage movement, or those involved in broader areas of social reform. Despite Link's inattention to women reformers, the question he posed about the progressive movement in the twenties should be asked of the women's movement as well. What happened to feminism during the decade after the political goal of suffrage had been achieved?

Failure to consider the women's movement in the nineteen-twenties is not an uncommon oversight among historians. Even students of women's history, such as Eleanor Flexnor, Andrew Sinclair, and Aileen Kraditor, conclude their accounts with the passage of the nineteenth amendment.[2] Until very recently, this tendency to ignore post-1920 women's history has fostered the repetition of a standard image of American women in the twenties. Frederick Lewis Allen's 1931 account is representative:

> The revolution [in manners and morals] was accelerated . . . by the growing independence of the American woman. She won the suffrage in 1920. She seemed, it is true, to be very little interested in it once she had it; she voted, but mostly as the unregenerate men about her did. . . . Few of the younger women could rouse themselves to even a passing interest in politics: to them it was a sordid and futile business, without flavor and without hope. Nevertheless, the winning of the suffrage had its effect. It consolidated woman's position as man's equal.[3]

William E. Leuchtenburg reached a similar conclusion nearly three decades later:

> The new woman wanted the same freedom that men had and the same economic and political rights. By the end of the 1920's she had come a long way. Before the war, a lady did not set foot in a saloon; after the war, she entered a speakeasy as

From _The Journal of American History_ LXI (Sept. 1974), 372-393. Reprinted by permission, _The Journal of American History_, Indiana University, Bloomington, Indiana.

thoughtlessly as she would go into a railroad station. . . . In the business and political worlds, women competed with men; in marriage, they moved toward a contractual role. . . . Sexual independence was merely the most sensational aspect of the generally altered status of women.[4]

These and other accounts have attributed the following characteristics to the "New Women" of the 1920s: they failed to vote as a block or in greater numbers than did men; their manners and morals differed sharply from those of previous generations; and their legal and economic position had so improved that for the first time in history, women had become the social and economic equals of men.

An examination of the record, however, reveals that historians have repeated these descriptions not because research and analysis have confirmed their validity, but because no new questions have been asked about women in the 1920s since the initial impressionistic observations were made. The fact that these interpretations have been handed down for forty years with very little modification makes them suspect, and closer analysis confirms that several important historical questions have remained unanswered. Who precisely was the New Woman; what was her fate after 1920; and how does her history relate to that of women's movement? Specifically, historians need to claify when and why the organized women's movement lost its influence; whether enfranchisement affected women's efforts for social reform and for equal rights for their sex; precisely what economic gains women made; and how widely and deeply the moral revolution reached.

Original and creative use of primary resources is obviously necessary to answer these questions. But before this research is undertaken, it is essential to understand what has already been written about women in the twenties. This essay will provide such an historiographical framework by tracing interpretations of the new woman from the 1920s to the early 1970s.[5] The influence of historical events will be of central concern, as will the shift of conceptual frameworks from the analysis of the 1920s to the contemporary revival of women's history.

For years, historians agreed with Mary Beard's claim that women are a positive "force in history." They praised the post-1920 woman as an active participant in American politics and economic life, as if trying to correct what Arthur Meier Schlesinger had termed "the pall of silence which historians have allowed to rest" over women's "successes and achievements."[6] Women's history was merely an effort to include more women and their successes in the history books. In later years after social scientists rediscovered the "woman question" in the 1950s, historians groped towards a feminist perspective. This approach to women's history, as Gerda Lerner has explained, finds that women have been unable to contribute fully to American society — even after suffrage — because they have remained the oppressed victims of history.[7] If the latter view prevails, women's history must become the study of a unique interest group, a study which requires new forms of research and new conceptual models.

Since historians were relatively silent on the question of the new woman during all but two periods—from approximately 1927 to 1933 and from 1964 to the present—broad accounts and textbooks must suffice as evidence for parts of this review of the literature. Towards the end of the long period of neglect, scholars in other disciplines began to question the validity of the image of women in post-World War I America. By the time a revival of interest in the subject had reached popular dimensions (coincident with but not necessarily related to the 1963 publication of *The Feminine Mystique*), historians too had begun to review their conceptions of the new woman. Numerous revisionist interpretations can now be expected; from what historiographical traditions do they proceed?

Social commentators of the late 1920s and early 1930s reached mixed conclusions in their evaluations of the first decade of woman suffrage. Concentrating on political and economic measures of emancipation, they praised women's participation in American society, in spite of strong indications that women had not, in fact, achieved equality.

As might be expected, many analyses reflected presuffrage positions. In a 1927 *Current History* symposium on "The New Woman," Charlotte Perkins Gilman found extensive evidence of women's political, literary and economic achievement since enfranchisement, and Carrie Chapman Catt wrote that the vote had been used profitably to remove discrimination on the state level and to improve legislation for women and children.[8] Former opponents of woman suffrage found very little to praise in articles decrying "Woman's Encroachment on Man's Domain," and the "Evils of Woman's Revolt Against the Old Standards."[9] Ida Tarbell, an "anti" in the early suffrage debate, wrote in 1930, "I don't feel that women have contributed anything new or worthwhile. . . . I maintain that this ten years experience has proved that women have become the tools of party leaders, just as men have."[10]

Positive but apologetic evaluations of women's progress appeared in a special 1929 issue of the *Annals of the American Academy of Political and Social Science* devoted to "Women in the Modern World." A regional director of the League of Women Voters argued that it would take more than eight years to break a tradition of exclusion from public affairs. Therefore the contribution of women should not be measured by the size of their vote. Another contributor proclaimed that already "women have successfully stepped from social life into the political realm," even as she felt it necessary to assure her readers that women politicians did not shirk their domestic duties.[11]

Journalists, too, concentrated on political progress. Although generally favorable, their analyses were usually qualified by an apologetic tone. "Not many of our editors seem enthusiastic over the showing made under the Nineteenth Amendment," a *Literary Digest* survey found; "Yet on the other hand, few are pessimistic." A representative editorial comment came from the Winston-Salem *Journal:*

> The women have acquitted themselves well during this first ten years of their political enfranchisement. But even greater results will be expected during the next decade. During the ten years just passed the women have been laying a foundation. The superstructure of achievement now remains to be built.[12]

Social scientists reported few substantive gains for women since suffrage, but they were not without sympathy for the problems the new voters faced. The authors of a statistical study of the 1920 election found that women had not utilized the ballot to the same extent as men, nor had they voted predictably. However, they suggested that women were politically handicapped — not by a psychological incapacity for politics, as some critics claimed, but only by lack of experience. "When participating in politics has become through habit as natural to women as to men . . . women will undoubtedly participate in all phases of political life on a basis of actual as well as nominal equality with men."[13]

Although most authors stressed political progress, a few also evaluated women's economic and personal rights. Editor V. F. Calverton believed that "woman's economic independence has been a far more important item in her emancipation than [has] her political enfranchisement." He was impressed by the increasing number of married women who were working and by the effects of the growing women's labor force in fortifying single women's desires for independence. However, he duly noted the pervasive discrimination against women workers, particularly that of organized labor against married women in industry.[14]

Other writers who explored the possibilities of social and cultural emancipation of women in the twenties found, like Calverton, that antifeminist attitudes persisted. George Britt wrote that "it is possible for the Southern girl now to an extent never permitted before to . . . become a person and not just another woman." But, after citing individual examples of professional women in the South, the growth of women's clubs during the 1920s, the changes in personal habits such as smoking, and the involvement of women in social reform, Britt concluded: "The Southern girl may like to earn a little money and have her fling, but the ideal in the back of her head is a nice house in the home town and a decorative position in society."[15]

Former Judge Ben Lindsey drew on his experiences counselling youth in the 1920s to evidence a moral revolution: premarital sex, birth control, drinking, and contempt for older values. Yet almost every case he cited revealed a strong conflict between the appeal of flamboyant freedom and the sense of sin it still engendered. Lindsey suspected that in a few years each lively flapper would become "a happy, loyal wife with several children."[16]

In spite of indications that only a few political rights and not many broader feminist goals had been achieved in the 1920s, the optimistic writers of the decade generally hailed the end of discrimination against women. Typical of their strained efforts was a 1930 essay by feminist Chase Going Woodhouse. She maintained an overly enthusiastic tone even as her evidence wore thin. Women had made significant advances in education, Woodhouse wrote, particularly "outstanding improvements in nursing education," but Harvard still refused to train women for law and medicine. Employment figures "increased steadily," she claimed, although for the period after 1919 she had to juggle figures to include housewives among the "gainfully employed." Women advanced in the professions, but mainly in teaching, and mostly before 1920. Despite the fact that in education, industry and politics, "despair and resentment" characterized women's responses, Woodhouse claimed "steadily gained recognition" for women.[17]

Certainly women had made some advances by the end of the 1920s, although few commentators explained how their economic and political gains measured in comparison to the previous decades or with feminists' larger goals of economic and social equality. In politics, women writers claimed significant progress, while men graciously excused women's supposedly poor voting record. Most observers ignored entirely women's legislative achievements of the early 1920s. A few writers recognized the limitations of women's roles, but most strained to emphasize the positive, although often superficial, aspects of women's history in the twenties — slight increases in political office holding and nonprofessional jobs, and greater sexual freedom. Nevertheless they confidently portrayed the period as one in which feminist goals were well on their way to fulfillment.[18] By proclaiming emancipation a *fait accompli* and denying the existence of discrimination, they helped to discourage further efforts for social change.

Meanwhile, historians began to incorporate the 1920s into their works. They too stressed positive roles and women's increased participation in American history. Although published in the early 1930s, the first histories reflected the tone of the years before the crash rather than that of the depression. Charles and Mary Beard, Frederick Lewis Allen, and Preston William Slosson echoed the feelings of the generation which had seen both the presuffrage woman and the new woman, and their predepression accounts emphasized the changes in woman's social position during the 1920s.

"Women," the Beards wrote in *The Rise of American Civilization*, "now assumed an unquestioned role in shaping the production of goods, material, humanistic, literary and artistic." The ballot had enlarged women's influence in politics, while economic power, education and social freedom had made women "powerful arbiters in all matters of taste, morals and thinking." The Beards seemed pleased with these successes, but they were also apprehensive about some of the consequences of women's emancipation — the decline in the authority of fathers, defiant and divorce-prone women, and the "more intransigent" demand for "'absolute and unconditional equal opportunity' in every sphere" of an equal rights amendment.[19]

Preston William Slosson reported in *The Great Crusade and After* the "complete acceptance of American women in political life" and even greater progress, if that was possible, in economic status and social prestige. But Slosson's main concerns were topics traditionally defined as part of women's sphere. In a chapter entitled "The American Woman Wins Equality," Slosson devoted six pages to economics and politics and twenty-two pages to the family, home, and fashions. Shorter skirts, more comfortable undergarments, shorter hair, the use of cosmetics, smoking, drinking, and the "breezy, slangy, informal" flapper characterized the era for him. As suffrage "disappeared from politics," women became content, he wrote, with the exception of "the more doctrinaire type" who pressed for equal rights.[20] Women's history was reverting to women's spheres of home, fashions, and sex and finding there little or no oppression.

According to Frederick Lewis Allen, women did not vote in the 1920s, but they did work, if not in offices or factories, then as "professional" homemakers. But the job, or the potential for earning, created a feeling of comparative economic independence in women, which, for Allen, threatened husbandly and parental authority. Even with all of this, woman wanted more: "She was ready for the revolution" — sexual freedom, as enhanced by Sigmund Freud, the automobile, and Hollywood. Changes in fashion, Allen implied, were signs of deeper changes in the American feminine ideal.[21]

With these three historical views, women in the 1920s began to be presented as flappers, more concerned with clothing and sex than with politics. Women had by choice, the accounts suggested, rejected political emancipation and found sexual freedom. In the long run, however, they settled down to home and family. The term feminism nearly disappeared from historical accounts, except in somewhat pejorative references to the Woman's Party. While critics claimed that women had achieved equality with men, they issued subtle warnings of moral and family decay.

At the same time, many women who wrote about the 1920s were more concerned about political and economic equality than the flapper and the moral revolution. In 1933, Inez Haynes Irwin offered *Angels and Amazons*, an all too glowing chronicle of the advancement of women in American history. Looking back over the first decade of new freedom, Irwin found four organized feminist activities "worth remembering": work for child welfare, self-education as voters, influence on world peace, and the struggle for equal legal status for women.[22] None of these subjects had been discussed yet by historians, and Irwin left the moral revolution entirely to them.

In the same year Sophonisba Breckinridge, a social scientist from the University of Chicago, offered a more sophisticated approach to women's history. In a monograph prepared for the President's Commission on Recent Social Trends, a document which Henry F. May has called a "monument of the chastened social science of the thirties,"[23] she quantified and analyzed women's organizations, occupations, and politics. The volume, *Women in the Twentieth Century*, is an invaluable aid for the study of American women and a sobering contrast to the superficial treatment of the topic in other texts.

Breckinridge's conclusions suggested that perhaps women were not the emancipated, satisfied participants in American society that historians were describing. While an increasing number of women worked, she found that they were severely restricted in their range of employment. In the realm of public activity, Breckinridge reported that "the moment seems an unhappy one at which to attempt to take account of stock." Women had become disillusioned with the ballot and had to turn to government agencies and educational institutions for bases of emancipation. They had not as yet been successful in obtaining political power. Breckinridge described women's lobbying efforts and their roles in the national parties, but her picture is nowhere as promising as either Irwin's account of public life or the "progress" implied in Slosson's or Allen's description of the flapper. The Breckinridge study provided the data which might have prompted historical revisions on women's emancipation in the 1920s. On the contrary, with one exception in the mid-1930s, her work seems to have been unconsulted for several decades. The new woman remained an assumption rather than a subject for historical inquiry.

The one exception was *The American Woman: The Feminine Side of a Masculine Civilization* (1937)[24] by Ernest R. Groves, a sociologist of marriage and the family who stressed the economic roots of feminist activity. Groves outlined the effects of industrial employment during World War I in raising women's expectations and in "heightening of the feelings of self-interest." Groves was aware that the growth of a female labor force did not automatically change attitudes towards working women and the family. He suggested that the continued existence of a temporary female work force contributed to the exploitative double standard of wages geared to non-permanent help. While the vote had quickened the trend to legal equality and reinforced lobbying activities,[25] women were not yet, in Groves' view, active and equal subjects in history. Later writers would agree with him that women were a special class, treated unequally, the "feminine side of a masculine civilization."

From the mid-1930s through the late 1940s feminism was not a popular subject among historians. A country struggling through a prolonged depression viewed woman's emancipation and her entry into the job market in a very different light than had an earlier, more prosperous society. Working women were being asked, if not forced, to leave their newly acquired positions and return to the home, either to allow men to take up their jobs or at least to offer moral support to families in a time of crisis.[26] When rearmament and the war provided new jobs for women, American society had ample reason to readjust to working women; but by no means had a consensus been reached on the proper place of women in American society. The postwar years witnessed renewed debate over women's roles.

It is not surprising that during these crisis-ridden years, historians were either silent or ambivalent about the emancipation of women. The only sense one can get of their interpretations must come from textbooks and broad surveys of American thought, most of which contained brief sections on the new woman.[27] While no one seemed to doubt that emancipation had occurred, several historians were unsure whether to welcome or denounce the new woman.

Historians often cited the relationship between urbanization and the emancipation of women to explain economic opportunities in the 1920s. A rising standard of living, more household appliances, and compulsory public education provided women with unprecedented leisure time which enabled them to join women's clubs or to enter the work force.[28] These developments in turn influenced family life, the texts claimed, as evidenced by a declining birth rate and a climbing divorce rate. At this point historians often highlighted woman's new role of "professional homemaker." For example, Dwight Lowell Dumond's 1937 college text explained that feminists in the nineteenth century had made only small gains, but "Since then household electrical appliances have done more to emancipate women than all the generations of agitation by militant suffragettes." Consequently, "Women were living in a new and happier world.... The joy of home-making replaced the drudgery of housekeeping...."[29] Merle Curti's image of women in the 1920s displayed ambivalence toward working women. While he found that women's magazines devoted space to careers "in the big world outside the home," he added that they "naturally" gave more space to the efficient management of the home.[30] Foster Rhea Dulles's one page on the emancipation of women related increasing opportunity in business and professions to divorce rates, as well as to the development of independent social lives for women.[31] Harvey Wish discussed women's employment outside the home and then cited Robert and Helen Lynds's Middletown study to demonstrate the weaknesses in modern marriage — the loss of companionship in marriage, the use of birth control, and the new manners (smoking, drinking, and masculinized fashions) of women.[32]

These authors may not have intended to link working women with family decline, but often the proximity of the two statements, if not an explicitly drawn connection, brought them together in the mind of the reader. Similarly, historians in the 1930s and 1940s viewed the "moral revolution" in more negative terms — as a threat to the family — than it had been seen in the late twenties. Then the short skirt and bobbed hair had been used as symbols of emancipation.

Once again, historians disagreed about the political effects of enfranchisement. Some believed that voting rights for women had little or no effect.[33] Others claimed that women had won total equality, as in John D. Hicks's statement that even before 1920, "Legal discrimination against women, aside from suffrage, were brought near the vanishing point."[34] Similarly, Henry Steele Commager wrote that while the emancipation of women had begun in the 1890s with the typewriter, telephone exchange, and labor saving devices, it was "dramatized by the vote, and guaranteed by birth control."[35] Dwight Dumond pointed to women's political roles in the Women's Joint Congressional Committee and stated that "Their successes in securing state legislation for child welfare, women's legal rights, social hygiene and education have been little less than phenomenal."[36] A 1950 textbook by Curti, Richard Shryock, Thomas Cochran and Fred Harvey Harrington also acknowledged women's fight for progressive legislation and local good government in the twenties. Contrary to Dumond, however, it claimed that women rarely entered the political parties.[37]

Throughout the 1930s and 1940s, then, historians suggested that women in the 1920s were emancipated by the vote and by an urbanized, industrialized society, but chose to remain for the most part in the home. Textbook portrayals of satisfied professional housewives or unstable career women were doubtless both products of and reinforcements for the depression psychology which sought to take women out of the work force. While legal and political equality won praise, social and cultural emancipation evoked gentle reproaches. Rarely, however, did even the most liberal male historians recognize the persistence of discrimination against women.

Post-World War II American society faced a dilemma of women's roles: Would the many women who had gone to work during the war return to their homes? Popular literature on "woman's place" abounded after 1947.[38] Scholars, too, began to question women's roles in a way that would eventually change the direction of historical writing on the new woman. Once the existing discrimination against women was exposed, historians would have to reexamine their portrayal of the past decades as a period of emancipation.

Evidence of a reemerging intellectual curiosity about women can be found in the publications and reviews of the early 1950s. Alfred Kinsey's report on *Sexual Behavior in the Human Female* (1953) raised dormant issues of women's sexuality. More provoking, perhaps, was the 1953 English translation of Simone de Beauvoir's *The Second Sex*, which produced new hopes and fears of a revitalization of feminism.[39] In the same year, Mirra Komarovsky defended equal education for women in *Women in the Modern World*, and another sociologist, Sidney Ditzion, published

Marriage, Morals, and Sex in America: A History of Ideas. If these offerings were not sufficient to bring women to the attention of intellectuals, the very title of Ashley Montagu's essay, *The Natural Superiority of Women,* must have raised a few eyebrows (though probably not much consciousness).

These precursors of the new feminism appeared in the 1950s for several reasons. American women were ready for a revival of feminism. They had weathered the years of the depression and war without making new demands for equality. They now lived in an increasingly affluent society which was beginning to turn its attention to the question of racial equality, a subject which has historically heightened feminist concerns. Furthermore, the generation of women which came to maturity in the 1950s had not lived through and tired of an earlier feminist movement. These women were at a crossroads; would they return to the long interrupted battle for equality, or would they be seduced by the security promised to homemakers? Scholars looked back to the 1920s for clues and although they discussed politics, they emphasized social and cultural forces which defined women's roles.

In 1950, for example, Arnold W. Green and Eleanor Melnick asked "What Has Happened to the Feminist Movement?" They found that feminism had achieved the specific goals of suffrage and career opportunity, and it had given impetus to "the steady nurturing of the philosophy of the service state." But the feminist movement, they believed, had in a larger sense failed, for "about thirty years ago, in both politics and the job world, a fairly stable level was reached which the further passage of time has only indeterminately altered."[40] Three factors hampered women's efforts for further advancement. First was the "residue of prejudice against working women," especially in nontraditional women's occupations. In addition the feminists were ignorant "of the fundamental changes in social structure which must precede women's assuming positions of leadership." Finally were the class cleavages in the women's movement, which were exacerbated by the conflict over the equal rights amendment (the upper-class and professional women of the National Woman's Party supported the amendment, while lower- and middle-class women wanted protective regulation).[41]

The views that women had not yet achieved full equality and that social prejudices were at least partially responsible found even fuller expression in 1951 in a pivotal article by sociologist Helen Mayer Hacker. Elaborating on Gunnar Myrdal's comparison of woman's social position with that of Negroes, Hacker viewed women as a minority group that suffered collective discrimination, received separate socialization, and generally fit sociological definitions of minority group status and behavior.[42] Of particular interest to historians was Hacker's conceptualization of a "sex relations cycle," comparable to the race relations cycle hypothesized by Robert Park. She believed that the latter stages of the cycle of competition, conflict, accommodation, and assimilation had been reached with passage of the suffrage amendment. Hacker suggested prophetically that a new era of women's dissatisfaction was approaching.

The analogy of women with minority groups later appeared elsewhere, including Sidney Ditzion's *Marriage, Morals, and Sex* and in a reinterpretation of the flapper by B. June West. Rejecting the traditional view that women's fads and fashions in the 1920s were manifestations of freedom, West's literary analysis suggested that women's fashions were an aping of men, "as minority groups have always done . . . to the so-called superior group." Although the plays and novels of the 1920s depicted women in a variety of masculinized roles – the aggressor in sex, the divorcee – West cautioned that the literature "implied a moral disintegration that was quite likely more publicized than actually existent."[43]

Another reinterpretation of changes in women's roles in the 1920s which questioned historians' assertions of sex equality was *Women and Work in America* (1959) by Robert W. Smuts. The legal status of women, he found, shifted not after World War I but earlier with the passing of their frontier. By the end of the war the feminist movement was "rapidly subsiding." The war had led to a "remarkable liberalization of views about women's abilities and the propriety of their working outside the home," but the postwar decades were marked by women's lack of interest in many of the victories they had won. As evidence Smuts described a low level of interest in politics, a small increase in women working for pay, retirement from work at marriage, indifference of young women to feminism, and a failure to make significant gains in careers other than teaching and nursing.[44] His explanation for this demise of feminism in the 1920s was that feminists, never more than a small minority of women to begin with, had won their primary goals; their demands became less important as the status of men and women became less differentiated. Thus the women's rights movement had failed only in succeeding too well, and women turned from a search for political and economic equality to one for sexual and social identity.

How did historians initially respond to the postwar interest in the social roles of women? A few studies appeared, some inspired by the centennial of the Seneca Falls Convention, some worthless, and some very suggestive, such as Carl N. Degler's 1956 article on Charlotte Perkins Gilman.[45] For the most part, however, historians maintained the older view that women had lost interest in politics after attaining legal equality. Historians' interests in social emancipation remained confined to the "revolution in morals" concept.

Eric Goldman's 1952 history of reform, *Rendezvous with Destiny*, stated little more than that women's suffrage had made no difference, women failed to use the ballot, and when they did vote they didn't vote as women.[46] Arthur Link's 1955 text repeated the story of the revolution in manners and morals, claimed that women had achieved political and economic equality after 1920, and seemed relieved to announce that the "revolution in morals and customs had run its full course by 1930 [when] . . . [t]here seemed to be certain signs of returning sanity."[47] William Leuchtenburg argued in *The Perils of Prosperity* (1958) that "women's suffrage had few consequences, good or evil." Although millions voted and some held office, "the new electorate caused scarcely a ripple in American political life." Yet in business and social life Leuchtenburg described a period of accomplishment.[48]

Once again, these accounts are not necessarily mistaken, but they are glaringly inconsistent in their evaluations of the progress towards women's emancipation that was made in the 1920s. What is most interesting is that historians had not yet defined and attempted to resolve the controversies over the women's movement and the history of women after suffrage. Previous writers had claimed all things and nothing for women in the 1920s: that the vote was not used, that it had brought equality; that women became men's equals in the world of work, that they had remained in traditionally female occupations; that the sexual revolution had changed women's lives, that the revolution was more literary than actual. Either historians were indifferent to these issues in the early postwar years, or, perhaps, while other scholars pointed to new conceptual frameworks for viewing women's history, historians were contemplating the issues and beginning to design the research which was to take form in the next decade. If the latter was the case, it was a long time before their thoughts actually reached the public, for one must skip to the early 1960s to find them in print. By this time, concern about discrimination against minority groups was widespread. President John F. Kennedy had established a Commission on the Status of Women and several states and localities had followed suit. Civil rights legislation was being applied to women's rights. The Negro rights movement was about to turn toward Black Power. And, in 1963, Betty Friedan published *The Feminine Mystique*,[49] a journalistic polemic which was to sell over a million copies and help spark a revival of feminism in America.

As if to mark the beginning of serious interest in women in American history, two established historians published essays on the subject in 1964. Both works indicated a significant shift away from the view that women's emancipation had been completed in the 1920s and toward one that recognized the persistence of discrimination against women.

David Potter's comments on "American Women and the American Character" credited the city, the business office, and mechanization with the promotion of sexual equality, but acknowledged the barriers to full equality. Most important was the conflict between women's dual roles of career and domestic life, which made women's emancipation different from that of other oppressed groups.[50] Carl Degler also linked feminism with industrialization and urbanization. At first, Degler agreed with earlier commentators about the advances women had made. However, he retreated from unqualified congratulations by noting that no permanent increase in the female labor force was made after World War I, that women's occupational gains were not great in the professions, that sexual divisions of labor remained, and that women's educational position later regressed. Why, an historian finally asked, did feminism fail to consolidate and increase its gains after the 1920s? Changes in women's status, he explained, had occurred more through chance of war, depression, and technological change than through planned efforts.[51] American women, "like American society in general, have been more concerned with individual practice than with a consistent feminist ideology."[52] Thus, he suggested that only a strong ideological stand would enable feminists to recognize their goals consistently and continuously.

At the time that Degler and Potter made these generalizations about women, a small number of historians began investigating more closely women's political and social activities in the post-World War I decade. They discovered that there was more to the new woman than the image of the flapper had revealed, and their works offered compensatory balance to former interpretations. Harking back to emphasis on women's political activities during the late 1920s, the new studies still did not elaborate on the theme of women as an oppressed group, but they did present valuable discussions of women's political efforts and incidentally acknowledged the social barriers impeding emancipation.

One revision was implicit in Clarke A. Chambers's 1963 study of social service reforms.[53] Chambers did not discuss feminism *per se*, but he did find women in the 1920s actively working in settlement houses, lobbying for wages and hours regulations and for safeguards for earlier protective legislation, and educating women workers. Chambers proposed that progressive thought did not end in the 1920s, but was tempered, to be drawn on heavily by the New Deal. Anne Firor Scott's study of Southern women confirmed that women advanced Progressivism in the 1920s and weakened the historians' monolithic interpretation of the new woman as flapper. Suffrage, she found, greatly encouraged the political life of Southern women and prompted efforts for social and political reform. In several states Scott found women's organizations investigating labor conditions, securing children's and women's legislation, and even organizing for interracial cooperation. In Georgia, Tennessee, Virginia, and Kentucky, women's groups pursued state and municipal government reform. At odds with entrenched politicians, Southern women's political progress was "not one to gladden Mrs. Catt's heart," yet their efforts persisted through the decade. However, the 1920s did not witness a new morality in the South: "Through it all the outward aspect of the Southern lady was normally maintained as the necessary precondition of securing a hearing."[54]

James Stanley Lemons's book, *The Woman Citizen* (1973), showed how the women's movement "advanced progressivism in the period from World War I to the Great Depression." He cited successes such as the Sheppard-Towner Act, new marriage and divorce laws, independent citizenship (the Cable Act), and municipal reform, as well as organizations such as the National Women's Trade Union League, the National League of Women Voters, and the National Consumer's League and various professional women's groups.[55] The list of legislation which the Women's Joint Congressional Committee influenced successfully is a lenghty one, but most of its entries are dated before 1925, for, as Lemons shows, forces of reaction after 1925 shifted the emphasis of women's activities from goals of social justice to goals of efficiency. Red-baiting, the defeat of the child labor amendment, decisions of the Supreme Court barring protective legislation, and the rejection of the Progressive Party in the 1924 election placed progressive women on the defensive.[56] The equal rights amendment, Lemons believed, was "the hallmark of impatience in the 1920s, and it was an issue which helped fragment the women's movement and weaken the progressive impulse."[57] Although the newly enfranchised sex had achieved no great political gains in public office or party politics, women had continued to push for reforms, laying the groundwork for the New Deal.

Not unrelated to these new interpretations of women in the 1920s was an essay by James R. McGovern, which called into question earlier historians' periodization of the revolution in morals. McGovern cited Sophonisba Breckinridge's statistics on the prewar occupational status of women, pre-1910 advertisements depicting women, changing hair and cosmetic styles in the Progressive era, dance crazes, the practice of birth control, and use of automobiles to show that the flapper had been predated by events of the first decades of the century. If, as McGovern suggested, a moral revolution occurred before World War I, were the 1920s as "revolutionary" as they had been depicted, or in fact had a reaction taken place in which women returned to home and family?[58]

The works of Scott on the Southern woman's new political awareness, Chambers and Lemons on progressivism and women in the twenties, and the reinvestigations of the moral revolution by McGovern and others may differ on many counts, but they all point to a new attitude toward women's history. Prompted in part by the political and social movements of the 1960s, these authors looked more closely at the political lives of post-World War I women and more critically at the supposed moral revolution. While they were eager to praise the role women had played in political movements, their researches laid the foundation for recent works which are critical of the failures of the women's movement to achieve lasting reform. Two recent studies evidence the shift in view from woman as emancipated historical actor to woman as the victim of discrimination. William O'Neill places the bulk of the blame for feminism's demise on women; William Chafe faults American society for oppressing the "second sex."

Everyone Was Brave (1969), O'Neill's history of feminism, was originally subtitled "the rise and fall of feminism in America," a phrase indicative of the author's view of the 1920s:

The women's rights movement expired in the twenties from ailments that had gone untreated in its glory days. Chief among them was the feminists' inability to see that equal suffrage was almost the only issue holding the disparate elements of the woman movement together.[59]

O'Neill found that politicians abandoned the women's movement when no female voting bloc appeared. He also offered several criticisms of women's political activity. The author quoted — and made clear his agreement with — a blatantly antiwoman assessment of suffrage which claimed that the vote had done little more than to bring out such undesirable female traits as fussiness, primness, bossiness, and the tendency to make unnecessary enemies. O'Neill also claimed that although the radicals of the Woman's Party correctly understood the discrimination against women which existed after 1920, their "knowledge did them little good because the passions that led them to demand a feminist revival kept them from effecting it."[60]

Outside of politics as well, O'Neill noted little progress towards emancipation after 1920. The moral revolution had been rooted in the prewar years, and "sexual freedom had little effect on the life styles of most women," who still preferred the stability of home and family to the life of the flapper. Professionalism among women declined by the mid-twenties, he explained, because the novelty and "glamour" of the career experience was wearing out, discrimination in salaries and promotions became apparent to women, and the struggle between home and career exhausted working women.[61]

O'Neill believed that the feminine mystique of fulfillment through motherhood and home originated in the 1920s, when "feminism" came to mean merely sexual liberation within the confines of domesticity. Home economics became woman's professional realm, and femininity became the watchword for the "privatized young women."[62] Although the ideas of earlier feminists were kept alive by individuals such as Charlotte Perkins Gilman, Dorothy Bromley, Alice Beal Parsons, and Suzanne La Follette, by 1930 feminism had fallen, to remain dormant until the present revival.

The second recent interpretation and one of greater usefulness is Chafe's study, *The American Woman* (1972). In an effort to correct what Degler called the "suffrage orientation of historians of women's rights," Chafe began after suffrage. He has provided a broad and preliminary investigation of women in politics, industry, the professions, and other aspects of American life. Drawing on several of the studies discussed above, he explored the progressive legislative successes of women in the early 1920s and acknowledged the individual accomplishments of women in the peace movement, in the struggle for social welfare legislation, and in municipal government reform. But in general, Chafe found that women had failed to achieve political equality. After surveying the political and sociological literature on voting behavior, he attempted to explain women's political failure in terms of social forces — the cross-group pressures on women, discrimination rooted in the authoritarian family structure and the sexual division of labor, and the absence of a strong women's issue for the new voters to focus upon. Chafe acknowledged that economic advances by women were minimal. Although he believed that sexually women had "substantially increased the amount of equality," he realized that "shifts in manners and morals did not interfere with the perpetuation of a sexual division of labor." He dated the shift in emphasis from careers to homemaking at 1930 and suggested that the depression merely wielded the final blow to feminist hopes for equality. Although Chafe placed part of the blame for the decline of feminism on the feminists themselves, especially their factionalism over the equal rights amendment, his analysis emphasized social barriers to emancipation. "For economic equality to become a reality," he wrote, "a fundamental revolution was required in the way men and women thought of each other, and in the distribution of responsibilities within marriage and the family."[63]

In the last few years, the literature on women in the 1920s has reached a new level of historical inquiry. Historians are now trying to understand the decline of feminism rather than to deny the need for further emancipation. Although the revised version finds that women were politically active in lobbying for reforms in spite of failures at the polls, the latest accounts recognize that the 1920s were not the years of economic prosperity for women described so proudly earlier: professional gains were minimal, industrial wages discriminatory, and unionization difficult. Marriage and motherhood brought most women out of the labor force and, supposedly, home to domestic and sexual fulfillment. Historians have generally retained the notion of the revolution in manners and morals, although research on the prewar years and on literary stereotypes may indicate a need for revision. How the social freedom in clothing, manners, and sex contributed to deeper social change must be questioned further in light of the new view of women's history. Rather than proclaiming the contributions of "women as force" in recent history, historians now explain feminism's decline in terms of societal forces, such as family structure and political trends, the weaknesses inherent in the pre-1920 suffrage coalition, and legal and social discrimination against women as a group.

By further investigations of women's lives, historians can continue to correct their past errors, not only for the sake of historical accuracy, but also to begin to compensate for the disservice which earlier writings have rendered. The portrayal of the 1920s as a period of full equality, when actually discrimination in education, hiring, salaries, promotions, and family responsibilities was abundant, has perpetuated a myth of equality, one which has helped undermine women's attainment of group consciousness. Similarly, to write and teach — on the basis of insubstantial observations — that women were politically apathetic but sexually active during the 1920s is to provide sexually stereotyped historical roles for women. Historians' use of the "sexual revolution" as an explanation for women's history in the 1920s was, perhaps, an extension of their own inability to conceive of women outside of sexual roles. Furthermore, if the admittedly minimal evidence on writings in the 1930s and 1940s is substantiated, American historians' emphasis on woman's place in the home rather than her capacities for nondomestic careers may have contributed to the perpetuation of cultural stereotypes which helped weaken feminism since 1920.

The works of recent writers have begun the long overdue revision of historical attitudes towards women. Since 1970, studies by Lois Banner, William Chafe, Paula Fass, Peter Filene, Jacquelyn Dowd Hall, and Mary Ryan have shown the complexities of the historical experiences of women in the 1920s.[64] Younger scholars are heeding the advice of the pioneering modern historian of American women, Gerda Lerner, to study women both as a group and as members of specific racial, class, regional, and ethnic cultures. Only after investigating the lives of numerous women of the 1920s will historians discover patterns of women's history which will enable us to generalize about the new woman. Only then can we begin to judge the impact of suffrage and the extent to which women became active participants or struggling victims in American history.

Notes

1. Arthur S. Link, "What Happened to the Progressive Movement in the 1920's," *American Historical Review*, 64 (July, 1959), 833-49.

2. Eleanor Flexnor, *Century of Struggle: The Woman's Rights Movement in the United States* (Cambridge, 1959); Andrew Sinclair, *The Emancipation of the American Woman* (New York, 1965); Aileen S. Kraditor, *The Ideas of the Woman Suffrage Movement, 1890-1920* (New York, 1965). Also, Page Smith, *Daughters of the Promised Land* (Boston, 1970) and Ishbell Ross, *Sons of Adam, Daughters of Eve* (New York, 1969), both of which have very superficial treatments of the post-1920 years.

3. Frederick Lewis Allen, *Only Yesterday: An Informal History of the Nineteen-Twenties* (New York, 1931), 95-96.

4. William Leuchtenburg, *The Perils of Prosperity: 1914-1932* (Chicago, 1958), 159.

5. My conceptualizations in this essay were influenced by Gerda Lerner's early articles, especially "Women's Rights and American Feminism," *American Scholar* XXXX (Spring, 1971), 235-48.

6. Arthur Meier Schlesinger, *New Viewpoints in American History* (New York, 1922), 126.

7. Mary R. Beard, *Woman as Force in History* (New York, 1946). For a discussion of historiographical approaches to women's history and the distinction between Beardian and feminist views, see Gerda Lerner, "New Approaches to the Study of Women in American History," *Journal of Social History*, 3 (Fall, 1969), 53-62. Lerner rejected both approaches; she contended that women are too complex to be considered as a single group, although she recognized that they have been the victims of group discrimination.

8. Charlotte Perkins Gilman, "Woman's Achievements Since the Franchise," *Current History*, XXVII (October, 1927), 7; Carrie Chapman Catt, "Suffrage Only An Epic in Age-Old Movement," *Current History*, XXVII (October, 1927), 6; also, "Ten Years of Women Suffrage," *Literary Digest*, 105 (April 26, 1930), 11.

9. *Current History*, XXVII (October, 1927).

10. "Ten Years of Women Suffrage," *Literary Digest*, 11.

11. Marguerite Wells, "Some Effects of Woman Suffrage," *Annals of the American Academy of Political and Social Science*, CXLIII (May, 1929), 209; Dorothy Ashby Moncure, "Women in Political Life," *Current History*, XXIX (January, 1929), 639-43.

12. *Literary Digest*, 105 (April 26, 1930), 11.

13. Stuart A. Rice and Malcolm M. Willey, "American Women's Ineffective Use of the Vote," *Current History*, XX (July, 1924), 641-47.

14. V. F. Calverton, "Careers for Women: A Survey of Results," *Current History*, XXIX (January, 1929), 633-38; and V. F. Calverton and Samuel Schmalhausen, *Woman's Coming of Age: A Symposium* (New York, 1931), introduction.

15. George Britt, "Women in the New South," Schmalhausen and Calverton, eds., *Woman's Coming of Age*, 409-23.

16. Ben Lindsey, "The Promise and Peril of the New Freedom," Schmalhausen and Calverton, eds., *Woman's Coming of Age*, 447-71.

17. Chase Going Woodhouse, "The Status of Women," *American Journal of Sociology*, 35 (May, 1930), 1091-96.

18. A similar confidence among social scientists in the twenties has been described by Henry F. May in "Shifting Perspectives on the 1920's" *Mississippi Valley Historical Review*, XLIII (December 1956), 405-27.

19. Charles A. and Mary R. Beard, *The Rise of American Civilization* (New York, 1930), 753-58.

20. Preston William Slosson, *The Great Crusade and After: 1914-1928* (New York, 1931), 131-60.

21. Allen, *Only Yesterday*, 97-108.

22. Inez Haynes Irwin, *Angels and Amazons: A Hundred Years of American Women* (Garden City, New York, 1933), 411.

23. Sophinisba P. Breckinridge, *Women in the Twentieth Century: A Study of the Political, Social and Economic Activities* (New York, 1933); May, "Shifting Perspectives on the 1920's," 412.

24. Ernest R. Groves, *The American Woman: The Feminine Side of a Masculine Civilization* (New York, 1937).

25. Groves, *The American Woman*, pp. 364, 377. Legislation included the Women's Bureau, which became a permanent agency in 1920, and the Sheppard-Towner Act of 1921, which funded welfare and hygiene centers for maternity and infancy care. Groves also connected the sexual revolution with economic roots: because women's motives for marrying had become less economic, he reasoned, women had begun to "demand from the experience a fulfillment of personality which more and more includes satisfactory sexual relationships." (389)

26. According to the Lynds, the need for women to work to supplement reduced family incomes during the depression confused traditional roles and placed renewed emphasis on femininity and on the value of women as homemakers. Robert S. and Helen Merrel Lynd, *Middletown in Transition: A Study in Cultural Conflicts* (New York, 1937), chapter four. E. Wight Bakke, in *The Unemployed Worker* (London, 1940), also noted that although women worked during the depression, their

employment was always considered a necessity, and their proper place remained in the home.

27. Examples of the texts which had little about women in the twenties were: Jeannette P. Nichols, *Twentieth Century United States: A History* (New York, 1943); Samuel Eliot Morison and Henry Steele Commager, *The Growth of the American Republic*, Volume II (New York, 1942 edition), with one paragraph on the women's rights movement; and John D. Hicks, *The American Nation: A History of the United States from 1865 to the Present* (Boston, 1949), which had only the sentence quoted below.

28. See: Harold Underwood Faulkner, *American Political and Social History* (New York, 1937), 651-52; Foster Rhea Dulles, *Twentieth Century America* (Cambridge, Mass., 1945); 176-77; Dwight Lowell Dumond, *Roosevelt to Roosevelt: The United States in the Twentieth Century* (New York, 1937); 35; Merle Curti, Richard Shryock, Thomas Cochran, and Fred Harvey Harrington, *An American History* (New York, 1950), 452-60; Louis M. Hacker and Helene S. Zahler, *The United States in the Twentieth Century* (New York, 1952), 355-56.

29. Dumond, *Roosevelt to Roosevelt*, 35.

30. Merle Curti, *The Growth of American Thought* (New York, 1943), 700. Although Curti's account leaves the reader with the impression that women remained at home in the twenties as efficient homemakers, occasionally glancing up from the card table to take note of the world, he later looked back on the decade (during his discussion of the thirties) as a time of "expanding economic opportunities from which so many ambitious women had profited. . . ." The thirties, he claimed, "dealt blow after blow at women in the professions, in the arts and in business. Feminists regretted that the new turn of events undermined the progress women had been making. . . ." (721) When this progress had been made is unclear.

31. Dulles, *Twentieth Century America*, 176.

32. Harvey Wish, *Society and Thought in Modern America: A Social and Intellectual History of the American People from 1865* (New York, 1952), 445-47.

33. Hacker and Zahler, *The United States in the Twentieth Century*; Faulkner, *American Political and Social History*.

34. Hicks, *The American Nation*, 408.

35. Henry Steele Commager, *The American Mind: An Interpretation of American Thought and Character Since the 1880's* (New Haven, 1950), 46.

36. Dumond, *Roosevelt to Roosevelt*, 59-60. The WJCC worked for passage of the Sheppard Towner Act (1921), the Cable Act (1922, for the right of independent citizenship for married women), and dozens of other bills.

37. Curti, Shryock, Cochran, and Harrington, *An American History*, 462.

38. On the postwar confusion over women's roles, see: William Chafe, "From Suffrage to Liberation: The Changing Roles of American Women, 1920-1970," doctoral dissertation, Columbia University, 1971, especially chapter 10, "The Debate on Women's Place." He cites, for example, "American Woman's Dilemma," *Life*, 22 (June 16, 1947), 101-11.

39. The generally favorable reviews ranged in opinion from "a very lively thesis," (New York *Times*, February 22, 1953) to "borders on paranoid" (*Atlantic*, 191, April, 1953). Patrick Mullahy (*Nation*, 176, Feb. 21, 1953) and Ashley Montague (New York *Herald Tribune*, Feb. 22, 1953) predicted that the book would dispel myths about women and encourage reform. Elizabeth Hardwick (*Partisan Review*, 20, May, 1953) rather bitterly criticized the book as one which filled her "with a kind of

shame and sadness." Joint reviews on women's literature appeared in *Hudson Review*, IX (Summer, 1956) by S. Rudikoff, and *The Antioch Review*, 14 (June, 1954), by Robert Bierstedt.

40. Arnold W. Green and Eleanor Melnick, "What Has Happened to the Feminist Movement?," in Gouldner, Alvin W., ed., *Studies in Leadership: Leadership and Democratic Action* (New York, 1950), 283.

41. Green and Melnick, "What Has Happened to the Feminist Movement?," 296, 301.

42. Helen Hacker, "Women as a Minority Group," *Social Forces*, XXX (October, 1951), 60-69. The definitions which she used are those of Louis Wirth and Kurt Lewin.

43. B. June West, "The 'New Woman'," *Twentieth Century Literature*, I (July, 1955), 55-68.

44. Robert W. Smuts, *Women and Work in America* (New York, 1959), 142-43.

45. Eric J. Dingwall, *The American Woman: A Historical Study Since 1620* (London, 1956); Carl N. Degler, "Charlotte Perkins Gilman on the Theory and Practice of Feminism," *American Quarterly*, VIII (Spring, 1956), 21-39.

46. Eric P. Goldman, *Rendezvous with Destiny: A History of Modern American Reform* (New York, 1952), 292-93.

47. Arthur S. Link, *American Epoch: A History of the United States Since the 1890's* (New York, 1955), 274-75.

48. Leuchtenburg, *Perils of Prosperity*, 160.

49. Betty Friedan, *The Feminine Mystique* (New York, 1963). While Friedan's book is not an historical study, it does offer several hypotheses on the history of women after 1920 which require clarification. Friedan dated the end of the era of the New Woman—the woman who searches for her own identity—around 1949-50, when a change in emphasis to "femininity" created the feminine mystique of housewife-mother. Her argument is based in large part on analyses of short stories in women's magazines, in which she finds career girl heroines predominant in the 1930's, and housewife-mother heroines, who forsake careers for husband, home and family, in the 1950's. One explanation for the shift, Friedan asserted, was that career women editors of these magazines were either being replaced by men, or were so embarrassed by their own success that they tried to make other women accept a more traditional feminine role. "Did women really go home again as a reaction to feminism?" she asked; "The fact is that to women born after 1920 [and thus coming to maturity in the post-World War II period] feminism was dead history. It ended as a vital movement in America with the winning of that final right: the vote." (93) After 1945, the sexual sell of advertising further encouraged the role of homemaker-consumer. (200-5)

Friedan's argument overlooks the realities of women's history. She hypothesized a generation of liberated career women in the twenties and thirties, largely based on one short story published in 1939. She offered some basis for the fifties model from the magazine literature, but had no reason to suggest that the homemaker-consumer had not originated back in the twenties. After World War II, she admitted, statistics on working women show increased female employment.

For another use of the women's magazine literature, see Chafe, "From Suffrage to Liberation," 190-201, which finds domesticity and an attack on feminism in the 1930's if not earlier.

50. David Potter, "American Women and American Character," in John A. Hague, ed., *American Character and American Culture: Some Twentieth Century Perspectives* (DeLand, Fla., 1964), 69-82.

51. Carl N. Degler, "Revolution without Ideology: The Changing Place of Women in America," in Robert J. Lifton, ed., *The Woman in America* (Boston, 1967), 197.

52. Degler, "Revolution without Ideology," 207. Other research on women included several dissertations on individual feminists and on women in politics.

53. Clarke A. Chambers, *Seedtime of Reform: American Social Service and Social Action, 1918-1933* (Minneapolis, 1963), 82-83.

54. Anne Firor Scott, "After Suffrage: Southern Women in the Twenties," *Journal of Southern History*, XXX (August, 1964), 298-318; also, *The Southern Lady: From Pedestal to Politics, 1830-1930* (Chicago, 1970).

55. James Stanley Lemons, "The New Woman in the New Era: The Woman Movement from the Great War to the Great Depression," doctoral dissertation, University of Missouri, 1967, v, vi, 72-73.

56. Lemons, "The New Woman in the New Era," 77, 90-91, 100.

57. Lemons, "The New Woman in the New Era," 302. Another positive interpretation of women's political progress in the twenties is found in Martin Gruberg, *Women in American Politics: An Assessment and Sourcebook* (Oshkosh, Wisc., 1968), 8, 9ff.

58. James R. McGovern, "American Woman's Pre-World War I Freedom in Manners and Morals," *Journal of American History*, LV (September, 1968), 315-327; see also, Robert E. Riegel, "Women's Clothes and Women's Rights," *American Quarterly*, XV (Fall, 1963) on nineteenth century dress reform; William O'Neill, *Divorce in the Progressive Era* (New Haven, 1967), on prewar social and moral change; and Henry F. May, *The End of American Innocence* (New York, 1959).

On fashions and the function of women's new styles, see K. A. Yellis, "Prosperity's Child: Some Thoughts on the Flapper," *American Quarterly*, XXI (Spring, 1969), 44-64. Yellis noted that "the new woman seemed to go into eclipse during the period of anxiety [the depression], but the changed circumstances of World War II, including a manpower shortage, brought her out again." (64)

59. William O'Neill, *Everyone Was Brave: A History of Feminism in America* (Chicago, 1971), 264. Originally published in 1970. For a summary of O'Neill's distinction between "social feminism" and "hard-core feminism," see his essay "Feminism as a Radical Ideology," in Alfred F. Young, ed., *Dissent: Explorations in the History of American Radicalism* (DeKalb, Illinois, 1968). Another study which contributes to post-1920 women's history but does not explicitly discuss the decline of feminism is David M. Kennedy's *Birth Control in America: The Career of Margaret Sanger* (New Haven, 1970). On Sanger, see also Linda Gordon, *Woman's Body, Woman's Right: A Social History of Birth Control in America* (New York, 1976). On the decline of feminism, see Estelle B. Freedman, "Separatism as Strategy: Female Institution Building and American Feminism, 1870-1930," *Feminist Studies* 5 (Fall, 1979), 512-29.

60. O'Neill, *Everyone Was Brave*, 270-73, 291.

61. O'Neill, *Everyone Was Brave*, 306.

62. O'Neill, *Everyone Was Brave*, 313.

63. Chafe, "From Suffrage to Liberation," 56ff, 120, 185, 211-12.

64. Lois W. Banner, *Women in Modern America: A Brief History* (New York,

1974); William H. Chafe, *The American Woman: Her Changing Social, Economic, and Political Roles, 1920-1970* (New York, 1972) and *Women and Equality: Changing Patterns in American Culture* (New York, 1977); Paula S. Fass, *The Damned and the Beautiful: American Youth in the 1920s* (New York, 1977); Peter Gabriel Filene, *Him/Her/Self: Sex Roles in Modern America* (New York, 1974); Jacquelyn Dowd Hall, *Revolt Against Chivalry: Jessie Daniel Ames and the Women's Campaign Against Lynching* (New York, 1979); Mary P. Ryan, *Womanhood in America: From Colonial Times to the Present* (New York, 1975, 1979).

PART II

The Economic Context

The movement of married women into the work force continued throughout the interwar years, and by the 1930s the substantial increase in the number of working wives from middle-income families became apparent. Through a close analysis of evidence related to the buying habits of American families, Winifred Wandersee has discovered that in addition to social, demographic, and technological changes which eased this development, the definition of what constituted economic need for many families was undergoing change. Although the concept of economic need might be relative for middle-income families, it was the subsistence level of life that concerned the poor white and black female tobacco and cotton mill operatives studied by Dolores Janiewski. Utilizing oral history as well as more traditional sources, she examines in depth the interplay of race and gender with the paternalism of North Carolina factory owners and the traditionalism of union organizers. In the Southwest, Chicana workers also faced much of the same discrimination during the years of the first large-scale Mexican immigration, and in her article Rosalinda González focuses on the impact of industrial capitalism on these women's lives at home, in the fields, and in factories.

How and why did the standard of living for middle-income American families change? In the face of a severe depression, how did so many families maintain this new level of consumption? What were the similarities in the plights of black and white female operatives in Durham's cotton and tobacco factories? What factors divided these women from one another? Why did both groups express relatively low interest in union activities? How similar were the problems faced by the Chicana workers in the Southwest during this period? As these workers moved out of their homes into the work force, what kinds of changes might have taken place in family roles and structures?

2

The Economics of Middle-Income Family Life: Working Women During the Great Depression

_____ WINIFRED D. WANDERSEE _____

The history of women and work is becoming an increasingly fertile field of research for historians, and the interest in this topic has generated a great deal of valuable scholarship. If there is one theme that emerges, it is that women's work outside of the home has been an extension of their family role and a reflection of their economic need. From the historian's point of view, the "pin-money theory" is dead.[1] Long before the depression of the 1930s, married women left their homes to work in the factories and fields, in the homes of other women, and, increasingly during the twentieth century, in clerical and service occupations. In the decade between 1930 and 1940, the number of married women in the labor force increased by nearly 50 percent, while their numbers in the population increased by only 15 percent. By 1940 married women were 35 percent of the female labor force, in comparison to 29 percent in 1930 (see Table 1).

Thus, in spite of the oversupply of labor and the underemployment of the population as a whole, married women workers made substantial numerical gains during the depression decade. It would be a mistake to suggest that the 1930s represented a new direction; rather, the labor force behavior of these years was a continuation of long-term trends that had been developing since the turn of the century. In fact, the gains of the 1930s were not nearly as dramatic as those of two earlier decades — 1900 to 1910 and 1920 to 1930. What is significant is that they were made at a time of economic stagnation — at a time when women were under a great deal of public pressure to leave the labor market in order to avoid competing with men for the short supply of jobs.

The majority of married women workers during these years were working because of economic necessity. The investigations conducted by the Women's Bureau were devoted to proving that point, and even a cursory glance at the census data on the female labor force would support the bureau's interpretation. For instance, in 1930, about 3.9 million women combined the roles of homemaker and wage earner; nearly one million were from families with no male head. In that year, nearly 38 percent of all

From _The Journal of American History_, LXV (June 1978), 60-74. Reprinted by permission. _The Journal of American History_, Indiana University, Bloomington, Indiana.

married working women were either foreign born or black, and practically one-fourth were in domestic and personal service.[2]

Table 1   Number and Proportion of Women 15 Years Old and Over, Gainfully Occupied, by Marital Condition, for the United States, 1890-1940

Census Year and Marital Status	Total Number*	Gainfully Occupied		% Distr. of Gainfully Occupied
		Number*	Percent	
1890				
Females 15 and over	19.6	3.7	18.9	100.0
Single and unknown	6.3	2.5	40.5	68.2
Married	11.1	0.5	4.6	13.9
Widowed and divorced	2.2	0.7	29.9	17.9
1900				
Females 15 and over	24.2	5.0	20.6	100.0
Single and unknown	7.6	3.3	43.5	66.2
Married	13.8	0.8	5.6	15.4
Widowed and divorced	2.8	0.9	32.5	18.4
1910				
Females 15 and over	30.0	7.6	25.4	100.0
Single and unknown	9.0	4.6	51.1	60.2
Married	17.7	1.9	10.7	24.7
Widowed and divorced	3.4	1.2	34.1	15.0
1920				
Females 15 and over	35.2	8.3	23.7	100.0
Single, widowed, divorced and unknown	13.9	6.4	46.4	77.0
Married	21.3	1.9	9.0	23.0
1930				
Females 15 and over	42.8	10.6	24.8	100.0
Single and unknown	11.4	5.7	50.5	53.9
Married	26.2	3.1	11.7	28.9
Widowed and divorced	5.3	1.8	24.4	17.2
1940				
Females 14 and over**	50.5	12.8	25.3	100.0
Single	13.9	6.3	45.0	49.4
Married	30.1	4.6	15.3	35.5
Husband present	28.5	3.8	13.3	29.6
Husband absent	1.6	0.8	46.9	5.9
Widowed and divorced	6.5	1.9	29.2	15.1

* Numbers in millions.
** 1940 age category differs from other census years.
Source: 16th Census of the United States, 1940, *Population.* Vol. III: *The Labor Force: Industry, Employment, and Income.* Part I: *United States Summary* (Washington, 1943), Table 9, p. 26; 15th Census of the United States, 1930, *Population.* Vol. V: *General Report on Occupations* (Washington, 1933), Table I, 272; and Gertrude Bancroft, *The American Labor Force: Its Growth and Changing Composition* (New York, 1958), Table 25, p. 45.

Much attention has been given to the working women of lower-income families by the Women's Bureau, by social workers, and by recent historians.[3] But there has been a tendency to overlook another demographic characteristic of the 1930s: the rather substantial number of married women from middle-income* families who were also gainfully employed. By 1940, over 40 percent of the gainfully employed homemakers who lived with their husbands were married to men who had earned $1,000 or more in 1939 (see Table 4).

This statistic has little meaning unless placed into the context of family economics during these years. Tables 2 and 3 give the family income distribution for two different time periods, 1929 and 1935-1936. Neither of these time periods corresponds to 1939, a year for which there are no figures on income distribution. 1939 was probably a somewhat better year than 1935-1936, but not as good as 1929. In 1935-1936, the median family income was $1,160; 50 percent of all families made between $500 and $1,500 a year. Thus, an annual wage or salary of $1,000 or more could place a family in the middle-income range.

But what did it mean to be a "middle-income family" in the 1930s? It did not mean that the family had a large surplus income, but it did suggest a fairly comfortable standard of living. In the years between the 1890s and 1920s, average annual money earnings and the purchasing power of these earnings increased substantially for many classes of American society.[4] Thus, it would seem that married women in spite of evidence of economic need, were entering the labor market in the greatest numbers during a period of relative affluence. Although the statistics indicate that most gainfully-employed married women were working because of need, the number of working women from middle-income families was also increasing. The increase was related to complex social, demographic, and technological developments; to changes in the economic function of the family as it became town-based rather than rural; and to the factor explored in this article — the changing definition of economic need.

By the 1920s, American economic and social life reflected an awareness of what was commonly referred to as "the American Standard of Living."[5] The average American may have been unable to describe the precise meaning of this term, but nearly everyone agreed that it was attainable, highly desirable, and far superior to the standard of any other nation. Its nature varied according to social class and regional differences, but no matter where a family stood socially and financially, members set their aspirations beyond their means. A family defined its standard of living in terms of an income that it hoped to achieve rather than by the reality of the paycheck.

Thus, the American standard of living, influenced by the availability of

---

*The term "middle-income" will be used, as opposed to "middle class," which is a term much more difficult to define.

consumer goods and mass advertising, gave the term "economic need" a new definition. Instead of referring merely to food, clothing, and shelter, economic need came to mean anything that a particular family was unwilling to go without. When the American dream of prosperity came to an end in 1929, American families at all economic levels were hard hit. For those at

Table 2   Family Income Distribution, 1929

Income Level (in dollars)	No. of Families (in thousands)	Percent at Each Level	Cumulative Percent
Under 0	120	0.4	0.4
0 to 500	1,982	7.2	7.6
500 to 1,000	3,797	13.8	21.5
1,000 to 1,500	5,754	21.0	42.4
1,500 to 2,000	4,701	17.1	59.5
2,000 to 2,500	3,204	11.6	71.2
2,500 to 3,000	1,988	7.2	78.4
3,000 to 3,500	1,447	5.3	83.7
3,500 to 4,000	993	3.6	87.3
4,000 to 4,500	718	2.6	89.9
4,500 to 5,000	514	1.9	91.8
Over 5,000	2,256	8.2	100.0
Total	27,474	100.0	

Source: Maurice Leven, Harold G. Moulton, and Clark Warburton, *America's Capacity to Consume* (Washington, 1934), 54.

Table 3   Family Income Distribution, 1935-1936

Income Level (in dollars)	No. of Families (in thousands)	Percent at Each Level	Cumulative Percent
Under 250	1,163	4.0	4.0
250 to 500	3,015	10.3	14.2
500 to 750	3,799	12.9	27.1
750 to 1,000	4,277	14.6	41.7
1,000 to 1,250	3,882	13.2	54.9
1,250 to 1,500	2,865	9.8	64.6
1,500 to 1,750	2,343	8.0	72.6
1,750 to 2,000	1,897	6.5	79.1
2,000 to 2,250	1,421	4.8	83.9
2,250 to 2,500	1,044	3.6	87.4
2,500 to 3,000	1,314	4.5	91.9
3,000 to 3,500	744	2.5	94.4
3,500 to 4,000	438	1.5	95.9
4,000 to 4,500	250	.9	96.8
4,500 to 5,000	153	.5	97.3
Over 5,000	793	2.7	100.0
Total	29,400	100.0	

Source: "Incomes of Families and Single Persons, 1935–36: Summary," *Monthly Labor Review*, 47 (Oct. 1938), 730.

the bottom, the Great Depression was an extension and intensification of the hard times they had always suffered. Families that had been marginally independent were pushed across the line into poverty and dependency. But even relatively affluent middle-class families saw their accustomed standard of living greatly diminished.

Expectations with respect to standards of living remained high, but the means to achieve these expectations declined. Some families borrowed, while others simply did not pay their bills. Some moved in with relatives and some went on relief. The most logical way to meet the economic crisis was to cut back expenditures; and although this measure was forced upon most families, many nevertheless managed to maintain a remarkably high level of consumption during the depression. Even in the face of unemployment, wage reductions, and general economic insecurity, people of middle incomes clung to certain material goods and life-styles that had become important elements in the new definition of economic need.

In 1935-1936, the Bureau of Labor Statistics and the Bureau of Home Economics, in cooperation with the National Resources Committee and the Central Statistical Board, did a national study on incomes and expenditures (hereafter referred to as the Consumer Purchases Study). The study was a random sample of about 336,000 families and a smaller sample of about 53,000 families to provide information on the consumption patterns of families not on relief and at different income levels. Since the information was being obtained primarily to provide a basis for indexes of living costs, it was felt that the information should not reflect the distorted spending of families whose incomes had been abnormally low or irregular.[6]

The Consumer Purchases Study revealed that postwar changes in family expenditures occurred during the 1920s—not the 1930s—and that these changes had had a profound effect upon consumption patterns of the 1930s, in spite of the decline of income during the depression. Faith Williams of the Bureau of Labor Statistics observed that most families of wage earners and clerical workers had higher standards of living in 1934-1936 than families of comparable income in the years 1917-1919: "Their diets more nearly approach the recommendation of specialists in human nutrition; they have homes with better lighting; many of them are able to travel more because they have automobiles. The change in the ideas of these workers as to how they ought to live has resulted in fundamental changes in their expenditure patterns."[7]

Comparisons were made in view of the price realignments that had occurred between the 1917-1919 study and the Consumer Purchases Study. The purchasing power of the worker's dollar was, on the average, slightly higher in 1934-1936 than it had been in 1917-1919. Food prices were consistently lower by as much as 16 percent to 38 percent in each of the cities covered by both studies. Clothing prices were also lower by 5 percent to 31 percent. Differences in the cost of rent, fuel, and light varied greatly from city to city. Furnishings and household equipment generally cost less in the later period, but miscellaneous items were more expensive in every city. The Bureau of Labor Statistics eliminated these price differences by applying the cost of items in the 1934-1936 period to the average expenditures of the families studied in 1917-1919.[8]

The basic change in expenditure at all economic levels was a shift away from essential items—food, clothing, and shelter—toward the miscellaneous items that signify an over-all higher standard of living. The pattern of change was very similar in each city. For instance, in twenty-four out of thirty-five cities, average expenditures for food were lower in the later period. This was because food prices were lower, enabling families to eat as well or better on less money. The average amount spent for clothing was down for each city, but expenditures for housing, which included fuel, light, and refrigeration, were higher in every city except one. A large proportion of the 1934-1936 families had electric lighting and modern plumbing, which accounted for the higher costs. Expenditures for furniture and furnishings varied from city to city. Finally, two-thirds of the cities showed a higher average expenditure on miscellaneous items, or everything not included under the above items.[9]

Economists, home economists, and even social workers, tended to be critical of the buying habits of American families; some suggested that Americans created their own economic problems through love of luxury and ignorance of money management. A home economist, Day Monroe, felt that even low-income families could improve their standards of living by wise spending, a criticism that should probably have been directed at middle-income families.[10] Although more intelligent buying habits might have resulted in a higher standard of living for some families, the problem was primarily related to changing values. While American families of all income levels raised their expectations, the expenditure pattern of an individual family depended on personal values rather than on the sophisticated opinions of economists and social workers.

Many families, especially those in the middle- to upper-income groups, made a conscious effort to plan their expenditures in response to wage reductions or changes in employment. Women's magazines and popular journals had special sections on budgeting. They published articles written by housewives who were budgeting and even ran contests for those who wished to advise the perfect budget. That this was definitely an upper-middle-class phenomenon is indicated by the incomes that these families had to budget—the lowest was $1,200, and they ranged to $3,000 and even $5,000. Most of the women (and it was always women) who wrote personal accounts of their budgeting experience did so in a manner that was both light-hearted and smug. Obviously there was something good and clean—even fun—in returning to the "plain living" of grandma's day, especially when that plain living was sustained on a $2,500 a year salary.[11]

In the mid-1930s, an income of $2,500 placed a family in the upper 12 percent income bracket (see Table 3). Even in 1929, at the height of affluence, only about 29 percent of all American families made more than $2,500. A budget implies that there is room for flexibility with respect to expenditures, and, although most families established priorities through the simple act of buying, few had a surplus requiring conscious decision or varied choices. As humorist Will Cuppy observed, "In order to run a budget, you have to have money. . . . I don't feel that I can afford one right now—there are so many other things I need worse." Many Americans would have agreed with Cuppy: "I'm not good at figures, but I know when I'm ruined, and I don't have to write it down on a piece of paper."[12]

Since about 42 percent of all American families were living on a marginal income basis, that is, below $1,000 a year, how did they manage to maintain a relatively high standard of consumption during the depression? The lower cost of living was one factor. Combined money income in 1931 was approximately seven-tenths that of 1929, but the cost of living for a workingman's family declined about 15 percent during the same period. This was not equal to the decline in money income, but the necessities of life, food, in particular, showed the most striking decreases.[13] Moreover, the rate of consumption did fall off considerably, especially during the early years of the depression. But for some, installment buying remained an important means of maintaining a facsimile of the standard they wished to achieve. Although consumption of durable goods fell off steeply during the early 1930s, by 1936 about $6 billion worth of automobiles, radios, and other goods were purchased on installment—an increase of 20 percent over 1929.[14]

Many families were able to maintain an acceptable standard of living by placing "additional workers" in the labor force. In spite of traditional American values that have supported the ideal of the one-wage earner family, most families have always depended upon the economic contributions of several members. Sometimes this contribution took the form of "unpaid family work," as in the case of the agricultural family or of the family that ran its own business. But wage-earning and salaried families also were often dependent on the efforts of all members able to work. There is evidence to suggest a direct relationship between income level and number of family earners.

Many middle-income families of the 1930s derived their status from the efforts of several family members. At the very low wage and salary levels — under $800—fewer than one out of five families had an extra wage earner, but nearly one out of four families earning $800 to $1,600 relied on an extra wage earner. A substantially larger ratio of families with extra earners occurred above $1,600. These categories did not represent an insignificant number of families; 22 percent of all urban and rural non-farm families had wage or salary incomes between $1,600 and $2,500 in 1939, and over one-third of these relied upon several family earners.[15] Thus, many American families owed their middle-class status not to adequate wages for one person, but to the presence of several wage earners in the family.

Most of the extra family wage earners were not wives and mothers, but other relatives of the head of the house, usually sons. In fact, even males under the age of eighteen were more likely to be listed as being in the labor force than were wives. But the nature of their employment suggests that young boys were less likely to bring in an extra paycheck than were married women workers: 47 percent were listed as "unpaid family workers" in comparison to 8 percent of all working wives and 22 percent of working girls under the age of eighteen.[16]

Thus, by 1940, married homemakers were more likely to be making an economic contribution through paid employment than were their children, either male or female, under the age of eighteen. The rapid decline of child labor during the twentieth century was probably a related factor in this development, but it is difficult to determine the direction of the causal relationship, assuming that there was one. That is, did women enter the labor market because older children no longer worked, or did older children remain out of the labor market, possibly in school, because their mothers were working?

The increased participation of married women in the work force reflected a variety of developments, including the decline of child labor, economic need at the poverty level, relative need at every other level, and the availability of more desirable jobs. There is no way of determining which of these factors predominated. The relationship of economic need to the gainful employment of married women was an issue that could not be resolved because it was a matter of individual interpretation. That is, each family decided for itself at which point it was willing to accept the inconvenience of a working wife and mother in order to achieve a better standard of living. But the investigations of working women that were conducted in the 1920s and 1930s were generally sympathetic to women and their right to work. Therefore, the investigators sometimes overstated the case for "economic need" by accepting at face value the reasons for work given by the women themselves.

A study in 1932 by Cecile T. LaFollette for Columbia University reflects this tendency to accept perhaps too wholeheartedly the economic need of working women. The group surveyed included 652 women of the business and professional class; 438, or 67 percent, gave economic necessity as their reason for working. Many of the other reasons given were really economic in character — to educate children, make payments on the house, pay for sickness or other debts, and raise standards of living. For instance, 320, or 49 percent, worked in order to provide the "extras" that would not have been possible on the husband's salary alone.[17] Many of the women who gave the reason "economic necessity" probably stretched the term to include some of these items. But LaFollette felt that the incomes of the husbands offered ample evidence that most of these women had to work. What she did not seem to realize was that most of these families were far better off than their contemporaries. Only 6 percent of them made less than $1,000 a year, compared to about 42 percent of all American families who made less than that in 1935-1936. About 32 percent had husbands earning less than $2,000 a year, but nearly 80 percent of all American families were under that income level. The median income of husbands in LaFollette's sample was $2,094, or about $1,000 more than the median for all families.[18]

Values, rather than absolute need, made the women in the LaFollette sample willing to go to work, in spite of the relatively high earnings of their husbands. These business and professional women were hardly representative of working women as a whole, however, and there is no question that there was a strong relationship between low income and married women in the labor force. Table 4 indicates that the women whose husbands were in the lower-income groups were over-represented in the work force. For instance, in metropolitan areas, about 23 percent of all husbands earned under $1,000 a year in 1939, but the wives of this income group contributed about 33 percent of the married women work force. In smaller urban areas, wives of husbands with low income were even more heavily over-represented.

The earnings of working wives could sometimes lift the family of a low-level wage earner into the middle class, but in most cases their wages were very low, undoubtedly because employment was often temporary or part time. The census data of 1940 reveal that low-paid women were most often

Table 4   Wage or Salary Income in 1939 of Husbands, for Married Women, 18 to 64 Years Old, with Husband Present, by Labor Force Status, in March, 1940*

Wage or Salary Income	Percent of Wives	% Distr. of Gainfully Employed	% of Wives in Labor Force
None and not reported	4.8	7.1	24.3
$1 to $199	1.0	1.7	27.6
$200 to $399	2.6	3.9	24.2
$400 to $599	4.0	5.6	22.7
$600 to $999	11.2	14.8	21.7
$1,000 to $1,499	17.5	20.3	18.8
$1,500 to $1,999	14.6	12.6	14.0
$2,000 to $2,999	11.5	6.5	9.2
$3,000 and over	5.0	1.7	5.6
Husbands without other income	72.2	74.4	16.7
Husbands with other income	27.8	25.6	14.9

* Data drawn from metropolitan areas of 100,000 or more.
Source: 16th Census of the United States, 1940, *Population: The Labor Force (Sample Statistics) Employment and Family Characteristics of Women* (Washington, 1943), Table 23, pp. 133–35.

married to low-paid men, and the more a woman earned, the less she needed it. Over a third of all married women workers were in families in which the husband made less than $600.[19] In contrast, over half of these women — 56.3 percent — had husbands who made from $600 to $2,000; over one-fourth of the husbands earned between $1,200 and $2,000.[20] It is in this broad middle range that values, rather than need, began to influence decisions regarding work. The decision must have been a complex one, related to personal family circumstances, including number and age of children, desired standard of living, and availability of suitable work; but it cannot be seen as a case of absolute need.

Another way to estimate the economic status of married women workers is to relate employment to occupational grouping and employment status of the husband. Occupational group is not as effective as the use of income level, because there is often a wide range of salaries paid to workers in a particular occupational field. Also, workers in certain kinds of work — skilled labor, for instance — often had values that prevented or inhibited wives from working, in spite of economic need. But, in a sense, that is exactly the point being made: values, as well as economic need, influenced the decision of women to work.

In 1940 women who were married to men in low-paying, low-prestige jobs, were more likely to be in the labor force than the wives of men in "middle-class" or white-collar occupations (see Table 5). For instance, over half of the wives of domestic service workers were in the labor force, probably as domestic workers themselves. Over one-fourth of the wives of service workers, including those in domestic and protective services, were in the labor force; but these two groups did not contribute a very large share of the female labor force, because there were not many husbands in these occupations. The column showing distribution reveals that 55.8 percent of all working wives were married to men who were proprietors, managers and officials; clerical and sales workers; craftsmen and foremen; or factory operatives. All but the last of these four categories could be considered middle class, two of them being white collar, and the third being skilled work requiring experience and bestowing a certain amount óf prestige. Thus, although women with husbands in low-paying jobs were more likely to be in the labor force, a large proportion of married working women were married to men in "middle-class" occupations — a fact that suggests that the occurrence of working wives was fairly widespread socially, even though it still affected only a minority of families in each occupational field other than domestic service.

There is no single answer to the question of why women worked during the 1930s. A number of related factors can be suggested, including the decline of child labor, the decline in the birth rate, the changing economic function of the home, economic distress, and desire to maintain a particular standard of living. Given the low incomes of the 1920s and especially the

1930s, and the rising expectations with respect to the standard of living, it is not surprising that married women were entering the labor force. What is surprising is that they remained a small minority. By 1940 there were over 4 million married women workers over the age of 14, but they still represented only 15 percent of all married women (see Table 1). Even at the lowest income levels, only one married woman in four was working. Since the great majority of Americans were living on low incomes during the depression, the question is not so much why a small minority accepted the employment of married women, but why such a large majority did not, in spite of the fact that they too experienced unsatisfied economic needs as a result of inadequate wages.

The answer lies partly in the cultural values held by most American families, by the poor as well as by the middle-class. One group that did not share the dominant value system, black families, had a much higher proportion than whites of wives and mothers in the labor force at all economic levels. For most white Americans, a working wife placed a stigma

Table 5   Employment Status and Major Occupation Group of Husband, for Married Women 18 to 64 Years Old, with Husband Present, by Labor Force Status in the United States 1940

Occupation and Employment Status of Husband	No. of Married Women Husband Present*	No. of Wives in Labor Force	% of Wives in Labor Force	% Distr. of Gainfully Employed
Total	26.6	3.7	13.8	100.0
Husband Employed				
(excluding emergency work)	22.3	3.0	13.7	100.0
Professional & semi-prof.	1.3	.2	13.7	4.8
Farmers & farm managers	3.8	.2	4.4	4.6
Proprietors, managers, & officials, excl. farm	2.7	.4	15.2	11.7
Clerical, sales, & kindred workers	2.7	.5	17.0	12.5
Craftsmen, foremen, & kindred workers	3.8	.5	12.4	12.7
Operatives & kindred workers	4.1	.7	16.8	18.9
Domestic service workers	.06	.03	56.4	.9
Protective service	.4	.04	10.9	1.1
Service workers, excluding domestic and protective	.8	.2	25.3	5.6
Farm laborers & foremen	.8	.1	11.6	2.4
Laborers, excluding farm	1.7	.3	16.3	7.8
Occupation not reported	.1	.01	14.4	.5
Husband on emergency work and seeking work	2.8	.4	13.6	10.2
Not in labor force	1.6	.25	15.7	6.8

* Numbers in millions.
Source: Census, 1940, *Employment and Family Characteristics of Women*, 164.

upon the husband and the family—a stigma that could not be easily removed, but one that might be justified by the presence of economic necessity. Also, during the 1930s many women simply did not have job opportunities, particularly those women of lower-income families who were less likely to have skills to sell on the labor market. Many housewives found it physically impossible to run a household and maintain a paying job. Over half of all housewives spent forty-eight hours a week at work in the home. An additional third spent over fifty-six hours a week. The "modern conveniences" argument has been greatly overworked with respect to its effect upon the amount of physical labor involved in keeping house.[21]

Nonetheless, the fact that there was an increase in the number and proportion of married women in the labor force between 1920 and 1940 indicates that traditional values were gradually breaking down in the face of other, more concrete, changes. That most families resisted change, in spite of economic straits, reflects their basic conservatism in the face of economic and social developments of enormous consequence. But the public discussion of women's roles in the family and in the broader community strongly suggests that an important minority of women and their families were willing to accept a new life-style in response to a personal recognition of economic realities. To the extent that these women were from middle-income families, where they could make choices, they were influenced by values as well as absolute need in their determination to work. This does not contradict the assumption that many, if not most, married women worked because of economic need; but economic need is a relative concept, and it becomes a reality for different families at different levels of exprience. Most women could argue that they worked because they had to work, but they defined their needs differently from the non-working wives whose husbands had similar incomes.

The life-styles adopted by working women continued to be based on traditional family values. The women who worked were working in response to their understanding of family need. Although they carried their economic role beyond the confines of their homes, the relationship between home, self, and job remained constant. That is, the work of the married woman usually reflected the primacy of her home life. She was working to pay for a home, keep her children in school, help her husband with his business, or pay for the "extras." It would be a mistake to assume that her home life remained unchanged, however. The question of the working wife's role and status within the family, and the extent to which they evolved in response to the economic "necessities" of the depression is another topic that must be given further consideration if scholars are to understand the real impact of the 1930s upon American women.

Notes

1. Several historians discuss the "pin-money theory" in the context of broader social issues. See Clarke A. Chambers, *Seedtime of Reform: American Social Service*

and Social Action, 1918-1933 (Minneapolis, 1963), 62-63; and William H. Chafe, The American Woman: Her Changing Social, Economic, and Political Roles, 1920-1970 (New York, 1972), 62-65. The relationship between work and family is the basic theme of several recent studies in women's history: Virginia Yans McLaughlin, "Patterns of Work and Family Organization: Buffalo's Italians," Journal of Interdisciplinary History, II (Autumn 1971), 299-314; Daniel J. Walkowitz, "Working-Class Women in the Gilded Age: Factory, Community, and Family Life among Cohoes, New York, Cotton Workers," Journal of Social History, 5 (Summer 1972), 464-90; Joan W. Scott and Louise A. Tilly, "Women's Work and the Family in Nineteenth-Century Europe," Comparative Studies in Society and History, 17 (Jan. 1975), 36-64; and Thomas Dublin, "Women, Work, and the Family: Women Operatives in the Lowell Mills, 1830-1860," Feminist Studies, 3 (Fall 1975).

2. There were numerous studies done by the Women's Bureau during the 1920s and 1930s that were expressly devoted to disproving the "pin-money theory." For a summary of the census data cited above, see Mary Elizabeth Pidgeon, "The Employed Woman Homemaker in the U.S.: Her Responsibility for Family Support," Women's Bureau, Bulletin, No. 148 (Washington, 1936), 17, 21. See also 15th Census of the United States, 1930, Population. Vol. V: General Report on Occupations (Washington, 1933), Table 8, p. 275.

3. In addition to the studies already mentioned, see Robert W. Smuts, Women and Work in America (New York, 1959), 51-58. Several recent collections of documents give attention to working women of low-income status. See W. Elliot Brownlee and Mary M. Brownlee, eds., Women in the American Economy: A Documentary History, 1675 to 1929 (New Haven, 1976); Rosalyn Baxandall, Linda Gordon, and Susan Reverby, eds., America's Working Women (New York, 1976); and Gerda Lerner, ed., The Female Experience: An American Documentary (Indianapolis, 1977).

4. Paul H. Douglas, Real Wages in the United States, 1890-1926 (New York, 1930), 584. For a good description of affluence in the 1920s, see William E. Leuchtenburg, The Perils of Prosperity, 1914-1931 (Chicago, 1958), 178-203.

5. Royal Meeker, "What is the American Standard of Living?" Monthly Labor Review, IX (July 1919), 1.

6. Faith M. Williams, "Changes in Family Expenditures in the Post-War Period," Monthly Labor Review, 47 (Nov. 1938), 968.

7. Ibid., 979.

8. Ibid., 973.

9. Ibid., Table 1, 969-72, 973. For detailed information on family consumption, see "Family Expenditures in Selected Cities, 1935-36," Vols. I-VII, Bureau of Labor Statistics, Bulletin, No. 648 (Washington, 1941).

10. Day Monroe, "Levels of Living of the Nation's Families," Journal of Home Economics, 29 (Dec. 1937), 670. For a fictional account that reflects a similar bias, see Josephine Lawrence, If I Had Four Apples (New York, 1935).

11. See, for instance, Alice O'Reardon Overbeck, "Back to Plain Living," Forum, LXXXVIII (Nov. 1932, 302-06; H.M.S., "The Family Problem: Two Salary Cuts Have Taught Us What a Budget's For," American Magazine, CXVI (Sept. 1932), 120-21; "How We Live on $2,500 a Year," Ladies' Home Journal, XLVIII (Oct. 1930), 104; and H. Thompson Rich, "How to Live Beyond Your Means," Reader's Digest, 34 (May 1939), 1-4.

12. Will Cuppy, "I'm Not the Budget Type," Scribner's Magazine, CII (Dec. 1937), 21, 20.

13. William A. Berridge, "Employment, Unemployment, and Related Conditions of Labor," *American Journal of Sociology,* XXXVII (May 1932), 903-04. The *Monthly Labor Review* ran a regular monthly account of the rise or decline in the cost of living with respect to particular commodities during the 1930s.

14. Henry F. Pringle, "What do the Women of America Think About Money?" *Ladies' Home Journal,* LV (April 1938), 100. See also Blanche Bernstein, *The Pattern of Consumer Debt, 1935-36* (New York, 1940), 10, 113-16. Blanche Bernstein argues that consumer credit was particularly important in expanding the purchasing power of lower-income families. Other studies that consider the broader effects of the relationship between consumer credit and the economy during the 1930s are: Gottfried Haberler, *Consumer Instalment Credit and Economic Fluctuations* (New York, 1942); Duncan McC. Holthausen, Malcolm L. Merriam, and Rolf Nugent, *The Volume of Consumer Instalment Credit, 1929-38* (New York, 1940).

15. 16th Census of the United States, 1940, *Population. Families: Family Wage or Salary Income in 1939: Regions and Cities of 1,000,000 or More* (Washington, 1943), 32-33. These figures are for families with no other income than wage or salary.

16. 16th Census of the United States, 1940, *Population. The Labor Force (Sample Statistics), Employment and Personal Characteristics* (Washington, 1943), Table 26, p. 133, and Table 27, p. 137.

17. Cecile Tipton LaFollette, *A Study of the Problems of 652 Gainfully Employed Married Women Homemakers* (New York, 1934), 29.

18. *Ibid.,* 31.

19. Census, 1940, *Population Families: Family Wage or Salary Income in 1939,* Table 12, p. 151.

20. *Ibid.*

21. Hildegarde Kneeland, "Woman's Economic Contribution in the Home," *Annals of the American Academy of Political and Social Sciences,* CXLIII (May 1929), 33-40; and Hildegarde Kneeland, "Is the Modern Housewife a Lady of Leisure" *Survey,* LXII (June 1929), 301-02. For a recent interpretation, see Ruth Schwartz Cowan, "A Case Study of Technological and Social Change: The Washing Machine and the Working Wife," Mary Hartman and Lois W. Banner, eds., *Clio's Consciousness Raised: New Perspectives on the History of Women* (New York, 1974), 245-53.

3

Chicanas and Mexican Immigrant Families 1920–1940: Women's Subordination and Family Exploitation

ROSALINDA M. GONZÁLEZ

The Mexican Revolution of 1910-1920 and U.S. entry into World War I in 1917 greatly stimulated the northward migration of Mexican families to the United States, a migration which reached a peak in 1920 and which by 1930 had brought one-twelfth of Mexico's population to the United States (close to 1.5 million immigrants). Three fundamental characteristics marked this migration process into the U.S. Southwest. First, it was a migration of families, as distinct from the male Chinese and other Asian immigration into the Southwest which had preceded Mexican labor. Second, it was a labor force recruited primarily by the monopoly corporations which since the 1880s had come to dominate the U.S. economy and state machinery at federal and local levels. And third, the migration of these families involved a class and cultural transition, from the peasant class and strongly feudal patriarchal culture of Mexico to the working-class (agricultural, industrial, or urban) and capitalist culture of the United States.

The significance of the interrelationship between these three characteristics becomes clear if we examine the role of Mexican immigrant women in domestic and social production. While Mexican and Mexican-American women have until very recently only rarely been the focus of historical literature, the 1920-1940 period offers a rich field for study of the Chicana experience.[1] This is the period for which the greatest amount of literature on Mexican labor in the Southwest is to be found, and rightly so, for it encompasses the first phase of large-scale Mexican immigration responding to the post-World War I labor demands; the growth of agricultural and other industries increasingly based on Mexican labor; the growing militancy and class consciousness of Mexican workers and their increased organizing efforts, resistance, and strike activity. It also encompasses the Depression years and the mass deportations and other changes that they brought.[2]

A study of the labor history of Mexican immigrant and Chicana women should help to clarify the economic conditions which underlay the social and political realities of their lives. In so doing, it will offer a concrete example of the manner in which sexual oppression, racial discrimination, and class exploitation have been interrelated. And it will serve to bring to light the experiences of an important sector of the U.S. population for these critical years of boom, despair, and political unrest in American history.

Pre-1920 Background

Prior to the outbreak of the Mexican Revolution in 1910, the penetration of U.S. railroad and mining corporations into Mexico under the Porfirio Diaz regime had begun the process of breaking up feudal relations in the Mexican countryside and recruiting and importing *peónes* to labor on the railroads of the United States Midwest and Southwest.[3] The experience of women in this disruption are poignantly captured in a "Biographical Sketch of the Life of an Immigrant Woman":

How many sunrises and sunsets has a person seen in seventy-eight years of life? How many times has one laughed? Cried? Hurt? How many miles has one traveled? How many meals has a woman prepared in a lifetime of being a housewife? How many tortillas can be made in seventy-eight years? How many? How many? How many?

No one knows I guess, because no one has ever really counted what to some are trivial things. But to a person that has such a life, these things/events are not trivial. Especially not when your worth is measured by how well you can "keep house," cook, and bear children.

Surely the female child born on July 1, 1898, on the hacienda of Peñuelas, state of Aguascalientes, Mexico, never thought about her life from that perspective. All she knew was that she was God's gift to her parents and that as such, she was indebted to them and had to obey them and, of course, her elder brother also. . . . Picture thus, a child that since the age of seven or eight was already helping to cook, to sew, to spin, to help her mother in all the household chores and her father in the field. . . . It didn't matter . . . that this family along with thousands of others, were being exploited. It didn't matter because the significance and impact were not understood! . . . Thus when this child's father moved the family to another hacienda because of a promise that he could "share-crop," and then the ENTIRE crop was appropriated by the hacendado—leaving them hungry and even more destitute; even then she could not vent her hurt, her sorrow!

She didn't cry when one fine day Zapata's revolutionaries suddenly appeared in the doorway of their hut asking for a bite to eat — "una tortilla con frijoles."

Nor did she cry when her father took her and the other young girls of the hacienda into the mountains to hide them and save them from possibly being raped and/or kidnapped. It is fitting to note, however, that to her recollection not a single girl or woman was raped or otherwise molested on her hacienda. The revolution destroyed the hacienda and thus the peones lost their "jobs" and what little security they had. Employment was offered by the Mexican railroad to the peones and was taken — the beginning of an era of wandering from one estación or encampment to another; raising derailed trains and/or laying or repairing tracks in the process. This child, now a young woman, was still wandering between Aguascalientes and Zacatecas in 1914; however, she was now married. By the end of 1914, however, husband and she, now swollen with child, had joined the rest of her family in Chihuahua, Chihuahua—still seeking roots, a better existence. In this case, however, existence coincided with bare survival! Chihuahua at this time was a city of refugees, of uprooted persons; all of them destitute, all of them hungry. . . . often reaching the door only to be told that the foodstuffs had run out, come back tomorrow!

What can one do to ease the crying, the ceaseless crying of children when they are hungry today . . . and hungrier tomorrow?

Under these circumstances, not a damn thing, except rock them and give them water; rock them when your own belly is swollen and bursting with a hungry life within! And when this life, a boy enters this world demanding to be fed and you cannot feed it because your own body has been so decimated by hunger that you have no milk . . . what do you do? How do you explain to this mewling little creature that you, his mother, have had nothing to eat for three days since his birth, existing solely on tea made from orange-tree leaves! Yes, how much hurt can one person endure in a lifetime? How many tears can one shed? Especially when you realize that you entered the world crying and that sixteen years later, you are still in tears.

Little wonder then that this woman-child eagerly followed her husband from Chihuahua to Texas and then to California. Again in hopes of a better life, again working for the railroad – this time however, in the United States. It must be rather disheartening, however, to suddenly find yourself with food and nothing to cook it in; with a home but with nothing to sleep on. Left in the middle of the desert in a country where you know neither the language nor the customs; where you know no one! Secundina adapted quickly however, and soon had food cooking . . . in clean empty coffee cans she had gathered along the tracks, along with firewood. . . . A woman . . . offered her a job washing the railroad workers' clothes . . . by hand, natu- rally. This offer was accepted and Secundina worked daily at this chore until she developed an allergy to the strong, caustic detergent she had to use.

She declined the offer of her employer, however, to buy her son since in the opinion of her employer, she was too young and naive to care for him properly! And besides, they could use the money . . . couldn't they?[4]

This biographical sketch of an immigrant woman captures the manner in which women's subjugation was intertwined with class exploitation under Mexican feudalism. In the words of the author, the two were inseparably "linked much as Siamese twins." The railroads brought these families to the United States, where women's subordination was continued under a new class system. From the railroads, many laborers were drawn to other indus- tries, primarily agriculture and mining.

Women and Family Labor in Agriculture

World War I transformed the United States into a world power; from being a debtor to European capital, it became the creditor for Europe. With its overseas possessions, markets, and raw materials assured, the U.S. internal economy was able to proceed along the monopoly-guided process of the transformation of production into assembly line mass production and the creation of mass consumption through credit, installment buying, and advertising.

World War I had provided a great stimulation to development in the Southwest. Increased urbanization and demand for food in the cities trans- formed truck gardening into a great agricultural industry with the growth of the canning industry and the refrigerated railroad car. The demand for labor that this economic expansion produced was made more acute by the migration of black labor to industrial centers during and after the war following the exclusion of European immigrants who had principally supplied cheap industrial labor. This labor shortage came at a time when there was a great inflation in agricultural land values resulting from the increased agricultural production that stimulated speculation and saddled many landowners with large interest payments, thus necessitating cheap labor as the only way to keep down production costs.[5]

At the same time, the deteriorating conditions in Mexico stemming from Porfirio Diaz's brutal regime which served to consolidate the feudal hacendado's stranglehold over the Mexican peasantry and the sacking of Mexico's mineral wealth by U.S. monopoly capital intensified the contrast in economic opportunities between the two countries.[6] A comparison of the national wage differences between 1900 and 1930 in Table 6 reveals that even as late as 1920, agricultural wages in the United States were five to twelve times as high as in Mexico, and industrial wages six to eight times as high.[7]

The Mexican Revolution decisively resolved the problem when it tore the *peones* from the land and supplied the new, cheaper labor force needed in the U.S. Southwest.[8] While this expansion of U.S. capitalist industry and agriculture served to stimulate the transformation of Mexican *peones* into wage laborers, the contradictory character of the monopolistic capitalist land ownership that predominated in the era trapped many Mexican families in feudal-type conditions. The growing phenomenon of the

Table 6   Average Daily Wages for a Common Laborer in U.S. Currency, 1900-1930

	Agriculture			Industry, Rails, Mines, Factories	
Year	Mexico	U.S. Border	U.S. Interior	Mexico	U.S. General
1900	$.20–.25	$ .50– .75	$ .75–1.00	$.40– .50	$1.00–2.00
1910	.20–.25	.50–1.00	1.00–1.50	.50– .75	1.25–2.50
1920	.20–.25	1.00–2.00	1.50–2.50	.50– .75	3.00–4.00
1930*	.25–.40	1.50–2.50	2.00–3.00	.50–1.00	3.50–5.00

*Before the impact of the 1929 stockmarket crash

Source: Based on a composition of data from Clark, "Mexican Labor"; Gamio, *Mexican Immigration;* Taylor, *Mexican Labor in the United States;* Paul H. Douglas, *Real Wages in the United States, 1890-1926* (Boston, 1930); *U.S. consular correspondence from Mexico.* National Archives, Record Group 59, File 811.111/Mexico, 1910-1929; Mexican consular correspondence in AHSRE, files IV/350 to IV/560.

Mexican tenant farmers in this period was due to the increased monopolization of agricultural land in the Southwest and the pattern of large absentee
landowners. Some landowners preferred Mexican tenant sharecroppers,
particularly as "halvers," since they could, in this way, secure cheaper wage
labor when needed throughout the year. They preferred Mexican to white
tenants because the wives and children of Mexican tenants worked in the
fields, while white tenant families (for example, Germans), did not.[9]

Childbearing was a major way in which the rural woman contributed
economically to her family. Large families were required by landlords
before they would rent to a tenant. In Texas, for example, cotton production, which requires much hand labor, was sustained by child labor. Landlords commented that a tenant must have "at least eight children and a wife
who worked in the field 'like a man'" and that "a woman who can't have a
child a year isn't worth her salt."[10] Ruth Allen, an economist who carried
out a comparative study of farm women in five Texas counties in 1920,
observed how this requirement adversely affected women. "In a large part
of the agricultural economy of the South the importance of children as a
force of workers, while making a woman an indispensable adjunct to a farm,
tends also to place her in a subordinate position as a means to an end and, in
the case of many farmers, degrades the mother to the position of a breeder
of a labor supply. In addition, the mother is for so large a part of the time so
physically unwell."[11]

For the Mexican tenant sharecroppers, of course, these arrangements
barely guaranteed a miserable standard of living, which reinforced their
competitiveness as a source of cheap labor against white and other groups.
They also served to retain the subordination of women and children within
the family and thus ensure the perpetuation of the sharecropping system of
exploitation. Because of the isolated backward conditions and serflike social
relations prevailing in rural areas, and the great poverty and ignorance they
engendered, patriarchal feudal relations were not easily broken down, and
even employment as a part-time wage laborer did not offer women the economic independence that weakened patriarchal relations as it did in town or
industrial employment.

Allen's study included a survey of 294 Mexican women who belonged to
tenant families, "croppers," or "halvers." Fifty-two percent of these women
were born in Mexico. The patriarchal family relations were very strong, to
the extent that women hired out as laborers to pick cotton were never paid
their own wages. This payment of women's wages to the family men served
to benefit the employers:

Even when the woman becomes a hired laborer, she has no individual economic
existence. Her husband, father, or brother handles the financial affairs. She does not
collect her own money; she does not know how much is paid for her services; she
seldom knows how much cotton she picks a day or how many acres she chops. The
wage paid is a family wage, and the family is distinctly patriarchal in its organiza-

tion. When family groups of from ten to twenty members may be secured to pick cotton, and the women keep house in the open air or in disreputable shacks, there is all of the advantage of group living and the employer profits therefrom. What effect would be had upon the cost of production of cotton if the price of picking were set by the individual laborer rather than for the group? How long could the group system continue if the Mexican women refused to practice their sphere under existing conditions?[12]

Agricultural wage labor, while an improvement over tenant farming, was still highly exploitative and, in many areas, also characterized by family labor. Texas again provided an example, containing not only tenant farming, but truck farming as well. Dimmit County of the Winder Garden district of South Texas had Bermuda onions as its main crop. Here, as elsewhere, the recurring characteristics of the Southwest are exhibited: domination of the industry by the big growers and bankers; use of cheap Mexican family labor; and antagonistic interests between small growers and large growers. A large amount of the field labor in Dimmit County was done by women and children who generally received lower wages. The abundance of cheap labor retarded the introduction of machinery. One merchant, describing the effects of cheap labor in arresting technological and social development, compared it to slavery in the Old South.[13]

In another Texas county, Nueces, the threat of introduction of machinery was used by the planters to keep workers in line. From its beginnings, large-scale agricultural production (cotton and vegetables) in Nueces County was tied in to the use of Mexican labor. The preference of planters for families was often expressed, "for it is maintained that children as a rule will pick as much cotton as grown-ups." The dependence of planters on Mexican labor was openly acknowledged.[14]

Employers continually sought to control and dominate labor as much as possible, by restricting the mobility of seasonal labor, by recruiting families who were less likely than single men to go off without paying debts, and by encouraging Mexican sharecroppers. The intent was above all to secure a large surplus army of laborers.

The political and economic advantages of family labor emerge most clearly in the sugar beet fields of the South Platte Valley of Colorado. This area was dominated by the Great Western Sugar Company — the paternalistic monopoly which coordinated labor relations between its growers (lessees) and the imported and resident workers. The relations of exploitation and wealth, labor and capital in the area were based on the company's monopoly control of the land, control of the beet-growing industry through ownership of the sugar manufacturing industry, and a close financial relationship with the banks.

Beet production in Colorado had historically relied heavily on family and child labor. In the early period of beet agriculture, "local boys and girls" did most of the field work. When it became necessary to bring in outside labor, German-Russian families were brought in. When the German-Russian flow was stopped by World War I, Japanese and Mexican-American "solos" (single men) were brought in "to increase the labor supply and to afford competition against the German-Russians in a certain district." By 1929, Mexicans dominated the beet labor group.[15]

The Great Western Sugar Company's recruiting policy strongly favored the recruitment of families. This practice of employing families rather than solos or groups of solos was economically cheaper for the company and provided them with a more stable force. In addition, it was easier to induce families than single men to settle and remain as a resident (and self-perpetuating) labor force. Fully aware of the benefits of resident family labor, the company took an active paternalistic role, trying to encourage its growers to adopt liberal attitudes toward their Mexican workers by providing better living conditions. It encouraged the establishment of colonies to provide housing for beet workers, the practice of giving "certificates for good work" and "prize gold buttons" for the more productive workers, and defended workers in dealings with town merchants. The company made its intentions clear to the growers when it pointed out that their workers were only machines and that it was in the best interests of the growers to see that their machines ran well.

Even more revealing of the real motivation behind this paternalistic concern was the company's attitude in regard to child labor. Mexican labor was paid lower wages than other groups, yet the company still found it necessary to encourage and defend child labor. Bankers, company officials, and merchants all had a stake in perpetuating child labor. Child labor was cheaper and lowered wages. While grower prices (and profits) on beets rose, the wages of the laborers producing this wealth suffered a relative decline.

Wage discrimination against women and children was not the only tactic used by growers to reap greater profits through the exploitation of Mexican families. Racial discrimination was also an important tool. California provided the classic example of this. California labor developed within the context of monopolization of the land and production and the growth of capitalist agriculture, or "agribusiness" as it is now more commonly known. The monopolistic patterns of landownership, which were established at the birth of California as a state, shaped the social structure of California and governed its agricultural history and farm labor relations. The growing importance and, finally, dominance of banking and financial institutions in California agriculture began with the financing of the vast irrigation projects needed for the development of intensive agriculture.[16]

Besides financing and irrigation, intensive agriculture requires large sources of cheap labor which, for the period between 1860 and 1930, was provided principally by foreign workers who were often ineligible for citizenship and thus easily deported if they organized or agitated for higher wages. The familiar pattern of exploitation of one racial group after another emerged in California. China, Japan, the Philippine Islands, Puerto Rico, Mexico, the Deep South, and Europe all provided cheap labor in large numbers, employable at below-subsistence wages. Racial antagonisms were fostered through the enforced competition for jobs and the resulting depression of wages. Except for blacks, Mexicans were consistently paid the lowest wages of the different groups.[17]

Government institutions were also manipulated to ensure the subordination of the Mexican labor force. In this desire for control, the potential danger of education was easily recognized by owners. In Texas, farmers and the boards of education cooperated in securing nonenforcement of attendance laws to prevent Mexican children from being educated and either migrating to cities or becoming conscious of their rights and fighting for them. One farmer stated, "If I wanted a man I would want one of the more ignorant ones—possibly one who could read and write and weigh his own cotton. Educated Mexicans are the hardest to handle. . . . It is all right to educate them no higher than we educate them here in these little towns. I will be frank. They would make more desirable citizens if they would stop about the seventh grade."[18]

Once in the schools, racial antagonisms were deliberately fostered between white and Mexican children. When education was advocated, it was primarily to socialize them to "accept their place." In California, child labor was also related to the low education levels of children. Cotton was the principal crop using child labor. School authorities often looked the other way in the enforcement of school attendance, as both the large growers in their greed and the Mexican families in their poverty relied on child labor. The early marriages and large families characteristic of rural and peasant families intensified the exploitation of child labor. Often the oldest girl would stay at home to help the mother who was "ill or overburdened with the work of a large family."[19]

Families engaged in migrant agricultural labor suffered even harsher exploitation:

For some of these the living conditions are indescribable. Houses which have been abandoned as unfit for human habitation, outhouses which have no preparation for housekeeping are their homes. The congestion of living quarters reaches almost the saturation point. . . . On the Western Plains with the weather at freezing temperature, they live in tents, in smokehouses, and in cars. There is no evidence that these conditions are harder upon the women than upon the men, but the babies pay a heavy tribute to King Cotton.[20]

Urban and Industrial Labor

By 1930, approximately 15 percent of Chicanas ten years old and older were wageworkers, a much lower percentage than for white women (20 percent) or black women (40 percent).[21] Large agricultural interests (beet, cotton, melon, grape, and lettuce) were the principal recruiters of women's labor, while the manufacturing industries were the secondary recruiters. A summary of 1930 census data in Table 7 shows the overall U.S. occupational distribution for Mexican women, Mexican men, and all white women.

While Mexican men were concentrated in agriculture, close to 60 percent were in other sectors, with over 26 percent in manufacturing and mechanical industrial employment. Mexican women were also employed outside of agriculture, but their greatest concentration, approaching 50 percent, was in "domestic and personal service." Still, a significant proportion was employed in industrial labor, close to 20 percent.

California statistics confirmed this trend. While large numbers of Mexican laborers and families were engaged in agricultural employment, a growing number of industries also relied on Mexican labor. Factories and laundries absorbed 45 percent of Mexican working women in California in 1930. Los Angeles County had the highest concentration of Mexican laborers in California industry (over 50 percent). The principal employers

Table 7.   Mexican Women, Mexican Men, and All White Women
Occupational Distribution in Percentages, 1930

Occupational Sector	Mexican Women	Mexican Men	All White Women
Agriculture	21.2	40.5	4.5
Manufacturing & Mechanical Industries	19.3	26.1	20.0
Trade	8.9	5.7	10.7
Professional	3.1	1.2	16.6
Domestic & Personal Service	44.3	4.2	22.6
Clerical	2.6	.9	22.4
Other	0.6	21.4	3.2
TOTAL	100.0	100.0	100.0

(Data taken from Lori Helmbold, "The Work of Chicanas in the United States: Wage Labor and Work in the Home, 1930 to the Present," paper delivered at West Coast Association of Women Historians Conference, April 1978, Santa Monica California, Table III and V. Compiled from the Fifteenth Census, 1930, Population, v. V, 74, 86-91.)

of Mexican women in Los Angeles in 1928 included the clothing and needle trades, packinghouses and canneries, and laundries. A survey of these industries indicated that most of these women were young, unmarried Chicanas. Two-thirds were sixteen to twenty-three years old, 90 percent were single, and 65 percent were born in the United States.[22]

Racial divisions were also observed among women in urban industries. In the fruit and vegetable canneries, for example, Mexican women were employed in the cutting and, occasionally, canning departments, but rarely in the packing departments where Anglo women were employed. This paralleled the practice in agricultural areas such as the Imperial Valley, where Anglo women were employed in the packing sheds and Mexicans were restricted to field work.[23]

Employment in restaurants and hotels, apartments and homes, and in mercantile establishments was also an important source of wage work for Chicanas. In Texas young Chicanas tended to be employed in towns, in stores and as domestics, rather than in the fields. Chicanas were preferred as clerks because they would perform more tasks, were paid lower wages, and were more "docile" than Anglo women.[24] In El Paso as early as 1900 an estimated 18 percent of Mexican families had a working woman and 15.5 percent of Mexican families had female heads of households. By 1920, Mexican working women comprised approximately 33 percent of the immigrant labor force, the majority employed as servants and laundresses. The importance of the servant category is shown by the fact that in 1918 El Paso established a local employment bureau with federal assistance whose main purpose was to place Mexican servants in the homes of El Pasoans. The entrance of an increasing number of Anglo women into the work force was subsidized with the labor of Mexican servant women. Domestic employment provided extremely low wages—four to six dollars a week. Employment in laundries offered similarly low wages. Service in the trade of prostitution was another way of surviving for some.[25]

The employment of women in industry was characterized by the payment of piecework—a favorite method of employers for extracting the greatest amount of labor at the lowest wages, using the greatest exploitation to produce the greatest profits. For Mexican women, racial discrimination served to drive their wages down even more. As early as 1902, Mexican women were already being employed in El Paso's garment factories at considerably lower wages than Anglo women. In one shirts and overalls factory, for example, Anglo American women received $10 to $14 a week while Mexican women were held to $9 or less.

Inhuman living conditions were forced on Mexican families by low wages. Their extremely difficult, congested, and unsanitary living conditions placed an additional heavy burden of hard physical labor on the women. In El Paso, for example, they had to haul water daily from the river because the city, claiming that Mexicans were not property owners, provided no water or other municipal services to the *jacales* (shacks). Disease, illness, and death took a heavy toll, especially on the children. Yet, rather than seeking to alleviate these conditions, the city of El Paso played on the availability of the large pool of Mexican labor at such low wages as a drawing point to attract industries.

Conditions in Los Angeles in 1921 were no different. Miserable living conditions were the product of the very low wages Mexican labor received. While wages had increased since the war, so had the cost of living, making it unlikely that real wages (purchasing power) had increased. High rates of tuberculosis and other diseases, poor and insufficient food, overcrowding, and lack of sanitation were common.[26]

The Depression hit Mexican families especially hard. In 1930 in Texas females comprised about one-fifth of the work force ten years of age and over. An analysis of the hours, wages, and conditions of work of Anglo, Mexican, and black women in major Texas industries for 1930 and 1932 revealed that five of the principal "women-employing groups" were factories, stores, laundries, hotels and restaurants, and telephone exchanges.[27] Industrial homework prevailed in some industries, including garment (principally children's wear) and pecan-shelling. Mexican women were employed primarily in the clothing industry — exclusively in plants making infants' and children's garments. They were also employed in laundry and meat packing plants and department and ready-to-wear stores as well as in hotels and restaurants. Mexican women received much lower wages than Anglo women. A large proportion of Mexican women workers were under twenty-five, and over half were single. In 1932, wages were lower for women as a whole as a result of the Depression, as was employment. Women were generally the first to be laid off. However, in some instances women were hired to replace men because they were cheaper.

Most of these industries paid on a piecework basis with the characteristically associated low wages. Excessive strain was placed on the workers, and they were subjected to conditions injurious to their health such as denial of seats and working machinery while standing up all day because "they could work faster standing up." Accidents often resulted from the hazardous working conditions.

The garment industry was the chief woman-employing industry in Texas. In the midst of the Depression, women garment workers worked under intolerable conditions and at below-subsistence wages. The children's clothing factories, an important part of the garment industry in Texas, were all located in the south near the Mexican border and employed Mexican women exclusively. These women tended to be older, with many children and heavy family responsibilities. The work involved exquisite, delicate handwork on tiny infants' and childrens' clothing and on handkerchiefs, including embroidery, and much of it was done in the workers' homes. The exploitation in this industry on the basis of piecework was especially intense, with the intricate, difficult, and time-consuming work often being rejected by the factory and having to be redone at the worker's expense. It took, for example, twelve hours of steady and concentrated work for a woman to finish one garment for which she received forty-two cents. These exquisite little dresses were then sold back east at eight dollars a piece.

Pecan shelling was another important Texas industry. In San Antonio it was dominated by the Southern Pecan Shelling Company, the largest employer in the city. Initially the industry had operated on the basis of hand shelling, but mechanization spread rapidly throughout the industry. During the Depression, many plants continued to mechanize, but in San Antonio, with a huge surplus army of unemployed Mexican migrant agricultural laborers and peasant immigrants, the Southern Pecan Shelling Company reversed the process. It abandoned the use of machinery and modern industrial production and regressed to hand shelling, intense exploitation of Mexican family labor, and take-home work. The pecan-shelling families suffered the abuses of a contracting system whereby the company paid contractors who often pocketed the wages of the laborers they employed. The people worked under primitive and unhealthful conditions, with as many as 100 persons packed into a twenty-five-by-forty foot room, no toilets or running water, and wages that fell as low as $1.29 per week for a 34.8-hour week. The National Recovery Administration (NRA) code for the pecan-shelling industry was never put into effect.[28]

The severe impoverishment suffered by the families during the Depression drove some young women to prostitution. The roots of this were recognized by a government study.

The relationship of poverty, such as that among the pecan shellers, to prostitution is made clear in the following statement by Mrs. R. Van Eaton, Salvation Army worker: "The girls in those houses don't want to be there. They do it only because they have worn themselves out looking for work. If they could get a job with a living wage, they would leave. Since the pecan industry has shut down, many new Mexican girls have come into the vice district. They come down there evenings to work, and take their earnings back to their parents. Sometimes their parents don't know where they go. The girls refuse to let their parents go hungry. In the last 3 months, since the shelleries shut down, there have been more under-age girls down there than ever before. Some of them are only 13 years old."[29]

The Los Angeles garment industry in the 1930s relied primarily on immigrant Mexican female labor.[30] Conditions in the garment industry in Los Angeles had greatly deteriorated with the onset of the Depression. Wages of as little as $3.00 to $5.00 a week were common, and the manufacturers had developed a series of tactics designed to cheat the workers, pressure more out of them, and destroy any organizing efforts. The companies found it easy to get away with gross illegal practices because they had the political support of government institutions. Rose Pesotta, an International Ladies'

Garment Workers' Union (ILGWU) organizer, explained that "in Los Angeles, the NRA office was supposed to be upholding the President's Blanket Code. Instead, that office was actually working hand-in-glove with the reactionary forces, including the Chamber of Commerce and the Better America Federation—a front organization enjoying the blessing of Harry Chandler's *Los Angeles Times*."[31] She quotes a bulletin put out by the Associated Apparel Manufacturers of Los Angeles attempting to block a proposed merger of the State Bureau of Labor and the Industrial Welfare Commission. It stated bluntly, "We have been able to overcome a lot of this resistance through the close co-operation of the Industrial Welfare Commission. However, if that department is merged with the Bureau of Labor . . . all this good work will be wiped out and *we will . . . be forced to strictly adhere to the minimum wage laws of California.*" (Pesotta's emphasis).[32]

One scholar observed in 1926 that "A group that is brought or lured here for purposes of economic exploitation will carry with it the stigmata of that exploitation. It is wanted for no other purposes, and it will soon find that there is no place for it under any other conditions."[33] He was referring to Mexican immigrants, and his words proved prophetic when, during the Great Depression, thousands of families, both Mexican and U.S. born, were shipped to Mexico to face an even more abject misery and starvation. One woman who was a child in a Mexican village during the Depression related how a large family was repatriated. The parents had been from the village, but all the children had been born in the United States. With no means of surviving, the children and the mother all died off, one by one, until only the father and a little girl were left, and then they too starved to death.[34]

The Mexican population in the United States in 1940 was almost half what it had been in 1930, as Table 8 reveals. This phenomenal decrease was due to repatriations and immigration restrictions.[35] By 1940, most of the Mexican population was urban, with a greater number of Mexican women than men living in urban areas.

Table 8. Mexican-Origin Population in the United States, by Sex, 1930 and 1940, and Urban and Rural, 1940

	1930 Total	1940 Total	Urban	Rural-Nonfarm	Rural Farm
Male	360,332	197,965	117,977	44,732	35,265
Female	278,685	179,468	120,008	35,111	24,349
Totals	639,017	377,433	237,985	129,834	59,614

Data taken and compiled from "Table 1--Foreign-Born White Population, Totals, and Latin-Americans by Place of Birth, by Sex, for the United States, Urban and Rural, 1940 and 1930," p. 124, in W. Rex Crawford, "The Latin American in Wartime United States," American Academy of Political and Social Science. Annals. v. 223, Sept. 1942, pp. 123-131.

Cultural Transformation and Class Struggles

In the early period of Mexican immigration, the feudal patriarchal attitudes that the families brought with them from rural Mexico served to inhibit the full economic participation of women in social production, while reinforcing their domestic labor responsibilities within the family. Correspondingly, the dominant position of the husband within the family was strengthened. This did not mean that women and children were mistreated, for even within their poverty, the men took pride in providing as well as they could for their wives and children.

Nevertheless, the perpetuation of these patriarchal attitudes among Mexican families in the United States reveals a very important conflict between U.S. social, political, and economic processes and the culture and class background of Mexican immigrants. Traditionally, capitalism developed by destroying precapitalist and preindustrial social relations, forms of production, political structures, and forms of thought. When industrial capitalism first developed in Europe, for example, it uprooted peasant families, forced them into towns where it broke up extended kinship relations, reduced the family to its nuclear core, and then drew women and children into factory production. As exploitative and degrading as this process was, it nevertheless represented an important step forward for the laboring classes and for women, because it at once freed the serfs and peasants from their bonds to the feudal lord and the land and liberated women and children from authoritarian patriarchal bonds by providing them with an independent economic existence in wage labor.[36]

In the U.S. Southwest, American capitalism broke the feudal bonds which had bound Mexican women and men in subjection to the *patrón* and also to a certain extent broke the bondage of women within the family to their fathers or husbands. But monopoly capitalism did not complete the process of liberating women from the patriarchal bonds of the family. Instead, the patriarchal bondage of women was perpetuated by such mechanisms as the family labor contract, the family wage paid to the male head of the family for the agricultural labor of women, and the isolation of Mexican peon families in labor camps. These conditions were forced upon the families by miserable below subsistence wages. Likewise in manufacturing and urban employment, women found themselves segregated in certain industries and at low occupational levels, and often paid by piecework wages. Like the family wage, piecework wages were an effective means of perpetuating poverty and the need for family labor. Thus monopoly capitalism, in practice, not only fostered sexism but encouraged the retention of feudal patriarchal attitudes in Mexican communities in the United States. This contradictory action of capitalism upon the social relations within Mexican immigrant communities stemmed, as we have seen, from the monopolistic character of land ownership and of industrial capital which predominated in the Southwest in the twentieth century when Mexican families first began to enter in large numbers.

Even in urban areas, the Mexican family retained its importance as a social institution. In the 1930s, Mexican women in Los Angeles told a labor organizer "that they too, would like to be Americans. In Mexico, they said, women still had no freedom; a married woman could not vote nor hold a job without her husband's consent, and the father was still the supreme ruler over unmarried daughters until they reached the age of 30. The poor were always overburdened with work, entire families toiling on the plantations owned by the rich."[37] Similar aspirations were expressed by Mexican farm women in Texas who desired independence, no longer for themselves, but for their daughters. While Mexican fathers opposed the daughters leaving the farm to seek domestic or other urban employment, the mothers secretly supported their daughters' efforts to leave the stultifying drudgery and hopelessness of rural farm life.[38]

A comparative study of black, white, and Chicana women in San Antonio, Atlanta, and New Orleans in the 1930s and 1940s reveals that in San Antonio in 1930, of the employed Chicanas fifteen years old or older, 50.3 percent were single, only 9.6 percent were married, and 41.1 percent were widowed or divorced. However, many married women were employed in homework such as pecan shelling and hand production of infants' clothing. According to the San Antonio study, "A survey of Mexican Americans who were children of the Depression indicated that Chicano families preferred to allow male children to enter the job market while keeping wives and daughters in the home." For the United States as a whole, only 14.8 percent of Mexican girls and women ten years old and older were employed in 1930.[39]

While the strength of the cultural values from peasant Mexican society tended to inhibit the assimilation of Mexican immigrant women into the American economy and society, this situation began to change for the American born children of immigrants, especially in urban areas under the influence of the schools. Table 9 is a sample study reporting illiteracy rates among Los Angeles's estimated 30,000 Mexican inhabitants in 1920.[40] While women's inability to understand or communicate in English was much higher than that of men, the English illiteracy of school age Mexican or Chicano children was drastically lower. School enrollment in the cities began to promote the assimilation of Mexican and Chicano children, but this assimilation was carefully guided to integrate Chicanos and Chicanas into their new class position as manual laborers, with a clear distinction in the training of boys for industrial participation and girls for domestic duties. A Chicano historian studying the Los Angeles schools' treatment of Mexican children between 1920 and 1930 shows how class, sex, and racial segregation were structured into the "progressive education" philosophy formulated to meet the needs of monopoly capital. He quotes the principal

Table 9.   Illiteracy Rate Among Los Angeles Mexicans, 1920

	Men	Women	Children of School Age
Unable to speak English	55%	74	11
Unable to read English	67	84	20
Unable to write English	75	85	24

of an all-Mexican school. "The girls will have more extensive sewing, knitting, crocheting, drawn work, rug weaving and pottery. They will be taught personal hygiene, home-making, care of the sick. With the aid of a nursery, they will learn the care of little children. The boys will be given more advanced agriculture and shop work of various kinds."[41]

Still, changes began to occur within the patriarchal family. In interviews with Mexican immigrants in the 1920s, Mexican men often expressed resentment against Mexican women who had lived and worked in the United States for a time. They became "like American women," independent, sassy, and no longer content to remain submissively at home.[42] This is revealing of one of the effects of capitalism on feudal relations: eroding the patriarchal relations in the home and "liberating" the woman by drawing her into industrial production, thereby making her economically independent.

The disorganization of family life under the pressure of economic conditions also contributed to the erosion of patriarchal authority. During the Depression some daughters were able to gain employment, as in Detroit, where many Mexican men were laid off by the giant automobile plants and subsequently were declared ineligible for Works Progress Administration (WPA) employment because of their alien status. Their places were taken by their American-born sons and in some cases by their daughters.[43]

The inability of fathers to support their families sometimes resulted in abandonment, thus forcing the female head of the household to become the breadwinner. In urban areas, the deterioration of family life because of adverse economic and social conditions often led to a loss of authority by the father or parents, the breakup of families, the rise of juvenile delinquency in some areas such as Los Angeles, and a rise in the number of young girls bearing illegitimate children.[44]

The loosening of patriarchal authority in urban areas, the educational system, and the increasing participation of women in industry thus contributed to a growing independence and transformation in the consciousness of Chicanas. As members of the working class, their involvement in labor struggles served to further develop their political awareness and to strengthen their desire for active social participation.

Although the increasingly antidemocratic political system under the control of monopolies and the institutionalization of racism and sexism combined with language and cultural barriers and residential isolation to keep Mexican immigrants and Chicanos and Chicanas politically powerless, nevertheless their new class interests served to draw them into political action.[45]

Some of these efforts were spontaneous responses to the low wages, miserable living conditions, and intense exploitation and abuses suffered by the Mexican workers. In 1927, for example, the *Confederación de Uniones Obreras Mexicanas*, an ethnic union influenced by the traditions of the Industrial Workers of the World [IWW] and the Mexican Revolutionaries, was formed in California. Other organizing efforts were supported by the radical or independent forces within the U.S. labor movement. These forces had broken with the reactionary American Federation of Labor (AF of L) bureaucracy which had been co-opted by the bribes of monopoly capital and the government. Under this tutelage, the AF of L had followed the class policies of its tutors: racism, sexism, opposition to industrial unions, immigrants, leftists, unskilled labor, and militant rank and file unions. It had therefore abandoned the organization of agricultural workers and of Mexican immigrant and Chicano and Chicana workers.

In contrast to this, the young Communist Party U.S.A. undertook a spirited organizing campaign among those sectors of the working class spurned by "Big Labor." The California Great Strikes involved spontaneous struggles and strikes led by various organizations, but the Communist party-led Cannery and Agricultural Workers Industrial Ur'on (C&AWIU) headed the majority and the most militant of the strikes. The drastic drop in wages during the Depression created great misery and suffering among agricultural laborers. At a time when the government considered an annual income of $780 to $850 as the minimum needed for subsistence, many migrant families were earning less than $100. In King County, a principal cotton-growing region, the 1938 infant mortality rate was 95.2 (per thousand)! A wave of strikes by migrant workers and families arose after the Depression began in 1929. They were met with bloody repression and fascist measures. In the most significant strike, the cotton strike of October 1933, families were evicted en masse, but found shelter in the camps erected by the C&AWIU. On 10 October, the strikers in Pixley and Arvin were fired upon by the growers. Dolores Hernandez, Delfino Davila, and a third person were killed; many were wounded and arrested. But rather than breaking the strike, this only served to provoke the strikers' anger and militancy.[46]

The conflict of interests between the workers and the growers was very clearly demonstrated in other ways. For example, in addition to continuous efforts to divide the workers, the growers had always provided substandard living quarters, used piecework wages, child labor, lower wages for women, and a long working day. The demands put forward by the C&AWIU, however, included wage increases, an eight-hour day, time-and-a-half for overtime, decent homes and sanitary conditions, abolition of piecework and contract labor, payment of wages by the hour, equal pay for women workers, and the abolition of child labor.[47]

In contrast to the growers' practice of deliberately fostering racial, sexual, and other antagonisms (between city workers and farm workers, skilled and unskilled labor, groups of adult workers and groups of families), the workers' efforts to defend themselves brought about the opposite practices. During the Great Strikes of the 1930s in California, in which many Mexican families participated, the activities and unions of the workers involved a united effort of solidarity between Filipino, Mexican, and Anglo workers of many nationalities. For example, in Los Angeles a meeting was held of women employed in walnut factories, "a huge meeting, with a dozen or more nationalities being represented. The chairman was a Russian girl, eighteen years old, who used a hammer for a gavel, and presided as a veteran. The remarks of the speakers had to be translated into many languages: Russian, Armenian, Spanish."[48]

These organizing efforts were violently and viciously repressed by the organized efforts of growers, banks, police and vigilante forces, and state government agencies. Conditions during the Depression worsened for the workers. Families were thrown off relief and forced to work for the growers at below subsistence wages. The government in collusion with corporate agriculture instituted forced child labor and, while prices continued to rise, workers' wages fell drastically. There was a growing degeneration of conditions for workers. By the end of the 1930s Anglo workers and families had replaced the bulk of Mexican workers and other minority groups in the California fields.

Nevertheless, in areas where Mexican families did remain, substantial improvements in their conditions were often attained by their organizing efforts. A 1935 study of child labor in the beet fields of the Midwest examined the living and working conditions in the sugar beet fields of Michigan, Minnesota, Colorado, Nebraska, Wyoming, and Montana.[49] In the areas studied, 65 percent of the families of beet workers were Mexican or Mexican-American. Large families and child labor prevailed, as did acutely low wages, arduous physical toil, inadequate food, poor shelter, and other adverse conditions. The labor policies of the industry had been responsible for the selection of large families with children old enough to work (six years old and up). Most employment was on the basis of the labor-contract system, which, the study pointed out, was particularly suited to utilization of the labor of wives and children. In contrast, the study noted the close correlation between relatively high earnings, low child labor, and high educational levels in areas with trade unions.

As in agriculture, Mexican workers in urban industry responded militantly to their exploitation by organizing. The Congress of Industrial Organizations (CIO) which split off from the AF of L in 1937 was involved in many of these organizing efforts. In the San Antonio pecan-shelling industry, when an additional one cent reduction was proposed to the already absurd three to eight cents per pound piece rate, the "docile" shellers walked off their jobs by the thousands. This strike, begun on 1 February 1938 and lasting thirty-seven days, was the biggest industrial struggle San Antonio had ever experienced.[50]

The workers had been organized into two unions, an independent union by the name of *El Nogal* and a company union, the Pecan Shelling Workers' Union of San Antonio. The strike was initially led by a militant and spirited young Chicana Communist, Emma Tenayuca. It was shortly taken over by the CIO's United Cannery, Agricultural, Packing and Allied Workers of America (UCAPAWA). The combined forces of the city officials, the local police and courts, the church, and the press quickly moved to break the strike through all legal and illegal forms of persecution. Over 1,000 strikers and picketers were arrested throughout the struggle, women as well as men. In the jails, according to one account, "as many as 33 women were confined to a cell designed for six people. Prostitutes and pecan shellers resided in the same cell. And although 90 percent of the prostitutes suffered from infectious diseases, all cellmates shared a common toilet and the lone drinking cup." The strike failed to change the lowered piece rates over which the workers had struck; they lost, not because of lack of courage and determined struggle, but because of a betrayal worked upon them by a "board of arbitration."[51]

In California, the UCAPAWA was also involved in organizing Chicanos and Chicanas. A leading role in this effort was played by Luisa Moreno, who had been active in the San Antonio strike. Born in Central America, Luisa became involved with the struggles of Mexican workers in the United States. In addition to the pecan sheller's organization, she helped organize Texas cotton pickers and Colorado-Michigan beet workers as well as California cannery workers. Luisa Moreno became an international vice-president of the UCAPAWA, a vice-president of the CIO executive board in California, and chairwoman of the California committee against discrimination in the labor movement. She was instrumental in drawing the California CIO council into the Sleepy Lagoon Defense Committee in 1943, and in 1938 played a key role in the organization of the National Congress of the Spanish Speaking People held in Los Angeles in defiance of the intense red-baiting and persecution in the country. The congress was explicitly political, involving Latinos from all over the United States: farm workers, steel workers, miners, educators, students, and professionals. It defended democratic political liberties, immigrants' rights, and the rights of workers to organize. It further affirmed its commitment "[to] the economic and social and cultural betterment of the Mexican people, to have an understanding between the Anglo-Americans and the Mexicans, to promote organizations of working people by aiding trade unions, and to fight discrimination actively."[52]

In the garment industry, important organizational efforts also took place.

The ILGWU organized various locals and waged strikes in Texas and California.[53] Rose Pesotta, a Russian immigrant, was involved in organizing Mexican and Chicana garment workers in Los Angeles in 1933. Fighting many antiunion tactics as well as pessimistic union views that the Mexican women who constituted 75 percent of the garment workers labor force "could never be organized," Pesotta undertook a militant organizing campaign whose principal objective was drawing in the Mexican workers. She prophetically predicted that Mexican workers might "well become the backbone of our union on the West Coast." The workers courageously defied the manufacturers, the police "Red Squad," and court injunctions in their strikes and work stoppages. At one point, a group of arrested pickets chose to go to jail rather than pay fines. Fourteen of them were locked up in the Lincoln Heights jail. The next day, the jail matron protested, "For the love of God, never leave a bunch like that in this place overnight again." The girls and women had prevented her from getting any rest by singing all night. These experiences also taught the strikers a political lesson. "Several of the girls, all American-born, told me later that not until they found themselves in a cell did they realize that men and women who had never committed any crime were often arrested in this land of the free, particularly in Los Angeles. Reading newspapers in the past, they had thought of arrested persons as thieves, murderers, prostitutes, swindlers, or gangsters. Now their knowledge was broadened. They expressed no regret that they had chosen to be jailed in a worthy cause."[54]

World War II brought changes in the conditions of life and work for Mexicans in the United States, as well as for all Americans. To satisfy agricultural labor demands, the U.S. government established contract-labor programs with Mexico and the West Indies that came to be known as "bracero" labor. The impact of the Bracero Program on the Southwest was substantial. Economically, it created millions in profits for large growers and facilitated their corporate consolidation, and allowed the Mexican government to alleviate its chronic unemployment by shipping thousands of poor braceros to be exploited at higher wages than they would have received in Mexico — if they could have found jobs — but much lower wages than American workers would be paid. Politically, the bracero program resulted in the formalization and legalization of what had been a "common-law marriage" between big business and big government and allowed manipulation of government regulations regarding the "protection of domestic workers' jobs against the braceros" to drive out and break up the domestic workers' organizing attempts.[55]

In spite of the racial and sexual conflicts engendered by the discriminatory labor division and cultural values in U.S. society and Mexican communities, the organizing efforts continued, and women continued to play an important role in the struggles waged. The classic example of this involves a strike which falls outside our time framework but which typifies the historic

response of Mexican and Chicana women to their situation in this country—
the 1950-1951 Empire Zinc Mine strike outside Silver City, New Mexico,
immortalized in the film *Salt of the Earth*.[56] This struggle is especially
illustrative because it involved the Chicanas who had grown up in the
period we have surveyed. Their participation was crucial in the strike,
waged by the predominantly Mexican miners, in which the women's
demands as housewives were rejected by their own men. In the process of
the strike a microcosm of the contradictions facing Mexican-American
women and men in their historic struggles in the United States was enacted:
the confusions of racism, sexism, and class oppression. The growing participation of women in the strike ultimately became decisive and won the
prolonged and violent battle—as well as the self-confidence of the women
and a new respect on the part of the men. This democratic equality which is
the necessary and indispensable basis for successful class unity among all
laboring peoples was forcefully argued by Esperanza when she told Ramon,
her husband,

Have you learned nothing from this strike? Why are you afraid to have me at your
side? Do you still think you can have dignity only if I have none?... The Anglo
bosses look down on you, and you hate them for it. "Stay in your place, you dirty
Mexican"—that's what they tell you. But why must you say to me, "Stay in *your*
place"? Do you feel better having someone lower than you?... Whose neck shall I
stand on, to make me feel superior? And what will I get out of it? I don't want anything lower than I am. I'm low enough already. I want to rise. And push everything
up with me as I go.... And if you can't understand this, you're a fool—because you
can't win this strike without me! You can't win *anything* without me!

Notes

   1. The terms "Chicanas" and "Mexican-American women" are used interchange-
ably in this essay to refer to the U.S.-born female children of Mexican immigrants or
to third generation U.S.-born females. "Mexican women" refers to immigrant
women. "Mexicans" or "Mexican workers" or "Mexican families" are generally used as
references to all Mexican immigrant *and* U.S.-born descendents in the United States,
since the majority of workers of Mexican descent in the United States at this time
were immigrants.
   2. While there are few works specifically devoted to the Chicana, a great amount
of literature exists which can be combed to examine Chicana labor history in the
period from 1920 to 1940. Several of the major classic works on Chicanos in the
Southwest deal with (and were written in) this period. Carey McWilliams's studies of
immigrant and migrant farm labor, Paul Taylor's studies on Mexican labor in the
United States, and Manuel Gamio's classic study of Mexican immigration all span
this period. There are also many government studies sponsored by the Works
Progress Administration, the Women's and Children's bureaus of the U.S.
Department of Labor, and state government studies all dealing with the labor of
families, of women, and of children in agriculture and industry. In addition, college

and university students produced much research dealing with Mexican labor in the Southwest and Mexicans in the United States. Many articles written in this period examined the situation of Mexican workers and Mexican communities and documented the great number of labor strikes and struggles that erupted and the vicious repressions that invariably followed, sanctioned and often encouraged by local and state authorities. A survey of these studies can be found in Rosalinda M. González, "The Chicana in Southwest Labor History, 1900-1975, (A Preliminary Bibliographic Analysis)," Mimeographed paper, Program in Comparative Culture, University of California at Irvine, August 1976.

Most recently, new work has begun to be produced by Chicana and Chicano scholars, some of which covers this period. Of special note are Martha P. Cotera, *Diosa y Hembra, The History and Heritage of Chicanas in the United States* (Austin, Texas: Information Systems Development, 1976); Maria Linda Apodaca, "The Chicana Woman: An Historical Materialist Perspective," *Latin American Perspectives*, Vol. 4, Nos. 1 and 2 (Winter and Spring 1977 double issue: "Women and Class Struggle") 70-89; Alfredo Mirandé and Evangelina Enriquez, *La Chicana, The Mexican-American Woman*, (Chicago: University of Chicago Press, 1979); and Marta Cotera, "Feminism: The Chicana and Anglo Versions, a Historical Analysis," in Margarita B. Melville, ed., *Twice A Minority, Mexican American Women* (Saint Louis, Missouri: The C. V. Mosby Company, 1980), pp. 217-234. An important unpublished recent paper is Lori Helmbold's, "The Work of Chicanas in the United States: Wage Labor and Work in the Home, 1930 to the Present," New College, San Jose University (California), May 1977. Two informative pictorial histories which cover the activities of Chicanas are Chicano Communications Center, *450 Years of Chicano History Through Pictures* (bilingual) (Albuquerque, New Mexico: 1977), and the San Francisco Women's History Group, *What Have Women Done? A Photo Essay on Working Women in the United States* (San Francisco: United Front Press, 1974). Two bibliographies that list other sources on Chicanas are *The Chicana, A Comprehensive Bibliographic Study*, compiled by Roberto Cabello-Argandona, Juan Gomez-Quiñones, and Patricia Herrera Duran (Los Angeles: University of California at Los Angeles, Chicano Studies Center, 1975); and *Bibliography of Writings on La Mujer*, compiled by Cristina Portillo, Graciela Rios, and Martha Rodriguez (Berkeley: University of California at Berkeley, Chicano Studies Library, December 1976).

3. Victor S. Clark, *Mexican Labor in the United States*. (New York: Arno Press, 1974 reprint of 1908 edition). For a graphic eyewitness description of conditions in Mexico under the Porfiriato, the role of U.S. monopoly capital in maintaining or generating those conditions, and the plight of women in those circumstances, see Frederick J. Turner's excellent *Barbarous Mexico* (Austin, Texas: University of Texas Press, 1980 reprint of 1905 edition).

4. José Santos Lona, "Biographical Sketch of the Life of an Immigrant Woman," in Maria Linda Apodaca, "The Chicana Woman: An Historical Materialist Perspective," *Latin American Perspectives* Vol. 4 (1977). Reprinted with the permission of Maria Linda Apodaca and *Latin American Perspectives*.

5. Max S. Handman, "Economic Reasons for the Coming of the Mexican Immigrant," *American Journal of Sociology*, 35 (January 1930), 601-611.

6. See Raul A. Fernandez, *The United States-Mexico Border: A Politico-Economic Profile* (Notre Dame, Indiana: University of Notre Dame Press, 1977).

7. Arthur F. Corwin and Lawrence A. Cardoso, "Vamos Al Norte: Causes of

Mass Mexican Migration to the United States," in Arthur F. Corwin, ed., *Immigrants – and Immigrants* (Westport, Connecticut, Greenwood Press, 1978), pp. 38-66. Table from page 53.

8. On Mexican immigration for this period, see Mark Reisler, *By the Sweat of Their Brow: Mexican Immigrant Labor in the United States, 1900-1940* (Westport, Connecticut: Greenwood Press, 1976). An excellent synthesis of legislative and policy treatment of Mexican immigrants is found in Dick J. Reavis, *Without Documents* (New York: Condor Publishing Co., 1978).

9. Paul S. Taylor, *An American-Mexican Frontier: Nueces County, Texas* (Chapel Hill, North Carolina: University of North Carolina Press, 1934). Ruth Allen, *The Labor of Women in the Production of Cotton* (Chicago: University of Chicago Library private edition, 1933, reprinted by Arno Press, Inc., 1975). Excerpts used with the permission of Arno Press, Inc. A summary of her material on Mexican women appears in "Mexican Peon Women in Texas," *Sociology and Social Research,* 16 (November-December 1931). Max S. Handman, "The Mexican Immigrant in Texas," *Southwestern Political and Social Science Quarterly,* 7 (June 1926), 33-41.

10. Allen, *Labor of Women,* pp. 71 and 64, respectively.

11. *Ibid.,* p. 71.

12. *Ibid.,* p. 234.

13. Paul S. Taylor, "Mexican Labor in the United States, Dimmit County, Winter Garden District, South Texas," in his *Mexican Labor in the United States,* vol. 1, pp. 293-464, July 31, 1930 (Berkeley: University of California Publications in Economics, vol. 6, 1928-1930, University of California Press, 1930).

14. Taylor, *An American-Mexican Frontier.*

15. Paul S. Taylor, "Mexican Labor in the United States, Valley of the South Platte, Colorado," in his *Mexican Labor in the United States,* vol. 1, pp. 95-235, June 12, 1929.

16. Documentation of the growth of monopoly industries in the Southwest can be found in: Carey McWilliams, *Factories in the Fields: The Story of Migratory Farm Labor in California* (Santa Barbara, California: Peregrine Publishers, 1971); Matthew Josephson, *The Robber Barons* (New York: Harcourt, Brace & World, 1934); and Jim Dann, "Communists Try to Organize 'Factories in the Fields'," *Progressive Labor,* Vol. 6, No. 6 (February 1969), 72-96.

17. McWilliams, *Factories in the Fields,* and Carey McWilliams, *Brothers Under the Skin* (Boston: Little, Brown & Co., 1964). Paul S. Taylor, "Mexican Labor in the United States, Imperial Valley," in his *Mexican Labor in the United States,* pp. 1-94, vol. 1, December 17, 1928. Clark, *Mexican Labor in the United States.*

18. Taylor, Nueces County and Dimmit County studies.

19. Taylor, Imperial Valley study.

20. Allen, "Mexican Peon Women in Texas", p. 138.

21. Lori Helmbold, "Work of Chicanas," p. 27.

22. *Ibid.,* pp. 32, 28, 29.

23. *Ibid.*

23. McWilliams, *Factories in the Fields;* Taylor, Imperial Valley study.

24. Taylor, Nueces County study.

25. Mario T. Garcia, "The Chicana in American History: The Mexican Women of El Paso, 1880-1920 – A Case Study," *Pacific Historical Review* 49 (May 1980), 315-337.

26. G. Bromely Oxnam, "The Mexican in Los Angeles from the Standpoint of the Religious Forces of the City," *American Academy of Political and Social Science Annals*, 93 (1921), 130-133.

27. Loretta Sullivan and Bertha Blair, *Women in Texas Industries* (Washington, D.C.: U.S. Department of Labor, Women's Bureau, Bulletin No. 126, GPO, 1936).

28. Seldon C. Menefee and Orin C. Cassmore, *The Pecan Shellers of San Antonio: The Problems of Underpaid and Unemployed Mexican Labor* (Washington, D.C.: WPA, Division of Research, Washington, D.C.: GPO, 1940, reprinted in 1974 by Arno Press in *Mexican Labor in the United States*).

29. *Ibid.*, p. 49.

30. Rose Pesotta, *Bread Upon the Waters*, edited by John Nichols Beffel (New York: Dodd, Mead, 1944), Chapter 2, "California, Here we Come!" Chapter 3, "Mexican Girls Stand Their Ground"; Chapter 4, "The Employers Try an Injunction"; Chapter 5, "Our Union on the March." Quote is from p. 26.

31. *Ibid.*, p. 23.

32. *Ibid.*, p. 31.

33. Handman, "The Mexican Immigrant in Texas," p. 40.

34. Related to me by my mother, Guadalupe Carrasco Mendez. The village is an *ejido*, La Concordia, in Chihuahua, Mexico.

35. On repatriations, see Abraham Hoffman, *Unwanted Mexican Americans in the Great Depression, Repatriation Pressures, 1929-1939* (Tucson: University of Arizona Press, 1974), and Mercedes Carreras de Velasco, *Los Mexicanos Que Devolvio La Crisis 1929-1932* (Mexico: Secretaria de Relaciones Exteriores, 1974).

36. For a discussion of the effects of capitalism on women, see Terry Fee and Rosalinda González, "Women in Changing Modes of Production," 38-47, and "Imperialism, the State, and Political Implications for the Liberation of Women," 120-134, in *Latin American Perspectives* Vol. 4, Nos. 1 and 2 (Winter and Spring 1977 double issue: "Women and Class Struggle").

37. Pesotta, *Bread Upon the Waters*, p. 26.

38. Allen, *The Labor of Women in the Production of Cotton.*

39. Julia Kirk Blackwelder, "Women in the Work Force: Atlanta, New Orleans, and San Antonio, 1930 to 1940," *Journal of Urban History*, 4 (May 1978), 331-358. Quote from p. 339. U.S. statistics from Helmbold, "Work of Chicanas," 27.

40. "Mexicans in Los Angeles," *Survey*, September 15, 1920, 715-716.

41. Gilbert G. Gonzalez, "Racism, Education, and the Mexican Community in Los Angeles, 1920-30," *Societas*, 4 (Autumn 1974), 287-301. Quote from p. 300.

42. Manuel Gamio, *The Life Story of the Mexican Immigrant: Autobiographic Documents* (New York: Dover, 1971) contains seventy-six interviews, seventeen of which were with women. An extensive review of these cultural conflicts as reflected in songs and literature of the period can be found in Helmbold, "Work of Chicanas."

43. Norman D. Humphrey, "Employment Patterns of Mexicans in Detroit," *Monthly Labor Review*, 61 (November 1945), 913-923.

44. Emory S. Bogardus, "Second Generation Mexicans," *Sociology and Social Research*, 13 (January 1929), 276-283; Robert C. Jones, "Ethnic Family Patterns: The Mexican Family in the United States," *American Journal of Sociology*, 53 (May 1948), 450-452; Norman D. Humphrey, "The Housing and Household Practices of Detroit Mexicans," *Social Forces*, 24 (October-May 1946), 433-437.

45. Documentation of these struggles is to be found in Carey McWilliams, *North*

From Mexico: The Spanish Speaking People of the United States (New York: Greenwood Press, 1968); Rodolfo Acuña, *Occupied America: The Chicano's Struggle Toward Liberation* (San Francisco: Canfield Press, 1972); Cotera, *Diosa y Hembra*; and Chicano Communications Center, *450 Years of Chicano History*.

46. Dann, "Communists Try to Organize"; Margie Marin, "An Historical View of Chicano/Chicana Unionizing," *Cadre*, 2 (Spring 1975), 49-56.

47. McWilliams, *Factories in the Fields*.

48. *Ibid*.

49. Elizabeth S. Johnson, *Welfare of Families of Sugar-Beet Laborers: A Study of Child Labor and Its Relations to Family Work, Income, and Living Conditions in 1935* (Washington, D.C.: U.S. Department of Labor, Children's Bureau Publication No. 247, GPO, 1939).

50. Harold A. Shapiro, "The Pecan Shellers of San Antonio, Texas," *Southwestern Social Science Quarterly*, 32 (March 1952), 229-244, reprinted in Renato Rosaldo et. al. eds., *Chicano: The Evolution of a People* (Minneapolis, Minn.: Winston Press, 1973), pp. 193-202.

51. Shapiro, "Pecan Shellers," in Rosaldo, *Chicano*, p. 197. See also Chicano Communications Center, *450 Years of Chicano History*, p. 100.

52. Acuña, *Occupied America*, pp. 196-197; Mirandé and Enriquez, *La Chicana*, pp. 230-232; and Luis Leobardo Arroyo, "Chicano Participation in Organized Labor: The CIO in Los Angeles 1938-1950. An Extended Research Note," *Aztlan*, Vol. 6, (Summer 1975): 277-304; Miguel Tirado, "Mexican-American Political Organization: The Key to Chicano Political Power," *Aztlan* 1 (Spring 1970): 59-60.

53. Pesotta, *Bread Upon the Waters*. For an analysis of some of the problems involved in the predominantly male and Anglo leadership of the ILGWU organizing drives among predominantly female Mexican garment workers in Texas, see George N. Green, "ILGWU in Texas, 1930-1970," *Journal of Mexican-American History* 1 (Spring 1971), 144-69.

54. Pesotta, *Bread Upon the Waters*, pp. 21, 32, 52.

55. Documented in McWilliams, *Factories in the Fields*; Ernesto Galarza, *Merchants of Labor: The Mexican Bracero Story* (Santa Barbara: McNally & Loftin, West, 1978).

56. Herbert Biberman, *Salt of the Earth* (Boston Press, 1965) is a detailed chronicle of the political and economic events surrounding the strike and the making of the film, with equally rich accounts of the participation and views of the miners and their families in the process of the strike and the filming. A more recent analysis and reassessment is found in Deborah Silverton Rosenfelt's Commentary in Michael Wilson and Deborah Silverton Rosenfelt, eds. *Salt of the Earth* (Old Westbury, New York: Feminist Press, 1978) pp. 93-168. Both books contain the entire script of the film.

On earlier organizing efforts in New Mexico and Arizona mines and women's roles, see the following articles in *Southwest Economy and Society*, 3 (Winter 1977-1978): Mike Casillas, "The Cananea Strike of 1906," 18-32; Harry R. Rubenstine, "The Great Gallup Coal Strike of 1933," 33-53; and *ibid*, 4 (Fall 1978), Monica Eklund, "Massacre at Ludlow," 21-30. See also Raymond Otis, "Union in New Mexico," *New Masses* (May 24, 1938), 18-19; and Richard Melzer, *Madrid Revisited: Life and Labor in a New Mexican Mining Camp in the Years of the Great Depression* (Santa Fe, New Mexico: The Lightning Tree, Jane Lyon, Publisher,

1976). On the labor and role of women in New Mexico villages, a subject we have not even touched on in this essay, see Charles P. Loomis, "Wartime Migration from the Rural Spanish Speaking Villages of New Mexico," *Rural Sociology,* 7 (December 1942), 384-395.

4

Flawed Victories: The Experiences of Black and White Women Workers in Durham During the 1930s

DOLORES JANIEWSKI

Observing women's experiences as tobacco and textile workers in Durham, North Carolina, during the depression era offers a way to illuminate some of the most critical issues facing women workers. These women lived within the constraints imposed by class, sexual, and racial structures of domination. Embedded within the built and human environment, these structures shaped the patterns of daily life inside and outside the factories. Inevitably, they also shaped the workers' efforts to organize. In fact, the one mode of domination that did not impinge upon all the women in the same way — racial domination — divided the very women who were trying to organize as workers against their employers. Nevertheless, their victories, however flawed by defense of male and white-skin privilege, testified to the vitality that characterized their efforts as workers to challenge their employers. Deprived of the benefits that flow from a common culture and community, these women, together with their male counterparts, managed to organize some of the few union locals still surviving in the hostile climate of the South.[1]

Their experiences test the commonplace notion that women have been exceptionally difficult to organize by examining the ways women's lives were shaped by their sexual and racial identities. Analysis of the Durham experience suggests that the issue might be more appropriately phrased by seeking an explanation for the unions' failures to espouse policies that would transform the unequal power relationships between men and women, blacks and whites, built into the workplace and the surrounding community. Rather than blame the women who saw the union as irrelevant to vast areas of their daily life, the inadequacy of a class-based strategy which ignored the racial and sexual divisions among its constituency is the focus of this study.

Durham, a city created by rapid industrial development in the post-Civil War period, provided an environment in which its residents lived and worked in racial, class, and sex-ordered categories.[2] Race and industrial affiliation largely determined its spatial orientation. White textile workers lived in the company-owned mill villages on Durham's eastern and western

The article is based upon a section of the author's dissertation, "From Field to Factory: Race, Class, Sex, and the Woman Worker in Durham, 1880-1940," Duke University, 1979.

flanks. White tobacco workers lived in various parts of the city including central Durham neighborhoods where their neighbors ranged from middle-class professionals to laboring whites.[3] The poorest whites, unemployed, female-headed families, or demoralized, lived, like the poorest blacks, in low-lying areas called "bottoms," which precisely described the place occupied by their inhabitants in the social order. Black tobacco workers lived in Hayti, the main black ghetto, and in pocket ghettos scattered on the east and west sides of town below the railroad tracks which sliced through Durham.[4] By the 1930s, the white men who ran Durham's factories had removed themselves from proximity to their workplaces, residing in the exclusive residential sections of Forest Hills and Hope Valley.[5] Constrained by racial segregation, the black elite lived along the main street in Hayti where the grandeur of their homes indicated their status.[6]

The intricate mosaic of differentiated communities which composed the cityscape manifested itself in the minds of its inhabitants where it marked their position in Durham's hierarchy of prestige and power. The presence of the Bottoms bordering on more respectable neighborhoods warned the more vulnerable members of those adjacent communities of their potential fates if they were to lose their respectability and their jobs. One textile worker from the West Durham mill village expressed her fears in 1938, "A person don't ever know what they'll be brought to in this life, but I sure hope I'll never have to move to Monkey Bottom."[7] Tobacco workers who lived in East Durham carefully defended their own claims to respectability by distinguishing their neighborhood from the depressed mill village communities in the Edgemont section of Durham.[8] At the top of Durham's social order the elite lived in areas whose names and locations symbolized the distance they sought to preserve between themselves and the workers whose labor they controlled.

Race, class, and sex supplied the basic structuring mechanisms in Durham's major mills and factories. The Erwin Cotton Mills Company, the Liggett and Myers Tobacco Company, and the American Tobacco Company used existing forms of labor segmentation while reinforcing and adapting those divisions in their labor force to their need to control their workers and the manufacturing process itself.[9] Erwin Cotton Mills and the tobacco companies began the process of segmenting by hiring from separate labor markets. The mills, like most southern textile companies, employed workers primarily in family groups. By the 1930s most of these workers had previous textile experience or had grown up in the West Durham mill village.[10] The tobacco industry, on the other hand, selected white workers for its skilled and semiskilled positions on the basis of individual skills and family background.[11] The companies filled the more numerous unskilled and laboring positions with black workers selected largely from the lines of people who stood outside the factory gates.[12] Their jobs, especially the positions employing the greatest numbers of black women, were subject to seasonal fluctuations as well as to the instability common to unskilled work.[13]

Once employed, the workers fitted into the elaborate factory hierarchy in accordance with their socially defined characteristics. White college-educated men from managerial families predominated in mill and factory management at the highest levels.[14] White men monopolized the supervisory and skilled positions down to the position of loom fixer in textiles and making-machine operator in tobacco. White men and women then divided the semiskilled operative positions which constituted the rest of the manufacturing process. Black men took on the arduous jobs involving lifting and hauling which they performed in gangs. Black women performed the tasks requiring dexterity in preparing the tobacco leaf for the actual manufacturing process and general cleaning jobs in the main factory where they cleaned white workers' bathrooms and performed work deemed unsuitable for white women.[15]

The very layout of the mills and factories replicated the sexual, racial, and class divisions. A few departments at Erwin Mills – the card room, dye house, and machine shop – employed men primarily while blacks were excluded from the mill almost totally. Black tobacco workers usually worked in separate buildings where the leaf departments and smoking tobacco departments were housed, on different floors, or in carefully defined positions such as cleaning ladies. Although white men and women might work in the same departments in the tobacco industry, they did not perform identical functions: the women assisted the men. In the mill, on the other hand, men and women worked at equivalent tasks below the level of loom fixer although some women holding more skilled jobs did not receive the same respect as did men holding equally skilled positions.[16] Segregated restrooms in tobacco factories coupled with the most unpleasant working conditions in those factories reinforced black workers' subordinate position.

Not unsurprisingly, workers came to be valued by their supervisors and coworkers in conformity with the same criteria used to order the industrial environment. White women operatives at Liggett and Myers, who had to maintain their reputations for chastity as a job requirement, prided themselves on belonging to a "better class of people" than the workers at American Tobacco, where employers usually tolerated sexual exploitation rather than enforce a morals code as a condition of employment.[17] Tobacco workers looked down upon mill workers. Meanwhile some female textile workers drew satisfaction from their position among Erwin Mills's chosen people in stark contrast to those disrespectable people who had been banished from West Durham to live in Monkey Bottoms or other slums.[18] Almost without exception, white textile and tobacco workers took for granted their social superiority to black workers whom some of them bullied in much the same way as did their foremen.[19] Like their men, white women tobacco workers did not believe they could or should do male-designated tasks nor that blacks could work as productively as whites. Indeed, like their social betters, these women often did not classify black workers as men or women like themselves, but as an undifferentiated mass, contented and well adapted to doing the dirty work white women would refuse to do.[20]

Black workers, too, developed their own hierarchy of respectability, but it was obtained by church membership and moral conduct rather than by industrial affiliation.[21] Often acutely conscious that other people discriminated against them, these workers in turn evolved their own conceptions of self-respect and respectability in which race, industrial affiliation, skill, and personal conduct played as prominent a role as they did in the managerial policies that governed their respective workplaces.

Although major companies sought to divide their work forces in terms of recruitment and in the manufacturing process itself, their labor management policies differed in the emphasis placed upon racial and sexual divisions and, consequently, in their impact upon workers. The textile manufacturing process, which flowed horizontally rather than vertically like cigarette manufacturing, produced a less elaborate hierarchy of skills, function, and control. The absence of black workers in textile mills combined with greater equality in tasks and pay between men and women to produce a more unified labor force. At Erwin Mills a persisting tradition of mill village paternalism aided by the cohesiveness of the mill village community made it easier for workers to see themselves as a collective whole rather than competing groups. The Erwin Mills brand of mill village paternalism as espoused by its first manager, W. A. Erwin, reinforced these unifying factors by using a familial ideology in which Erwin himself represented the father or patriarch of the village. Before his health began to fail in the late 1920s, Erwin also performed the role of religious teacher for his workers in a regular Sunday school class. Thus combining the traditional roles of the paterfamilias as priest, father, and owner, Erwin evoked filial loyalty from the people whose labor he commanded.[22]

The tobacco companies, except for somewhat more paternalistic policies on the part of Liggett and Myers, evolved bureaucratic methods of control which emphasized coercive labor discipline rather than appeals to personal loyalties. Their line of command extended from the time clerk to the factory superintendent to managerial headquarters in New York City, where the general company policies originated. Untempered by any lingering traditions of paternalism, these companies practiced the more modern forms of labor control which subjected workers to the rhythms dictated by the ever-accelerating speed of the manufacturing process. In contrast to the application of the most modern technological innovations, the actual methods used by foremen in day-to-day operations relied upon the use of arbitrary power to hire and fire rather than rationally derived work rules or sophisticated methods of psychological manipulation to keep their employees working.[23]

Compelled by their superiors, foremen often resorted to abuse to force their subordinates to make production.

The women, who bore the brunt of the interwoven forms of domination and managerial policies, were first or second generation migrants. Pushed from nearby tobacco or cotton farms by loss of land and male labor power or by the impact of agricultural depression,[24] these female migrants had come to Durham where employers valued their labor and offered better wages than the rural, cash crop economy which could not sustain its population. A National Recovery Administration (NRA) survey reported that about 70 percent of the white women tobacco workers in Durham and 55 percent of the employed black women came from the country.[25] Oral history interviews confirmed that proportion for the forty-year period from 1900 to 1940. Tobacco workers, in contrast to textile workers, typically had come directly from their rural homes to find work in Durham's tobacco factories.[26] White women tobacco workers lacked experience in any other industry or in any paid employment, but about half the black women interviewed had worked as domestics, in tobacco factories, or in other industries before coming to work in Durham's cigarette factories. In about one-third of the cases female textile workers either began working at smaller mills outside Durham or had parents who worked in the mills, so that they had acquired greater experience in industrial employment as individuals and as members of families than had their white counterparts in the tobacco industry.[27]

More detailed analysis of these migration patterns demonstrated the declining importance of family considerations in influencing young women's decisions to migrate to Durham. Of the female workers interviewed who arrived in Durham before 1920 all had accompanied their families. After 1920, young women frequently made the decision to become tobacco workers for themselves.[28] Their reasons for doing so verify the results of a survey conducted in Durham in the mid-1920s which reported that "rural girls" came to the city primarily looking for work and secondarily in response to family commitments.[29] All the women who migrated to Durham as individuals were white. Black women continued to travel with their families, and white textile workers, reflecting the basic recruitment policies in that industry, also moved from mill to mill in family groups.[30]

These female migrants, with few industrial skills and little book learning, had early learned lessons that their industrial masters would seek to reinforce. As the daughters of tenants and small landowners, they had already realized the necessity, if not the virtues, of hard work for the sake of the entire household rather than for self-satisfaction.[31] Some may have been fleeing the severe discipline imposed by that family economy, but they continued to fulfill certain family responsibilities even at a distance.[32] They had matured in a segregated rural society where blacks and whites, men and women, tenants and landlords, ideally never performed the same tasks or

received equivalent rewards. Racial etiquette governed the personal interactions between whites and blacks so as to insure black subordination.
Women in the poorest tenant and farm laborer households frequently
"crossed over" to carry on tasks customarily assigned to men such as plow-
ing and other arduous fieldwork.[33] As the household's prosperity and
prestige increased, women's participation in work outside the house correspondingly declined. The men in landowning families and the more independent tenant farmers controlled the production of the chief cash crop,
took it to market, and spent the proceeds. In such families women's public
role did not exist. The white families that could afford to make distinctions
hired black labor to take on the less prestigious forms of field work and
housework.[34] Rural whites unable to demonstrate their racial superiority by
employing black labor tended to ignore their black neighbors or to bitterly
insist upon strict observance of racial etiquette.[35] Women born into textile
families early learned to associate blacks with menial labor like yard work,
cleaning out privies, or doing the wash.[36] Consequently the women who
became Durham tobacco and textile workers came equipped with deeply
engrained notions about the proper occupations for men and women,
blacks and whites. White men were supposed to perform the most symboli-
cally important tasks calling for skill, judgment, and authority; black
women, at the other end of the social hierarchy, did the most degraded and
unskilled work. When necessary, white women could do "public work," but
care had to be taken to distinguish their work and their status from that of
black workers lest the family's status, already jeopardized by their loss of
economic independence, should be further degraded.[37]

Depending upon the decade of their arrival, women combined household
duties and public work in different patterns over their life cycles. White
women in the early twentieth century typically followed the pattern
denoted by the phrase "family wage economy."[38] Young girls began working
as soon as their families needed their wages and continued working until the
combined wages of their husbands and children could support the family.
The average female worker under this system was young and unmarried.
The factories also chose child labor over adult labor, preferring to hire
fatherless children rather than put widows to work. The gradual elimination of child labor by legal restriction and company policy began in the
1910s. Some children continued to work as unpaid assistants to their
mothers or older sisters during that decade,[39] but North Carolina state law
in 1919 officially ended the employment of children under age fourteen.
Erwin Mills and the Durham tobacco factories apparently obeyed this
law.[40] Because black families had generally never been able to afford the
luxury of keeping an adult woman out of the labor force, the legal end to
child labor did not make so drastic a change in black patterns of labor force
participation as it did for white women. Black women, especially widows
and female heads of households, continued to face the burdens of combin-

ing child care, housework, and wage earning throughout the thirty-year period.

By the 1930s the typical female employee in tobacco and textile factories was a married woman in the middle years of her child-bearing cycle who had probably begun working in mid or late adolescence (Table 10).[41] Compared to the typical female textile worker in the early 1900s,[42] these women faced the greater burdens entailed by dual responsibilities as workers and housewives. Mothers were now forced into the workplace on a massive scale to support their children. The higher proportion of older and married women in the tobacco labor force, according to the 1930 census, reflected the high percentage of black women in that industry. A survey done in Durham in 1934 found that 52 percent of black female tobacco workers were married compared to 41 percent of white women employees.[43] An additional 20 percent from each group listed as widowed or separated may have born the still greater burden of supporting an entire household without the benefit of male wages.

Table 10. Marital and Age Characteristics of the Female Workforce Employed as Operatives in N. C. Tobacco & Textiles 1930-1940

	Tobacco Operatives	Textile Operatives
1930	57.9%	48.9%
1940	66.8%	71.8%

	Widows	
1940	14.6%	7.6%

The Ages of Female Operatives in North Carolina

Ages	Tobacco Operatives		Textile Operatives	
	1930	1940	1930	1940
15-24	49.3%	22.9%	59%	27.8%
25-44	45.9%	69.8%	35.7%	63.6%
45+	4.7%	6.2%	5.2%	8.6%

U. S. Census of Population: 1930, Vol. IV, Occupations.

U. S. Census of Population: 1940, Vol. III, The Labor Force.

The women working in Durham mills and factories in the 1930s clearly represented a new type of woman worker who had begun to assume, like most black women, that they were permanent workers. No longer single, these workers were mature women whose families needed their wages. The conditions they experienced in their workplaces could no longer be dismissed as brief inconveniences from which marriage would rescue them after a few years. Deprived of the labor of their children, these adult wage earners had to earn a living for an entire household. Because the average wages paid to male tobacco workers required two incomes to earn a minimum standard of living for a family, workers had to receive higher wages if their families wanted to do better than merely subsist.[44] The low level of wages in the textile industry, brought still lower by wage reductions in the early 1930s, made improvements in that industry even more critical for the workers involved. Women, now mature breadwinners, began to face these issues in the 1930s and seek ways to resolve them.

Predictably, in the straitened circumstances exacerbated by the economic crisis, households closest to the subsistence line suffered most. Black female-headed households, given the racial and sexual differentials in pay and working conditions, experienced the most impoverished conditions.[45] Many such households, already struggling on wages that averaged one-fourth to one-third of the minimum necessary to pull a family above the poverty line, saw their incomes fall to below one dollar per member per week. By 1935 nearly 60 percent of the black tobacco households in Durham were receiving public assistance compared to about one-fifth of their white counterparts.[46] White textile workers, displaced by unemployment or managerial displeasure from the West Durham mill village, found it similarly difficult to survive. A life history written in 1939 by a member of the Federal Writers' Project described one extended household subsisting in Monkey Bottoms. The author depicted one female member of this "confused family" as its moral center who had not grown discouraged in spite of her circumstances. After a year's unemployment, she remained in Durham tagging company sacks, a major Durham home industry for otherwise unemployable people.[47] The same writer interviewed a neighboring family who also lived "from meal to meal" while the mother tagged tobacco sacks. On combined wages of $14.00 per week the family fed and housed twelve people.[48] This woman had fallen into cheerful apathy because she could see no way out but dependence upon the charity of others.

Whether women found factory work or tagged sacks at home like the women in Monkey Bottoms,[49] they had to utilize the major household resource — the wage-earning power of its members. Maintaining that labor force through cooking, clothing, and keeping the working members clean and ready for work was usually the woman's responsibility. A typical day for a black female tobacco worker, married or separated, began at 5:30, when she prepared breakfast and left without seeing her children. The oldest child, boy or girl, cooked the breakfast for the other children. At night, when she came home at 5:30 or 6:00 P.M., ". . . the mother has the night meal to cook, the laundry, cleaning, and care of the children to do, which, if she [is] conscientious, will take well toward midnight before it is completed."[50] Benefitting from the racial differential in wages and access to employment, a white tobacco or textile worker could hire a black woman to assume many of her household responsibilities for a third of her own wage. Black women, like the woman in the previous example, had either to find women too old for regular employment outside their homes or to rely upon the help of their overworked husbands, their children, or neighbors no better off than they.[51]

The absence of many household conveniences made housework and child care more difficult for the already overburdened woman. Clothes often had to be washed in pots in the yard. Food had to be cooked on a wood- or oil-burning stove. The poorest people continued to eat the filling but nutritionally limited characteristic rural diet of meal, molasses, and salt pork because their budgets and culinary training perpetuated that routine. Bathing had to be done in a basin or tin tub because many homes lacked bathrooms. Indoor toilets were a rarity in black tobacco households, making sanitation and personal cleanliness still more difficult to achieve. The lack of garden space in the poorest neighborhoods prevented those people from providing fresh vegetables in their daily meals.[52] The absence of paved streets in many working class neighborhoods made housecleaning more burdensome. Substandard housing—inadequate plumbing, oil lamps, wood- or oil-burning stoves—increased women's difficulties in providing a healthy and comfortable environment for themselves and their families.

A tobacco worker survey in 1935 showed that the burdens of inadequate housing were not equally distributed. A little over one-third of black households used electricity in that year compared to almost three-fifths of white households. The others apparently used oil lamps and oil or wood-burning stoves. White households were more than twice as likely to have indoor toilets as were black households (87 versus 38 percent) and sixteen times as likely to have bathtubs (81 versus 5 percent). Only in terms of home ownership and running water did the two groups of tobacco workers enjoy similar advantages. Almost 90 percent in both cases rented their homes; almost 100 percent had running water. The same survey evaluated white tobacco worker housing in Durham as among the best in six tobacco manufacturing centers but described black housing as "unsightly, closely-packed congeries of cheaply constructed and worn-out dwellings."[53] Although black workers paid rents quadruple those paid by West Durham mill workers and comparable in terms of their total income to those paid by white tobacco workers, they lived in houses whose con¹itions made women's work, inside and outside the home, difficult, if not impossible, to accomplish. White women shouldered a double burden of domestic labor, but white-skin privilege and wage-earning work made their lives easier.

Racial domination was more than simply a matter of inconvenience or poorer living conditions. It cost the lives of black women and their children. As national life tables revealed, in 1929 a white female child could expect to live almost sixty years compared to a newborn black female who could expect to live less than fifty years.[54] Black women in Durham in the early 1930s died in childbirth at almost twice the rate of white women, and their children were more than twice as likely to die before reaching one year of age than were whites.[55] Declining white fertility rates during the 1930s and increasing black fertility rates also suggested that white women could control their fertility to a greater extent than black women.[56] Other painful demographic realities including greater susceptibility to typhoid, tuberculosis, and pneumonia intensified the anxieties black women already experienced due to frequent unemployment, racial hostilities, and inadequate income.[57]

At the individual level the intersection of demographic and social inequities induced an attitude one observer described as "physical tenseness and helplessness . . . disorganizing to family stability and sustained efforts."[58] Such deprivations could also produce an attitude of dignified endurance, neither passive nor militant, which took pride in small triumphs. A widowed black tobacco worker accepted the poverty in which she and her two children lived as a part of God's plan. She did not complain because she had to cut up her own dresses to make Sunday school clothes for her children. She sent them to church and remained at home blaming no one for her troubles.[59] Such women lived according to the words of Psalm 90:

> The days of our years are threescore years and ten
> and, if by reason of strength, they be fourscore years,
> yet is their strength labor and sorrow; for it
> is soon cut off, and we fly away.
>
> Make us glad according to the days wherein thou hast
> afflicted us, and the years wherein we have seen evil.[60]

They found release from their struggles for bare subsistence in religious faith. A few women verbally defended themselves against abusive foremen and white coworkers but most women could not risk losing their jobs. Instead, they simply endured.[61]

White women, for the most part, never questioned the justice of the racially-stratified system. If they considered the black woman's situation at all, white women preferred to think that blacks were as satisfied with race relations as whites desired them to be.[62] White women expressed a greater variety of attitudes when it came to questions related to their employers, their fellow workers, and their actual working conditions. White female tobacco workers, more highly paid and more independent from the family economy than black women or the majority of female textile workers, seemed to be most concerned with maintaining their relatively privileged status. Women who had met the Liggett and Myers standard for moral character and family background felt threatened by the disrespectful and coercive methods foremen used to speed production. Though they did not necessarily personally experience abuses such as punitive layoffs for minor mistakes, many women sympathized with workers who did.[63] The pride that the company had attempted to instill in them as a working elite made them resent company policies that threatened that self-respect. While women workers at American Tobacco could not claim the same standards of respectability, they prided themselves on their greater daring in resisting managerial compulsion.[64] Rooted in their measurably greater sense of their rights to respect and decent treatment, the white women employed at American Tobacco and Liggett and Myers found it easier to assert their claims than did their more constrained black coworkers. Generational differences in attitudes among textile workers also seemed related to changes in managerial methods. Women who began work as children identified more closely with mill management than women who had not learned to conceive of their employers in a paternal role.[65] Younger women whose socializing experiences had occurred in school as well as in the mill or the patriarchal farm family defied managerial authority more readily than did their older coworkers.[66] While former child workers approved the Erwin Mills policy of expelling unmarried mothers and their families from the village, the friendship networks formed by younger women tried to shield a pregnant friend from managerial discipline.[67] Thus white women employed in both industries had begun to develop loyalties to their fellow workers which could come into conflict with managerial authority.

The industrial response to the depression further eroded women's faith in the good intentions of their employers. As workers lost their ability to move from job to job when they became dissatisfied, mill and factory foremen took advantage of the increased competition for jobs. Threatening workers with the loss of their jobs, foremen demanded greater productivity and subservience. They used their power to hire and fire at will to its maximum extent. Both textile and tobacco workers suffered under the system they called the "stretch-out,"[68] but which their employers preferred to call the "extended labor system,"[69] or by the more neutral term "scientific management." Industrial engineers and time-study men applied the methods originally developed by time-and-motion study pioneer Frederick W. Taylor to speed up production, assign more machines to each worker, eliminate jobs, reduce the skill level for each occupation, and increase production quotas workers had to achieve to keep their jobs. Minimum wage and maximum hour legislation encouraged Durham employers to accelerate their production process by replacing the now more costly human labor with faster machines. The partial elimination of racial and southern differentials in wages by the Fair Labor Standards Act (FLSA) in 1938 drastically affected the proportion of black workers in the tobacco labor force in North Carolina (Table 11).[70] Black women, who made up 55 percent of the total work force in 1930,[71] lost a disproportionate share of the jobs because the cutoffs occurred in the stemmeries where they worked.[72] The leaf department at Liggett and Myers contributed to this trend by discharging half its employees in a three-year period in the late 1930s.[73]

Table 11. Percentage of Black Workers in North Carolina Tobacco Industry
1910-1940

1910	1920	1930	1940
73.9%	74.2%	76.2%	64.8%

Source: U. S. Census of Population:

1910:   Vol. IV, Occupations, Table 7.
1920:   Vol. IV, Occupations, Table 1.
1930:   Vol. IV, Occupations, Table 11.
1940:   Vol, III, The Labor Force.

The NRA hearings in August 1934, intended to draw up a code for the tobacco industry, heard several white Durham workers testify about the speedup in progress in Durham factories. C. D. Whitfield, a tobacco worker, explained that instead of three and a half women per machine, one girl could operate a new machine at a speed close to twice the older machine.[74] An American Tobacco worker reported that their new wrapper used one girl instead of the two who used to operate its predecessor.[75] A year later, a black woman stemmer noted the contradictory results of the NRA code: "They laid off one-fourth of the people in my room after the last raise we got."[76] Still another told the investigator, "I'll tell you, don't write this down, I don't think it's right to put in them machines to take work away from us poor people."[77] Many years later, another black woman formerly employed by American Tobacco Company tersely summed up those years. "It was Hell," she said.[78]

Erwin Mills introduced its own version of the stretch-out stricter work rules, higher standards of productivity, and increasingly onerous work discipline. The mill increased the work load for loom fixers in 1931. The managers did not increase the fixers' pay but promised, instead, "to try to keep from reducing" their wages.[79] The mill did not alter the work load requirements for spinners, largely a female occupation, because their wages were so low that it would have been impractical to hire assistants to do the cleaning. Textile workers' wages lagged behind increased productivity, as general industry figures indicated (Table 12).[80]

Following the first implementation of the NRA, textile prosperity briefly revived in 1933 before a downturn in demand combined with worker unrest over the stretch-out produced the first serious labor trouble at Erwin Mills

Table 12. Wage Increases and Increases in Productivity in Textiles, 1928-1937 and 1937-1940

	1928-1937	1937-1940
Percent increase in output per worker	40%	14%
Percent increase in wages	27%	0%

in thirty years. Blaming "unprincipled agitators" for a September 1934 strike, Erwin Mills president K. P. Lewis assured his stockholders that he would continue the policies which had provoked worker protests. Fearing that the mills would "have more trouble fighting competition than ever before," Lewis declared that the company would continue to modernize its machinery and production methods as rapidly as possible.[81] Thus Erwin Mills reproduced the same tendencies toward overproduction and fierce competition that had plagued the industry for nearly fifteen years. During the next seven years the mill management and employees would become increasingly locked in a struggle marked by the installation of new machinery, the imposition of new work loads, the displacement of some workers, and work protests against these undesired changes in their work culture. Short periods of improved demand for Erwin products would periodically relieve the pressure, but successive wage cuts, curtailed production, and layoffs would then precipitate renewed worker discontent.[82]

Women, as a majority in the tobacco labor force and a near majority in the textile work force, bore the full brunt of technological change and stricter forms of labor discipline. The key workers aside from skilled loom fixers leading worker protests were women battery fillers and sewing room personnel.[83] A fixer at Liggett and Myers testified in the 1934 hearings to the harmful effects the speedup imposed upon female tobacco operatives in his department. "The girls up there, on my line . . . are nervous, a nervous wreck with the fast machine. . . . If you do speak to them . . . they jump all to pieces."[84] White tobacco workers also complained about the insensitivity and abusive treatment foremen inflicted upon them or their coworkers in their drive to increase production. They deeply resented the curse words some supervisors used to make them work as much as the partiality displayed toward some women at American Tobacco in exchange for sexual favors.[85] They questioned the justice expressed in sending a woman home for several days without pay at Liggett and Myers because of some minor mistake. Women at Erwin Mills protested the insecurity of their employment in the sewing room and the arbitrary treatment they received. Some women, for example, apparently could take pregnancy leave and return to their jobs without difficulty; others could not.[86]

Because the changes in technology and work discipline flowed along the lines of social cleavage, black women experienced the most severe hardship.

Their already insecure claims to employment were attenuated as the hand processes in which they had been employed began to mechanize. However bitterly they may have felt the injustice of their situation, they did not express their resentment directly, then or later.[87] Instead, they phrased their complaints obliquely by praising a foreman with words that might damn him in the ears of a sympathetic and perceptive listener. Several hand stemmers at Liggett and Myers, for example, spoke about fear of layoffs or being "cut off" but did not blame their foremen as a white woman might have done. "They liable to tell you to go home any time," one black woman said, "but the foreman is as fine a white man as I ever seen to work for." Such a statement could signify that she was too accustomed to poor treatment from her white bosses to complain.[88] Only two women, one black and one unusually sympathetic white, openly denounced the tobacco foremen's abusive attitudes toward black women. Voicing a common complaint about the company reluctance to allow black people to earn above a certain amount, one stemmer said, "If you are doing more than they want to pay you for, the boss will come around and find all manner of fault and act just as hateful as he can. That makes you nervous and scared and then you naturally can't do as well and that naturally makes you slower."[89] The white woman, employed at American Tobacco in the 1930s, remembered the brutal way white workers as well as white supervisors bossed black women around. She explained that many of her coworkers would not talk about conditions back then because they did not like to remember their suffering.[90]

As relationships between workers and management grew more strained, workers began to create stronger bonds among themselves rooted in their common plight. Communities grew out of the policies employers had devised to divide and control workers along racial and sexual lines. The planned community built by Erwin Mills provided a territorial basis for a tightly knit community of workers where commitments and identification with each other began to supplant fast-eroding loyalties to the company. The more dispersed white tobacco worker population began to meet in secret and by 1935 in public. Only black workers, who certainly bore more than their share of the indignities imposed by factory discipline, did not develop a cohesive, autonomous, working-class community. Outside the workplace, racial domination imposed a solidarity upon the black community where black elites lived together with black workers. But hostility or indifference toward organization tended to inhibit working-class militance in the black community after most of the churches closed their doors to black workers desiring to meet together.[91] Although white workers tried to encourage blacks to organize, their refusal to meet as a group with black workers made it still more difficult for blacks to conceive of themselves primarily as workers in opposition to their employers. Denied a common meeting place, in both a spatial and a cultural sense, the three communities of workers never evolved a sense of their collective identity as members of the same community, but they did begin to articulate their common interests in the 1930s and to act upon them.

The labor unions which tried to channel the strong currents of discontent into organizational forms took on a formidable task. The actual records of the national tobacco and textile unions did not auger well for their success in Durham in the 1930s in spite of worker dissatisfaction. Neither the excessive timidity of the Tobacco Workers International Union (TWIU) nor the overly rash activism of the United Textile Workers (UTW) had sustained organization in the South during earlier campaigns. The difference in approach—the union label emphasis of the TWIU versus the strike emphasis of the UTW—merely influenced the ways in which the two unions had failed. Nearly inactive since the 1910s in any public way,[92] the TWIU had ceased to involve its members through organizing campaigns, union conventions, a union journal, or even election of its own officers for at least a decade.[93] The UTW trailed behind them a series of defeats culminating in a bitter strike at Danville, Virginia, in early 1931. The unions' failure to develop an approach to organizing women and black workers that would recognize the structures separating them from white male workers magnified their already apparent weaknesses so as to militate against any successful organizing drives. The Textile Workers Organizing Committee (TWOC) replaced the discredited UTW in Durham in 1937. It did not carry the loser's image associated with the TWIU or its own predecessor, but its leaders, like most male trade unionists, saw men as the key group of workers to be mobilized.

Confronting the organizers were the visible, if not fully analyzed, obstacles of company antagonism and racial division within the labor force. The companies, particularly Erwin Mills, vigorously opposed any demands from workers for collective bargaining rights. All three companies adamantly refused to concede their power to control the labor process and, thereby, the labor force.[94] The unions, moreover, essentially shared the assumption of the employer's prerogative to determine the pace of technological change and the composition of his labor force. They did not seek to challenge capitalist control but sought a more equitable wage scale for tobacco and textile workers. The TWIU, in fact, continually affirmed that company interests and workers' interests were essentially identical.[95] On the race question, which concerned the TWIU directly, the union appealed to white workers on largely pragmatic grounds by pointing to the majority status of blacks in their industry. White tobacco workers had to help organize black workers if the organization was to succeed, but the union locals remained segregated so that blacks would not outnumber and outvote white members.[96] As a consequence, black and white workers never met together to discuss the organizing campaign or to deal with mutual concerns. White organizers attended black union meetings, but black and white women never associated together under union auspices.[97] TWIU locals in Durham thus replicated the segregationist patterns already deeply embedded in the workforce.

The unions never came to grips with the issue of male domination in spite of its obviously crippling effect upon women's participation in the locals. Limited access to public space combined with household duties to make it more difficult for women to assume leadership roles, attend meetings, and serve as union officials.[98] Their absence from the decision-making process contributed to the union's failures to incorporate issues appealing to women in their demands. Women members, in turn, responded to the union less enthusiastically than their male counterparts. Female tobacco workers, especially black women, consistently expressed less interest in unions than men. When asked about unions, black women typically voiced disinterest or suspicion. As one black woman summarized her opinions about unions, "It would be a pretty hard job to set up a union in this town because colored people have been treated so dirty."[99] Most of the women who joined TWIU locals took no active role in organizing or deciding the union's goals.[100] In the TWOC locals, which became affiliates of the Textile Workers Union of America (TWUA) in 1939, women served as local secretaries but did not participate in union negotiations. Office-holding, moreover, tended to involve single women rather than the married majority among the union membership.[101]

The unions' organizing tactics at the national level did not encourage women's participation on an equal basis with men. The spokesmen for the UTW, the TWIU, and the TWOC/TWUA remained almost exclusively male and white throughout the 1930s. Their policies and their organizers did not take seriously the question of women's special needs despite the frequent complaints about the difficulties involved in organizing women.[102] Suspicious of the feminist and leftist views espoused by women who tried to encourage female union activism,[103] unions continued to organize women as though they were men while denying them an equal voice because they were women. In Durham, for example, a female tobacco worker educated at the Bryn Mawr Summer School for Women Workers refused to take an active part in the union at American Tobacco because she disliked the attitudes of the men who dominated that local.[104] Middle-class feminists and churches, not unions, provided the first meaningful assistance for working mothers by opening day-care centers in Durham.[105] Even the more progressive textile workers local did not take minimal steps to groom women for union leadership until the mid-1940s.[106] Neither union, moreover, did anything to encourage women to take on the more skilled, better-paying positions designated for men. As in the case of race, the unions reinforced the divisions in privilege and control which employers had originally introduced.

The unions' apparent isolation from the important community meeting places of church and family further hindered their organizing efforts. Generally excluded from the churches by elite pressure and the southern church's opposition to the reform-minded adherents to the Social Gospel,[107] unions could not appeal directly to the strong religious traditions that provided workers with their orientation towards the world. Indeed, they often appeared as alien. Ministers at best acted as a neutral force in Durham, and at least one minister warned workers against becoming involved in any disruptive actions.[108] Although families were drawn into the union campaign, the union locals apparently made no attempts to link their efforts explicitly to family needs or to appeal to nonworking members in each household. Because these institutions were often more central to women's than to men's lives, the unions' estrangement from family and church undoubtedly deprived them of much-needed support from many women.

In spite of these obstacles, worker discontent proved strong enough to sustain successful organizing campaigns in Durham. White workers at the tobacco factories became the first to organize successfully. Forced by the federal government to bargain with its workers, Liggett and Myers signed the first contract with the white Local 176 in 1935. Black locals at Liggett and Myers found it tougher going. Local 194 took five years to organize black stemmery workers after its inception in 1934. Black men employed in manufacturing departments established Local 208 in 1937 and won a contract the following year. The local then cooperated with the white local in the 1939 strike that succeeded in closing down L & M plants across the nation because the closing of the Durham stemmery stopped the flow of tobacco. Local 194 members, however, were largely passive observers of the strike who stopped work when the stemmery closed. The TWIU locals secured a preferential shop agreement from L & M when the company agreed to ask its workers to join the TWIU. Union organizing at American Tobacco lagged behind the L & M campaign in the face of more determined company opposition, but eventually the union locals won bargaining rights while establishing the same segregated organization.

The succession of unions who campaigned to enlist Erwin Mills workers faced strong but relatively restrained resistance from the company. During the early 1930s the company relied on its tradition of paternalist welfare policies to sustain the loyalty of its workforce. Indeed the unions had to overcome many workers' deeply engrained loyalties toward William Erwin and the company which had employed, housed, and directed many workers from early childhood. The death of W. A. Erwin in 1932, however, enabled some longtime Erwin workers to become involved in the union drive without feeling disloyal. "W. A. Erwin," said one worker who became a union leader, "considered the employee along with the business. Now K. P. was strictly a businessman."[109] Once K. P. Lewis took charge of the company and introduced more modern methods of production, workers did not feel obliged to transfer their devotion to Erwin's successor. As the continuing disruption of their accustomed work culture proceeded, more and more Erwin workers began to agree that the mill no longer considered their interests "along with the business." At the same time Lewis did not use all the weapons at his command. Although the Erwin management employed a spy to seek out union activists in the spring of 1934, the company did not resort to mass firings after the General Textile Strike in September closed down all the textile mills in Durham.[110] Like other manufacturers, the company used the National Guard to protect non-striking workers at its Coolemee plant but did not use Guardsmen as strike-breakers in Durham where the workers were more united. Instead K. P. Lewis sought to regain control over his restive workforce by speeding up the pace of technological and managerial change, the very forces that were undermining workers' security. Three years later the workers voted in the TWOC. After years of fruitless negotiation, the union struck the company in March 1940. A year later the company, forced to bargain by the War Labor Board, signed the first union contract with the TWUA local.[111]

Durham workers, aided to an important degree by the federal government's intervention on their side, had won union victories in Durham's major industries, but those victories proved seriously flawed in terms of their effects upon women's subordinated place in the industrial labor force. Led almost exclusively by white men who monopolized the public, decision-making arena by virtue of their sex and race, the unions did not alter the structures of domination which placed black women at the bottom of the social hierarchy. Women workers joined the tobacco workers' locals once the unions had become firmly established, but the locals did not defend black women's jobs in the face of white determination to maintain a monopoly over the prospering sector of the tobacco industry.[112] The unions also kept white women tobacco workers from entering the male-designated, higher paying jobs, but those women continued to receive higher wages and better working conditions than black men or black women. Erwin women, benefitting from the more progressive orientation of the TWUIA had a greater voice in union policy than women in the TWU, but decision-making power and the better-paying jobs continued to reside largely in male hands in the union as well as in the company.

In spite of the union victories, many workers' positions had deteriorated by the end of the 1930s. Black women had already begun losing their jobs in the tobacco industry to machines which would eventually result in their becoming a tiny minority in an industry they had once dominated. The Textile Workers Union proved unable to halt the process which called it into being. Its leaders, like the TWIU leadership, believed that technological innovation would prove beneficial to workers as well as employers in the long run. The speed-up continued. Outside the workplace, women continued to assume primary responsibility for household and family duties. The women who had been able to keep their jobs could now afford household conveniences, but the women who had lost jobs, primarily black women, found work once more in other women's kitchens. Asked a question about the advantages brought by the union, one woman said, "Now they have upped the wages a lot, but it's killing the people so what has been gained by it?"[113]

What indeed had been gained by the struggle of these workers to organize? The unions essentially replicated the structured inequalities already dividing the workers they organized. Moreover, unions did not alter the balance of power between workers and employers. In the very process of bargaining, the unions allied the workers' interests more closely with those of the company, giving workers a vested interest in their own continued subordination. Improved wages and working conditions did help workers, but the companies gained a still more powerful tool to use in the continuing struggle to control their workforce. The structures of sexual, racial and class domination continued to shape the human environment in which women lived, worked, and interpreted their world. It would appear that so little had changed as to call into question the very notion of "victory" for women workers in Durham.

Something will have been gained, however, if we can understand the reasons for their failure to restructure the work described as "killing the people." Participants in that struggle did not consciously recognize or challenge the structures of racial and sexual domination because those structures were so deeply interwoven into the fabric of their lives as to seem natural or inevitable. The women most subordinated by the combined forces of class, sexual, and racial domination were least able to confront them because the daily struggle for subsistence absorbed most of their physical and emotional resources. The relatively privileged position accorded to other participants by that system provided them with concrete advantages which obscured their own subordination to sexual and class domination. White women accepted a system of racial domination where the prestige of the superior depended upon the coerced respect of the inferior even though that system imprisoned them along with their black subordinates. Accustomed to forms of domination in their daily life, Durham workers could not construct a thorough-going critique of their employers' right to control their labor without an analysis which could expose the assumptions they shared with the dominant class. Like the men who employed them, these workers—at least the white majority—assumed the necessity and even the justice of a social hierarchy of race, sex, and class which forced black women to the bottom. Their unions, moreover, failed to provide the analysis needed to challenge these pervasive assumptions, because they limited their efforts to achieving narrowly-defined economic goals. Attacking only the most apparent symptoms of class domination, these unions won victories which the system of interlocking dominations could absorb without serious disruption. Denied an opportunity to articulate their common interests, women workers remained separated and subordinated members of a dominated class. The fact, however, that they did begin to resist one cause of their domination, makes their story one of victory as well as defeat.

Notes

1. E. P. Thompson in his introduction to *The Making of the English Working Class*, (New York: Vintage, 1966) describes the proleterianizing process in a society where class and culture coincided in contrast to the Durham example.

2. For Durham history see William K. Boyd, *The Story of Durham: City of the New South*, (Durham, N.C.: Duke University Press, 1927); Robert Durden, *The Dukes of Durham*, (Durham, N.C.: Duke University Press, 1975); and Nannie May Tilley, *The Bright Tobacco Industry: 1869-1929*, (Chapel Hill, N.C.: University of North Carolina Press, 1939).

3. Based upon sixty-four interviews conducted by the author and twenty-nine additional interviews conducted by associates.

4. These patterns, already firmly established in the 1890s according to the Mangum City Directory (1897), prevailed throughout the period in question as the U.S. Census on Population, *1940: Special Survey on Housing: Durham, North Carolina*, (Washington, D.C.: GPO, 1942) attests.

5. Kemp P. Lewis Papers, 1916-1940, in the Southern Historical Collection (SHC), Wilson Library, University of North Carolina, Chapel Hill, North Carolina. Lewis, who became president of Erwin Mills in 1932, moved from the mill village to Forest Hills in the mid-1910s, and then became involved in the Hope Valley development project in the mid-1920s along with many prominent Durham businessmen. Hereafter cited as Lewis Papers, SHC.

6. This residential pattern for the black elite continues today as it has for the past eighty years.

7. Quoted in Ida L. Moore, "Description of a Mill Village," September 17, 1938, Durham, in the North Carolina Writers' Project Papers, SHC, Wilson Library, UNC.

8. Interview with a white woman tobacco worker, January 1979.

9. Richard C. Edwards, Michael Reich, and David M. Gordon, eds., *Labor Market Segmentation*, (New York: Heath, 1975).

10. Based upon interviews with four female textile workers and three male textile workers.

11. Based upon interviews with five female tobacco workers and three male tobacco workers who were all white.

12. Based upon interviews with five female tobacco workers and two male tobacco workers who were all black.

13. C. Tinsley Willis, "Negro Labor in the Tobacco Industry in North Carolina," (M.A. thesis, New York University, 1931), and Herbert R. Northrup, *The Negro in the Tobacco Industry*, (Philadelphia: University of Pennsylvania Press, 1970.)

14. Information derived from Lewis Papers, SHC.

15. Based upon Willis, "Negro Labor"; Northrup, *Negro in the Tobacco Industry*, and above-mentioned sets of interviews with black tobacco workers.

16. For information about the sexual division in labor and skill in the textile industry, see Senate Document 645, 61st Congress 2nd Session, "Report on the

Condition of Women and Child Wage-Earners in the United States," Vol. 1: Cotton Textile Industry (Washington, D.C.: GPO, 1910); U.S. Women's Bureau Bulletin 111, Ethel L. Best, "Hours, Earnings, and Employment in Cotton Mills" (Washington, D.C., 1930); U.S. Women's Bureau Bulletin 52, "Lost Time and Labor Turnover in Cotton Mills," (Washington, D.C., 1926); and Jennings Rhyne, "Some Southern Cotton Mill Workers and Their Villages" (M.A. thesis, University of North Carolina, 1930).

17. Based upon interviews with three white women tobacco workers: one employed at Liggett and Myers, one at American Tobacco, and one by both companies.

18. Mentioned by Helen Worthington Smith in her history of the Bryn Mawr Summer School for Women Workers.

19. Mentioned by two sympathetic white tobacco workers at American Tobacco Company.

20. Based upon interviews with four female and one male tobacco workers.

21. According to Glenn Hinson, an oral historian of black culture in Durham, employed by the North Carolina Department of Cultural Resources.

22. Based upon interviews with the same set of textile workers previously mentioned.

23. Discussed by five tobacco workers and Robert C. Weaver, "The Tobacco Industry in North Carolina", unpublished study in National Recovery Administration (NRA) records, Industrial Studies Section, Tobacco Workers, National Archives, Washington, D.C.

24. Unpublished study by Charles S. Johnson, "The Tobacco Worker," Vol. 2, 387, in NRA records, Industrial Studies Section, National Archives, Washington, D.C.

25. Out of twenty-eight tobacco workers interviewed by the author, twenty-one had migrated from rural areas into Durham.

26. Johnson, "Tobacco Worker," p. 400, discusses occupational experiences among different sexual and racial groups in Durham tobacco factories.

27. Based upon interviews with thirty textile workers. Erwin Mills, as the biggest mill, apparently hired more workers with previous textile experience rather than hiring workers directly from the farm by the decade covered in the article.

28. Based upon analysis of forty-four interviews.

29. Orie Latham Hatcher, *Rural Girls Come to the City for Work*, (Richmond, Va.: Garnett & Maine, 1930).

30. Based upon the interviews cited. One young woman who travelled into Durham on her own found her first job at Erwin Mills, but she moved on in less than a year to Liggett and Myers.

31. Margaret Jarman Hagood, *Mothers of the South: Portraiture of the White Tenant Farm Woman* (1939; reprint, New York: Norton, 1977) and Willis, "Negro Labor," for black women.

32. Hatcher, *Rural Girls.*

33. Quoted from an interview with a rural black woman and described in Hagood, *Mothers of the South*, for white tenant farm women.

34. Several incidents reported by Hagood, *Mothers of the South*, point to the bitterness and/or deliberate omission of black people on the part of poor whites.

36. Described in oral history interviews concerning life in West Durham, where

the principal black character was the man who cleaned out the privies; other interviews dealing with other mills speak of black women doing domestic work.

37. "Public work" originally referred to men's work on public roads but came to signify any kind of nonagricultural, paid employment for men and women. The phrase recurred in numerous oral history interviews, apparently indicating the innovative quality of these relatively new forms of employment for the people involved.

38. Louise Tilly and Joan Scott, in *Women, Work and Family*, (New York: Holt, Rinehart and Winston, 1978).

39. Reported in one oral history interview and in U.S. Children's Bureau records, unpublished survey on child labor in Durham 1917, National Archives, Washington, D.C.

40. The law required children aged eight to fourteen to attend school for the entire term and forbade employment of children under fourteen. According to an interview with William Ruffin, last president of Erwin Mills, no children worked at Erwin Mills from the 1920s onward.

41. Calculations based upon data in U.S. Census of Population, 1930, Vol. 4, "Occupations"; and U.S. Census of Population, 1940, Vol. 3, "The Labor Force."

42. Described in the "Report on the Condition" for textile industry, and in subsequent volume, 18, "Employment of Women and Children in Selected Industries," for tobacco industry.

43. Johnson, "Tobacco Worker," Vol. 2, p. 390.

44. According to Johnson, "Tobacco Worker," Vol. 1, pp. 52, 149, the annual wages for Durham tobacco workers followed a definite racial and sexual hierarchy: white males averaged $726, white females $646, black males $543, and black females $430. He used $1,500 per year as the basic income needed for an average family to subsist without going into debt.

45. *Ibid.*; Willis, "Negro Labor"; U.S. Women's Bureau Bulletin 76, "Negro Women in Industry in 15 States" (Washington, D.C., 1929); and U.S. Women's Bureau Bulletin 127, "Hours and Earnings in Tobacco Stemmeries" (Washington, D.C., 1934).

46. Johnson, "Tobacco Worker," Vol. 2, p. 446.

47. Ida L. Moore, "The Haithcocks," July 7, 1938, West Durham, N.C., Federal Writers' Project, Southern Historical Collection (SHC).

48. Ida L. Moore, "The Dunns," July 12, 1938, West Durham, N.C., Federal Writers' Project, SHC.

49. Tagging tobacco sacks was called "tagging bulls" because the work involved putting a Bull Durham tag on each sack.

50. Quoted in Hugh P. Brinton, "The Negro in Durham: A Study of Adjustment to Town Life," (Ph.D. dissertation, University of North Carolina, 1930).

51. Described in two oral history interviews with one black woman and the child of two tobacco workers.

52. Brinton, "Negro in Durham," p. 220.

53. Johnson, "Tobacco Worker," Vol. 2, pp. 440-445.

54. Table 17—Infant Mortality Rates in U.S. Bureau of the Census, *Negroes in the United States, 1920-1932* (G.P.O.: 1935).

55. N.C. State Board of Health, Bureau of Vital Statistics, Reports for 1932-34 and 1939.

56. Based upon comparison of North Carolina State Board of Health, Bureau of Vital Statistics, Reports for 1932-1934 and 1939.

57. *Ibid.*

58. Brinton, "Negro in Durham," p. 119.

59. Interview with black woman tobacco worker, December 1978.

60. Quoted at meeting of American Tobacco Retirees Club, November 1978.

61. Described by two sympathetic white tobacco workers, December 1978.

62. Only one white female tobacco worker out of all those interviewed appeared to sympathize with black peoples' circumstances.

63. Attitudes of Durham workers discussed in Johnson, "Tobacco Worker," Vol. 2, pp. 418-422, and in my own interviews conducted with six women who worked at Liggett and Myers.

64. According to one woman employed at American Tobacco.

65. According to two interviews with women who began working as children.

66. Based upon analysis of the seniority records of Erwin Mills strikers in the Erwin Cotton Manufacturing Company Papers, Manuscript Collection, Perkins Library, Duke University.

67. Interview with one woman textile worker who became active in the union.

68. The weavers and fixers of No. 1 Weave Room at Erwin Mills sent a petition to the Erwin Mills management in April 1929, protesting the "new system, known as the 'stretch-out,'" and the tobacco workers at Liggett and Myers sent a report to the NRA, Industrial Studies Section, on changes in the Making Department at Liggett and Myers which said, "Our first stretch out came in 1928. . . ." The petition was found in the K. P. Lewis Papers; the report in the NRA Papers, Industrial Studies Section, Tobacco Code, National Archives, Washington, D.C.

69. Quoted from K. P. Lewis to W. A. Erwin, February 27, 1931, K. P. Lewis Papers, SHC.

70. Northrup, *Negro in the Tobacco Industry.*

71. U.S. Census of Population, 1930, Vol. 4, "Occupations."

72. Described for Durham women in Leo Davis, "The History of the Labor Movement among Negro Tobacco Workers in Durham, North Carolina with Specific References to AF of L Locals 194, 204, 208," (MA thesis: North Carolina Central College, 1949).

73. *Ibid.*

74. NRA Hearings: "Code of Fair Competition for Cigarette, Snuff, Smoking and Chewing Tobacco Industry," August 21, 1934, NRA Records, p. 210, National Archives.

75. *Ibid.*, p. 216.

76. Quoted in Johnson, "Tobacco Worker," Vol. 2, p. 408.

77. *Ibid.*, p. 421.

78. Reported by a retired white tobacco worker.

79. K. P. Lewis to W. A. Erwin, February 27, 1931, Lewis Papers, SHC.

80. According to Herbert J. Lahne, *The Cotton Mill Worker* (New York: Farrar and Rinehart, 1944).

81. K. P. Lewis, "Report to the Stockholders and Directors of Erwin Cotton Mills Company," January 26, 1935, Lewis Papers, SHC.

82. *Ibid.*

83. *Ibid.*, and confirmed by interview with one female textile worker who was a battery filler and the daughter of a loom fixer.

84. NRA Hearings, p. 211.

85. Cursing discussed in Johnson, "Tobacco Worker," Vol. 2, pp. 418, 421-422;

sexual abuse described by two white tobacco workers.

86. Described by one female textile worker. Complaints about pregnancy leave policies also appeared in records of committee meetings with the union local in Erwin Cotton Mills Company Papers.

87. Black women often refused to be interviewed or interviewed on record concerning their experiences in tobacco factories.

88. Quoted in Johnson, "Tobacco Worker," Vol. 2, p. 420.

89. *Ibid.*, p. 421.

90. A white female tobacco worker employed at American Tobacco and now a member of American Tobacco Retirees Club.

91. Reported in Davis, "History of the Labor Movement," which was based upon oral history interviews with the participants conducted in 1948.

92. According to correspondence between K. P. Lewis and W. Carmichael of Liggett and Myers, between 1925 and 1929 union organizing was being attempted at Liggett and Myers. It never emerged publicly because the company bribed at least one union official and intimidated the others. A few leaders lost their jobs. Lewis Papers, SHC.

93. Northrup, *Negro in the Tobacco Industry.*

94. Described in a confidential memorandum such as the one William Ruffin wrote to K. P. Lewis on August 2, 1939, in which he discusses the Erwin Mills anti-union strategy which he asked Erwin to destroy after "giving it consideration." Lewis Papers, SHC.

95. Based upon a reading of the TWIU journal, *Tobacco Labor,* 1900-1922.

96. Motive suggested by Northrup, *The Negro in the Tobacco Industry,* who also suggests that the TWIU became revitalized in the 1930s due to pressure from tobacco workers in Winston-Salem who led a revolt against the conservative leadership.

97. Noted by John Rice, "The Negro Tobacco Worker and His Union in Durham, North Carolina" (M.A. thesis: University of North Carolina, 1941), who remarked upon the racism prevalent among the white rank and file.

98. Mentioned in interviews with one male and one female union official in each industry.

99. Quoted in Johnson, "Tobacco Worker," Vol. 2, p. 414.

100. Revealed in every interview conducted with black women. Apparently the black women active in organizing the union who had been interviewed by Leo Davis had died or left Durham.

101. Based upon analysis of the records of the strike drawn up by Erwin Mills to present to the National Labor Relations Board, in Erwin Cotton Manufacturing Company Papers.

102. Based upon interviews with four male union officials.

103. Described by Mary Frederickson, "The Southern Summer School for Women Workers in Industry: A Female Strategy for Collective Action in the South," (paper delivered at the Berkshire Conference in Women's History, August 1978).

104. Based upon an interview with a female tobacco worker, February 1979.

105. Mary O. Cowper Papers, Manuscript Collection, Perkins Library, Duke University.

106. Discussed in an interview with one female textile worker who protested her exclusion from training programs for union members.

107. The issue of the church's attitude towards unions, particularly among southern

textile workers, was discussed by Liston Pope, *Millhands and Preachers: A Study of Gastonia* (New Haven: Yale University Press, 1942) and specifically for Durham by Spencer Miller, Jr. and Joseph F. Fletcher, *The Church and Industry* (New York: Longmans, Green, and Co., 1930). Leo Davis in "The History of the Labor Movement in Durham . . ." mentions the general indifference or hostility by black churches tobacco worker elicited this explanation of the ministers' attitudes. He explained that they thought only of the "inner man" and forgot to consider the "outer man."

108. Davis, "The History of the Labor Movement," and Rice, "The Negro Tobacco Workers."

109. As quoted in H. Lanier Rand, "'I had to like it': A Study of a Durham Textile Community," BA Honors paper, University of North Carolina, Chapel Hill, 1977.

110. Lewis papers.

111. Erwin Cotton Mill Company papers.

112. Jean M. Cary, "The Forced Merger of Local 208 and Local 176 of the TWIU at the L & M. in Durham, N.C.," MA Thesis, Duke University, Chapel Hill, N.C., 1977, describes the embittered reaction of black workers as they lost their place in the company and then their local.

113. A white female textile worker quoted in Rand, "'I had to like it.'"

PART III

Images — Female, Feminine, Feminist

In the 1920s, many women were concerned about the multiplicity of roles that seemed to be offered to them. Mary P. Ryan utilizes one form of popular culture, the movies, to explore the ways in which women and girls were socialized and their reactions to the "new woman" as she was portrayed in films. From this study, several themes emerge clearly. Julie Boddy's article on Marion Post Wolcott offers not only the contrast of rural women's life-styles but also that of a career woman; a professional photographer. Another alternative, that of the intellectual, is explored by Norma Pratt in her description of the struggles of Yiddish women writers to engage in radical political activism during the 1920s and 1930s. Ruth Schwartz Cowan's analysis of advertising trends in the women's magazines during the same period indicates that important changes were taking place both in the nature of housework and in the expectations placed upon women in the home.

How does Ryan make the connection between mass cultural image and actual social behavior? What were the important themes which emerged from her study of the movies during this period? How were expectations about women's roles in the home shifting? In what ways did this affect the nature of housework? What similarities and differences might be found in rural women's lives? For native born career women and Yiddish women intellectuals, obstacles blocked the way to full participation in American life. What explains their failure to be accepted fully by the movements in which they participated? How did they react to that failure?

5

The Projection of a New Womanhood: The Movie Moderns in the 1920's
MARY P. RYAN

The ideal of femininity was changing so dramatically around the third decade of the twentieth century that contemporaries began to speak of an entirely "new woman." In 1925 the mothers of Middletown recognized the transformation in their own daughters: "Girls aren't so modest nowadays; they dress differently," "Girls are more aggressive today. They call the boys up to try to make dates with them as they never would have when I was a girl." "When I was a girl, a girl who painted was a bad girl—now look at the daughters of our best families "[1] Historians have called attention to the same transformation of the female image in popular literature, advertising, and the graphic arts, underway even before World War I.[2] Historians have not been as diligent, however, in culling another rich body of imagery regarding the new woman—the moving pictures, which vividly record the full flavor of the flapper's personality, complete with her characteristic gestures, energy, and activism. Although many of these early films have been destroyed, enough remain from which to piece together a schematic moving portrait of the new woman.

Careful analysis of popular movies, furthermore, offers the historian access to the dream-life of past generations, male and female. By the 1920's, movie making had become a smoothly functioning industry, capitalized at over one billion dollars and tooled for the mass production and distribution of fantasies. The output of the major studios (Paramount, Fox, MGM, Universal, Warner Brothers) was manufactured by an army of directors, technicians, writers, and businessmen, all working under the imperative of pleasing an audience that numbered as many as 100 million viewers a week, gathered together in over 18,000 theatres all across America.[3] The understandable result of this collective process was a standardized product that could be simply classified by such formulas as the adventure story, western, comedy, and love story. The success of each popular genre depended upon striking a responsive cord in the mass audience, reaching

This article is reprinted from *Our American Sisters: Women in American Life and Thought*, 2d ed., Jean E. Friedman and William G. Slade, eds. Boston: Allyn and Bacon, Inc., and appears by permission of the author.

some common denominator in the experience, hopes, and fears of Americans. This juncture of dream and reality on the silver screen provides the historian a multidimensional cultural document.

Cinema also provides an ideal vantage point from which to observe the making of the new woman. Screen femininity in the twenties was often the creation of woman scenarists, like Bess Meredyth, Anita Loos, Frances Marion, Jeanie MacPherson, and June Mathis,[4] who worked in teams and at a frantic pace to construct captivating images and compelling plots. Their formulaic stories reached an audience which included millions of women often in their formative years. One survey concluded that females between the ages of eight and nineteen attended the movies an average of 46 times a year[5] in the twenties.

Perhaps the crucial link in this female cultural chain was the star. Well before the studios were willing to identify their actresses by name, the mails were flooded with chatty letters to familiar screen personalities. When Universal revealed the "biograph girl" to be Florence Lawrence, this first starlet was immediately mobbed in St. Louis, hounded by fans begging her autograph and ravaging her clothing.[6] The star was a unique cultural phenomenon, an actress whose personal style enlivened a multiplicity of familiar but fictional roles, blending the real with the imaginary in one glamorous individual. She was, as Stanley Cavell phrases it, an "individuality" that "projects particular ways of inhabiting a social role."[7] By the 1920's national surveys revealed that movie stars had replaced political, business, and artistic leaders as the favorite role models of American youth.[8] In the twenties, the female social role was projected on the screen by such personalities as Madge Bellamy, Clara Bow, Joan Crawford, and Gloria Swanson, all vivid embodiments of the new womanhood, known to contemporaries as "the moderns."

By the mid-twenties the sweet heroines of the late Victorian age had been totally banished from the screen by these new women. The cinematic staples of the pre-war era, both the one-reelers that stocked the nickelodeons in working-class neighborhoods and the prestigious features directed by D. W. Griffith, featured actresses like Lillian Gish and Mary Pickford who reveled in motherly sacrifice, sexual purity and shy submission. Another woman who enacted such parts, Linda Arvidson Griffith, described her typical roles as "the peasant, washwoman and tenement lady" staunchly protecting her babes from starvation, and her virginity from despoilment by rich and vulgar villains. When Mrs. Griffith wrote her memoirs in 1925, however, she woefully acknowledged that such true womanhood was regarded as old-fashioned and had been replaced by an antagonistic set of mores: "We were dealing in things vital in our American life and not one bit interested in close-ups of empty-headed little ingenues with adenoids, bedroom windows, manhandling of young girls, fast sets, perfumed bathrooms or nude youths heaving their muscles."[9] Such permissiveness in the display of the female body and the treatment of sexual themes was the most obvious hallmark of the new woman.

Nonetheless, early cinema had not been as asexual as Arvidson liked to remember. One of the first scandals of the screen was the 1896 "Anatomy of a Kiss" which drew out that intimate act to a full 42 frames. As the medium advanced from merely photographing natural phenomena to full-fledged story-telling, sex became a favorite theme, albeit veiled in moralistic condemnations of the villainous roué and the hapless prostitute. It was in the hey day of Griffith, in fact, that female sexuality struck its most aggressive pose in the screen antics of Theda Bara—"The wickedest face in the world, dark, brooding, beautiful and heartless"—luring unfortunate males to self-destruction. Theda Bara made no less than 40 films on the torrid vamp theme in the three years after her first appearance in the 1915 film *A Fool There Was*.[10]

Although the vamp was too extreme a caricature to endure, she had cleared the air of the dangerous vapors of female passion and cleared the way for a more respectable brand of sex appeal. The arrival of the new woman on the screen was clearly apparent by 1919 when she intruded into the wholesomely titled film made by the most Victorian of directors, Griffith's *True Heart Susie*. The heroine, played by Lillian Gish, radiated nineteenth-century womanhood as she worked, sacrificed, and waited in the blush of innocence for the boy next door. Yet True Heart Susie was a much beleaguered heroine in 1919. In fact she temporarily lost her hero to a member of the fast set, whose city ways included a painted face, short clinging skirts, and a wiggling walk that the camera followed with delight. Even True Heart Susie was momentarily tempted to powder her face with corn starch and hitch up her skirt. The contrived nature of the plot also illustrated the obsolescence of Victorian values. The old virtues did not triumph until Susie's rival had been exposed as a bad cook, sloppy housewife, an unfaithful wife, and then died of pneumonia. The last shot of the film underscored the nostalgia for the old morality and the old code of femininity: as the reunited couple walked into the sunset their images faded into a photograph from their rural childhood.[11]

The backward-looking ethic of *True Heart Susie* becomes even more distinct when the film is compared with the box-office sensation of 1919. It was in that year that Cecil B. De Mille, in collaboration with screenwriter Jeanie MacPherson, transposed the *Admirable Crichton* into a film entitled *Male and Female*. Under De Mille's direction the play became little more than a sexual display whose centerpiece was the female body. The movie audience was invited to share the hero's fantasy of sexual domination, to gaze upon Gloria Swanson's naked thighs and surging breasts in the frenzy of a shipwreck and watch in amazement as the star gingerly steps into the bath.[12] *Male and Female* grossed the extraordinary amount of one and one-quarter billion dollars, and ensured that sex appeal would become a favorite movie theme. Partial female nudity, excused by the bath or draped only in lingerie, became a staple of cinema in the decade to come. De Mille was its undisputed master: "He made of the bathroom a delightful resort . . . a mystic shrine to Venus and sometimes to Apollo. . . . Underclothes became visions of translucent promise."[13] Most every star who came to popularity in the twenties played a lingerie scene, which placed her in a languorous pose with soft, body-hugging silk around her torso. Clara Bow played the familiar lingerie salesgirl in *It* (1927); critics raved about Bebe Daniels' "negligible negligee" in *Stranded in Paris* (1926); *Bertha the Sewing Machine Girl* (1926) was described by William Fox Productions as "A Love and Lingerie Edition of the Great Melodrama"; and Joan Crawford modeled lingerie with matchless sensuality in *Our Blushing Brides* (1930).[14]

The exposure of the star's limbs was but one harbinger of the new woman. The women in lingerie were more than mannequins. They were the personification of the "moderns," females whose whole projected personalities had a new vitality and aura. Whether they played the upper-class flapper as did Gloria Swanson and Norma Talmadge, or the working girls characteristic of Clara Bow and Madge Bellamy, the same spirit surrounded them.[15] The new movie woman exuded above all a sense of physical freedom — unrestrained movement, confident gait, abounding energy — the antithesis of the controlled, quiet, tight-kneed poses of Griffith's heroines. These women moved confidently into a once male world. With a dashing spontaneity they rushed onto dance floors, leapt into swimming pools, and accepted any dare — to drink, to sport, to strip as Bow did in *Saturday Night Kid* (1929). They entered the world of work and college as well as the social circle, dashing down the city streets to offices, shops and classrooms with aplomb and self-assurance. They were an ambitious group, determined to use their bodily charms to make their way in the world.

The Hollywood ingenues enthusiastically embraced the remodeled image of women and imbued their new roles with a spirit of independence. Joan Crawford's scintillating Charleston sequence in *Our Dancing Daughters* (1928) is a case in point. Although the editor cut periodically to lustful male faces, the camera emphasized Crawford's gusto and liveliness, rather than eroticism. When the dancing Crawford ripped off her skirt, it was as if to remove a constricting garment, to facilitate freedom of movement and release of energy, not to entice male admirers. Her Charleston consisted not of bumps and grinds, but of jumps and starts at a frantic pace. Her sheer vitality and self-confidence were at the forefront.[16] In the role of "Dangerous Diana" Crawford upheld the new standard of movie virtue. In contrast, it was the "evil women" of *Our Dancing Daughters* who portrayed shy innocence, a mere ruse to captivate an old-fashioned hero.

The type of sex appeal labeled *It* by Elinor Glyn and presented on film by Clara Bow in 1927 had a similarly wholesome cast. Bow rendered this trait of the new woman as spirited bravado; she seduced her prey at an amusement park and captured her man in the course of a boyish prance through the fun house. The essence of Bow's screen presence was recognized by contemporary critics. Agreeing that Clara Bow had "it," or "good old-fashioned sex appeal," one reviewer described her as "an amusing little person, a slam-bang kid, full of vitality and an easy, none too subtle appeal."[17] The movie modern did indeed project more of the aura of the slam-bang kid than that of the femme fatale or the vamp. It was her mischievous vivacity that most emphatically eclipsed the old woman.

Yet the stars vitality only embellished a rigidifying set of movie stereotypes; the twenties' films gave precise details on how to become *correctly* modern. Gloria Swanson performed the requisite transformation in *Why Change Your Wife* (1920). In one extravagant gesture she tore off her old garb, draped herself in plumes and lamé, and realigned her shapely form in a stylized seductive posture. The popular stars of the twenties excelled in such movements and poses, the hands placed low on the hip, the jaunt in the walk, the cock of the head that made the new woman a lively reality. The education in the mannerism of the flapper was undertaken with special self-awareness by a shopgirl named Nora (Madge Bellamy) in *Ankles Preferred* (1926). The portion of her anatomy mentioned in the title propelled the plot and mesmerized the camera. Nora regarded the first compliment to her ankles as a lecherous insult. When she retired to her apartment, however, she gazed at her legs with a new interest and pride. Her narcissism reached its fullest development in a situation common to many movies of the era, the heroine's fist modeling experience. Goaded on by two lascivious old shopkeepers, Nora tried out a sexy strut, a self-caressing gesture and a heightened hemline. Once the modern style of self-projection had been acquired, Nora's bosses put her to work seducing first the male customers and then a business tycoon from whom they sought financial assistance.[18] This objectification of the female before male admirers was lodged deep in the scenario of the flapper film, and was depicted with entrancing finesse by movie moderns.

These cinematic personalities are more than an historical depository of female images. In the twenties they served as a means of propagating new values and translating popular images into social behavior. As a consequence the movie moderns claim a part in the making of modern womanhood with all the sex roles and sexual stereotyping it entailed. Their initial function was simply didactic and instructional, to train the female audience in fashionable femininity. The movies of the silent era were inherently stereotypical, relying on extravagant images, bold-faced titles and enthralling musical accompaniment. Thus, they were particularly suited to shaping women's aspirations in a uniform direction. Many of the first cinematic lessons were very rudimentary. DeMille's *Why Change Your Wife*, made in 1920, was a simple parable admonishing women to discard the remnants of Victorian womanhood and embrace the flapper model. The audience assimilated this advice through the example of Elizabeth Gordon, played by Gloria Swanson, who at the beginning of the film was a staid, bespectacled wife who reads books on "How to Improve Your Mind" and listens to classical music. The error of her ways was proclaimed by her husband's grimaces at her glasses and chaste attire, and his vulnerability to the wiles of a new woman armed with perfume, short skirts and a panoply of gadgets designed to entrap men. When Robert Gordon divorced his wife to marry this coquette, the first Mrs. Gordon vowed to cling to the old ways, to devote herself to charity, claiming she "hates men and clothes." Upon overhearing a conversation that attributed her divorce to her matronly attire, however, Elizabeth made an abrupt about-face: she exclaimed that she would go the limit to regain her spouse and ordered a "sleeveless, backless, transparent, indecent" wardrobe. The heroine, of course, succeeded in regaining her husband, and their second wedding night found her thoroughly remodeled, dressed in an inanely fashionable gown and dancing a foxtrot.[19] By the mid-twenties, this scene of female transformation had been replayed so many times that one reviewer could write of *His Secretary* (1926): "so cliched and worn was it all we finally fell from our seat suffering from some ancient atavistic complaint that the ennui of this theme always rouses in us."[20] The point had been made over and over again: to win husband and happiness, women must join the competition on equal terms with the American flapper.

Such basic lessons were not lost on the movie audience. Studies of female movie-goers, financed by the Payne Fund and conducted between 1929 and 1933, revealed that young women paid close attention to the star's appearance and behavior. Of a Joan Crawford film, one girl said, "I watch every little detail, of how she's dressed, and her make-up, and also her hair." Another surmised, "I'll bet every girl wishes she was the Greta Garbo type. I tried to imitate her walk, she walks so easy as if she had springs on her feet." This young woman's attempt to mimic Garbo succeeded only in provoking laughter, a fate that also befell a black girl enamored of Clara Bow. "After seeing her picture (*It*) I immediately went home to take stock of my personal charms before my vanity mirror and after carefully surveying myself from all angles I turned away with a sigh, thinking that I may as well want to be Mr. Lon Chaney. I would be just as successful." Such an observation suggests the active, often good-humored ways in which young women might interpret the movie message.[21]

Young moviegoers of the twenties were educated in other, more personal, matters as well. One college girl told the Payne Fund interviewers that "movies are a liberal education in the art of making love." She went on to recount such specific benefits of this cinematic education as learning "how two screen lovers manage their arms when they are embracing; there is a definite technique; one arm over, the other under." This young woman was grateful to the movies for providing a remedial education in a subject avoided by her straitlaced parents, while another found cinematic instructions in love-making "more suggestive and effective than I could possibly find in any book by say Elinor Glyn on 'How to Hold Your Man.'" The adolescent girls who flocked to the movies each week were getting their sex education through the prism of the Hollywood clinch, a training which culminated in erotic awareness if not in actual necking parties. The magic of the movies brought one teenager a rich fantasy life: "Buddy Rogers and Rudy Valentino have kissed me oodles of times but they don't know it, God bless 'em!" Whatever the behavioral consequences of this education, its cultural impact cannot be denied. Movies were handmaidens to the modern preoccupation with intimate heterosexual relations. Moving pictures were clearly more effective than static literary images in detailing the active components of flapper sexuality. One sixteen-year-old girl came to these apt historical conclusions: "No wonder girls of older days, before the movies, were so modest and bashful. They never saw Clara Bow and William Haines. . . . if we did not see such examples in the movies, where would we get the idea of being 'hot'? We wouldn't."[22]

It would be very difficult, on the other hand, for a movie-going girl to receive the idea that sexual promiscuity was an approved form of behavior in the nineteen-twenties. The movie heroine was always chaste at heart. Whatever extremes of brash free-living Bow or Crawford might portray, they preserved their virginity until marriage. Likewise, infidelity among the upper classes, so often sanctioned in the films of Cecil B. De Mille, was prescribed only as a means of retrieving a lost spouse or enlivening a spiceless marriage. Sex in the films of the twenties existed as a readiness to display physical attractions, not as a willingness to give in to the yearnings of the flesh; it heightened sexual awareness without promising ultimate gratification.

Sexiness was in fact associated more with apparel, make-up, and perfume than with the body itself. While movie morality kept sexuality within traditional bounds, materialistic desires were given bountiful gratification in the cinema of the twenties. Hollywood fed consumer lusts through its stock of production values—epitomized by the spendthrift De Mille who surrounded his heroines with furs, jewels, modish clothes, and modern household artifacts. Fashion shows and tours of modern homes and apartments became staples of the new woman's movie world. In the 1920's, whole films were devoted to the new joys and pitfalls of consumption with titles like *Charge It, Ladies Must Dress, Gimme.*[23] Thirty-eight films detailed the career of the fashion model, another convenient method of inculcating consumerism. The expansion of the consumer sector of the American economy in the twenties called for an accelerated tempo of shopping and the movies provided incentives and instruction for yet another updated female role.

Movies offered to the women of the twenties, and reveal to historians, something more dynamic than packaged instructions about the new femininity and new female roles. The object of the Hollywood craftsman was to arrange images into engrossing stories. To the movie audience, gathered together in darkness and anonymity, the moving picture offered a vicarious dream life. This cinematic experience has been aptly defined by Raymond Durgnat: "For the masses the cinema is dreams and nightmares, or it is nothing. It is an alternative experience freed from the tyranny of the 'old devil consequences'; from the limitation of having only one life to live. One's favored films are one's unlived lives, one's hopes, fear, libido."[24] Movie fantasies are nonetheless inextricably intertwined with the realities of the age in which they are produced. Films, after all, as Stanley Cavell has pointed out, are composed of photographs, images that reproduce the world outside the theatre. Moreover the basic events presented in contemporary dramas are at least conceivable, perhaps even probable, in the lives of viewers. This evocative mixture of reality and dream, furthermore, is concocted by an industry whose imperative is box office profits. The popular film formula is constructed around the aspirations and anxieties of the contemporary audience. The relation of the world on the screen and American realities has been elegantly described by Barbara Deming. After viewing up to one-fourth of Hollywood's productions between 1942 and 1948, Deming reached this conclusion: "The heros and heroines who are most popular at any particular period are precisely those who, with a certain added style, with a certain distinction, act out the predicament in which we all find ourselves — a predicament from which the movie-dream then cunningly extricates us. But the . . . moviegoer . . . need never admit what that condition really is from which he is being vicariously relieved."[25]

The historian's task, given this interpretation of film culture, is to identify the predicaments which underlie the popular film, to analyze the condition from which the viewer is "being vicariously relieved." In the case of the woman's film, the superficial problem is quite obvious: to win and keep a husband's love, and to secure the social and economic status which accompanies marriage. The Payne Fund survey of movie themes between 1920 and 1933 found the most common plot theme to be winning the loved one. Through six decades of cinema history the problems of the unmarried woman and the neglected wife have been "resolved" in thousands of happy endings, enacted by characters from every walk in life and every social station. One variation on this theme was particularly germane to the twenties, however, and deserves special attention: the predicament of the working girl.

In point of fact the work force had been a familiar environment for young women well before 1920. The rate of female employment skyrocketed in the teens and increased at only a moderate rate, if at all, between 1920 and 1930 when over ten million women were at work outside the home. Most of these women, like their impersonators on the screen, were under thirty years of age and single. The employed women of the twenties were apt to congregate in a relatively new segment of the work force, deserting factories and domestic service to take up white-collar employment. The number of female clerks had increased almost 300 percent between 1910 and 1920; the number of stenographers and typists more than doubled, making women the majority in those occupations.[26] These facts were also reflected in the films of the era. In the twenties the American Film Institute Catalog listed only four films made about factory workers, while only 46 concerned housemaids, most of them in minor roles. On the other hand the catalog lists 49 sales clerks, 28 stenographers, and no less than 114 secretaries who appeared on the screen between 1921 and 1930.[27] On occasion, the film detailed this historical progression in female work roles. For example, *Bertha The Sewing Machine Girl* (1926) carried the heroine from her factory job, to the role of telephone operator, then model, then fashion designer.[28] The movie camera tended to skirt the mundane aspects of white-collar work, preferring to dwell on the glamour of a setting full of consumer goods, entertainment, and eligible men, all of which the young woman could pursue without parental interference. The demand of the economy for women's labor in this job sector, as well as women's responsiveness to this need, was nonetheless very real. By 1925, 34 percent of high school girls in Middletown, for example, aspired to be clerical workers.[29] Fan magazines took pains to associate movie stars with these prosaic roles, pointing out that Joan Crawford was once a shop girl in Kansas City; that Janet Gaynor clerked in a shoe store; and that Frances Marion earned $25 a week as a stenographer before she became a star, then screen writer.[30] Early films no doubt facilitated the transformation of the female work force, reflecting, endorsing, and legitimizing women's assumption of new roles.

By the late twenties, Hollywood seemed to take the work experience of young females for granted. No longer bothering to issue tantalizing invitations to enter the work force, they planted heroines firmly behind desks and counters. At this point, the focus of the film shifted to grappling with the specific complaints of working women. In fact several films began with a sharp critique of the routine and rigid nature of the work situation. The opening shot in *Ankles Preferred* featured Madge Bellamy at a department store counter, annoyed at the customers, bored with her work, and anxiously gazing at the clock. The monotony of woman's work was emphatically underlined by the superimposition of a clock upon Bellamy's forlorn countenance, followed by her jubilation at closing time. The clock motif appeared again in *Our Blushing Brides*. This 1930 film opened with a close-up of the time clock as a long line of workers, mostly female, filed into a department store. Throughout the film the alarm clock stood as the exasperating symbol of work which the women dreamed of throwing out the window forever. The regimentation associated with the conscription of women into the modern work force was presented in other ways as well. The assembly line nature of work in these white-collar occupations was painstakingly delineated in *Our Blushing Brides*. In the opening sequence the camera panned across a massive, dreary locker room as hundreds of women scurried past. They amassed behind the mirror until a clamorous bell sent them rushing to their assigned places at the consumer counter. Once in their stations, the mechanical and impersonal nature of sales work was underscored by the supervisors; one girl was addressed only as number 36, another as number 42.[31] In this department store film and in secretarial films like *Soft Living* (1928), special care was taken to show the working girls laboriously filling out forms and adding up columns of numbers. The movies took cognizance of the discipline imposed by the modern work place, a regimen which the women of the twentieth century rarely escaped by retaining a life-long place in the home.

The work world so bleakly pictured in these films also encroached upon the private lives of the female characters. It established their tedious week-day schedule, composed of a frantic struggle on the subway, hasty meals, and shattered nerves. The homes which these women entered at the end of a work day were a tribute to their meager earnings on the job. The movie set included a carefully constructed working girls' apartment: cramped quarters, shabby furnishings, a tiny table where the roommates took their frugal meals. Silent filmmakers did not hesitate to insert titles expressing the girls' complaints about these conditions, the implicit lot of their sex and class. In fact they frequently used an intertitle to announce the specific wage rate for female labor, usually between $25 and $35 a week. Once the essential features of woman's work had been established, the thrust of the heroine's dream was obvious—escape.

Impermanence was built into the work situation of these screen heroines. The cheerful camaraderie and spunky optimism characteristic of the working-girl flapper stemmed from the assumption that her job tenure would be brief. The avenue of escape was predictable enough: matrimony. Yet there were a variety of ways to secure a husband while on the job. The bluntest technique was the aggressive use of sexual attractions as employed by the ubiquitous gold digger. No less than 34 films were made on this theme between 1921 and 1930.[32] The most famous movie in this genre, *Gentlemen Prefer Blondes* (1928) written by Anita Loos, approvingly recounted the heavy-handed tactics of Lorelei Lee, who entrapped America's richest bachelor.[33] *Soft Living*, made the same year, traced gold digging directly to the plight of the working girl. The heroine, played by Madge Bellamy, was secretary to an attorney specializing in divorce cases. She embarked upon her hunt for a millionaire after comparing her weekly salary of $35 to the thousands in alimony carted away each week by a deft gold digger. Her original intention was to remain a "kissless bride,"file for divorce on trumped-up charges, and retire on her alimony. The typical sexual shyness beneath the flapper exterior was revealed on the heroine's honeymoon when she cowered in the upper berth of the train to avoid viewing a pajama-clad husband. In the end, love triumphed over avarice, and the secretary and millionaire settled into a bone fide love nest. Nonetheless, the fantasy was clear, the secretary had won her millionaire; in the parlance of the day she had "slapped a trap on a sucker's bank roll."[34]

More typically the working girl of the twenties' cinema won her retirement through the promptings of love and trusting submission to her man. Charm, poise, virtue and the advantage of close proximity to eligible men were ingredients in the scenario that captured many a wealthy mate. Secretaries were particularly successful in this regard, placed as they were in close association with their boss. But salesgirls did equally well despite the odds against their meeting millionaires across department store counters. Joan Crawford achieved this success in *Our Blushing Brides*, proving her worth by rejecting the owner's son as an illegitimate lover, later to win him as her spouse. Other working women found rich men in the most unlikely places. The character in the title role of *Five and Ten Cent Annie* (1928) married a street cleaner who conveniently inherited a fortune. A theatre cashier came upon her affluent husband at the box office in *The Girl in the Glass Cage* (1929).[35]

The working girl's fantasy as manufactured by Hollywood was not always this extravagant. In numerous movies of the twenties, heroines found their happy ending in the arms of a man of their own class. A subway guard was the perfect match for both *The Girl From Woolworth's* (1929) and *Sub Way Sadie* (1926).[36] Such alliances were often formed after females had given up their daydreams of independent success, be it as showgirls or department store buyers. The homely solution to this variety of working girl drama was epitomized by *Ankles Preferred*. Madge Bellamy's success in the retail trade took her into the company of many wealthy men, all of whom wanted only the pleasures of her body. Disillusioned by status climbing of this sort Bellamy turned her attention to a more trustworthy young man, who shared her own social world, the lower-class boarding house. Clara Bow illustrated the same sensible solution in *Kid Boots* (1926). She chose as her spouse a humble tailor played by Eddie Cantor, convinced, as a title clearly announced, that unlike many foolish females she craved a man who was "just reliable." The climax of this picture also conveyed the boyish *joie de vivre* with which these marriages were forged. Bow recited her marriage vows to Cantor at the end of a comic chase, attired in disheveled pants and running behind a speeding automobile containing the judge.[37] The role pattern which the movie moderns embraced so ebulliently was mundane reality to millions of American women, the youthful female labor force that retired en masse upon marriage henceforth to rest, however insecurely or impecuniously, on the income of their mates.

The magic of these movies, and their meaning to the historian, lie as much in the anxieties which precede the domestic denouement as in the happy ending itself. Movie fantasies have a double-edged quality, are both

"dreams and nightmares" as Raymond Durgnat puts it. At times the nightmares constitute the direct and central themes of the movies; more often,
particularly in women's films, fearful visions provide the cutting edge of the
romance itself. Imbedded in the images and plots of the movie moderns are
a prevalent set of tensions, unfulfilled promises, and unhappy endings for
minor characters. These tragic subplots provided the essential dramatic
tension in the films of the twenties. Many women lost out in the marriage
competition, and not even the most optimistic melodrama tied up every
female character in a neat wedding knot. In most working girl stories at
least one of the roommates was required to function as a negative example
for the audience. In *Our Blushing Brides* the gold digger Frankie was
punished for her mercenary sexuality by the discovery that her hard-won
husband was a gambler whose expensive gifts were quickly confiscated by
the police. A second roommate, a naive and trusting sort named Connie,
was deceived into the unsavory position of a kept woman, only to have her
concubine marry one of his own class. In this film the odds were two to one
against a successful marital alliance. The third roommate, Jerry, played by
Joan Crawford, succeeded only because she was painfully cautious in
bestowing her love. In fact, the disastrous fate which befell Connie was in
many ways the emotional pivot of *Our Blushing Brides*. The forsaken
woman happened to turn on the radio to hear an on-the-scene report of her
lover's engagement party. Her lost love and lost status were detailed simultaneously in a merciless account of what the fashionable entourage was
wearing on this occasion. The finale laced suspense with maudlin sentimen-
tality as the prostrate Connie swallowed poison amid intercuts to her speeding rescuers, while the radio blared cruelly away in the background. This
death scene was prolonged to full melodramatic length as the evil male was
carted against his will to Connie's bedside, allowing her to die with her
romantic illusions intact. This bittersweet story was designed by Bess
Meredyth, a woman who created hundreds of such dream portraits. The
successful formula, steeped in a pessimistic female consciousness and a
cynical view of men, exposed the underside of modern romances. Might not
this movie cliché suggest that some women secretly yearned to escape the
whole tortuous labyrinth of the sexual marketplace?

Another empathic ploy of these films preyed on the apprehension that
marriage itself does not put an end to woman's anxiety. In fact in the twenties almost 300 films were made on the theme of infidelity.[38] In addition to
their titillating value these movies harped upon the insecurity of the married
woman, inevitably aging and losing her girlish charms within a world constantly replenished by a stream of attractive flappers. Over and over again
wives were charged with rejuvenating their appearance in order to retrieve
husbands from flirts and gold diggers. One woman's success on the
marriage market was all too often another's failure. A dowdy wife was poor
competition for the young workers who shared her husband's store or

office. The anxieties of upper-class wives were endlessly exploited by De Mille, and by the mid-twenties even Theda Bara was placed in the predicament of the shunned wife (*Unchastened Woman*, 1925).[39] Alternately, the older woman was made the object of ridicule. In *Ankles Preferred*, for example, the wives of the shopkeepers were introduced into scenes by their ankles—fleshy, drooping, with sagging stockings—clearly identified as dinosaurs in the modern movie era. On the other hand a few films of the twenties recognized, in a roundabout fashion, that the married woman might be discontented with her role, as well as fearful of losing her husband. One remarkable film, *Dancing Mothers* (1926), ended as the wife defiantly leaves home. Two films of 1922, *The Real Adventure* and *A Woman's Woman*, portrayed older women whose boredom with housework and lack of appreciation from their husbands drove them into business. Although their successful careers culminated either in marital disaster or restoration to the fireside, these themes suggested to at least a few movie-goers the further problems that lay beyond the happy ending.[40]

These dark shadows were further accentuated by the characterization of male-female relations throughout these films. In most movies the male characters were very limply drawn; their chief role was to express, often in a puppylike fashion, the love sickness inspired by the heroines, some of whom overtly manipulated them into marriage. Seen through the woman's eyes, moreover, the movie male was often the object of distrust, even disgust. As Gloria Swanson set out on a second courtship of her ex-husband, her underlying view of the opposite sex was baldly announced in the title: "The more I see of men the better I like dogs." In the course of her uneven courtship in *Our Blushing Brides*, Joan Crawford displayed deep-seated cynicism about men, which she repeatedly pounded home to her roommates. This attitude was expressed to her prospective spouse in the most virulent attacks on his manhood. When she labeled his sweet-talk "ridiculous rubber-stamped lines," he responded: "When it comes to the matter in question I don't trust any modern girl." On their next encounter, when the boss's son intruded upon her in her underwear, she hurled further insults at his masculine ego, saying he wasn't "man enough" to take advantage of the situation, and that it made her "deathly ill" to have him touch her. Crawford's working girl also takes this opportunity to allude to the contradictions of class as well as sex: "I suppose your position entitles you to these little privileges." All in all the animosities in the courtship process cast considerable doubt on the quality of male and female relations after the happy ending.

The relations between female characters were also distorted by the new sexual mores. The sisterly solace associated with Victorian womanhood lingered on in many of these films, as working girls and roommates freely embraced to express sympathy and share joys. Yet the divisions between women were subtly and not so subtly indicated. The fragility of sisterhood was a movie cliché often expressed in a shot of a lonely girl in an empty apartment on evenings when her roommates had dates. The most heart-felt sympathy between women, furthermore, arose to salve the wounds inflicted by males. Female friendship appeared as a supportive by-product of heterosexual relations, not as a primary female bond. The fragmenting effect of the preoccupation with personal attractiveness was symbolized in another recurrent movie image, that of females gathered together before a mirror, obsessed with their own images and oblivious to one another. The conversations that ensued often bordered on the vicious, replete with snide attacks on one another's appearance or reputation. Then, of course, cinema delighted in portraying the most extreme negation of female friendship, the vitriolic "cat fight." This movie cliché was perfected by 1920 when the female rivals in *Why Change Your Wife* scratched, kicked, and threatened to throw acid in each other's faces, par for the course in movie man-hunting.

The melodrama's happy ending could not entirely efface all these peripheral failures and inherent contradictions. As Stanley Cavell observed in another connection, "The walk into the sunset is a dying star; they live happily ever after — as long as they keep walking."[41] The audience that emerged from the darkened theatre in the twenties, to gaze upon mundane reality and perhaps their own quite ordinary mates, might feel a disquieting let-down. The thrills of the film had been built on the activism and gay abandon of the flapper figure, a style that hardly jibes with the unacknowledged denouement into a world of dishes and diapers. At best the female viewer would return to the security of her work-a-day womanhood, content with only a brief relief and catharsis to be renewed in a week or so at the movies. Yet it is unlikely that modern maidens and dancing daughters, the Clara Bow's and Joan Crawford's, could survive unchanged in such a humdrum atmosphere.

As the reality of modern womanhood eclipsed the initial optimism of the flapper era, these dreams themselves came to seem extravagant, even dangerous, too hedonistic for women returned home and fighting off a depression to boot. Accordingly, the star of the flapper declined precipitously in the thirties. Its demise was already apparent in *Our Blushing Brides* (1930), the last in a series of Joan Crawford vehicles which included *Our Dancing Daughters* and *Our Modern Maidens*. At the outset of this film, Crawford's effervescence had been reduced to a sparkle in her eye and a spring in her step as she entered the department store. Back home in her sparsely furnished apartment she battered the high hopes of her roommates by calling attention to the chill reality of the working girl's predicament, a stance that she commended because "at least it's real." The stoical Jerry (Crawford) then spent the bulk of the movie ministering to disasters bred by the recklessness of the film's flappers. She became progressively more ridden with cares, looking more like a beaten-down worker than a dashing modern. Jerry's ultimate rescue from work and spinsterhood came suddenly and improbably. Her triumph was rent by contradictions. Her engagement to the boss's son was announced by an act of male posessiveness, her fiancé's genial threat to beat up a male caller. This announcement, furthermore, was made in her lover's hideaway, the scene of his previous seductions and a ferocious argument with the heroine, who is now attired in a costume she once modeled while an employee of her husband-to-be. This is a rather tawdry fantasy — that the working woman can win by marriage the very commodities and privileges that were expropriated from her labor. The screenwriters were making a telling if subtle point about modern womanhood.

Clara Bow exited from the twenties in an equally somber fashion. The thirties found her a box office wash-out attempting a come-back in abysmal roles like that of Nasa in *Call Her Savage*. Although Bow retained her characteristic volatility, it was given a completely different interpretation in this film of 1932. Her devilish pranks lost their gaiety, were judged symptomatic of uncontrollable wildness in her temperament which persisted despite her longing "to be like other girls." The exuberant charms that once won the screen heroine an ideal mate now invited bad matches, broken hearts, alcoholism and loneliness. The flapper had become perverse by 1932, and had to be explained away. Hollywood devised an uncanny solution, tracing Nasa's abnormality to heredity, the fact that she was indeed a savage, descended from an Indian.[42] Such was the ignoble end of the "it girl" as the zesty young actresses of the twenties went the way of the Charleston and the hip flask into a soberer and still unliberated era.

Very few of the stars of the twenties weathered the fashions in womanhood that followed. One sturdy actress fought her way through the Hollywood jungle for forty years only to secure less than savory female roles. She was, of course, Joan Crawford. In 1959 after a series of movies in which she played neurotic, lonely women, Crawford found herself back in the world of the working girl in a film entitled *The Best of Everything*.[43]In many ways the plot of this film replicated the working girl's formula of the twenties. The setting moved to the typing pool and editorial offices of a publishing firm, but the drama was familiar: three young women searching for an honorable escape from the workforce through matrimony. Crawford, however, was too old, too hardened by some 51 years experience of womanhood to have a central role in this plot. As Amanda Farrow she stood on the sidelines, admonishing women against the careerism which made of her a bitter, nasty, carping boss, left only a sterile relationship with a married man. Ironically, however, the very devastation of this woman's life entitled her to some stature and legitimacy in the business world. Crawford made one last-ditch attempt to reform, giving up her lucrative job for marriage in hopes that home life would "soften" her frustrated personality. Yet her marriage was casually allowed to fail. When Amanda returned to her editor's job it was with a new equanimity. In a genuinely warm gesture she extended her businesswoman's hand to the female work force, represented here by the central female character (played by Hope Lange) who we are led to believe will give up her career for marriage and launch another generation on a familiar "happy ending." Yet Joan Crawford's role bespoke another reality of womanhood in the 1950's. Her fans from the twenties had most likely returned to the labor force after a career of homemaking. The typical working woman was no longer an ingenue but a middle-aged, married woman — who, unlike Amanda Farrow, could secure only low-paying clerical and retail jobs. The aging of the new woman left at least this fanciful imprint on the screen.[44]

This modern adjustment of woman's roles was insinuated into the minds of millions of movie-goers beginning in the 1920's. But statistics concerning female employment and marriage rates hardly require this kind of confirmation. The fantasies which movies wove around common female experiences contain richer historical meaning. The moviegoer did not merely travel through a remote fantasy land but briefly inhabited a well-contrived make-believe role. In the case of the movie moderns, that role was a glamorous rendition of the social options open to women. Those vicarious lives could channel female expectations in a socially acceptable direction and then reconcile women to their lot, providing both relief and reinforcement in the guise of routine entertainment. The twenties marked the solidification of a new pattern of female roles characterized by a dynamic equilibrium between work, home, and consumer activities. The movies not only fixed these new priorities in the American woman's mind, but simultaneously prepared her for the discontinuities of a woman's life as she traversed the facile transformations of the typical scenario. The movies, particularly in periods like the twenties when female roles were undergoing a major remodeling, constituted a powerful cultural force, shaping individual choices within the boundaries of social and economic possibilities, thus assisting in the creation of a new womanhood. The movie moderns project the historical reality of the American woman's dream.

Notes

1. Robert S. and Helen Merrell Lynd, *Middletown: A Study in Modern American Culture* (New York, 1929) 140.

2. Kenneth A. Yellis "Prosperity's Child: Some Thoughts on the Flapper" *American Quarterly*, 21 (Spring, 1969), 44-64; James R. McGovern, "The American Woman's Pre-World War I Freedom in Manners and Morals," *Journal of American History*, 55 (September 1968), 315-333.

3. Kenneth McGowan, *Behind The Screen* (New York, 1965), 256.

4. Lewis Jacobs, *The Rise of the American Film, A Critical History* (New York, 1949), 328-329; MacGowan, 264.

5. Henry James Forman, *Our Movie-Made Children* (New York, 1933), chapter I.

6. Jacobs, 86-87.

7. Stanley Cavell, *The World Viewed: Reflections on the Ontology of Film* (New York, 1971), 33.

8. Fred I. Greenstein, "New Light on Changing American Values: A Forgotten Body of Survey Data," *Social Forces*, 42 (1964), 441-450.

9. Linda Arvidson Griffith, *When the Movies Were Young* (New York, 1969), 198.

10. Marjorie Rosen, *Popcorn Venus, Women, Movies and the American Dream* (New York, 1973), 59-67; Jacobs, 267.

11. *True Heart Susie*, directed by D. W. Griffith, 1919, Film Department, Museum of Modern Art (hereafter MOMA).

12. *Male and Female*, directed by Cecil B. De Mille, 1919. MOMA.

13. Benjamin B. Hampton, *History of the American Film Industry* (New York, 1970), 249; MacGowan, 261-2.

14. Clipping File, MOMA, under *Bertha the Sewing Machine Girl*, title index.

15. Molly Haskell, *From Reverence to Rape: The Treatment of Women in the Movies*, (New York, 1973), 75-82.

16. *Our Dancing Daughters*, MGM, directed by Harry Beaumont, 1928, "The Charleston Episode" MOMA.

17. Clipping file, MOMA, under *It*, title index.

18. *Ankles Preferred*, Fox, directed by J. G. Blystone, 1919, MOMA.

19. *Why Change Your Wife*, directed by Cecil B. De Mille, 1920, MOMA.

20. Clipping File, MOMA, under *His Secretary*, title index.

21. Forman, 141, 145, 225.

22. *Ibid.*, 151, 154, 167.

23. Jacobs, 407.

24. Raymond Durgnat, *Films and Feelings* (Cambridge, Mass., 1967), 135.

25. Barbara Deming, *Running Away from Myself: A Dream Portrait of America Drawn from the Films of the Forties* (New York, 1969), 2.

26. William Chafe, *The American Woman, Her Changing Social, Economic and Political Role 1920-1970* (New York, 1972), 48-50; Joseph A. Hill, *Women in Gainful Occupations, 1870-1920* (Washington, 1929), 42-47.

27. *The American Film Institute* (AFI) *Catalog, Feature Films, 1921-1930*, Vol. F2 (New York, 1971), 1523, 1545, 1615, 1619, 1631.

28. *AFI Catalog*, 51.

29. Lynd and Lynd, 50.

30. Margaret Thorp, *America at the Movies* (Arno Reprint, 1970 original, New Haven, 1939), 100.

31. *Our Blushing Brides*, MGM directed by Harry Beaumont, 1930, distributed by Films Incorporated.

32. *AFI Indexes*, 1538.

33. *AFI Catalog*, 285.

34. *Soft Living*, Fox, directed by James Tinley, 1928, MOMA.

35. *AFI Catalog*, 249, 292.

36. *Ibid.*, 291, 775.

37. *Kid Boots*, Paramount, directed by Frank Tuttle, 1926, MOMA.

38. *AFI Indexes*, 1549-1551.

39. *AFI Catalog*, 842.

40. *Ibid.*, 636, 992-993.

41. Cavell, 49.

42. *Call Her Savage,* Fox, directed by John Francis Dillon, 1932, MOMA.

43. *The Best of Everything,* Twentieth Century Fox, Directed by Jean Negulesco, 1959, distributed by Films Incorporated.

44. See Valerie Kincade Oppenheimer, *The Female Labor Force in the United States* (Berkeley, 1970).

6

Culture and Radical Politics: Yiddish Women Writers in America, 1890-1940

NORMA FAIN PRATT

Contemporary historians of East European Jewish immigration have noted that the cultural life brought to America was transformed within the first two decades of the twentieth century. However, neither in the past nor in the present have scholars paid sufficient attention to the variety of cultural changes. For example, historians have not explored deeply enough the diverse patterns of the new American Jewish culture; certainly they have not considered the extent to which changing Jewish cultural forms were an expression of class and gender. This study of the lives and works of immigrant East European Yiddish women writers confronts these issues of diversity, class difference, and especially gender as providing different developments in the new American Jewish society.

This study is based on information, collected during the last few years, that deals with the lives of about fifty Yiddish women writers (Appendix 1) whose extensive literary works appeared in the United States during the first half of the twentieth century and who have been ignored by historians.[1] These fifty writers shared certain common characteristics and may therefore be classified as a group by the social historian, although each writer was unique, and in this generation women writers did not consider themselves to be a distinct female group apart from male Yiddish writers in America.

What does a simple prosopographic portrait reveal about these writers? First, they were all women who came from the poorer classes of East European Jewry. A few were daughters of impoverished merchant families; others were raised in an artisan environment; but most came from the proletarianized Jewish classes of recently industrialized Russian Poland and the Austro-Hungarian Empire. Their parents, particularly their mothers, were almost illiterate. Few received advanced formal education either in Eastern Europe or in America. Yet in America they became journalists, poets, short story writers, and novelists — and represent a first generation of Jewish women, immigrant and poor, who interpreted their own lives in their own language.

*The author acknowledges the kind assistance of Hillel Kempinski of the Jewish Labor Bund Archives and Dina Abramowicz of the Yiddisher Visnshaftleiher (YIVO) Institute for Jewish Research. A version of this paper was published in the *American Jewish History*, Fall 1980.

Emigrating mainly in the years between 1905 and 1920 and settling in large urban centers (New York, Chicago, and Los Angeles), they wrote exclusively in Yiddish for audiences who still communicated primarily in *mameloshn*. Only a few individuals, like Fradel Stock, Anna Rappaport, and Hinde Zaretsky, experimented with English but failed to make the linguistic transition. The works of all fifty women writers appeared in those Yiddish newspapers and literary journals that both advocated radical political ideologies and espoused some form of secular Jewish life in America. The Jewish anarchist, socialist, Yiddish avant-garde, and, later in the 1920s and 1930s, the Jewish Communist presses regularly accepted the literary work of women, although much of this literature did not deal directly with contemporary political subjects. These literary productions dealt more with female, Jewish, and working-class identity and with adjustment to immigrant life.

Consequently, along with their male counterparts, these writers were spokeswomen for a politically radical Jewish subculture which existed within the general American Jewish society but at the same time possessed its own outlook and its own political, social, and cultural institutions. This Jewish subculture, consisting mainly of needle trades workers, small businesspeople, clerks, students, teachers, and artists, expressed one form of secular Jewish existence in America. These people were known as the *veltlikhe yidn* ("secular Jews"): the *radikaln* of the Jewith Left. They rejected Orthodox Judaism with its rituals and rabbinical leadership and in its place accepted a Jewish identity, *yiddishkeit*, which was committed to the preservation of the Yiddish language, the celebration of historic Jewish holidays, and the cultivation of Jewish loyalties. Their *yiddishkeit* also included a special devotion to the Jewish working class, the international working class, and America, their adopted home. Their ideology posited a belief in the possible creation of a distinct Jewish society as part of a culturally pluralistic society in America. They wanted to be American without assimilating; they wished to express politically radical ideals, especially in matters social and economic; and they hoped to remain linguistically Yiddish speakers and cultural Jews.

In the ideological paradigm of the *veltlikhe radikaln* ("secular radicals"), these diverse goals and loyalties did not seem contradictory. Rather, with these purposes in mind this Jewish subculture created Jewish radical political parties (the Anarchists, the socialist Verband, the Communist International Workers' Order, the Zionist-socialist Poale Zion) which in turn maintained Yiddish newspapers (*Tsukunft, Fraye arbeter shtime*), Yiddish literary journals (*Brikn, Signal, Hamer*), literary-political discussion groups, choruses, mutual insurance groups, drama clubs, recreational camps, children's Yiddish schools, and summer camps. It was an immigrant's society and an immigrant's dream that attracted thousands of people, at its center and at its margins, for several decades from the end of the nineteenth century until at least the fourth decade of the twentieth century. Women were an active force in creating and maintaining its institutions and Yiddish women writers were the visible and vocal representatives of their gender.[2]

Yet those same women writers, although an important group, were also isolated from men and from each other. Their participation in the radical Yiddishist culture was not the same as male participation. Although members of the same anarchist, socialist, or Communist parties and contributors to the same newspapers and journals, women writers functioned differently than men within the institutional structure of Jewish radical society. The hundreds of volumes of their fiction and nonfiction remain a distinct body of literature which documents, articulates, and serves as a guide for understanding the perceptions of an entire generation of immigrant women who came of age in the United States before the Second World War.

Had the fifty immigrant writers under discussion remained in Europe, they might have had some opportunity for educational and literary development since East European Jewish society was becoming increasingly secularized at the turn of the century. Girls attended gymnasium; some even took higher degrees at the university level.[3] A vital Yiddish literature was also developing in twentieth-century Europe, not only in America. Yet, as late as the 1930s only a few exceptional women, like Kadia Molodowsky in Warsaw and Devorah Fogel in Lemberg, had attained any literary reputation of consequence.[4]

In America, on the other hand, a much larger number of Jewish women achieved an artistic and intellectual existence, albeit a circumscribed one. The emergence of women as writers was part of the blending of old and new social and intellectual forces at work in American Jewish life which provided a favorable climate for the acceptance of a female intelligentsia. Some of the Jewish women immigrants had already participated in cultural activities in Eastern Europe in the 1890s. This was especially true of the socialist, Zionist-socialist, and anarchist immigrants. In addition, immigrant society in America was in need of interpreters of its new experiences, and intellectuals and critics, with little formal education but with insight into the contemporary scene, were perceived as authentic spokesmen. There was an enormous growth of Yiddish publications, and talented and persevering women without academic credentials, like men in similar circumstances, were encouraged to express their views in print.

Furthermore, during the Progressive Era American ideas of female emancipation reinforced favorable existing radical Jewish attitudes toward female intellectuality and competence. But most important of all, theoretical ideas of equality were concretized by the behavior of Jewish women, particularly working women, who belied all contemporary stereotypes of immigrant women as passive victims of industrial American society. In the period between 1909, the year of the famous shirtwaist makers' strike, and the 1920s, when Jewish women workers and trade unionists helped organize the garment industry unions, Jewish immigrant women were militant and tenacious. Therefore, those women who spoke on their behalf directly or indirectly received a hearing.

Under what circumstances did East European Jewish women become Yiddish writers? Scanty information exists in Yiddish biographical lexicons, rare autobiographies, and several oral history interviews.[5] From these sources, it appears that most of the immigrant Yiddish women writers began to write before they left Europe for America.

Most of the fifty writers were born in small towns in Eastern Europe in the late 1880s and 1890s into Orthodox Jewish households. Their fathers often worked at a trade or were poor merchants and devoted part of their time to talmudic scholarship. Their mothers were barely literate. Tending house, the women uttered prayers, the *tehines*, written especially for women and used by women in the privacy of their homes to ask God for personal, family, and community happiness.[6] Orthodox Judaism as practiced in Eastern Europe severely circumscribed the role of women in public worship and in communal affairs, although women were permitted and even encouraged to practice a trade outside the home. Many women, in fact, supported the household while their husbands devoted their lives to religious study.[7]

The women born in the last decades of the nineteenth century were the first generation of East European Jewish women to receive a formal secular education.[8] Several of the writers began their literary careers as children, encouraged by teachers in the Yiddish *folk shules*, the state Russian schools of the Pale of Settlement, or by Hebrew tutors. For example, Zelda Knizshnik, one of the earliest Yiddish women poets, who was born in 1869 near Vilna, wrote her first poem in Hebrew at the age of nine. Her first Yiddish poem was published in 1900 in a Cracow literary journal, *Der yid*. Married at a young age, Knizshnik was unable to pursue a literary career because of poverty and domestic responsibilities, but she began to write again in her later years. Her poems were personal laments upon her sad and lonely fate:

My husband is in America
A son is in Baku;
Another son is in Africa,
A daughter — God, I wish I knew!

Sent away, my little bird,
Exiled from her tree,
And I too wander, drift and dream
Where, where is my home?

A mother's heart is everywhere,
The soul fragments and tears —
I have, oh, so many homes
But rest I do not have.[9]

Even though girls were sent to school, parents quite often disapproved if
the young writers took their literary interests too seriously. At times parents
regarded writing itself to be an irreligious act. For instance, Malke Lee, one
of the few Yiddish poets to write an autobiography, recalled with intense
bitterness that her father, a pious man, secretly burned her entire portfolio
of poetry in the family oven because he believed it was against God's will
that a girl write.[10] The same attitude is found in the reminiscences of Hinde
Zaretsky. In an interview, she described how at the age of six or seven she
was awarded a special candy at a Russian school for making a clever verbal
play on the Russian word *tchelovyek* ("human being"). Dividing the word
into two, Hinde recalled she created "*tzelyi vyek*, the whole world. It was
my first intuitive experience with imaginative writing." Her parents were
proud of her achievement but her grandmother disapproved: "When my
bobe heard that I had written *tzelyi vyek*, the whole world, she came over
and slapped me. She was my first critic. 'Why did you slap her when she
was awarded a candy by the teacher?' my mother asked her. *Bobe* said, 'I
will not be a partner with God. The world was created by Him and not by
Hinde.'" But her grandmother's slap did not stop Zaretsky. "When I came to
America I carried a notebook . . . wide . . . and long. With rhymed verses
and small poems, inspired by, I do not know myself. The customs official
took it from me. I cried, but nothing could be done. He thought I wrote
revolutionary things. And I wasn't yet sixteen."[11]

Unlike Zaretsky, a considerable number of the women writers became
radicals in Eastern Europe and their writing was part of a more extensive
political consciousness. Often the initial step toward political radicalism
came with the rejection of traditional Orthodox Jewish values. Many of
these writers, while still quite young, were repelled by standards set for
female behavior. Lilly Bes recalled in an angry poem:

Within me has burst my grandmother's sense of modesty
Revolt burns in me like effervescent wine.
Let good folk curse and hate me,
I can no longer be otherwise.[12]

In their adolescent years in Europe, several writers either joined illegal
radical Jewish political organizations or had a relative who belonged. These
political groups were particularly important for those young women,
mainly manual workers, who did not receive a secondary education, the
group providing the place of the school. Furthermore, at the turn of the

century, European Jewish radicals lauded women as fellow workers and fellow intellectuals, in contrast to the manner in which they were regarded by the Orthodox male leadership. The Bund hymn, the *Shvue* ("Oath"), which was intoned at every mass meeting and at strikes and demonstrations, called upon *"Brider un shvester fun arbet un noyt* ("Brothers and sisters, united in work and in need"). Within the Bund, there were special worker education groups where women without much education were given positions of importance. Women were appointed to the Bund's executive committees; acted as union organizers, prepared propaganda leaflets, and disseminated revolutionary literature.[13]

At the turn of the century, the women in the Bund did not attempt to organize separate socialist women's groups. Feminism, as an ideology, was considered to be bourgeois, serving the ambitions of middle-class women. As workers, these women identified primarily with the Jewish proletariat, although they were aware of the special problems of women workers, such as unequal pay, work-related health problems, and double work at home and in the factory. It was not until the 1920s, when the Bund became a legal party in Poland, that women's organizations were founded.[14]

Nevertheless, Jewish women in radical groups felt they had broken tradition and were acting outside the female roles assigned them in Jewish society. Their poets expressed these feelings. For instance, Kadia Molodowsky, poet, essayist, and editor of literary-political journals in the United States from the late 1930s until the early 1970s, described her estrangement from traditional Jewish life in her famous poem "*Froyen lider*," written in Poland around 1919. Ambivalently, she expressed her sense of alienation which combined with feelings of strong ties to the women in her family. Adrienne Rich, the American poet and Molodowsky's translator, noted that the poem voiced the difficulty of escaping old models of womanhood and the need to find new concepts of self.

> The faces of women long dead, of our family,
> come back in the night, come in dreams to me saying,
> We have kept our blood pure through long generations,
> we brought it to you like a sacred wine
> from the kosher cellars of our hearts.
>
> And one of them whispers:
> I remained deserted, when my two rosy apples
> still hung on the tree
> And I gritted away the long nights of waking between my white teeth.
>
> I will go meet the grandmothers, saying:
> Your sighs were the whips that lashed me

and drove my young life to the threshold
to escape from your kosher beds.
But wherever the street grows dark you pursue me —
wherever a shadow falls.

Your whimperings race like the autumn wind past me,
and your words are the silken cord
still binding my thoughts.
My life is a page ripped out of a holy book
and part of the first line is missing.[15]

East European radicalism made a powerful impact upon those young Yiddish women writers who participated in these movements which gave their lives direction. In extreme instances, women who were trained in the underground Bund engaged in illegal revolutionary activities and were forced to emigrate to the United States in order to escape police arrest. Among them were Esther Luria, Shifre Weiss, Eda Glasser, and Rachel Holtman.

Esther Luria is particularly fascinating, since her life reflects a type of Jewish woman revolutionary transplanted from Eastern Europe to the United States. Little is known about her life or her disappearance and possible death. Born in Warsaw in 1877, she was one of very few Jewish women not only to complete a gymnasium education but also to graduate from the University of Bern, Switzerland, with a doctor of humanistic studies degree in 1903. In Bern she joined the socialist movement but returned to Russia to help fellow Jews as a member of the Bund. Involved in revolutionary activities in Warsaw, she was arrested several times and, in 1906, was sent to Siberia, from where she escaped in 1912 and fled to New York City.[16]

Luria discovered that the socialist movement in America was very different than it was in Europe. Socialists in America were permitted to establish legal parties and a free press and had access to public gatherings. Socialism was not an underground movement whose members were sent into exile for inciting revolution. In fact, American socialists were part of the general reform movement of the Progressive Era and often encouraged alliances with and support of middle-class reformers. This was especially true for women's issues. In Eastern Europe, where no one voted, socialists isolated their party from liberals and feminists. In the United States, on the other hand, where only men voted, socialists supported liberal and some feminist causes. At the height of the American suffrage movement, between 1914 and 1920, Jewish socialists, especially in New York, made a special point of supporting women's suffrage, and the socialist Yiddish press frequently published articles on working women and the vote.[17]

Esther Luria tried to earn a living by writing for the Yiddish socialist press in New York: the *Jewish Daily Forward, Tsukunft,* and *Glaykhhayt,* the

Yiddish edition of the International Ladies' Garment Workers' Union paper *Justice* (ILGWU). Her articles about Jewish salon women in Germany, the poet Emma Lazarus, and the sociologist Martha Wolfenstein were meant to impress her working-class readership with the fact that women, even Jewish women, had made important contributions to society outside the home.[18]

After 1920 and the passage of the Nineteenth Amendment, Luria's articles appeared with less frequency. She then tried to support herself by lecturing on general socialist topics, but there was no interest in her views that did not pertain to women's issues. Unmarried and without family, she lived in terrible poverty and died alone in the Bronx, New York. Even the *Leksikon* records her death as "192?"

The Earliest Writers: Before the 1920s

At the turn of the century and well into the second and even third decades of the twentieth century, Yiddish women writers were considered by literary critics to be rare phenomena or, as Kadia Molodowsky noted sarcastically, "gentle, often exotic flowers of the literary garden."[19] Editors of Yiddish newspapers and journals, especially the anarchist and socialist press, were eager to publish the work of women poets and short story writers. Women's literature was both a symbol of modernity and a way of increasing circulation. Women wrote about women, a subject which seemed to sell papers. Editors and literary critics who were concerned with the quality of the emerging American Yiddish literature and felt that women might make a special contribution to this genre encouraged female writers. Among this latter group were the literary editor and socialist Abraham Reisen, the anarchist editor of the *Fraye arbeter shtime* Sh. Yanovsky, and the poet and literary critic A. Glanz.

The place of women in Yiddish literature was rarely discussed, however, during this period. An article by A. Glanz which appeared in *Fraye arbeter shtime* on 30 October 1915, entitled *"Kultur un di froy"* ("Culture and the Woman"), was one of the very few on that subject. Glanz lamented the fact that culture had become stagnant because it was a lopsided product of male creativity; Yiddish culture had therefore become impotent. "Women are not in our culture, neither her individuality nor her personality." Women had a "new power, a new element" which, if introduced into literature, would also liberate the male and revitalize male originality. Men suffered from egoism and from blind selfish individualism; they thought only of themselves. Women were the opposite of men: "By nature women are not egoistical. By nature women are bound organically to other lives. Out of her body new life comes. Another kind of knowing exists for her. She has a second dimension and understands nature. She is a mother in the deepest sense of the word. Men are ephemeral, women are concrete." Therefore, "If these female characteristics are introduced into our literature a true revolution would result."[20]

The revolution Glanz envisioned was, however, slow to arrive. In fact, most of the literary careers of young women writers, although received with some initial enthusiasm, really never matured. This was especially true for the writers of the period before the 1920s but was true to some extent later as well. The lives of two poets, Anna Rappaport and Fradel Stock, and one short story writer, Yente Serdatzky, are typical of women writers of this early period.

Anna Rappaport has been called "the first woman social poet" by literary historian Nahum Minkoff. Born in 1876, Rappaport emigrated to the United States from Kovna as a girl. Her father had been a famous rabbi in Kovna and her brother was studying for a medical degree at Columbia University. Anna went to work in a sweatshop and, after experiencing a personal sense of outrage because of conditions, she became a socialist. In 1893, a year of depression and unemployment when male poets like Morris Rosenfold and David Edelstadt were already well known for their social-protest poetry, which expressed their responses to immigrant American life, Rappaport made her literary debut in the Yiddish socialist newspaper *Di arbeter tsaytung*. Her first poem, *"A bild fun hungers noyt in 1893"* ("A Picture of the Hardship of Hunger in 1893"), was of this social protest genre, describing the unemployment problems of Jewish women in New York City. Other poems followed, portraying the conditions of women in the factories and preaching a new world order through socialism. All her poems describe the painful plight of immigrant Jewish women, especially their attempts to control their own lives in the world of terrifying social realities. One of her most interesting poems, *"Eyn lebnsbild"* ("Picture of Life") relates how mother love becomes corrupted with opportunism in an industrial society and leads to the destruction of a daughter. The mother convinces her daughter to marry a man the girl does not admire. "You will be free of the machine and you will grow to love him," advises the mother. But the marriage ends in failure. The daughter explains her difficulties in the last stanza. The Yiddish style is intentionally simple, childlike and almost captures the mood of a folksong:

> Noch nit genug vos kayne ru
> Hob ikh fun kind un hoys
> Tsaylt er mir yede penny tsu
> un tsaylt mir tsores oys.

("It is not enough I have no rest / from child and house / /He counts out the pennies / and counts out trouble too.")[21] Rappaport ceased to write in Yiddish after 1919. For a time she wrote a comic column for the socialist

English-language New York *Call* but at that point she disappeared from the literary horizon.[22]

Fradel Stock did not write in the then popular genre of didactic social realism. Although her poetry appeared in the anarchist *Fraye arbeter shtime*, she wrote sonnets and lyric poems which explored the institution of marriage and the relationships between men and women. Erotic, exotic, turbulent, and audacious, her poetry challenged the passivity of women in love relationships. Courtship was central to her poems but women playfully dominated the interactions.

> A young man like you, and shy
> Come here. I'll coddle you like a child.
> Why are you shy? Such a young man afraid of sin?
> Come on, you can hide your face in my hair.[23]

Beautiful, young, and witty, Stock became a popular figure in the literary cafes of the Lower East Side frequented by the Jewish intelligentsia. Both women and men admired her poetry and her romantic appearance.[24] In 1916 she began to publish short stories in the *Jewish Daily Forward* and in the new daily *Der tog*. In fact, the great demand for short stories in the growing Yiddish press provided opportunities for several other Yiddish women writers, such as Rachel Luria, Sarah Smith, and Miriam Karpilove, whose stories about women in the *shtetl* and in contemporary modern America began to appear regularly after 1915-1916.[25] But Stock was most admired, and a collection of her short stories, *Ertseylungen*, was published in 1919.[26] Many of the stories were subtle psychological studies of ordinary people caught in the anguish of a culture in rapid transition. Unfortunately, the reviews were unsympathetic, her severest critic being Glanz in *Der tog* on 7 December 1919. Glanz expressed the deepest disappointment in his unfulfilled expectations of women writers, and even intimated that Stock was really a minor poet. An apocryphal story circulated in the literary cafes —that upon reading the Glanz review Stock went to the editorial offices of *Der tog* and slapped her critic. But it is a fact that after her poor reception Stock stopped writing in Yiddish. Her first and only novel in English, *For Musicians Only*, appeared in 1927. Its plot involved the obsessional love of a young married Jewish woman for an Italian vaudeville orchestra leader. It was poorly written and not well received by American literary critics. Sometime in the late 1920s Stock was institutionalized for mental illness.[27]

The fate of Yente Serdatzky, also a writer of short stories whose earliest work was published before the 1920s, was considerably different in that she remained a Yiddish writer despite adverse criticism and long periods of unproductiveness. In 1969, Sh. Tennenbaum, an essayist and short story writer, wrote a laudatory essay about Serdatzky called "Queen of Union Square." He portrayed her as cantankerous, articulate, intelligent, and still politically radical as she reigned in the proletarian public park of New York's Union Square in the 1960s.[28]

Serdatzky was born in the *shtetl* of Alexat, near Kavnas, Poland (Russia) in 1879. Her father was a furniture dealer and talmudic scholar who provided his daughter with an education which included a knowledge of Yiddish, German, Russian, and Hebrew. Their home was a central meeting place for young Yiddish poets, and Abraham Reisen was a frequent visitor. Before 1905 Serdatzky married, gave birth to two children, and was the proprietress of a small grocery store in Alexat. The revolution of 1905 stirred her literary imagination and was also her reason for moving to Warsaw. Her first short story, "Mirl," was published in Warsaw in the journal *Veg* (1905). The famous writer I. L. Peretz was the editor. In 1907 she emigrated to New York, where she became a well-known writer, especially for the *Fraye arbeter shtime*. Her stories portrayed the fate of revolutionary Jewish women in the American environment. Isolated, left without ideals, often having sacrificed family life for the revolution, these women experienced mental depression, poverty, and lonely deaths. The stories written in the 1908-1920 period reflect an unwillingness by the author to adjust to American life. Her central theme remained one of relentless estrangement. Critics abounded; she was excoriated for the thinness of her plots, the sameness of her characters and, as in the case of Fradel Stock, male critics expressed their disappointment in the long-awaited Yiddish women writers. In the 1920s she stopped writing and returned to shopkeeping, only to reappear as an author in the 1940s.[29]

The 1920s and 1930s

Although mass East European immigration to America ceased in the mid-1920s with the official termination of an open U.S. immigration policy, Jewish immigrants did not all become "Americanized" at that time. Nor was Jewish social mobility into the middle class a uniform phenomenon that accompanied the Americanization process. It is certainly a fact that Yiddish cultural institutions, along with their radical political ideologies, survived the decline of Jewish immigrants, withstood the Red Scare, and even survived the internecine warfare between the Jewish socialists and the Jewish Communists after the Bolshevik revolution. In fact, this was the very period when the Jewish Left, now separated and identified as Communist, socialist, socialist-Zionist, and politically unaffiliated cultural Yiddishist created more structured cultural institutions. More fervently than ever, the Left defended its right to a Jewish existence in America within a radical Yiddish culture.

The twenties also witnessed the emergence of large numbers of women writers whose work appeared with greater regularity in the Yiddish press and in anthologies and whose individual writings were no longer regarded as extraordinary events. These women writers fell into two major categories: Yiddishist writers, many experimenting with avant-garde techniques, who were not formal members of a particular political party (for example, Anna Margolin and Celia Dropkin, who wrote "pure" literature although they were published in anarchist and socialist papers as well as in such journals of modernism as *Insikh*); and a group of mainly Communist writers whose literary work was motivated by the propaganda needs of the party and by the new ideals of writing a Yiddish proletarian literature.

At this time a Yiddish writer considered herself to be a "radical" intellectual; that is, a person who combined the quest for social justice with a search for personal authenticity, whether she actually belonged to a specific political group or not. She wrote for an audience of other intellectuals, primarily from the Jewish working class, although there were loyal Yiddishists whose economic circumstances would certainly have excluded them from this category. Occasionally, women writers, like some male writers, prided themselves on being "worker-poets" remaining in the factory and participating in trade union activities, but this was rare. Only a few women actually did manual labor for a living. Writing was one way of escaping the factory without abandoning the ideals of working-class solidarity.[30]

However, the increase in women writers during the 1920s is not an accurate indication of the extent of their integration into radical politics and society. Despite their intense dedication, most women encountered difficulties in being accepted as equals by the Jewish male intelligentsia. Yiddish-speaking radicals treated women with ambivalence. While women's work appeared in socialist, Communist, and anarchist papers, not one woman was permanently employed on a radical paper as part of its editorial staff. And when articles were accepted, they were almost never about general political or economic matters, but about "women's issues." If men found it difficult to earn a living by writing, women found it impossible.

Generally, women writers married and had children. The common pattern was for women to write before marriage and after widowhood. Intellectual isolation was something very real for them. There was little camaraderie among women writers, in sharp contrast to the long-term friendships and the intimate groups created by male writers. Women were only marginally tolerated in these crircles. One had to be a wife, a sister, or a lover to gain admission into the inner sanctum of literary society where one could then share common intellectual and political interests. Many women writers did of course marry men who were active in Jewish Left political and literary circles, but the husbands were usually more famous than their wives, and in some instances wives depended upon their husbands' positions for their own publication. For example, Rachel Holtman married and later divorced Moishe Holtman, an editor of the Communist daily *Frayhayt*. During their marriage she edited the Sunday women's page but apparently lost the position when their marriage was dissolved.[31]

Immigrant Jewish women intellectuals did not respond to their exclusion from the centers of power or the implicit sexism of their male comrades by demanding access to power or by questioning the relationship between the sexes; nor did they organize a radical feminist movement. There were many reasons for this, rooted in the structure of immigrant American society. The women's isolation from and reliance upon men, as mentioned earlier, was one factor. Traditionally, Jewish men had been *the* intellectuals and despite the late nineteenth century ideals of equality, echoes of earlier views could still be heard in radical circles. Cultural asymmetry was prevalent, and this meant that male, as opposed to female, activities were always recognized as having greater importance, authority, and value, even when women and men were engaged in the same activities. There were other factors as well. In the 1920s Jewish cultural life was undergoing transformation toward Americanization, and the Yiddishists were beleaguered. Many Yiddish women writers supplemented their incomes by teaching in the Yiddish folk schools, which the children of socialist and Communist parents attended in the afternoon following the public school program. These women focused their energies on keeping the next generation from defecting culturally. Championing Yiddish studies and contending with children might have contributed to their noncontentiousness relative to their own position as women.

In general, radical Jews did not feel secure in their newfound homeland in the 1920s. Political radicalism itself was under attack from the American government during the Red Scare. The radical movement was split into warring factions, and there was the added fear of anti-Semitism. These problems, faced by women as well as men, exacted a certain measure of solidarity.

Nevertheless, most women believed themselves emancipated and on an approximately equal basis with men in America. In contrast to the positions of their grandmothers and mothers, they were breadwinners, voters, "legal" revolutionaries, and cultural workers. No one seemed to notice that in the 1920s separate women's auxiliaries institutionalized the separate functions of the sexes in both socialist and Communist organizations. It became accepted that men did the political work and women did the social and cultural work, although individual men and women transcended the barrier.

Individually, women writers explored their dissatisfaction with this state of affairs. New themes and experimental forms were introduced into Yiddish literature by both male and female writers in the twenties. Some women writers, encouraged to express themselves openly, described their intimate feelings as women and their criticism of traditional Jewish values. Anna Margolin and Celia Dropkin typified the intensely personal and iconoclastic tone of the twenties when they wrote about life's disappointments, ambivalent feelings, their sexual interest, and their hostility to conventional behavior and clichéd emotions.

Margolin's life was unconventional. She had lovers, was twice married, and left an infant son in the permanent care of its father.[32] Her sharp wit and intellectual acumen antagonized many of her male contemporaries and made it difficult for her to earn a living as a writer; they rejected her aggressive, self-confident behavior. It is particularly interesting that in her only book of collected poems, *Lider* (1929), Margolin chose as her first selection a poem entitled *"Ich bin geven amol a yingele"* ("I Once Was a Little Boy") and as her second selection *"Muter erd"* ("Mother Earth").[33] Like other women of her generation who could not accept disdain even when they were unconventional, she eventually grew to pity herself. She wrote her own epitaph, a lament for a wasted life:

> She with the cold marble breast
> and with the slender illuminating hands,
> She dissipated her life
> on rubbish, on nothing.
>
> Perhaps she wanted it so, perhaps lusted after
> unhappiness, desired seven knives of pain,
> And poured life's holy wine
> on rubbish, on nothing.
>
> Now she lies broken
> the ravaged spirit has abandoned the cage.
> Passersby, have pity and be silent.
> Say nothing.[34]

Celia Dropkin's life was more conventional. She married, reared five children and kept house while, as her daughter said, "she worked on pieces of noodle paper, on scratch paper, on total chaos, on figuring out time."[35] Dropkin accepted the traditional role of women, but in her poetry she expressed the ambivalence of anticipating freedom and fearing its consequences. Her poem *"Ich bin a tsirkus dame"* ("I Am a Circus Lady") illustrates this dichotomy.

> I am a circus lady
> I dance betwixt
> Sharp knives that are fixed,
> points up, in the arena.
> If I fall I die,
> But with my lithe body I
> Just touch the sharp edge of your knives.

People hold their breath as my danger they see
and someone is praying to God for me.
The points of your knives seem
To me like a wheel of fire to gleam,
And no one knows how I want to fall.[36]

Dropkin also expressed hostility toward men — a theme rarely expressed in Yiddish literature.

I haven't yet seen you asleep
I'd like to see
how you sleep,
when you've lost your power
over yourself, over me.
I'd like to see you helpless, strung-out, dumb.
I'd like to see you
with your eyes shut,
breathless.
I'd like to see you
dead.[37]

Both Margolin and Dropkin wondered in their poetry whether they were not under the influence of some "pagan" power. Anxiously, Margolin wrote in 1920: "With fright, I hear in my mind, the heavy steps of forgotten gods." Dropkin was more enthusiastic in *"Dos lid fun a getsendiner"* ("Poem of a Pagan"): "Silently, I came to the temple / today before dawn / Ah, how beautiful was my pagan god / Bedecked with flowers."[38]

In the 1920s the women who wrote for the Communist press rarely dealt with such sensuous themes as did those who published in the anarchist and socialist papers. The Communists tended to be puritanical and very much concerned with developing a "correct" working-class literature. But they were often more direct than other radicals in their distaste for female oppression. They openly advocated solidarity among women and pride in womanhood. In their poetry Esther Shumiatcher, Sara Barkan, and Shifre Weiss urged women to combat powerlessness by seeking self-respect and by acting in unison. In the December 1927 issue of *Hamer* Shumiatcher called upon women to "Free yourselves from the dark lattices that imprisoned generations." In the late twenties, she and her famous playwright husband Peretz Hirshbein took an extended trip to China, India, Africa, and the Middle East. In a series of poems, *"Baym rand fun khina"* ("At the Border of China"), she lamented the plight of women: "Wife and mother / at the border of China / Baskets, filled with your sadness and weariness, hang from your shoulders. . . ."[39] Sara Barkan, who had begun working in a factory at the age of nine and whose life was seriously affected by daily toil for herself and her daughter, wrote *"Mir arbeter froyen"* ("We Working Women"), dedicated to International Woman's Day in 1925:

> We, working women
> We are raped in Polish prisons
> We are decapitated in China;
> And we forge hammers out of our fists,
> In every part of the world, in each country
> we have cut the rotten cords of yesterday's dark oppression.
> Small, delicate our hands have become hard and muscular. . . ."[40]

Los Angeles poet Shifre Weiss also wrote about working women in *Hamer*, but in a somewhat different context:

> We women,
> We rebuilt the house and let in the sun
> . . . equal captains
> With our comrade husbands and brothers
> We help pilot the ship
> To eternally new lands
> Hand and hand at the steering wheel.[41]

Although the social status of women in Jewish radical circles did not change in the 1930s, a new, more aggressive tone, criticizing male behavior, emerged in some women's writings. Golde Shibke, in an article entitled *"Di arbeter froy un der arbeter ring"* ("The Working Woman and Workman's Circle"), blames her male comrades for limiting the role of women in that socialist "fraternal" organization to a mere women's auxiliary. Since women worked equally hard alongside men in the factories, it was unfair to discriminate against them in a socialist organization.[42]

Kadia Molodowsky, who emigrated to New York City from Warsaw in 1935, provided a role model for other radical women writers in the late thirties. Considered a serious journalist, poet, and intellectual among the Jewish intelligentsia in Poland, she was unhappy to discover that the New York radical literati considered women authors as "exotic flowers of the literary garden for whom direct and powerful thinking was alien." She protested the male categorizing of women as a breed apart. "Writing is more an expression of the spirit than of sexual gender," she insisted in her article *"A por verter vegn froyen dikhterin"* ("A Few Words about Women Poets"), which appeared in the New York Communist literary magazine *Signal* in 1936. While admitting that there were some differences in male and female literary style, word conception, and personality presentation, she maintained that women writers were the equals of men in their insightfulness, outspokenness, political and social awareness, and in their search for a profound understanding of reality.

Molodowsky herself wrote some poems about critical political issues of the 1930s. One about the Spanish Civil War, *"Tsu di volontirn in shpayne"* ("To the Volunteers in Spain"), was published in *Hamer* in 1938:

At night
when the moon burns above you with death
She awakens me
And calls me to the window
And the sky spreads itself
with stars
and a pricetag. . . .
And the debt is so great
And your blood falls on my mind
heavy and red.[43]

In that same year, one year before the Hitler-Stalin pact which destroyed the illusions held by great numbers of Jewish Communists about the anti-fascist stance taken by the Soviet Union, *Hamer* also published poetry in praise of the Russian experiment in revolution. Both Sara Barkan's "Near Your Picture, Lenin" and Shifre Weiss's "Biro-Bidjan Bride" sentimentally expressed the great expectation held by radical Jews for the success of the Bolshevik revolution and the possibilities of an autonomous Jewish state in the Soviet Union.[44]

It is difficult to assess in what way themes about women or poetry about politics affected the female readers of the radical Yiddish press and literature. Rachel Holtman's autobiography offers a rare glimpse into women's responses. In the mid-1930s Holtman traveled to Los Angeles, a city with a population of over 45,000 Jews. Most of the East Europeans had arrived in the First World War period. The city contained branches of the Workmen's Circle, locals of the ILGWU, the Amalgamated Clothing Workers, groups of the Communist International Workers' Order and their Industrial Union, plus the literary magazines *Zunland* and *Pasifik*. Los Angeles could even boast a leftist youth organization, the *Arbeter klub* with 100 "non-partisan" members.[45]

Holtman found that there were ten women's study circles affiliated with the International Workers Order which held meetings at least weekly and where members studied Yiddish literature. The women read both the Yiddish classics as well as works from contemporary Yiddish writers and discussed current political issues. Holtman described these women, most of whom were dressmakers and militant trade unionists. "The women in these study groups are quite another sort of woman—a *mentsh* (human being), who consciously educated herself. It is a pleasure to discuss things with her. She is sensitive, talented, understanding, straightforward. She takes a fine fresh look at the world."[46] Shifre Weiss, a member of one such Los Angeles study circle, shared her work with her group. Her writings include poems about Rosa Luxemburg, Edna St. Vincent Millay, and one "To My Black Sisters." She also wrote a poem entitled *"lern krayzn"* ("Study Circles"):

> We met as a *minyan*
> Eighteen or more;
> Building edifices of our culture
> Erasing the traces of tears and of pain
> Our dream shall come true
> By creating and recreating.
> Happiness, Justice and Peace
> Shall come to this world.[47]

It is clear that immigrant Yiddish women writers created an extensive literature which expressed their experimental and highly complex perceptions. As Kadia Molodowsky said, they were not exotic flowers of any literary garden. Rather, they were a first generation of immigrant Jews, an emerging female intelligentsia whose self-analysis and critical awareness are well worth exploring further. It is also clear that they experienced the profound contradiction faced by most other radical women in the early twentieth century — living within a pattern of seeming acceptance combined with implicit exclusion. They did not always directly do battle with this contradiction.

The literature of radical Jewish women has virtually vanished. By the end of the Second World War, Yiddish was hardly read by the majority of the Jewish population who had become linguistically assimilated. Anarchism, socialism, and Communism, the radical movements that attracted significant numbers of Jewish American workers and intellectuals, were also in deep decline. The literature produced by radicals lost its audience. Every effort must be made to rescue this literature from oblivion, not only for its intrinsic value, but also because it and the lives of those who created it provide us with a much broader insight and deeper understanding of the cultural transformation of East European Jewry in America.

APPENDIX
This list is representative; it is not complete.

	Birthdate	Year of Immigration
Bach, Pessie	1904	1916
Badanes, Ida	1874	
Barkan, Sara	1890	1907
Belov, Fraydel	1899	1908
Birek, Dora	1897	1912

Bordo-Rivkin, Minnie	1897	1927
Burstin, Liba	1901	1921
Charney, Freidl	1891	1926
Cooperman, Hasye	1907	American born
Dropkin, Celia	1888	1912
Fell-Yellin, Sarah	1895	1920
Gallin, Rivke	1890	1907
Gerbert, Sonia	1896	1906
Glass-Fenster, Rayzel	1910	1923
Glasser, Eda	1893	1909
Goldworth, Bella	1902	1921
Guterman, Silva	1914	American born
Gutman, Rosa	1903	1939
Halpern, Frume	1888	1905
Hofman, Leah	1898	1913
Holtman, Rachel	1882	1913
Kahan, Malcha	1897	1906
Kahana, Pesi	1895	1908
Karpilove, Miriam	1895	1905
Katz, Esther	1892	1906
Kaufman, Leah		1922
Kling, Bertha	1885	1899
Kudly, Berta	1893	1917
Lee, Malke	1904	1921
Liebert, Sarah-Leah	1892	1902
Levy, Shafra-Esther	1892	1910
Locker, Malka	1887	
Luria, Esther	1877	1912
Luria, Rachel	1886	1898
Margolin, Anna	1887	1906
Miller, Esther	1896	1912
Molodowsky, Kadia	1894	1935
Nevadovski, Rosa	1899	1928
Newman-Wallinsky, Rosa	1911	1915
Pomerantz, Bessie Hershfield	1900	1913
Rappaport, Anna	1876	1890
Safran, Chane	1902	1916
Shumiatcher, Esther	1900	1911
Serdatzky, Yente	1879	1907
Smith, Sarah	1888	1903
Stock, Fradel	1890	1907
Tarant, Deborah	1898	1923
Tussman, Malkna Heifetz	1896	1912
Vartzel, Chana	1872	1902
Veprinski, Rachele	1895	1907
Weiss, Shifre	1889	1905
Zaretsky, Hinde	1899	1914
Zunser, Miriam Shomer	1882	1891

Notes

1. A major portion of the biographic information can be found in *Leksikon fun der nayer yiddisher literatur* (New York, 1956-1968); Zalman Reisen, *Leksikon fun der yiddisher literatur, prese un filologye* (Vilna, U.S.S.R. 1927-1929); Ezra Korman, *Yidishe dikhterins* (Detroit, Mich.: 1928); Shmuel Roszinski, *Di froy in der yidishe poezie* (Buenos Aires, Argentina: 1966); and Ber Green, "*Yidishe dikhterin*," *Yidishe kultur*, December 1973, January 1974, March 1974, and April-May 1974.

2. Not all individual Jewish radicals were in favor of a special Jewish cultural expression. Some Jewish radicals joined the American anarchist, socialist, and Communist organizations without defining themselves as Jews. Other Jewish radicals participated in all Jewish radical groups but believed that the use of Yiddish and the perpetuation of Jewish culture were merely propaganda strategies to attract Jewish workers. Such Jewish radicals believed the "revolution" would solve cultural as well as class differences. For greater discussion on Jewish American radicalism see Arthur Liebman, *Jews and the Left* (New York, 1979); Melech Epstein, *Jewish Labor in U.S.A.*, 2 vols. (New York, 1959); and Nora Levin, *While Messiah Tarried: Jewish Socialist Movements 1871-1917* (New York, 1977).

3. Celia S. Heller, *On the Edge of Destruction: Jews of Poland Between the Two World Wars* (New York: 1977), pp. 211-247.

4. Biographical information on Kadia Molodowsky (1896-1975) can be found in her serialized autobiography "*Mayn elter zoydes yerushe*" ("My Great Grandfather's Inheritance"); *Sviva*, March 1965-April 1974 and in the Kadia Molodowsky Papers at the YIVO Institute for Jewish Research. For Devorah Fogel (1903-1943) see Melech Ravitch, *Mayn Leksikon* (Montreal, 1945), pp. 188-190; Ephraim Roytman, "*Di amolike Devorah Fogel*," *Israel shtime*, May 7, 1975; and I. B. Singer, "A Polish Franz Kafka," *New York Times Book Review*, July 9, 1978, who in discussing the writer Bruno Schulz mentions that "Schulz wrote a number of his stories as letters to a woman friend, Dr. Devorah Vogel, who lived in Lvov and wrote poetry in Yiddish. I knew Deborah Vogel and I also read her poems. In the Yiddish Writers' Club she was thought of as a brainy poet – an intellectual writer in contrast to one who writes with the 'heart.' I don't remember her poems now, and I wouldn't be able to say what their value was. I only recall that the more conservative poets mocked and mimicked her obscure style."

5. For autobiographical information see Rachel Holtman, *Mayn lebns-veg* (New York: 1948); Malke Lee, *Durkh kindershe oygn* (Buenos Aires, Argentine, 1958); and Molodowsky, "*Mayn elter zeydes yerushe*." In August 1978 this author interviewed the poets Rachele Veprinski, Rosa Gutman, Esther Shumiatcher, Reyzel Zychlinski, and Hinde Zaretsky and the literary critics Meyer Stiker and Ber Green in New York City.

6. Interview with Hinde Zaretsky.

7. Charlotte Baum, "What Made Yetta Work? The Economic Role of Eastern European Jewish Women in the Family," *Response*, 18 (Summer 1973), 32-38.

8. Heller, *On the Edge of Destruction.*

9. Korman, *Yidishe dilchterins* pp. 57-58. Unless otherwise noted, the translations are by the author.

10. Malke Lee, *Durkh kindershe oygn* p. 25.

11. Interview with Hinde Zaretsky.

12. Lily Bes, "*Fun eygene vegn,*" *Frayhayt*, January 20, 1929.

13. For women in the Bund see Anna Rosenthal, *"Di froyen geshtaltn in Bund,"* *Unzer tsayt* 3-4 (November-December, 1947), 30-31; and Harriet Kram, "Jewish Women in Russian Revolutionary Movements" (Master's thesis, Hunter College, The City University of New York); and Mordechai V. Bernstein, *"Di brider un shvester-zeyer yikhes un vi alt zey zenen,"* *Forois* (June 1963), 11-12.

14. Interview with Dina Blond, one of the leading women in the Bund, December 1978.

15. Kadia Molodowsky, *"Froyen lider,"* translated by Adrienne Rich, in Irving Howe and Eliezer Greenberg, eds., *A Treasury of Yiddish Poetry* (New York, 1969), p. 284; *The Other Voice: Twentieth Century Women's Poetry in Translation,* (New York, 1976).

16. *Leksikon fun der nayer yidisher literatur,* vol. 5, p. 30.

17. For Jewish socialist support of women suffrage in New York see Norma Fain Pratt, *Morris Hillquit: A Political History of an American Jewish Socialist* (Westport, Conn., 1979).

18. *"Berimpte yidishe salon froyen,"* *Tsukunft,* 19, no. 2 (February 1914), 189-195; *"Berimpte yidishe froyen in America und England,"* *ibid.,* 20, no. 9 (September 1915), 835-838; *"Emma Lazarus," ibid.,* 21, no. 9 (September 1916), 792-797; *"Martha Wolfenstein," ibid.,* 22, no. 4 (April 1917), 233-234.

19. Kadia Molodowsky, *"A por verter vegn froyen dikhterin,"* *Signal* (July 1936), 36.

20. A. Glanz, *"Kultur un di froy,"* *Fraye arbeter shtime,* October 30, 1915.

21. Nahum Minkoff, *Pionirn fun yidishe poezie in America* (New York, 1956); vol. 3, pp. 57-80. *"Eyn lebnsbild"* is quoted on p. 68. Reprinted with the permission of Hasye Cooperman Minkoff.

22. Anna Rappaport, *"Flashlights,"* *New York Call,* September 12, 1915, September 19, 1915, September 20, 1915, October 10, 1915, and December 19, 1915.

23. Fradel Stock, *"Sonnet," Di naye heym* (New York, 1914), p. 5.

24. Interview with Rashelle Veprinski.

25. Miriam Karpilove, *"Dos leben fun a meydl,"* *Yidishe arbeter velt,* June 30, 1916; Rachel Luria, *"Di groyse kraft," Der tog,* June 13, 1919; Sarah Smith, *"Der man vil hershn," ibid.,* July 23, 1916.

26. Fradel Stock, *Ertseylungen* (New York, 1919).

27. A. Glanz, *"Temperment," Der tog,* December 7, 1919; M. Olgin, *"Pesimizim," Di naye velt,* January 9, 1920; Melech Ravitch, *"Gezamelte ertseylungen," Khoydish bibliografikal zhurnal,* 1923; Dovid Zeydenfeld, *"A marionetn-molern," Renesons,* 1920; interview with Meyer Stiker. Also see Jacob Glatstein, *"Tsu der biografie fun a dikhterin," Der tog,* September 19, 1965.

28. Sh. Tennenbaum, *Geshtaltn baym shrayb-tish* (New York, 1969), pp. 47-51.

29. Reisen, *Leksikon,* vol. 2, pp. 684-685. Z. Zylbercweig, *Leksikon fun yidishn teater* (Warsaw, Poland, 1934), vol. 2, pp. 1524-1525.

30. Two poets who regarded themselves as workers were Sara Barkan and Rashelle Veprinski. Ber Green, *"Yidishe dikhterin," Yidishe kultur,* December 1973, 33; *Leksikon fun der nayer yidishe literatur,* vol. 3, p. 491, and interview.

31. Holtman, *Mayn lebns-veg,* pp. 79-100.

32. Reuben Iceland, *Fun unzer friling* (Miami Beach, Fla., 1954), pp. 129-172.

33. Anna Margolin, *Lider* (New York, 1929), pp. 5-6; Adrienne Cooper Gordon, "Myths of the Woman as Artist: A Study of Anna Margolin," Paper presented at the

YIVO Institute of Jewish Research Annual Conference, November 11-14, 1979.

34. Iceland, *Fun unzer friling* p. 172 (Author's translation).

35. Interview with Esther Unger, Celia Dropkin's daughter, August 1978, in New York City.

36. Celia Dropkin, *"Ich bin a tsirkus dame,"* translated by Joseph Leftwich in *The Golden Peacock: A Worldwide Treasury of Yiddish Poetry* (New York, 1961), p. 672.

37. Dropkin, *"Poem,"* translated by Adrienne Rich in Howe and Greenberg, *Treasury*, p. 168.

38. Anna Margolin, *"Fargesene geter,"* Di naye velt, July 23, 1920; Celia Dropkin, *"Dos lid fun a getsendiner,"* ibid., May 16, 1919.

39. Esther Shumiatcher, *"Tsu shvester,"* Hamer (December 1927), 17; *idem.,* *"Baym rand fun khina, ibid.* (July 1927), 5; interview with Esther Shumiatcher.

40. Sara Barkan, *"Mir, arbeter froyen,"* Signal (January 1925), 2; interview with Ber Green.

41. Shifre Weiss, *"Mir, froyen,"* Hamer (September 1928), 50; Reisen, *Leksikon,* vol. 1, p. 961.

42. Golde Shibke, *"Di arbeter froy un der arbeter ring,"* Lodzer Almanak, 1934.

43. Kadia Molodowsky, *"Tsu di volontirn in shpayne,"* Hamer (February 1938), 2.

44. Sara Barkan, *"Lebn Lenins bild,"* Hamer (February 1938), 40; Shifre Weiss, *"Biro-bidjan kale," ibid.* (November 1938), 57.

45. *"Notizen," Los Angeles Pasifik,* 1 (March 1929), 45-50.

46. Holtman, *Mayn lebns-veg,* pp. 152-153.

47. Shifre Weiss, *Tsum morgndikn morgn* (Los Angeles: 1953), p. 59.

7

Photographing Women: The Farm Security Administration Work of Marion Post Wolcott

_____ JULIE BODDY _____

> We are learning that the writing of women into history necessarily
> involves redefining and enlarging traditional notions of historical
> significance to encompass personal, subjective experience as well
> as public and political activities.
>
> Ann D. Gordon, Mari Jo Buhle, and
> Nancy Schrome Dye
> "The Problem of Women's History"[1]

The photographs taken by the Farm Security Administration (FSA) during the Depression are graphic and poignant records of American life, experience, and vistas. But these still images reflect more than subject matter. They are also statements and visions by the people who stood behind the cameras, photographers who had found a means of personal and political expression and a new, expanding area of gainful employment. Women were particularly active in the developing field of photojournalism. By focusing on one of these women, it may be possible to suggest ways in which photography mediated between speculative experience and paid, active work.

Many members of the full-time staff of the FSA are well known to historians of photography and of the New Deal. Marion Post Wolcott, in spite of the volume of her work, is not among them. The number of her photographs in the FSA files testify to her fruitful work within that agency, but the quality has been underestimated. While she is recalled primarily as the photographer who made beautiful landscapes, this genre, in fact, was a very small part of her total work.

The visual archive is full and varied: photographs showing how people made sorghum syrup; what a packing house looked like and how work was carried on within it; how members of different ethnic groups used their traditions to adapt their households to life in the mining areas of West Virginia; what fund-raising events among rural people looked like; how the work of cotton picking was organized; the unpaid work that children did in West Virginia or in the migrant camps in Florida. A complete list would be very long, for Wolcott's curiosity and perception seemed to have few restraints.

Not all Wolcott's photographs were work oriented. The nearly informal portraits most clearly revealed a quality characteristic of all her work: persistently respectful, appreciative, and frequently tender perceptions of women. Altogether, the consciousness that went into making the photographs can best be described as feminist.

But viewing the photographs as, first and foremost, the product of feminist consciousness raises a number of questions. What sense might there be in identifying as "feminist" work that was done at a time when the feminist movement was wracked by setbacks and dispersions, done in a solitary fashion, and done for a government-sponsored reform agency? Could such an interpretation merely reflect feminist sensibilities of the 1970s and 1980s? Where, outside the photographs themselves, might be the corroboration that, when she made the photographs, Marion Post Wolcott shared concerns that were feminist in nature?

Examination of transcriptions of interviews with Wolcott, her quasi-official field correspondence, perusal of FSA documents at the National Archives, published discussions of the FSA, the New Deal, and agricultural labor, novels written by women during the thirties, feminist art criticism, and the history of photography have all been helpful in providing a general context. Nonetheless, a method of relating her photographs to feminism remained elusive. Conversations with Marion Post Wolcott in December 1976 confirmed the supposition that a powerful feminist influence had gone into her FSA photographs. Finally, recent scholarship on the history of the women's movement and in labor history furnished the necessary perspective.

Before she became a photographer, Marion Post Wolcott seemed to veer between two kinds of projected work. She enrolled in an early childhood education program in college while intensifying an already serious effort to become a professional dancer. Teaching would provide a steady income; dancing would let her spirits soar. She acted as if she believed she had a right to both.

According to the claims raised by women some twenty years earlier, she did. "Bread and Roses," first voiced by the striking textile workers of Lawrence, Massachusetts, in 1912, was a concept that related directly to Wolcott's early experience and subsequent work. It was a collective claim for objective and emotional well-being through struggle against exploitation and oppression, and the interaction of both carried over into the photographs Wolcott made nearly thirty years later. The character and conduct of the strike that gave rise to "Bread and Roses" revealed the power of this understanding.

The strike had begun when a group of Polish women who worked in a woolen mill walked out of the mill crying "short pay, short pay!"[2] Their persistence rallied over twenty other ethnic groups into a strike force of 25,000 women, men, and children who worked in the textile mills of

Lawrence. These strikers gained the support of canny strategists of social reform, such as Jane Addams, and they drew upon the expertise developed in socialist organizations in coordinating strike actions. The Industrial Workers of the World facilitated organization, promoted the participation of women and children, and encouraged the striking population in non-violent direct action. Margaret Sanger was one person who travelled to Lawrence to bring young children of strikers to the safety of the homes of New Yorkers who supported the uprising. She was soon to use the organizing skills she developed during the strike in launching her struggle for birth control.

Together the strikers and their allies maintained the strike for three months, until they won their demands. Winning required a massive confrontation with the interests of the mill owners, but the length of the strike and the level of strike activity encouraged indirect but widespread support of the strikers' goals. Newspaper reports reached people across the country; word of mouth brought the message home to other mill towns.

The boldness and resourcefulness deployed in Lawrence led to other strikes where women were the instigators and the main force. The Lawrence victory touched off a wave of insurgence among mill workers in the next eighteen months which spread across New England and into New Jersey. It was only to be quelled by the increased layoffs produced by a depression in the next year.[3]

As a memory of what could be done and how things should be, the impact of the Lawrence strike continued through a far more severe depression, for it became part of the heritage of women. It was transmitted directly to Marion Post Wolcott through her mother, who worked as a nurse in the birth control clinic that Margaret Sanger began fighting for soon after the Lawrence strike.

By her own account, nearly sixty-five years later, Marion Post Wolcott has strong, warm recollections of her mother. There was first the pride that her mother made the decision to be self-supporting and that she worked with Sanger during the early years of the clinic. Her mother's encouragement of physical and, specifically, sexual self-expression was something she emphasized. She recalled with delight the fantastic costumes her mother designed and the ease and comfort of the bloomer outfits she made for everyday wear. Remembrances such as these are redolent of "Bread and Roses."

The encouragement of physical self-possession, which Marion Post Wolcott attributed to her mother, was intensified and abstracted into an art form — dance — during the first three decades of the twentieth century. Here too, women were largely influential in the initiation and development of this process. As an art form, dance had the dominance and rigidity of the classical ballet to contend with. To gain legitimacy reformers turned first to ancient Greece for suggestions of a still more "classical" source of dance tradition, then to alternatives presented by nonindustrial cultures as sources of vitality and method, and to dances popular in industrial society such as the cancan. They sought systematic principles through scientific study of human kinetics.

The diversity of the dance movement's origins and the scope of the transformations it intended to inspire can be glimpsed through the objectives espoused by the dancers with whom Marion Post Wolcott chose to study. The first of these dancers was Ruth St. Denis, whose most conscious influence came from Eastern dance. She was able to enlarge her contacts through the increasing number of dancers that began to come to the United States both as cultural emissaries and as immigrants. As her reputation grew, she engaged in serious study in places as far away as Java. From these sources she enriched the dance movement—soon to be known as "modern dance"—with costumes, gestures, and more fluid movement accomplished by a more profound mobilization of the female body. By the time Marion Post Wolcott studied with St. Denis she was devoting most of her energies to teaching the method that she had evolved. The Denishawn School, which she had established with her husband, dancer Ted Shawn, provided the only serious and intensive training in the new dance available in the United States until the late 1920s. After that, several new dancers took up where St. Denis left off.

Doris Humphrey, with whom Marion Post Wolcott studied next, had spent years at the Denishawn School. In 1928 she left it to promulgate the particular contributions she brought to dance—best summarized as disciplined thought about dance principles including a stress on dance form and a concomitant insistence on the importance of the inner organization of a group of dancers. In so doing, Humphrey was militating against the stars-and-their-backdrop form of organization which was emphasized by traditional ballet, and for an active interaction with space that fully involved the entire group. The scope of her concern with dance principles is very well articulated in her own words:

In choosing a theme for a dance, theoretically, I claim the world, at least the Western World, as possible material. By this I mean to include the arts, the industries, the legendary, history, and the sciences, even to biology and physiology of modern and ancient times. Also, I have my own interior world of sensation to work with and the meaning of my experience. . . . Now movement is the very blood and bones of the modern dance and must first, last and always be dominant in it.[4]

Marion Post Wolcott studied with Humphrey in the early 1930s while a student at New York University. By the end of Wolcott's sophomore year she had decided to study dance full time. Probably with the encouragement of Humphrey, she left New York for Germany, where Mary Wigman was introducing still other sources of vitality into the dance movement.

Perhaps at the heart of dance as Mary Wigman understood and performed it was her ability to translate paralytic despair into movement. Facing the aftermath of the First World War and the ruinous reparations forced upon their country, young Germans countered the destitute prospects before them, in part, by developing a social program that used physical exertion to raise their spirits and increase their stamina. Wigman moved beyond this popular program, called *tanzgymnastic*, and immersed herself in a study of the sciences of human anatomy and locomotion as they related to dance. When she returned to public performance, her work revealed an intense awareness of social grief and a commitment to do her utmost through dance to provide people with relief from the pangs of grief.

As her work developed she became aware that her ideas would be expressed more forcefully through a group of dancers, and so she organized a collective group. In 1930 the group performed a dance made possible through the aid of the city of Munich. Described as a memorial to the men killed during the world war, the dance was made vivid by the mourning of mothers, wives, and sisters. By 1934 the group was performing "dances of women." "Now a woman was dancing," said one commentator, "a woman of this world, whose sorrow, whose happiness, whose fate, whose life we all share."[5]

After joining this exhilarating movement briefly, Wolcott developed pneumonia. Following her recovery she left Germany for France and a job caring for the children of an American friend who was suffering from nervous collapse. After a few months her friend returned home, and Wolcott had earned enough money to go to Vienna, where her sister, Helen Post, was a student.

At the time when Wolcott arrived in Vienna, students exerted a potent political force, and the influence of feminists in nearby Germany and in the newly established Soviet Republic of Hungary was still strong. Through their alliance with militant working people, students took part in making sweeping changes in a city famous for its political conservatism.

As in other German-speaking cities, photojournalism had become an important means of political education. Local groups of worker-photographers had organized, in part through the auspices of the Workers' International Relief (WIR), an agency of the Communist International (Comintern). Perhaps because it was a relief organization, women gained powerful official positions within the WIR. From such positions they coordinated the struggle being waged at the time for control of communications.[6] In 1928 the worker-photographers had established a magazine, *Die Arbeiter-Fotografi*, and had mounted several small exhibitions which won widespread praise from the public and from professional photographers. Self-criticism of one of these exhibits suggests active participation by women in the worker-photographer groups. "Technically good throughout, some things excellent, but . . . where was the material from the working class, where the wide coverage of social conditions? Apart from pictures of miserable housing and women on sewing machines, nothing!"[7] By 1931 there were at least 100 local groups with 2,412 registered members. Their photographs were being published in periodicals with national circulation and in community, sports, and union papers. In Berlin, the International Office of Worker Photographers of the World was distributing their photographs to publications in other countries.

Vienna had long been a center of innovation in photography. Technical development as a process of collaboration and photography as a trade were especially valued there.[8] Through one of the self-employed photographers in the city, Trude Fleishman, with whom her sister was an apprentice, Marion Post Wolcott began an active interest in photography. Fleishman figures very warmly in Wolcott's recollections, as a model and as a photographer who provided her with her first use of a camera and with praise for the photographs she took with it.

Wolcott's involvement with photography and student politics in Vienna was short-lived, however. Increased Nazi aggression, which had driven the worker-photographers underground in Germany, assumed critical proportions in Vienna in 1934. In response to increasing provocation the workers declared a general strike, and sympathizers joined in support of their action. After four days of bloody struggle, they were defeated. Survivors were sent to concentration camps, and the Social Democratic party was declared illegal. Within a matter of months, Nazis seized the chancery and murdered the prime minister. As the confrontations became more violent and defeat more certain, Wolcott made the decision to return to the United States and get a job as a teacher. Despite the reversals she had experienced, she was well prepared for hard times ahead. She had a pride in the heritage of women, the examples set by other women, and the courage they had offered her. She had the will to move — the belief deeply instilled by women's dance that oppression could be acknowledged and transformed through action. She had an experienced awareness of the brutal force underlying social injustice, illuminated by the bold and persistent struggles that she had witnessed in Vienna. She also wanted to acquire a new skill — photography — which would allow her to translate these experiences into graphic statements.

Back in New York, Marion Post Wolcott got a job teaching in a progressive private school a few hours outside the city. With a steady income now in hand, her interest in photography continued and grew, strengthened by associations with cultural groups in New York. At first she concentrated on photographs of theatrical performances, bringing the perception of dramatic tension that she had gained as a dancer to subjects readily available to her, through performances at the school where she taught and through association with the Group Theatre in the city.

Her work with the Group Theatre cultivated her awareness of social issues presented through expressive forms. Like the Wigman troupe and other dancers with whom she had had earlier experiences, the Group Theatre emphasized the internal collaboration of its members. Yet, the Group Theatre did not fully share the social consciousness Wigman declared when she identified herself as a people's dancer, not a dancer's dancer. It identified itself more simply as professional. In that respect it achieved recognition as the most technically advanced, the most professional in its aims and social orientation; but it did not develop a sustained audience independent of Broadway and consequently became dependent on Broadway producers.[9] During its heyday Wolcott found much to photograph, and ready customers for her work among its members.

The Group Theatre had ties with another group that Wolcott began to frequent, the Film and Photo League. The Film and Photo League had begun about 1930 as the Workers' Camera Club, a group of about fifty who held meetings once a week. One member was a professional photographer and the others earned their livings as food workers, in restaurants, and through housework. Their occupations suggest that this group included a large proportion of women, as seemed to be the case with the German worker-photographers, at least in their resources. Reports describe the fourth annual exhibit of the Workers' Camera Club as scenes of May Day, demonstrations of food workers, laborers at construction work, a factory, and fishermen. In the spring of the same year, the Workers' Camera Club joined forces with International Labor Defense (ILD), which itself was an agency of the WIR. This new organization generated pictures for the *Labor Defender*, the publication of the ILD, and through its auspices exchanged photographs with worker-photographer groups in other countries. In December of that year it gained direct sponsorship of the Workers' International Relief and with it increased international ties and funds for a film program. Accordingly, the group changed its name to Workers' Film and Photo League.

The goals of the photo section were to provide militant workers (both employed and unemployed) with the skills to create photographic records of class struggle, to assure a flow of records for radical publications, to help publicize the work of the WIR, the ILD, and other Communist-led organizations, and to orient established professional photographers more to the left. In 1933 the photography section assembled a collection of photographs intended to portray the social and economic transformations in the United States following the stock market crash. Subjects to be included were unemployment, housing, militarism, and child misery, again suggesting that women exerted a strong influence. As the exhibit was further formulated, the subjects expanded to include industry, farming, stagnation, reforestation camps, child labor, political speakers, and the New Deal. Although the focus of activity was New York City, other chapters were established throughout the country, so that for this exhibition the New York league confidently called for photographs from the North, South, and West. Another indication of the league's effectiveness was the National Photo Exchange which it formed in response to requests from the workers' press, magazines, book publishers, and other picture services. In 1934 it was supplying an average of sixty photos per month to publications that included the *Daily Worker, Freiheit, Der Arbeiter, Labor Unity,* the *Labor Defender, Better Times* magazine, *Fortune,* the *Jewish Daily Bulletin,* and *Survey Graphic.* Demand was so great that they believed they could place three times as many. League members attributed their success to the activity of the labor movement and to their members' closeness to labor activities.

The National Photo Exchange supplied the Workers' Film and Photo League with a much-needed source of income, for the Berlin-based WIR had been largely destroyed by the Nazis when Hitler had become chancellor in the previous year, and events abroad continued to present problems. When the Comintern met in 1935, it attempted to meet the crisis of growing Nazi power by changing the policy of "united-front-from-below," with its emphasis on self-organization and collaboration among all working people, to one of a united front of all social classes against fascism, and it dissolved the WIR. Adapting to these changes, the league dropped "Workers'" from its name. Despite this setback, the popularity of its public lectures, symposia, workshops, and exhibitions continued to increase. Through *Photo Notes,* its mimeographed journal, the organization provided people across the country with what was declared to be the best critical commentary available.[10] Through its many activities the league influenced the work of many of the most influential photographers of the twentieth century, including Bernice Abbott, Helen Levitt, Margaret Bourke-White, and Lisette Model. From faraway California, Dorothea Lange became a member and later subsidized a scholarship. Roy Stryker lectured there as director of the FSA Photographic Unit. At one time or another almost all the FSA photographers directly benefitted from the Film and Photo League. It was there following a lecture he had given that Wolcott met Ralph Steiner, who later gave her assistance in applying for her FSA job.

After teaching for one year Marion Post Wolcott submitted her resignation. She had decided to spend full time establishing herself as a free-lance photographer. Backed by savings from her salary and a small inheritance provided after her father's recent death, she moved to New York and began sharing an apartment and a darkroom with her sister.

The market for photographs had been growing despite the Depression, particularly in publications with mass circulation. In the past these publications had used photographs mostly for promotional purposes and especially for advertising. Such photographs tended to be removed from any particular time and place, divorced from everyday life and the sources of production. But people wanted information about the very things such photographs left out, as the success of the National Photo Exchange had demonstrated. What people wanted was a major determinant in circulation, and an increase in circulation meant an increase in advertising revenues. If only for these reasons, mass circulation journals paid careful attention to public opinion, and so did mass circulation news services. To meet these circumstances, the Associated Press (AP), the largest of the news services, bought out Pacific and Atlantic Press Associates, distributors of photographs from all over the world. In 1935 it intensified photo coverage by putting in operation a device for transmitting photographs by wire, and by so doing co-opted local competitors. The success of this campaign was impressive. Taking note of it and also the success of illustrated periodicals in Europe, two large publishers launched two new weekly magazines which were based on photojournalism: *Life* and *Look*.

Photojournalism required special skills: an active interest in and knowledgeable awareness of what was going on and the people taking part in it, and the ability to make clear pictures, quickly, under diverse conditions in place of lengthy manipulation in front of the camera or in the darkroom. For worker-photographers, it was a skill quite readily acquired; for photographers who had studied hard to learn the conventions of visual art, it could pose enormous problems.

There were few people in the United States who had paid experience in such work. One possible exception was Margaret Bourke-White, who had been a photographer for *Fortune* magazine since 1929. Her great strength was based on her love of machinery, but her style of representation came from her work as an advertising photographer; in all her later years of work she was only rarely able to overcome it. From Europe, Gisele Freund, a German emigrant to France, photographed some assignments for *Life*. In Germany, photojournalism had developed into a profession.

The free-lance photographers who worked for the illustrated press in Germany provided an example that photojournalism could be very good work — responsive to initiative, useful, and well paid. Picture editors gave consideration of the photographers precedence over management concerns. These photographers were predominantly young men, students, professionals, or skilled technicians. They took good advantage of their situation. They could travel, and they did, bringing back photographs from all over.

Photojournalism assumed a major importance for mass circulation in 1929. Papers in Munich and Berlin fiercely competed and both published photo stories to win readers away from the other. The Munich paper published photographs from the Mother House of the Trappist Order, where inmates lived cut off from the world and from each other, bound to vows of silence. The Berlin paper published a series of photographs of the struggles of the Spartacus League in 1919. Other periodicals began to follow suit. They included reports on American workers, the youth movement, migrant labor, and theatrical performances, among many others. When the Nazis came to power, they destroyed the mass-circulation illustrated press along with the worker-photographer groups. Most of the photographers were Jewish; some of them found refuge in the United States. The size of the communications industry in the United States precluded diversity such as that which briefly flourished in Germany; few photographers in the United States were able to work with a similar degree of self-determination. Even so, the pre-Hitler German press stood as a model for photojournalism.[11]

Photo reportage, or documentary photography, as it is sometimes called, affected a wide range of photographers whether or not they worked as photojournalists. It was as old a way of making pictures as photography itself, and photographers drew from that tradition as well as contemporary examples as they changed their styles of work. Imogen Cunningham turned to a sharp-focused style which she used to photograph celebrities for fashion magazines. Doris Ulmann kept a soft focus and opaque image but turned her large view camera from portraits of businessmen to black people on the Georgia Sea Islands and mountaineers of the Appalachians, the customs they followed, the work that they did. Bernice Abbott abandoned making portraits of artists and wealthy patrons in Paris to undertake a photographic survey of New York City. Dorothea Lange turned her camera from wealthy patrons to the immigrants pouring into California. Barbara Morgan intensified her work as a photographer through her photographs of modern dance. As a field investigator for the Works Progress Administration (WPA), Eudora Welty took photographs of a world she had only glimpsed when growing up in Mississippi. And these are only the photographers whose work has been published.[12]

Only Cunningham, and to some extent Lange, made a living from this work. The prospects for paid, self-directed work melted away for photographers as they had with most of the population. In this respect women were especially hard hit. Though women's employment rose during the 1930s, their employment in sex-typed, subordinate positions increased even more. The women-generated social service organizations, such as settlement houses, were absorbed into state-run bureaucracies. The American Birth Control League became dependent on wealthy patrons and introduced management experts into the organization. The nursing staff, who had once run the clinic, responded by organizing. Marion L. Post, Wolcott's mother, took an active part in laying the groundwork and in representing their grievances before management.

Wolcott herself put aside plans of being a free-lance photographer and applied for a position on the staff of the *Philadelphia Evening Bulletin*. She was hired in 1937, just as the Depression took a sharp turn for the worse. 1937 was also the year that Hitler annexed Austria and the Film and Photo League, stymied by tensions, split into a film group and a photo group. In the face of these discouraging events, she took up her new job with relish. For a while she was the only woman photographer on the staff. But before long she was the only photographer doing "women's work"—fashion and light features—and so she turned to a friend, Ralph Steiner, whom she had met when he lectured at the Photo League, for suggestions of something better. Through him she learned of an opening in the photographic unit of the FSA and got his recommendations to the director. She was interviewed, her portfolio carefully inspected, and quickly hired.

In many respects the agency she now began work for was an offshoot of the Workers' Film and Photo League—"Workers'" Film and Photo League because under that name the organization had developed a distribution service and close ties to the purposes of the WIR. The distribution of photographs concerning FSA services justified the existence of this photographic unit, which was more comprehensive in its scope and operation than any government-sponsored operation before or since, with the exception of photography related to military operations. The FSA photo unit's file was the main source of this service. Though frequently photographs would be contracted out directly to other agencies, such as the Public Health Service (PHS) and state and local groups, the file represented the collection as a whole. A Film and Photo League proposal provides a good general description of the FSA-sponsored file as it developed:

We want to seek subjects that are powerful and representative factors in the present struggle of social forces. We want bankers, workers, farmers (rich and poor), white collar workers, policemen, politicians, soldiers, strikers, scabs, wandering youth, and so on. We want to see them in relation to these things they do, where they live, how they work, how they play, what they read, and what they think.[13]

The larger organizations that the photography groups were connected to also had significant similarities. The WIR, begun in 1921 to provide relief to people suffering from famine in Russia, quickly expanded its program to provide aid to all workers in need, such as the families of strikers and the unemployed. The FSA was also designed to provide aid to destitute people, employed as well as unemployed, many of whom had recently gained bargaining status through Section 7(a) of the National Industrial Recovery Act. Both relief organizations encouraged workers' self-organization. For the WIR self-organization was a general policy, articulated by the Comintern. FSA policies included government-built camps for migrant workers, which provided them not only with shelter and assembly halls, but with protection from vagrancy charges and vigilante violence; worker cooperatives set up on government-owned plantations in the Deep South or planned communities such as Hightstown, New Jersey; and various forms of assistance to tenant farmers trying to free themselves from domination by landlords and supply merchants. Both organizations carried out their work through far-flung networks of cooperating agencies. Yet another similarity, between the two photography groups, was the collaboration with filmmakers. The U.S. Film Service had been established in the same year as the photographic unit and both were sections of the Division of Information of the FSA. The photographic unit assisted the film service a number of times; Dorothea Lange supplied stills for *The Plow That Broke the Plains*.

Marion Post Wolcott worked for the FSA between September 1938 and March 1942. At first she supplied her own camera; later the FSA supplemented her equipment. In all, she worked with a press camera (Speed Graphic), a twin-lens reflex camera (Ikoflex), and a 35mm range finder Leica. Developing negatives was done in a lab built by the FSA. The lab saved her tedious labor, but the delay in seeing her exposures limited her ability to assess what worked. Quite a few hours were spent writing captions for the finished prints.

Having a car was a requirement for the job, for Wolcott spent most of her time on the road. She was involved in "covering" the southeastern region — everything east of the Mississippi and south of the Mason-Dixon line. She travelled thousands of miles from project to project, to proposed sites of FSA work and to operating programs, photographing what caught her eye in between. She was often completely on her own in unfamiliar situations. She sometimes stayed with FSA contacts. The photograph of a baby being fed by a maid (Figure 3) was made at the home of Dr. Howard Odum, professor, author, and an authority on changing patterns of land use. Wolcott showed many of the contradictions in FSA operations: the family dropped from a program because of ill health; the contrast in attitudes between FSA professionals and their clients; the indignity to women of having familiar household equipment replaced by machinery whether or not they wanted it.

Wolcott learned from the photographs of others on the staff, especially from Dorothea Lange, and she contributed special qualities to the project. Her awareness of light often caused her to begin work at sunrise — the time when many of her subjects began work and also a time when the sun illuminated flat stretches of land with particular clarity. Other qualities of light, such as an abrupt and jagged beam through the ceiling of a packinghouse, were integral to a picture of what was going on inside, as the long shadows of late afternoon heightened women's wait for work at packinghouses while their children remained untended.

Wolcott spent a lot of time with the people she photographed, helping with the housework or dressing a baby, for example. She often had to respond to requests from local officials or to their suggestions of what she should photograph, but she soon learned how to deflect excessive official pressures. The one thing she never had was enough time to do her work as well as she wanted to do it.

She was bold in her ideas of what to photograph. Her photograph of a white man, his face contorted, thrusting money at a black woman dancing with a partner (Figure 9), must have taken nerve to make; there were many times where she confronted outrageous things straight in the eye. Her photographs acknowledged the fury of people at what they had to put up with, as in the little girls on the porch of the sharecropper's cabin in Mississippi (Figure 2). She was also well attuned to the beauty of the people she photographed — the lovely dignity of an Indian woman and her three sons; the grace of women waiting in line for pay; the warm affection expressed while making dinner in the midst of dirt and disrepair. Tenderness between mothers and daughters threaded through her work.

Very carefully, she showed the concrete details of work and the different ways work was organized: cottage industry, factory organization, cooperative work, part-time and full-time day labor. She took frequent note of young girls' many household responsibilities. Most often she photographed the work done by women young and old — "women's work," as well as field work performed by both men and women. She consistently noted women's volunteer work; the social services they provided: fundraising for a school, organizing a church picnic in an abandoned mining town. She clearly pointed out time and again that it was women who did the cooking and the serving while the men sat idly by. She made pictures of idleness — the arrogant lounging of a boss in a small southern town, or the dispirited young woman sunbathing in Miami.

Wolcott worked outside of her assigned region twice. In the dead of winter she travelled to Vermont, New Hampshire, and Maine, operating and maintaining her equipment in below-zero temperatures. There she made a photograph of a wistful, lone young woman at a New England town meeting (not reproduced here). She made the other trip shortly before she resigned. That assignment took her through the Midwest and into the Rocky Mountains. Her mountain landscapes were awesome, the wilderness splendid despite the mines and polluted lakes to be found in its midst.

Another assignment views the tobacco industry from the bedroom of a farmhouse where a family is processing their harvest, through tobacco warehouses, to a Chesterfield cigarette factory. Seen in sequence, her photographs present comprehensive, well-unified perspectives. One such sequence shows the diversified penetration of the coal industry in West Virginia through company housing, company stores, railroad tracks for a main street, enormous slag heaps smouldering indefinitely and the burnt-out ones where children steal fuel for their houses.

Taken as a whole, Marion Post Wolcott's photographs for the FSA represent professional photojournalism at its best. They carry on practices developed by worker-photographers and free-lance photographers in close concert with a social and political movement and inform that movement with fresh bursts of feminist insight and perception. Though Wolcott's subjects and photographs were lost from sight, this work has remained accessible, in the public domain. They provide a connection between the good work that preceded them, some of it destroyed, some of it yet to be recovered, and the growing body of work by socially-conscious groups of photographers around the world today.

Notes

1. Berenice A. Carroll, ed., *Liberating Women's History: Theoretical and Critical Essays* (Chicago: University of Illinois Press, 1976), p. 89.

2. Ellen Cantarow, *Moving the Mountain: Women Working for Social Change* (Old Westbury, N.Y.: Feminist Press, 1980), p. 155.

3. David Montgomery, *Workers Control in America* (New York: Cambridge University Press, 1979) pp. 91-95.

4. Doris Humphrey, *The Art of Making Dances* (New York: Grove Press, 1959), p. 38.

5. Artur Michel, "The Development of the New German Dance," in Virginia Stewart, ed., *Modern Dance* (New York, 1970) p. 11.

6. Terry Dennet, "England: The (Workers') Film and Photo League" in *Photography/Politics* (London: The Photography Workshop, 1979), pp. 101-117.

7. W. Korner and Stuber, "Germany: Die Arbeiter-Fotografie" in *Photography Politics* (London: The Photography Workshop, 1979), p. 74.

8. Josef Maria Eder, *History of Photography* (New York: Columbia University Press, 1945), pp. ix-xii, and 720-728.

9. Norman Stevens, "More From The Group Theatre," *New Theatre and Film,* July 1936, p. 5.

10. Milton Meltzer, *Dorothea Lange: A Photographer's Life* (New York: Farrar, Straus, Giroux, 1978), p. 204.

11. Tim N. Gidal, *Modern Photo Journalism: Origins and Evolution, 1910-1933.* (New York: Macmillan, 1973). Gisele Freund was catapulted into her career on the occasion of her escape to France in 1933. A novice with a camera but active in the student outcry against early Nazi atrocities, she fled to Paris with documentary evidence of Hitler's rise to power.

12. For more on women photographers see *Women of Photography: An Historical Survey* (San Francisco Museum of Art, 1975). The bibliography is a good starting point for further inquiry.

13. Russell Campbell, "America: The (Workers') Film and Photo League" in *Photography/Politics,* p. 97.

Photographs of
Marion Post Wolcott

1. Members of the family of a Negro wage hand on his porch of the Knowlton plantation. Sacks of cotton are piled on the porch. *LC-USF 33 30572-M3. Perthshire, Miss. October, 1939*

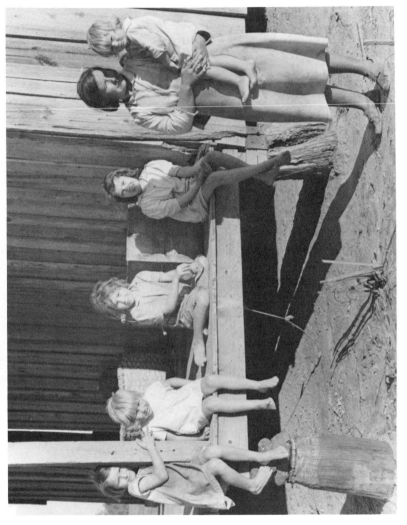

2. Members of the Melody Tillery family, a rural rehabilitation client family, on the porch of their home. *LC-USF 33 30333-M4.* Troy (vicinity), Ala. May, 1939

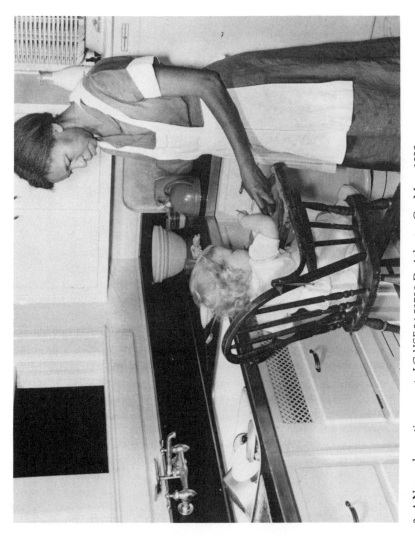

3. A Negro domestic servant. *LC-USF 34 51738-D*. Atlanta, Ga. May, 1939

4. A woman migrant packing house worker and her oldest child preparing supper. She has three other children. *LC-USF 34 50904-D.* Belle Glade, Fla. January, 1939

5. A Mexican woman picking cotton on the Knowlton plantation. She is one of the seasonal laborers brought in from Texas for the cotton-picking season. *LC USF 33 30536-M2*. Perthshire, Miss., in the Delta area. October, 1939

6. A woman from New Jersey picking beans. Hampers are very heavy and must be moved along as one picks. *LC-USF 34 51050-E.* Homestead, Fla. January, 1939

7. Day laborers on the Hopson plantation. They are hired in nearby towns and get paid at the rate of 75¢ to $1 per day plus transportation. *LC-USF 34 54980-C*. Clarksdale, Miss., in the Delta area. August, 1940.

8. Italian workers from Trenton and nearby area grading and bunching asparagus in the packing house at Starkey farms. *LC-USF 34-57559-D*. Morrisville, Penna. May, 1941

9. Jitterbugging in a Negro juke joint on Saturday evening in the Delta area. *LC-USF 34 52596-D.* Clarksdale, Miss. November, 1939

8

Two Washes in the Morning and a Bridge Party at Night: The American Housewife between the Wars

———— RUTH SCHWARTZ COWAN ————

The "feminine mystique" has been part of American cultural life for quite a long while, far longer than Betty Friedan and others have believed; its origins go back to the period after the First World War, not the Second.[1] Political tracts very often idealize the past, and *The Feminine Mystique* was no exception; the norms for American women between the wars were not nearly as bold and adventurous as Betty Friedan would like to think.[2] The cult of true womanhood—that marvelous Victorian combination of Christian sentimentalism and sexual repression[3]—had indeed died by the early 20's, but the ideology that replaced it was, to all intents and purposes, the same "feminine mystique" that Friedan attributes to the 40's and 50's. Whatever it was that trapped educated American women in their kitchens, babbling at babies and worrying about color combinations for the bathroom, the trap was laid during the roaring 20's, not the quiet 50's.

Friedan bases her appraisal of the period between the wars on the fiction that appeared in women's magazines. To some extent her appraisal is correct; those stories often dealt with adventurous, athletic and unconventional women—many of them pursuing a career. But Friedan neglects two aspects of those stories that are just as significant: the career girls were always single and the unconventional ladies were always attended by a truly unconventional number of servants. The housewives who were reading those stories could not possibly have seen themselves mirrored therein; in fact, those stories, with their exotic settings and fanciful plots, were frankly escapist literature. When they weren't about strong-minded career girls, they were often about baronesses, debutantes and Hollywood stars. Why tastes changed after World War II, why—as Friedan accurately noted —postwar fiction tended to be about housewives and not baronesses, is anyone's guess, but the fact remains that the fiction in the women's magazines in the 20's and 30's is not a reliable indicator of the attitudes and problems of the vast majority of American women. This does not mean, however, that the mass circulation women's magazines are not a reliable source for social history, but it does suggest that we should look at the non-

Reprinted from *Women's Studies* 1976, Vol. 3, pp. 147-172. ©Gordon and Breach Science Publishers Ltd., Printed in Great Britain. Used with permission.

fiction to find a more accurate reflection of what was happening to American women — not in fields of glorious endeavor, but in front of their kitchen sinks, which is where they happened to be. In the advertisements, the informative articles and the advice columns of *The Ladies' Home Journal,* *McCall's, American Home,* and other similar magazines, a careful reader can watch the feminine mystique descending upon the minds and hearts of American women during the two decades between the wars.

That mystique, like any system of cultural norms, was a complex and subtle affair, continuous with previous ideologies, yet clearly different from them. The mystique makers of the 20's and 30's believed that women were purely domestic creatures, that the goal of each normal woman's life was the acquisition of a husband, a family and a home, that women who worked outside their homes did so only under duress or because they were "odd" (for which read "ugly," "frustrated," "compulsive," or "single") and that this state of affairs was sanctioned by the tenets of religion, biology, psychology and patriotism. Hardly a surprising ideology to be found between the covers of women's magazines, past or present. The feminine mystique differed from previous value systems in its prescriptions about the details — who might reside in that household, how many children that happy family might contain, what the relationship between husband and wife, mother and children, housewife and household ideally might be.

The ideal housewife of the 20's and 30's did not have servants, or to put it another way, the servants she had were electrical, not human. In *The Ladies' Home Journal* for January 1, 1918 "The Householder's Dream of a Happy New Year," had been a cartoon: "Mandy Offers to Stay for Life and Takes Less Wages."[4] Throughout the monthly issues that year, in advertisement after advertisement, Mandy was repeatedly depicted: if you wanted to sell flannel baby's clothes to the readers of *The Ladies' Home Journal* you drew a baby held by a nursemaid; if you wanted to sell fabric, you drew a maid pinning up hems; shampoo — a maid washing her mistress's hair; talcum powder — "Nurse powders baby;" washing soap — a laundress hanging up clothes. All this in a year when, according to the editorial columns of the magazine, domestic help was scarce because of the wartime restrictions on immigration and the attractive salaries offered to women in industry.[5] By the time a decade had passed Mandy had retreated from the advertisements; by 1928 she had almost entirely disappeared into the realms of fiction. In that year if you wanted to sell radiators to the readers of *The Ladies' Home Journal* you drew a housewife playing on the floor with her children; if you wanted to promote supermarkets, women were shown doing their own shopping; cleansing powder — a housewife wiping her own sink; floor wax — an elegant lady polishing her own floor; hand cream — "They'll never know you mopped the floor yourself;" washing machines — "Two washes in the morning and a bridge party at night."

Even before the Depression struck, at a time when prosperity was widespread, American advertisers idealized the woman who was going to buy their product as a housewife, well dressed, to be sure, neatly coiffed and elegantly manicured, but a housewife who cheerfully and resolutely did her housework herself. The only servant in a full-page ad depicting every aspect of housework, an ad for Ivory Soap which appeared in *The Ladies' Home Journal* in 1933, was a confinement nurse.[6] Mandy had not disappeared entirely. She was still an important character in women's magazine fiction. *American Home* still published house plans that included a maid's room,[7] and *Parents' Magazine* still worried about the ways in which servants influence children,[8] but the days when a housewife of moderate means fully expected that she would have at least a maid of all work, and probably a laundress and nursemaid, were clearly over.[9]

On the matter of servants the feminine mystique was a reversal of older attitudes. The servantless household had once been regarded as a trial and a tribulation; now it was regarded as a condition dearly to be wished. Adequate household help had always been a problem in America and women's magazines had repeatedly offered advice to housewives who were, for one unfortunate reason or another, coping with their homes single-handedly. The emphasis in those articles was often on the word, "unfortunate;" the housewife was told, for example, that if help is scarce, it is easiest to serve children the same food that adults are eating, and at the same time — although clearly it would be better for their digestion and your temperament if they ate with a nursemaid in the nursery; hopefully the servant shortage would soon pass.[10] Occasionally a lone voice (often male) would remind the housewife of her patriotic obligations (wouldn't it be more democratic to fire the servants and have the family pitch in and do the work?) or would appeal to the higher reaches of her intellect (think how much chemistry you could learn if you would only do the cooking yourself!)[11] but the housewives apparently managed — somehow — to resist such blandishments. Housework was regarded as a chore, albeit a necessary one, and if it could be palmed off on someone else, so much the better. If one can gauge from the content and tone of advertisements, advice columns and letters to the editor, the American housewife clearly preferred to employ servants whenever economic and demographic conditions permitted her to do so.

This attitude began to change in the years after the First World War. Housework was no longer regarded as a chore, but as an expression of the housewife's personality and of her affection for her family. In past times the housewife had been judged by the way she organized her servants; now she would be judged by the way she organized her kitchen. If she were strong and proud of herself her workroom would be filled with labor-saving devices, meticulously cleaned and color coordinated; if she were insecure, frustrated and lonely, woe to her kitchen — it would be disorderly, dim and uninviting.[12] When the kitchen had been dominated by servants it had been a dreary room, often in the basement of the house. Now that the kitchen had become the housewife's domain it had to be prettied up.

Time was when kitchens were big and dark, for keeping house was a gloomy business. . . . But now! Gay colors are the order of the day. Red pots and pans! Blue gas stoves! . . . It is a rainbow, in which the cook sings at her work and never thinks of household tasks as drudgery.[13]

Laundering had once been just laundering; now it was an expression of love. The new bride could speak her affection by washing tell-tale gray out of her husband's shirts.[14] Feeding the family had once been just feeding the family; now it was a way to communicate deep-seated emotions.

When the careful housekeeper turns from the preparation of company dinner to the routine of family meals, she will know that prime rib roast, like peach ice cream, *is a wonderful stimulant to family loyalty*, but that it is not absolutely necessary for every day.[15] (Italics mine.)

Diapering was no longer just diapering, but a time to build the baby's sense of security; cleaning the bathroom sink was not just cleaning, but an exercise for the maternal instincts, protecting the family from disease.

Clearly, tasks of this emotional magnitude could not be relegated to servants. The servantless household may have been an economic necessity in the 20's, as the supply of servants declined and their wages rose, but for the first time that necessity was widely regarded as a potential virtue. The servantless housewife was no longer portrayed as "unfortunate;" she was happy, revelling in her modern home and in the opportunities for creative expression that it provided.

The fact is that the American home was never a more satisfying place than it is today. Science and invention have outfitted it with a great range of conveniences and comforts. . . . All this is, in the main, women's work. For the first time in the world's history it is possible for a nation's women in general to have or to be able to look forward to having homes and the means of furnishing them in keeping with their instinctive longings. The women of America are to be congratulated, not only in the opportunity but because of the manner in which they are responding to it. When the record is finally written this may stand as their greatest contribution.[16]

And what opportunities there were! In earlier years American women had been urged to treat housework as a science; now they were being urged to treat it as a craft, a creative endeavor. The ideal kitchen of the prewar period had been white and metallic—imitating the laboratory. The ideal kitchen of the postwar period was color coordinated—imitating the artist's studio. Each meal prepared in that ideal kitchen was a color composition in and of itself: "Make Meals More Appetizing by Serving Foods that Have

Pleasing Contrast of Color."[17] Ready-made clothes could be disguised by adding individual hand sewn touches; patterned towels could be chosen to match the decorative scheme in the bathroom; old furniture could be repainted and restyled. The new housewife would be an artist, not a drudge. The new housewife would also be a consumer, not a producer.

A woman's virtue and excellence as a housewife do not in these days depend upon her skill in spinning and weaving. An entirely different task presents itself, more difficult and more complex, requiring an infinitely wider range of ability, and for those very reasons more interesting and inspiring.[18]

That task was, of course, buying. The words come from an article about shopping for linens, but they could have been taken from any one of the numerous articles on wise buying—clothes, sheets, rugs, blankets, silverware, appliances—that began to appear regularly in women's magazines through the 20's.[19] In earlier days the young housewife had to be taught to make things well; in the 20's she had to be taught to buy things well. Magazines and manufacturers created new devices to teach her how to be a "professional" buyer: product testing services, gadget buying services, home shopping guides, home demonstrators, new packages, new grading systems. Apparently the devices worked; scores of sociologists and economists have noted that consumption is now the most important social function still performed by families.[20] Unlike so many familial functions, consumption has been expanding, not contracting; the 20's appear to be the decade in which the expansion began.[21]

In her physical appearance the new housewife looked quite different from her older counterparts. In earlier days the ideal American matron had been plump; corset makers were happy to send her garments that would add inches to her *derrière* if she were unfashionably skinny. After World War I the corset makers changed their tune; the emphasis was on reducing, not increasing. By the end of the 20's advertising campaigns were predicated on the American woman's passion for slenderizing: Sunkist oranges are nutritious, and non-fattening; Fleischman's yeast will aid your digestion and prevent constipation if you are dieting; Postum should be substituted for coffee while dieting because it calms the nerves.[22] By the end of the 20's articles about exercising to keep fit had become a regular feature in *The Ladies' Home Journal*; before the war they had been unknown.[23]

She was thin, this ideal lady, and she was also elegant; her hands were long and well manicured, so were her legs. If she worked hard at her housework during hot weather, she remained "personally irreproachable"— thanks to cream deodorants. She wore a fashionable wool suit with a fur collar to visit her local A & P and applied Pompeian Night Cream to keep from looking tired after an exhausting night of bridge. If life was creating problems for her she knew that one or two dabs of Raquel Orange Blossom

Fragrance would guarantee eternal bliss. This particular form of hidden persuasion, the notion that cosmetics can guarantee happiness, seems to have been invented in the 20's.[24] The cosmetics industry must have entered a boom phase after World War I — if the number and size of its advertisements are any gauge of its economic well-being.

Child rearing was the single most important task that this new housewife had to perform. Experts agreed that a child raised by nursemaids was a child to be pitied. The young boy tended by servants would never learn the upright, go-getting resourcefulness of the truly American child, would never become a useful member of the egalitarian republic, and would — horror of horrors — probably fail in the business world.[25] His sister, deprived of the example of her mother, would not know how to manage the myriad appliances of the modern kitchen; she would never learn how to decorate a pineapple salad, or how to wash silk underwear in an electric machine, and consequently — horror of horrors — she would never attract and keep a truly American husband.[26] Even more worrisome was the thought that children raised by nursemaids might never reach adulthood because they would not be tended by persons who were familiar with the latest medical and nutritional information. American mothers, anxious about infant mortality, were advised not to leave their offspring in the care of illiterate, untutored servant girls. In 1918, the editor of *The Ladies' Home Journal* rejoiced in the knowledge that, if present trends continued, the post-war generation of American children would be the first generation to be raised by its mothers; they would be healthy in mind and body and, as a result, they would lift the sagging fortunes of the race.[27] There was very little Freudianism in this new child psychology; mothers were to take over the rearing of their children, not because of the psychological traumas of separation, but because mothers were likely to be better informed and better educated than nursemaids.[28]

Spending time with her children seems to have been as much a moral imperative for the housewife of the 20's as spending time on Christian good works was for her mother. There were no more socks to be knitted for missionaries, or elderly sick relatives to be visited, or Bible classes to attend; instead there were basketball games to watch with her children, card games to play with them, and piano lessons to help them with. Togetherness had become a fact for middle-class Americans long before the editors of *McCall's* coined the term in 1954.[29]

I accommodate my entire life to my little girl. She takes three music lessons a week and I practice with her forty minutes a day. I help her with her school work and go to dancing school with her. . . .

There are now never ten days that go by without my either visiting the children's school or getting in touch with their teacher. I have given up church work and club work since the children came. I always like to be here when they come home from school so that I can keep in touch with their games and their friends. . . .

I certainly have a harder job than my mother did; everything tends to weaken the parents' influence. But we do it by spending time with our children. I've always been a pal with my daughter, and my husband spends a lot of time with the boy. We all go to basketball games together and to the State Fair in the summer. . . .

We used to belong to the Country Club but resigned from that when the children came, and bought a car instead. That is something we can all enjoy together.[30]

The advent of the Depression apparently accelerated this trend. Magazine editors noted that families were being forced to rely upon their own devices for entertainment; the end of prosperity meant the end of meals in restaurants and parties in hotels. *American Home* published essays on turning basements into playrooms; *The Ladies' Home Journal* discovered the barbecue; *Parents' Magazine* began denoting with an asterisk the articles that would be of interest to progressive fathers (i.e. those who wished to take a hand in rearing their own children).[31]

Life was not always a bed of roses in the model American household, but if the lady of the house had any complaints, she refrained, whenever possible, from discussing them with her husband. "She must never bring her troubles to the table;" dinner time was a moment of sweetness and light in her husband's weary day; he came home from the office to be greeted with a cheering cup of Steero bouillon; his children were scrubbed ("Self respect thrives on soap and water") and anxious to tell him about their day in school (they have done well because they did not forget to have hot cereal for breakfast).[32] Woe unto the housewife who would mar this scene by reminding her husband that he had failed to clean his hair out of the sink that morning – or other such domestic trivia. She was almost always cheerful, this modern housewife; in fact, the constellation of emotions that she was allowed to display in magazines was really rather limited. She could be happy, loving, tender or affectionate; occasionally she was worried, but she was never, never angry. What, after all, did she have to be angry about?

Only one anxious emotion ever creased her brow – guilt, she felt guilty a good deal of the time, and when she wasn't feeling guilty she was feeling embarrassed: guilty if her infant didn't gain enough weight, embarrassed if her friends arrived to find that her sink was clogged, guilty if her children went to school in soiled clothes, guilty if she didn't eradicate all the germs behind the bathroom sink, embarrassed if her nieces and nephews accused her of having body odor, guilty if her son was a laggard in school, guilty if her daughter was not popular with the crowd (her mother having failed to keep her dresses properly ironed).[33] In earlier times a woman could have been made to feel guilty if she had abandoned her children or been too free with her affections. In the years between the wars American women apparently began to feel guilty if their children were seen in public in scuffed shoes. Between the two sources of anxiety there seems a world of difference. Advertisers may have stimulated these guilt feelings, but they could not have created them singlehandedly; the guilt must have been there or advertisers would not have found that they could be successful by playing upon it.

In 1937 Emily Post coined a name for the new American housewife: Mrs. Three-in-One, the lady who is cook, waitress and hostess at her own dinner parties.[34] In almost every essential, Mrs. Three-in-One was no different from the housewives that Betty Friedan described in *The Feminine Mystique.* She was fairly well educated and somewhat sophisticated. Her family was smaller than her mother's, but more attention was lavished upon it. Her infants were weighed every day and their nutritional intake carefully planned. The development of her youngsters was carefully watched and the social affairs of her adolescents carefully — but discreetly — supervised. She drove a car, played bridge and took vacations. She had very few servants, or none at all. In the morning she served her family a light breakfast; lunch was a can of soup for herself. She shopped by telephone, or in a small supermarket, bought most of her clothes ready-made, wore silk stockings, and tied her hair in a neat scarf when doing housework. She could nurse a child through the measles, repair a dripping faucet, decorate a kitchen, discourse on vitamins, give a speech before her ladies' club or entertain her husband's business associates — all with equal facility. She was always cheerful, healthy, up-to-date, and gracious, never angry, frustrated, sick, old-fashioned or — perish the thought — gainfully employed. She was content with her life and had no doubts about her femininity; if she wished for anything it was another appliance or a better rug for the living room. She had the vote, but rarely discussed politics; believed in divorce, but was not herself divorced; practiced birth control but did not discuss sex with her daughter.

No doubt there were more Mrs. Three-in-Ones after World War II than there had been before. The feminine mystique probably became more pervasive after 1945; before that it was a social ideology to which only the middle classes — perhaps only the upper middle classes — could possibly pretend. But the ideologies of the upper middle classes eventually percolate down to everyone else in our society and I would venture to guess that that is precisely what happened to the feminine mystique in the late 40's and early 50's. As families moved up the economic and social ladder the signs of their success were the signs that the mystique had arrived on their doorstep: the wife stops working; the house becomes neater; new rooms are added; the children wear ready-made clothes; they stay in school longer, take piano and ballet lessons; slenderizing becomes a passion; nails must be manicured; choices must be made between muslin and percale sheets, double-oven or single-oven stoves, wool or nylon carpeting. The mother who had once complained about back-breaking toil to make ends meet now has a daughter who complains that despite her appliances she still works 16 hours a day, seven days a week — and doesn't quite know why. This pattern must have been repeated in millions of American homes after World War II, but the underlying ideology that produced it was formed in the decades between the wars.

Social ideologies are responsive to changes in economic and demographic conditions. The advent of the feminine mystique was a major ideological change and there must have been major social and economic changes that produced it. Friedan believed that the mystique arose after the Second World War and consequently her list of causal conditions—higher education for women, widespread prosperity, domestic disruptions attendant upon the Depression and the war, functionalism and Freudianism in the social sciences, the advent of new marketing and advertising techniques— warrants reexamination. One crucial aspect of the new ideology was its emphasis on the servantless household; changes in the supply of domestic servants are likely, therefore, to have been an important precondition.

Household labor was generally performed by five different types of workers in the early years of the 20th century: the housewife herself, her children (primarily her daughters), other female relatives (a maiden aunt perhaps, or a grandmother), dayworkers, and servants who lived in. Data on changes in the number of any of those types of labor are rather hard to come by, or are likely to be quite unreliable when we have them. Domestic servants are one of the most difficult categories of workers to enumerate as their labor is often transient, or part-time, or unreported. In the early decades of this century social commentators believed that in every category (except the housewife herself) the supply of labor was declining, and the data that are available tend to support this conclusion. Certainly wages for paid household employees were rising. Lynds estimates that in 1890 a live-in cook received about $4.00 a week in wages (this does not count the expense of room and board); in 1920 this would have increased to $25.[35] The Lynds estimate that in 1924 a single day's work for a day laborer cost the Muncie housewife approximately what a week's labor would have cost her mother.[36] Similarly the Lynds found that the business-class housewives in Muncie had roughly half the number of household servants that their mothers had had; according to the Federal Census for Indiana, the number of families per servant increased from 13.5 in 1890 to 30.5 in 1920.[37] Using nationwide statistics as a guide, it appears that most of this increase occurred in the decade from 1910 to 1920; the number of families per servant was roughly 10 in 1900, 10 in 1910 and 16 in 1920.[38] These data do not, of course, tell us anything specific about the *supply* of labor, but they are suggestive; if wages were rising and the proportion of workers to households falling, contemporary social critics may have been right in their assumption that the supply of household servants was declining because of the twin pressures generated by fewer immigrants and more attractive industrial wages.[39] Data on the other two categories of household help, children and female relatives, are, to all intents and purposes, nonexistent, but here again the remarks of social critics may be suggestive. Many observers noted tendencies toward less available labor from those sources as well: grandparents were not as frequently moving in with their married children (in part because houses were smaller); grown daughters seemed inclined to have apartments and jobs of their own before marriage; maiden aunts, like their unmarried nieces, were apparently living alone and liking it more.[40]

The odd thing about these social commentaries is that they are recurrent American themes. Household help has always been a sore point in American life; servants were constantly disappearing from the labor market or otherwise behaving recalcitrantly, and the daughters of the middle classes, if they weren't actually out working at Macy's, were often balking at household labor. Yet none of the other periods in which this scarcity of household labor was proclaimed produced an ideology like the feminine mystique, an ideology which put a premium on the servantless household. Consequently we must assume that the declining supply of servants (paid or unpaid) although it must have been part of the preconditions leading to that ideology, was by no means the whole story.

The story becomes more complete if we look at what was happening to domestic technology during those years. For the first time in the history of the republic there was, after 1918, a viable alternative to the labor of housewives, domestic servants, maiden aunts and adolescent daughters — the machine. It was a classic American solution: when in doubt, try a machine. For several years before the war, home economists had been pressing for the rationalization of household labor. After the war, as electrification and assembly-line production of consumer goods increased, that rationalization seemed to be at hand.

Almost every aspect of household labor was revolutionized during the 20's; in good part this was due to electrification. In 1907 (the first year for which data are available) only 8% of dwellings in the U.S. had electric service; by the time we entered the war this had risen to 24.3% and by 1925 more than half the homes in America (53.2%) had been wired. If we consider the data for urban and rural non-farm dwellings the figures are even more striking: almost half of those homes had been electrified by 1920 (47.4%) and more than two-thirds by 1925 (69.4%).[41] During this period the price of electricity fell from 9.5 cents per kilowatt hour to 7.68 cents (for an average monthly use of 25 kilowatt hours, which is the order of magnitude then used in homes).[42] The amount of money spent on mechanical appliances grew from $145 millions in 1909 to $667 millions in 1927, an increase of almost 500%, while at the same time expenditure on clothing increased only 250% and on furniture, 300%; similarly the dollar value (in current prices) of electric household appliances produced for domestic consumption soared from $11.8 millions in 1909 to $146.3 millions in 1927.[43]

With the spread of electrification came the spread of electrical appliances: a small motor to power the family sewing machine, a fan, an electric iron (the earliest models had no thermostats, but they were still easier to use than the irons heated on cooking stoves), a percolator, perhaps a toaster, a waffle iron or portable heater. Automatic refrigerators went on the market in 1916 (at roughly $900); in 1921, 5,000 units were sold, but by 1929 that figure had risen to 890,000 units and the price had fallen to roughly $180.[44] A study of 100 Ford employees living in Detroit in 1929 revelead that 98 families had an electric iron, 80 had electric sewing machines, 49 had electric washing machines, and 21 had electric vacuum cleaners.[45] The benefits of technology were clearly not limited to the upper middle class.

As household habits were being changed by the advent of electricity so eating habits were being changed by the advent of the metal can, the refrigerated railroad car and new notions about diet. Before World War I an average American family ate three extraordinarily hefty meals a day.

Steak, roasts, macaroni, Irish potatoes, sweet potatoes, turnips, cole slaw, fried apples, and stewed tomatoes, with Indian pudding, rice, cake or pie for dessert. This was the winter repertoire of the average family that was not wealthy, and we swapped about from one combination to another, using pickles and chow-chow to make the familiar starchy food relishing.... Breakfast, pork chops or steak with fried potatoes, buckwheat cakes, and hot bread; lunch, a hot roast and potatoes; supper, same roast cold.[46]

In 1908 an article appeared in *The Ladies'Home Journal* describing an ordinary family lunch; were that meal to be served today it would be regarded as a state banquet.[47] By the middle of the 20's such meals were no longer the rule: breakfast had been reduced to eggs and/or cereal; lunch was essentially one course, or perhaps soup and a sandwich; dinner was usually no more than three. Commercially canned fruits and vegetables made variations in the classic winter menu possible. Some canned goods (primarily peas and corn) had been on the market since the middle of the 19th century, but by 1918 the American housewife with sufficient means could have purchased almost any fruit or vegetable, and quite a surprising array of ready-made meals, in a can: Campbell's soups, Heinz's spaghetti (already cooked and ready to serve), Libby's corned beef and chili corn carne (heated directly in its package), Stokeley's peas, corn, string beans, lima beans, tomatoes, succotash, LeChoy's bean sprouts, Beechnut's chili sauce, vinegar, and mustard, Purity Cross's creamed chicken, welsh rarebit, lobster à la newburg, Van Camp's pork and beans, Libby's olives, sauerkraut and Vienna sausages, DelMonte's peaches, pineapples, apricots and plums. In the morning the American housewife of the 20's could have offered her family some of the new cold cereals (Kellogg's Corn Flakes, or Krumbles, or Post's Grape Nuts Flakes); if her family wanted pancakes she could have prepared them with Aunt Jemima's pancake mix. Recipes in the women's magazines in the 20's utilized canned goods as a matter of course: canned peaches in peach blancmange, canned peas in creamed finnan haddie. Very often the recipes did not even include the familiar rubric, "canned or fresh," but simply assumed that "canned" would be used. By the middle of the 20's home canning was on its way to becoming a lost art; the business-class wives of Muncie reported that they rarely put up anything, except an occasional jelly or batch of tomatoes, whereas their mothers had once spent the better part of the summer and fall canning.[48] Increased utilization of refrigerated railroad cars also meant that fresh fruits and vegetables were appearing in markets at reasonable prices all through the year.[49] Fewer family meals were being taken at home; restaurants and businessmen's clubs downtown, cafeterias in schools and factories, after-school activities for teenagers—all meant that fewer members of the family were home for meals.[50] Cooking was easier, and there was less of it to be done.

Part of the reason that cooking became easier was that the coal or wood-burning stove began to disappear. After World War I the women's magazines only carried advertisements for stoves that used natural gas, kerosene, gasoline or electricity; in Muncie in 1924 two out of three homes cooked with gas.[51] The burdensome chore of keeping a coal stove lit and regulated —and keeping the kitchen free of the resultant soot—had probably been eliminated from most American homes by the 30's. The change in routine that was predicated on the change from coal stoves to oil or gas stoves (electric stoves were inefficient and rarely used in this period) was profound; aside from the elimination of such chores as loading the coal and removing the ashes, the new stoves were simply much easier to regulate. One writer in *The Ladies' Home Journal* estimated that kitchen cleaning was reduced by one-half when coal stoves were eliminated.[52] As the coal stove disappeared from the kitchen, the coal-fired furnace also started disappearing from the basement. By the late 20's coal furnaces were no longer being advertised in home equipment magazines and homeowners were being urged to convert to oil or gas or electricity, "so that no one has to go into the basement anymore." A good number of American homes were centrally heated by the mid-20's; in Zanesville, Ohio 48% of the roughly 11,000 homes had basement furnaces in 1924.[53]

As the routines of meal preparation became less burdensome in the 20's, so did the routines of personal hygiene. The early 20's was the time of the bathroom mania; more and more bathrooms were installed in older homes and new homes were being built with them as a matter of course. Sixty-one percent of those 11,000 homes in Zanesville had indoor plumbing and bathrooms in 1924.[54] In Muncie in 1890 ninety-five out of every hundred families took baths by lugging a zinc tub into the kitchen and filling it with water that had been pumped by hand and heated on the stove; by 1924 three out of four Muncie homes had running water.[55] The rapid increase in the number of bathrooms after World War I was the result of changes in the production of bathroom fixtures. Before the war those fixtures were not standardized and porcelain tubs were routinely made by hand; after the war industrialization swept over the bathroom industry: cast-iron enamelware went into mass production and fittings were standardized. In 1921 the dollar value of the production of enamelled sanitary fixtures was $2.4

million, the same that it had been in 1915. By 1923, just two years later, that figure had doubled to $4.8 million; it rose again, to $5.1 million, in 1925.[56] The first one-piece, recessed, double-shell cast iron enamelled bathtub was put on the market in the early 20's; by the time a decade had past the standard American bathroom had achieved its standard American form: a small room, with a recessed tub, tiled floors and walls, brass plumbing, a single-unit toilet, and an enclosed sink.[57] This bathroom was relatively easy to clean, and — needless to say — it helped revolutionize habits of personal cleanliness in America; the body-odor fetish of the 30's can be partly attributed to the bathroom fetish of the 20's.

Similarly, the "tell-tale gray" syndrome of the 30's had its roots in the changing technologies of clothes washing. Soap powders and flakes arrived on the market in the early 20's, which meant that bars of soap no longer had to be scraped and boiled to make soap paste. Electric washing machines took a good part of the drudgery out of the washing process, although they required a considerable amount of time and attention to operate, as they did not go through their cycles automatically and did not spin dry.[58] There was more variation in methods of handling household laundry than in any other domestic chore; the Lynds noted that on the same street in Muncie, families of the same economic class were using quite different washing technologies: hand washing, electric machines, commercial laundries, laundresses who worked "in," and laundresses who worked "out."[59] Advertisements in the women's magazines do not give a uniform picture either: sometimes showing old-fashioned tubs, sometimes depicting machines. Commercial household laundries entered a boom period in the 20's; they began to expand their services (wet wash, rough dry, etc.) and began to do more personal laundry (as opposed to flat work) than they had in past years;[60] nationwide, the number of power laundries doing more than $5,000 business a year rose from 4,881 in 1919 to 6,776 in 1929, and their receipts more than doubled.[61]

While the processes of cooking, heating, cleaning, lighting and washing were revolutionized, other processes — just as much a part of the housewife's daily routine — were changing, but not quite as drastically. The corner grocer, the door-to-door merchant and the curb-side market were slowly being replaced by the telephone and the supermarket. In 1918 *The Ladies' Home Journal* referred to supermarkets as "The New Stores Without Clerks;"[62] by 1928 there were 2,600 Piggly Wiggly markets across the country.[63] Telephone shopping had become routine in many households by the end of the 20's. Instead of purchasing whole cases of canned goods or bushels of apples and onions to be stored and used over the months, housewives were now telephoning daily orders and having them hand-delivered: 1 head of lettuce, 1 pat of cream cheese, 1 can of string beans, ¼-pound of mushrooms.[64] Hardwood floors were replaced by linoleum; instead of tedious hand polishing, only a mop, soap and water were now required. Heavy cast iron pots and pans were giving way to aluminum and Pyrex. Ready-made clothes were no longer thought "poor-folksy;" by 1928 a good part of each monthly issue of the better women's magazines was devoted to photographs and drawings of clothing that could be bought off the rack. Home sewing, home mending, the once ubiquitous practice of making over dresses—all became vestigial crafts; young women were now being taught how to shop for clothes, not how to make them.[65] Home baking also disappeared; the bakers in Muncie estimated that, depending upon the season, they supplied between 55% and 70% of the city's homes with bread.[66]

Many factors must have contributed to the revolution in household production that occurred during the 20's. On the whole those were prosperous years and prosperity made it possible for many people to buy new equipment for their homes. Vast industrial facilities which were created during the war were converted to the production of consumer goods during peacetime. The apparent shortage of servants and the rise in their wages must have encouraged householders to try the new appliances more readily than they would otherwise have done. The growth of magazines devoted to the interests of modern housewives no doubt encouraged the trend, as did the growth of consumer credit arrangements. Whatever the causes were, the event itself seems indisputable; profound changes in household technology occurred between the end of the First World War and the beginning of the Depression—whether we measure those changes by the number of individual innovations or by the rate of their diffusion. Certain changes did occur after the Second World War: the standard American kitchen achieved its present form, with standardized fixtures and continuous counter space; the automatic washing machine (which could spin and go through its cycles itself) became widespread; the laundromat replaced the commercial laundry; the supermarket replaced the grocery store; frozen foods to some extent replaced canned foods; the dishwasher and the home dryer became more reasonable in price; the ranch home with its open room plan became more popular. However, all those changes pale to insignificance when compared to the change from oil lamps to electric lamps, coal stoves to gas stoves, coal furnaces to gas and oil furnaces, kitchen heating to central heating, outdoor plumbing to indoor plumbing, not having a bathroom to having one, canning tomatoes to buying canned tomatoes, making dresses to buying them, baking bread to buying it, living with servants and living without them.

Thus, a fundamental productive process was revolutionized by the introduction of new technologies; almost simultaneously an ideology developed which insured that those new technologies would be used in very specific and rather limited ways. In the early days the new technology could have been used to communalize housework. The first vacuum cleaners were large mobile units; they were brought into a home by a team of skilled operators to take over the housewife's cleaning chores.[67] The new washing machines could have been placed in communal laundries where paid employees would take over the housewife's washing chores, and the editors of *The*

Ladies' Home Journal advocated that this be done.[68] Those same editors also advocated retention of the wartime communal kitchens, so that the wasteful process of cooking each family's meals separately would be eliminated.[69] Many of the early luxury apartment houses had, along with elevators, communal nurseries on their roofs.[70] Within a very few years, needless to say, those visions of communal housekeeping had died a not very surprising death; this was America, after all, not Soviet Russia. The new domestic technology, communalized or not, could have freed American women to do productive work outside their homes; the growth of the feminine mystique insured that they would not do it.

The advertising industry cooperated in this endeavor, even if it did not invent it. As the size and number of women's magazines increased in the 20's, the amount and the variety of advertising increased also. The American woman was becoming the American consumer *par excellence;* automobile manufacturers, cigarette producers, life insurance companies (not to speak of the advertisers whose wares were of traditional interest to women) all discovered the virtues of the women's magazines. The magazines, of course, found ways to encourage this custom. They used their non-advertising space to advertise in subtler ways: listing new products by their brand names, adopting editorial policies that encouraged women to buy, creating "shop at home" columns for mail-order purchasers, sponsoring consumption oriented contests.

> Home building, home decoration and furnishing, *home making,* in fact, is the most outstanding phase of modern civilization. . . . The magazines of today have played an important part in this; they have carried on an intensive sincere campaign for better homes. But an even greater part has been that of the manufacturers. . . . Not only has beauty and convenience and efficiency of home equipment been carefully studied to meet the demand of the modern housewife . . . but back of all this stands the guarantee of the maker of his goods.[71]

Late in the 20's those earnest manufacturers (and their sincere advertising agents) discovered that they could sell more gadgets by appealing to the housewife's fears than by appealing to her strengths; advertisements stopped being informative and started pandering to status-seeking and guilt. An advertisement for soap in 1908 was likely to talk about the clean factory in which the soap was produced and the pure ingredients from which it was made; a similar advertisement in 1928 was likely to talk about the psychological trauma experienced by children who go to school with soiled clothes.[72] It would be difficult to prove that manufacturers and advertising agencies invented the feminine mystique, but it would be equally difficult to deny that they did everything they reasonably could to encourage it.

In a quite different way the proponents of the child health movement also helped to encourage the mystique. The infant mortality rate in the United States in 1915 was 100 for every 1,000 live births, one of the highest in the world. There were very few families who were not touched, in some way, by the spectre of infant death. After the war, with its discouraging reports about the health of young recruits, various public agencies began a concerted effort to improve the health and the physique of America's young people, particularly by disseminating information about proper nutrition and proper care of children during illness. The women's magazines were prime agents in the dissemination of this information; *The Ladies' Home Journal,* for example, started a Babies Registry so that the mothers of registered babies could receive monthly instructional booklets. Professional organizations, such as the Child Study Association (which organized child study groups in cities across the country and began publishing *Parents' Magazine* in 1926), and the federal government were also active in the campaign to improve the health of the young. By the end of the 20's advice to parents on the physical care of their children could be had at every turn: in magazine articles, in thousands of new books, in advertisements, in government pamphlets. The health of children became an overriding, perhaps even a compulsive concern for parents; they were urged to buy GE Mazda Sunlamps to provide Vitamin D for their children, to learn which foods would be most helpful in preventing anemia, to keep Vicks VapoRub on hand in case congestion should develop, to wear masks when they entered a sick child's room, to cleanse their bathrooms with BonAmi because the other (scratchier) cleansers would leave places for germs to breed, to guard against pink toothbrush, to watch for the signs of eczema, to use Castoria for constipation, Listerine for sore throats, and Vapo-Cresoline for whooping cough.[73]

This new concern for the health of children was no doubt necessary, and some of it no doubt worked; the infant mortality rate fell to 65 per 1,000 live births by 1930, before the age of the miracle antibiotics — but the burden that it placed upon the new American housewife was immense. Children had to be kept in bed for weeks at a time; bedpans had to be provided and warmed, "since even the slightest chilling is to be avoided carefully;" in some diseases excrement had to be disinfected before being discarded; food had to be specially prepared; leftovers had to be burned after the sick child's meal; utensils had to be boiled, alcohol baths administered, hands scrupulously washed, mouths carefully masked — and through all this the nursing mother was expected to "get plenty of rest and outdoor recreation," and remain unrelentingly cheerful, "for cheerfulness is needed in a sickroom and the attitude of a mother nursing an ailing child largely influences the speed of recovery."[74] Needless to say, mothers had to remain at home in order for all this nursing to be done; the death of a child whose mother had gone out to work was a recurrent theme in women's magazine fiction. In this sense, the child health movement was paradoxical; many women made careers out of convincing other women to stay at home and tend their children.

Oddly enough the Depression also served to reinforce the feminine mystique, although many commentators worried about what the economic disaster would do to the family as a social institution. The end of prosperity meant that entertainment outside the home had to be curtailed and it also meant that many families would be unable to pay for domestic servants. The genteel housewife who had formerly kept servants but who had let them go in the early years of the Depression became something of a social stereotype: ". . . a college girl who in recent years has been obliged to live the anxious, circumscribed life of the maid-of-all-work wife of a small-time lawyer with vanishing fees," as Anne O'Hare McCormick described a friend of hers in 1933.[75] "Doing it yourself these days?" asked the makers of La France Bluing over a stark picture of manicured hands immersed in a laundry tub; indeed, many American housewives were.[76] The need to economize to make ends meet meant that meals had to be planned carefully and cash had to be spent wisely; the editors of *American Home* advised their readers to stop buying over the telephone and go down to the shops in person to make certain they were getting good value for their money.[77] The editors of *The Ladies' Home Journal* were pleased to note that the new emphasis on home entertainment was leading families to remodel their homes – themselves.[78] To save money women learned how to fix electric motors, paint used furniture, sew curtains and – once again – remake last year's clothes. Manufacturers had to keep selling their goods, so prices came down and credit buying arrangements became more flexible. The more goods there were on shelves, the heavier advertising pressure on women became. Cash wasn't available, but time was – women's time – and since the prohibition against women entering the work force was particularly heavy during the Depression (they would, after all, be stealing jobs from unemployed men) the best place to spend that time was at home and the best way to spend it was in all those multitudinous little jobs that made up the daily routine of the housewife who was convinced that the feminine mystique made sense.

The feminine mystique, the social ideology which was formed during the 20's and solidified during the 30's, was quite a functional solution to real economic and demographic conditions. Servants were scarcer and their wages higher. Electricity could save burdensome labor and washday was unquestionably easier to face when the washing was done by machine than when it was done by hand. Infants' lives could be saved if care were taken to sterilize their bottles and balance their diets. In fact the feminine mystique worked; it kept women at home to do jobs that, in one way or another, American society needed to have done. Unfortunately, calling the solution functional does not mean that it was wise; it seems tragic that as a society we could not utilize all that new technology without constructing an ideology which oppressed half our citizens.

Notes

1. Betty Friedan, *The Feminine Mystique* (New York: Norton, 1963). Citations are to the paperback edition (New York: Dell, 1963). For Friedan's argument that the feminine mystique took hold after World War II, see Chapter 8. Other authors have adopted her chronology. See, for example, Sonya Rudikoff, "Marriage and household," *Commentary*, 55 (June, 1973), 61.

2. Friedan, Chapter 2.

3. Barbara Welter, "The cult of true womanhood, 1820-1860," *American Quarterly*, 18 (Summer, 1966), 162.

4. *The Ladies' Home Journal* (January, 1918), 4.

5. "Editorial," *The Ladies' Home Journal* (May, 1918), 4.

6. *The Ladies' Home Journal* (January, 1933), 2.

7. *American Home* regularly published house plans in every issue. About half the plans published between 1928 and 1933 had no maid's room, despite the fact that they were very expensive homes ($9,000 up).

8. Ruth Sapin, "For better or worse, sevants influence children," *Parents' Magazine* (January, 1929), 20.

9. The prevalence of household servants before World War I, and their disappearance thereafter, is discussed in Russell Lynes, *The Domesticated Americans* (New York: Harper & Row, 1957) Ch. 9. As just one example: an article in *The Ladies' Home Journal* (February, 1908), 44, described a young couple who were struggling along on the husband's meagre salary as a newspaper reporter; they did all the gardening, house painting, and repair work themselves and found various ways to economize on food — but they had a maid-of-all-work.

10. Paraphrased from, *The Ladies' Home Journal* (February, 1918), 49.

11. For an example of the genre see, S. M. Eliot, "The normal American woman," *The Ladies' Home Journal* (January, 1908), 15.

12. "What does your kitchen say about you?" *The Ladies' Home Journal* (March, 1933), 34.

13. "Editorial," *The Ladies' Home Journal* (April, 1928), 36.

14. Advertisement for Fels Naptha, *American Home* (June, 1937), 64.

15. *American Home* (April, 1931), 66.

16. "Editorial," *The Ladies' Home Journal* (February, 1928), 32.

17. *Parents' Magazine* (February, 1933), 33.

18. *The Ladies' Home Journal* (March, 1928), 43.

19. For example: "How to buy towels," *The Ladies' Home Journal* (February, 1928), 134, or "When the bride selects bed linens," *The Ladies' Home Journal* (January, 1928), 118.

20. On this point see, for example, John Kenneth Galbraith, *Economics and the Public Purpose* (Boston: Houghton Mifflin, 1973), 29-37.

21. Home economists were very much aware of the change, and of the need to educate women in their responsibilities as consumers. See, for example, Margaret Reid, *The Economics of Household Production* (New York: John Wiley, 1934), Ch. XIII.

22. These advertisements appeared regularly in the monthly editions of *The Ladies' Home Journal* in 1927 and 1928.

23. See, for example, "Keeping in shape," *The Ladies' Home Journal* (April, 1928), 191.

24. See, for example, *The Ladies' Home Journal* (March, 1928), 101.

25. "How we raise our children," *The Ladies' Home Journal* (March, 1928), 193.

26. "Christmas gifts for little girls," *American Home* (December, 1928), 227.

27. "Editorial," *The Ladies' Home Journal* (June, 1918), 4.

28. "Editorial," *Parents' Magazine* (October, 1926), 2.

29. Friedan, 41-42, attributes the concept to the editors of *McCall's*.

30. Remarks made by housewives of the business class in Muncie, Indiana in 1924. Robert S. Lynd and Helen M. Lynd, *Middletown: A Study in Contemporary American Culture* (New York: Harcourt Brace, 1929) 146-147. Excerpts are reprinted by permission of Harcourt, Brace Jovanovich, Inc.; Copyright 1929 by Harcourt, Brace Jovanovich, Inc., copyright 1957 by Robert S. and Helen M. Lynd.

31. *American Home* (November, 1931), 81. The idea of converting basements into playrooms was part of the magazine's campaign to encourage home remodeling so that jobs might be created during the Depression. The article on barbecues appeared in *The Ladies' Home Journal* (June, 1937).

32. "She must not bring her troubles to the table," was advice given in an article on Blue Monday, *American Home* (April, 1931), 14. The Steero bouillon ads ran in *The Ladies' Home Journal* in the mid 20's. "Self respect thrives on soap and water," was the motto of the Cleanliness Institute, which placed monthly advertisements in *The Ladies' Home Journal* in 1928.

33. This analysis is paraphrased and abstracted from advertisements in the women's magazines, 1923-1933.

34. Emily Post, *Etiquette*, 5th revised edition (New York, 1937), 823.

35. Lynes, 163 and 171.

36. Lynds, 169.

37. Ibid.

38. *Historic Statistics of the United States, Colonial Times to 1957* (Washington: U.S. Government Printing Office, 1960). These estimates were calculated from Series D 457-463, p. 77, "Private Household Workers Employed," and Series A255, p. 16, "Number of households." As the number of households was overestimated in 1910 and 1920 because of the inclusion of quasi-households in the count (rooming houses, dormitories, etc.) the figures are only a very rough guide.

39. See note 5, Lynes, 156, and Lynds, 170.

40. These phenomena were widely remarked upon. See, Lynds, 25, and 99. Edward Bok, "Editorial," *American Home* (October, 1928), 15, *The Ladies' Home Journal* (March, 1928), 35, an article on buying life insurance: "The old days when the maiden aunt or spinster sister was waiting patiently to take over wiping the noses . . . are rapidly passing. Sister is far too busy paying her own lunch check and insurance policies."

41. *Historical Statistics*, 510.

42. Ibid.

43. *Historical Statistics*, 179.

44. Data from Siegfried Giedion, *Mechanization Takes Command* (New York: Oxford University Press, 1948), 602, *Historical Statistics*, 417 (although the column is headed, "Refrigerators produced," in fact the figures are for refrigerators sold, as is explained on p. 407). The price in 1929 is derived from a Frigidaire advertisement, *The Ladies' Home Journal* (January, 1929), 140.

45. Hazel Kyrk, *Economic Problems of the Family* (New York: Harpers, 1933), 368, reporting a study in *Monthly Labour Review*, 30 (1930), 1209-1252.

46. Lynds, 156-157.

47. *The Ladies' Home Journal* (December, 1908), 46.

48. Lynds, 156. With regard to use of canned goods the Lynds made an interesting observation: "A prejudice lingers among these latter (housewives of the medium and smaller income groups) against feeding one's family out of cans."

49. Lynds, 157.

50. Lynds, 134-135, 153-154.

51. Lynds, 98.

52. *The Ladies' Home Journal* (January, 1908), 44.

53. Lynds, 96, citing a survey in *Zanesville and Thirty-Six Other American Cities* (New York: Literary Digest, 1927), 65.

54. Ibid.

55. Lynds, 97.

56. Giedion, 659-703.

57. Helen Sprackling, "The modern bathroom," *Parents' Magazine* (February, 1933), 25.

58. *American Home* (April, 1931), 64, describes, in some detail, how complex a process washing with one of these machines was.

59. Lynds, 174.

60. Ibid.

61. *Historical Statistics*, 526.

62. *The Ladies' Home Journal* (April, 1918), 29.

63. *The Ladies' Home Journal* (February, 1928), 170.

64. See, for example, *American Home* (April, 1931), 48 — for a typical shopping list.

65. Lynds, 164-167.

66. Lynds, 155.

67. On the earliest vacuum cleaners see, Giedion, 586.

68. "The after the war woman" *The Ladies' Home Journal* (June, 1918), 13.

69. "Editorial," *The Ladies' Home Journal* (May, 1918), 30; and, "The vanishing servant girl," *The Ladies' Home Journal* (May, 1918), 48.

70. Lynes, 107.

71. Edward Bok, "The American home, the joyous adventure," *American Home* (January, 1929), 287.

72. Compare advertisement for Ivory Soap, *The Ladies' Home Journal* (February, 1908), 5 with Fels Naptha advertisement (January, 1928), 35.

73. These examples were taken from a single issue of *Parents' Magazine* (February, 1933) in which 27 out of 79 advertisements were for drugs or health related items, and two out of the nine featured articles were about diseases.

74. All quotes are from Beulah France, "Home care of contagious diseases," *Parents' Magazine* (March, 1933), 26, 27, 57.

75. *The Ladies' Home Journal* (January, 1933), 13. For a fictionalized version of the same lady, see "Love flies out of the kitchen," *The Ladies' Home Journal* (January, 1933), 42.

76. *The Ladies' Home Journal* (February, 1933), 52.

77. *American Home*, (March, 1933), 50.

78. *The Ladies' Home Journal* (January, 1933), 42.

PART IV.

Organizational and Ideological Struggles

Historians have long been interested in the apparent decline in women's organizational activities after the suffrage victory in 1920. Although it is clear that many interrelated factors caused this decline, Joan M. Jensen discovered that at least one important sector of the federal government, the War Department, developed a specific antifeminist program in an attempt to divide and discredit women's groups. Divisions among organized women can also be traced to an ideological split between the social feminist reformers who supported protective legislation and the equalitarian feminists who sponsored the Equal Rights Amendment at home and the Equal Rights Treaty abroad. As Susan Becker notes, both the American and the international women's movements were enfeebled by this leadership struggle at the same time that working women generally experienced great economic insecurity. Yet, as Lois Scharf points out, the negative impact of many New Deal programs on women workers caused women's organizations to unite in opposition to economic discrimination, and an increasingly defensive feminism barely survived. Black women's organizations encountered interracial opposition that limited their impact and often caused racial issues to take precedence over feminist ones, while female socialists struggled to maintain their feminist identity within a male-dominated movement.

Why did the War Department perceive feminist activities as a threat to national security? What were the effects of the Red Scare on women's groups? To what degree and in what ways were women's organizations able to counteract these attacks? Why did the social and equalitarian feminists arrive at such different conclusions about the effects of protective legislation on working women? How crucial were these issues to black women? Why were these issues so important in the 1920s and 1930s? How and why did the divisions affect the international women's movement? What kinds of discrimination against women existed in major New Deal programs? What changes did women's organizations want, and how successful were they in obtaining them? What were the advantages and disadvantages of separate women's organizations?

9

All Pink Sisters:
The War Department
and the Feminist Movement
in the 1920s
JOAN M. JENSEN

The period from 1920 to 1929 was an age of pressure-group politics which American women entered as one of the best-organized interest groups in the country and from which they emerged battered and divided. A strong feminist movement existed with women organized around a wide range of social issues in 1920. By 1929, women's groups were disorganized, fragmented, and unable to agree on the best way to change their status in society.[1]

Historians have emphasized both external and internal pressures in explaining this decline of the women's movement. William Chafe stated the internal view most clearly when he wrote: "Fundamentally... women's political standing plummeted because the mass of female citizens failed to act in the cohesive and committed manner which the suffragists had predicted."[2] Chafe cited the lack of collective self-consciousness and argued that suffrage did not alter the structure of society, women's roles in it, or the sexual division of labor. Another group of historians, while not ignoring internal conflict, have emphasized external factors, especially attacks by rightists. J. Stanley Lemons, for example, argued that these attacks "weakened the progressive impulse as distrust and confusion crept into the feminist ranks."[3]

The history of the Women's International League for Peace and Freedom (WILPF) gives a good example of both the external and internal pressures to which the women's movement was subjected in the crucial first years after suffrage. The leadership, coalition politics, and ideology of this women's group and the attacks upon it by the War Department and various patriotic groups make it an ideal case study for analyzing women's politics during the early 1920s.

WILPF, organized first as the Woman's Peace Party in 1915 and reorganized by its new name in 1919, together with the National Woman's Party (NWP) and the League of Women Voters (LWV) of the United States are the oldest women's political organizations in this country. For more

The author would like to thank Bernice B. Nichols at the Swarthmore College Peace Collection and Timothy Nenninger at the National Archives for their assistance in locating documents used to research this paper. A shorter version was presented at the Fourth Berkshire Conference on the History of Women, Mount Holyoke College, August 1978.

than sixty-five years WILPF has fostered political activism on the part of women by encouraging their involvement in the formulation of foreign policy. Two Nobel Prize Winners — Jane Addams in 1931 and Emily Greene Balch in 1946 — worked through and headed this group. Perhaps best known for its work during the 1930s in fostering the Nye Senate investigation into the munitions trade, WILPF and its leaders had by that time more than a decade of experience behind them in dealing with problems of dissension within and attacks from without as they attempted to formulate programs of political action that would raise the consciousness of women about issues of foreign policy and galvanize them into political action.[4] The relationship of WILPF to other women's organizations as it attempted to rouse women to political activism is thus particularly relevant to any analysis of women's political role in the 1920s.

The Woman's Peace Party emerged in 1915 as the creation of a coalition of women's groups which felt the mixed male and female peace groups had been, in the words of Carrie Chapman Catt, "over-masculinized" and that women needed a separate group where they could formulate their own peace policies.[5] The first platform called for the democratic control of foreign policies, limitation of armaments, a conference of neutral nations to work for an early end to the European war (which had begun the year before), and universal woman suffrage, a cause to which all the women's organizations that sent representatives to this first convention were committed.

While women's organizations could rather easily agree on the necessity of coalition politics, the question of leadership proved more difficult. The prewar women's movement had been astoundingly successful in attracting a competent and articulate group of women to its ranks. Drawn together by consensus on the needs of women and the necessity of working together to achieve goals that would satisfy these needs, women nonetheless found that they differed greatly on strategy, tactics, and leadership style, all of which could drastically affect their ability to work together. Any political move-ment relies to a great extent on a type of personal leadership that promotes conversion of otherwise inactive but concerned people to political action. The suffrage movement had depended on this type of personal leadership to attract women to its cause.[6] At the same time, coalition politics involved convincing women with strong political persuasions that they shared a common ideology and could place their commitment to women above other political commitments or at least outside normal political alignments. Nonetheless, the women's movement, and consequently the women's peace movement, had its own distinctive political spectrum of left, center, and right.

Carrie Chapman Catt, who helped form the early Woman's Peace Party but withdrew during World War I, was the prototype of the right-wing leadership of the women's peace movement. This Iowa farm daughter who had worked her way through Iowa State College in the 1870s, married into wealth and soon widowed, had risen to head the National American Woman Suffrage Association (NAWSA) through a combination of an unusual speaking ability and a talent for gauging the political level of her potential followers. She had the capacity for developing strategy to take advantage of the easiest political terrain, then marshaling her suffrage troops in moderate and ladylike but persistent attacks on the political enemy. Catt's sheer physical toughness would take her through the last five grueling years of the suffrage battle to victory.[7]

But Catt's leadership style clashed with that of Alice Paul, a rising young leader in the women's movement who led a defection from NAWSA in 1912. While Catt practiced ladylike politics, Paul evolved a new militant confrontational style modeled on the tactics of the British suffrage organizations. Where Catt avoided meeting the antisuffragists head-on, Paul urged her followers in the Congressional Union (CU) to let men know that women were so determined to gain political power that they would be willing to disturb the political peace and be jailed for it.[8] Paul's organizers were skillful at publicizing the suffrage demands of women through activities that Catt considered outrageous. She would later accuse them of carrying "seditious banners" when they condemned "Kaiser" Woodrow Wilson during the war. Catt was careful to point out in private letters that members of NAWSA and the CU were "not all working together" and she opposed the CU leading the new Woman's Peace Party.[9] Paul would, in fact, hold herself and the later NWP aloof from the women's peace movement but many members were active in organizing the Woman's Peace Party and would remain active in WILPF when it reformed after the war. CU members like young and radical Crystal Eastman would form a left wing of the early women's peace movement.

A third type of leader, like veteran head of the powerful Massachusetts Woman's Suffrage Association Lucia Ames Mead, represented a centrist position. Mead understood the politics of coalition work. Indeed, she would help forge a powerful coalition of suffragists that later defeated John D. Weeks in his bid for the Senate. But she seemed to lack the ability to be "popular," a necessity at this stage of building the women's peace movement. Mead was able and well informed and had written several books on the abolition of war, but she was, again according to Catt, not popular. Left-wing women would later accuse Mead of being a reactionary.[10] Probably more moderate than reactionary, Mead nevertheless was the leader of a group of middle-class women who were considerably to the right of the New York women pacifists who were led by Crystal Eastman and formed the left wing of the women's peace movement.

Jane Addams was the one woman who seemed to be able to work successfully with Catt on the right wing of the peace movement as well as with the more moderate Mead and the radical Eastman. During Addams's years of political internship in Chicago, she had somehow developed a political style that allowed women of varying political views to work peaceably side by side. Her ability to keep strong women working together, women who had diverse politics on issues that did not involve women, decidedly divergent opinions on strategy, and almost irreconcilable tactical styles made her the logical leader of the women's peace movement.[11]

In the same way that a later generation of feminists would appeal to the bond of sisterhood, most of these early political leaders, regardless of political persuasion, appealed to what they called the bond of motherhood. The ideology of motherhood permeated the early women's movement to an extent that some later feminists would find embarrasing and others recognize as politically dangerous. In the early twentieth century, however, the appeal to a common potential experience, even for those who never married or bore children, provided a powerful bond as well as a rationale for separate organizations. In welfare reform, this ideology assumed that all women had special needs and that women had a special role in looking after women and children in society. When applied to war, this ideology assumed that women as the bearers and caretakers of life had a special sense of its preservation. The young unmarried Crystal Eastman expressed the attitude clearly in a letter to Jane Addams when she wrote, "From the beginning, it seemed to me that the only reason for having a Woman's Peace Party is that women are mothers, or potential mothers, therefore have a more intimate sense of the value of human life and that, therefore, there can be more meaning and passion in the determination of a woman's organization to end war than in an organization of men and women with the same aim."[12]

But this ideology of motherhood should not be overemphasized. Most WILPF leaders did not base their views about the relation of women to war on women's instinct and only a few saw opposition to war by women as the result of unique experiences. Addams summed up her views on women and war by saying that the basic human experience was perpetuating and cherishing the human race and that women had been the earliest custodians of the preventive human urgings "to foster life." Most of the women pacifists presented motherhood as a functional rather than an instinctual attitude and even this functionalism, although persistent, would not be a dominant theme in WILPF ideology after 1920.[13]

Expressions of the concept of motherhod are not easy to find. Anna Garlin Spencer, president of WILPF in 1920 appealed to the ideology of motherhood and its implication for separatism in her call to the second national meeting of WILPF when she said that women felt "a peculiar revolt" against the cruelty and waste of war and that women "may well for a while at least work somewhat by themselves until they become strong and commanding in their power of motherhood to declare that this obsolete legalizing of human slaughter must be outgrown. . . ." The Wisconsin state branch phrased the idea this way in the preamble of its constitution: "It is woman's function to conserve human life. Since she has acquired increased power in world affairs, she instinctively desires to utilize for humanity the knowledge and experience gained in the development of the race and thus help bring about conditions of permanent peace." Florence Allen, the WILPF member and first woman elected to the Ohio Supreme Court, said in a speech later circulated by WILPF that women's task was peculiar with regard to the abolition of war because they had the "emotion of the ideal – the power of working for a hope and dream." That spirit within women came, said Allen, "partly from our physical nature and partly from the long, sad training of the ages which has compelled us to achieve a masterly self-control." In personal letters, WILPF leaders occasionally talked about the "gospel of new world order of internationalism," or of "saving civilization," but mostly they did not dwell long on the causes of their own decisions to work for peace and to work in separate groups with other women. Once established, both the Woman's Peace Party and WILPF moved quickly on with little rhetoric to organize women politically to eliminate war.[14]

The lack of a systematic ideology about women and war would prove to be a disadvantage as the United States moved closer to World War I in 1917, less than two years after women had come together to form a separate peace group. Because women did not agree on what role women should have during wartime, the right wing of the women's peace movement defected, an event that had an important influence on the postwar WILPF. The clash between Eastman and Catt in the New York branch of the Woman's Peace Party both reflected and symbolized the split.

The Woman's Peace Party came together as a national organization composed of individuals rather than as a federation representing other organizations. Where there were a considerable number of members, the national board appointed women to call state conventions and elect state officers. When the women selected by the board to organize the New York state branch decided to postpone its first conference because of the war, Eastman – with at least the tacit approval of the governing board – took the initiative in calling a state conference. The conference elected Eastman, who was already head of the New York City branch, as president of the state group. It elected as officers socialists, feminists, and pacifists who believed that women should continue to organize during the war. When Catt announced in February 1917 that the New York women's suffrage association would help the governor in case of war, the New York Woman's Peace Party publicly censured Catt (she would later claim they revoked her membership), thus moving the peace group closer to the strategy of the CU which had also refused to follow Catt's lead and insisted on continuing its militant organizing. Catt resigned. So too did other women in the right wing of the Woman's Peace Party.[15] The defection of the right wing automatically strengthened the left wing of the party, but moderate reformers managed to maintain control of the national organization by formulating a middle way in which women could selectively participate in war work, especially in conserving food, a role that Addams felt women had performed traditionally in all societies.

The war drastically changed the political climate in the United States in which the leadership of women's groups had to work. Suffrage and the peace movement had both emerged on the crest of a progressive reform movement which had gained in strength from the presence of a vigorous, noisy, uncoordinated, and unpredictable left-wing movement. Soon after right-wing reformers severed their remaining contacts with liberals and radicals in 1917, the government began to suppress the civil liberties of left-wing groups. A few liberal male reformers managed to retain a foothold in the Wilson war administration, but they were unable to achieve power in the Democratic party in 1920. Progressive Republicans were likewise unable to capture political space in the Republican party after their defection in 1912 to form the Progressive party. The absence of a viable reform wing in either major party or a reform candidate for president undoubtedly were important factors in the decision of women leaders to remain aloof from partisan politics in 1920; to be, as Lucia Ames Mead wrote to Addams, "a balance of power."[16]

The attack on the left also made the moderate, or liberal, reformers much more careful of whom they allowed to become visible leaders in their own groups. Because they depended upon public opinion to publicize their reform goals and to elect progressive politicians to office, and because public opinion seemed to be moving against left-wing reformers, moderates abandoned their former left supporters. The accusations of the right during and after the war forced a clarification of political lines. The demonology of Germanism and then of Bolshevism worked effectively to force reformers into an independent role where earlier they had been able to work both within parties with more conservative politicians and outside of parties with more radical reformers.

The postwar radical political purge drove all but the most moderate socialists out of WILPF. Leaders were aware of the importance of maintaining civil liberties for their own political activities but, at the same time, WILPF elders felt uneasy having members like the brilliant and assertive Eastman remain visible leaders of their newly reformed organization. Eastman wanted to attend the 1919 International Congress of Women in Europe, but some of the board who had raised questions about her politics as early as 1915 now again questioned the wisdom of having her represent them internationally so soon after the war, particularly because of the public reaction against the left both in the United States and among western European governments that WILPF hoped to influence to accept a more moderate peace settlement. When a State Department representative said it would grant no passports to socialists, the older stalwarts rather quickly acquiesced and Eastman's defenders accepted the verdict. Two years later, when a board member recommended that Eastman be elected to the board, other members blocked the nomination from even coming to a vote.[17] Thus the more militant left was purged from WILPF leadership. The moderate left, including Emily Greene Balch, continued to work with WILPF and were especially comfortable working with the more radical international group. Even Balch, however, whose teaching position at Wellesley College had been terminated by its administration because of her socialist-pacifist politics, stopped referring to herself as a socialist. The war, she said, "had made me more skeptical of governments as such and much more afraid of trusting them with great new powers." She also felt that socialism now seemed to connote Marxism and Communist party membership, a political and economic view she rejected.[18] This shedding of socialist political identification for a type of individualist reform label was symptomatic of the postwar political climate that divided old allies.

Catt, Paul, and Addams emerged from the war as potential leaders of three strong and politically active women's organizations. Each seemed a logical political leader for the newly enfranchised women. Yet each held aloof from political office or party politics, and Catt and Addams withdrew to a great extent from the organizational structures they had helped to create. Each continued to believe that, despite enfranchisement, women must work in groups separate from men to achieve political influence. Given the political climate of 1920, that decision was perhaps as much based on practical political conditions as on an ideological commitment to separatism. There was no viable reform wing in either of the male parties.

Addams quickly recovered her national stature after being condemned by the press for her late and lukewarm support for the war effort. She and other members of the Woman's Peace Party held the ravaged group together during the war, collected sizeable pledges (over fifteen thousand dollars) from wealthy women to finance the 1919 International Congress of Women, and helped reorganize the group as WILPF in 1919.[19] Choosing Philadelphia for their first postwar meeting, the peace group drew much support from Pennsylvania Quakers and quickly reformed with plans for expansion. Addams, who had been elected president of the international section of WILPF, did not hold office in the U.S. group during the next five years but continued to be a member of the board. WILPF leadership often sought her advice, depended upon her popularity as a speaker and fund raiser, and on her abilities as peacemaker within their own group. Officers tried to arrange board meetings so that Addams could be present and always held their Chicago meetings at Hull House, the social settlement of which she was cofounder. Nevertheless, the U.S. WILPF was much more independent of Addams than either the media or other women's groups believed. WILPF consciously attempted to keep Addams above domestic organizational concerns while still keeping her informed on important events. By the early 1920s, WILPF leaders had already begun working to elevate Addams above politics to a symbolic status as leader of the peace movement.

The shearing of both right and left between 1917 and 1920 left WILPF with homogeneous, flexible leaders anxious to mobilize and expand rapidly. Most of the money collected during the war went to sponsor the 1919 peace congress, but with a few hundred dollars left in the treasury, a new president and secretary, and fueled by the experience of seeing German and French women embrace at their Geneva congress while men fashioned what they considered a harsh victor's peace at Versailles, leaders quickly sent out a call to old members to begin recruiting new ones. The leadership had not asked for dues in 1918, and by 1919 the group was down to fifty-two members. Twenty-five of the original eighty-five charter members of the Woman's Peace Party, including Belle LaFollette, Lucia Ames Mead, and Alice Thatcher Post, joined the new group and a membership appeal immediately brought more members, dues, and donations. By the second meeting, held in Chicago in April 1920, membership had climbed to nearly 500, with 300 members in Pennsylvania alone. Over the summer of 1920, 150 more joined. By April 1921, membership had more than doubled; by October there were six state groups, nine locals, and over 2,000 members. In January 1923, WILPF counted 2,500 members and by May 5,000 women were members.[20]

Money came flowing in with new members. Regular members contributed $1 in dues, college women 25¢, and wealthy women often pledged donations of up to $1,000. In March 1920, the treasurer reported only slightly over $200 in reserve, but a $1,000 donation from a California woman that month allowed the establishment of a national office, and contributions at the 1920 Chicago meeting brought in an additional $2,000. Office expenses rose to $500 a month in 1921; by the end of 1923 the national organization had a budget of $20,000 a year for domestic work. Between July 1923 and May 1924, WILPF spent $31,000 moving the office to Washington, D.C., and hiring seven full- and part-time workers.[21]

Among the women from the older Woman's Peace Party who worked to revitalize the new WILPF were Balch, the Wellesley economist not rehired by the college during the war because of her socialist pacifism; Mead, the Boston peace worker who had headed the Massachusetts women's suffrage organization; and Hannah Clothier Hull, a Pennsylvania Quaker. These women brought experience and knowledge to guide the expansion of the revitalized peace group. Balch, cut off at the height of her professional career, became a salaried executive secretary of the international office, then in 1924 worked for the United States section. Most of these mature women could depend on a network of emotional and financial support from families and friends and were hard workers and experienced organizers. They were able to attract younger women to their cause as well. Anne

Martin, a former CU organizer, joined the board, along with Harriet Connor Brown, who was active in planning strategy to defeat candidates pledged to increased armament, and Amy Woods, a Boston social worker who had spent fifteen months in Europe after the war with Balch, and who returned in 1922 to become a salaried executive secretary.

The younger women were more politically active and militant than the older women and yet the elders wanted to retain younger members. Even when disagreeing with the action the new militants advocated, the elders tried to give enough support and encouragement to keep them within the group. These younger women were from the East, with close ties to old Massachusetts and Pennsylvania pacifist families, many of whom were Quaker. Members in California, though offering financial and moral support, were too far away to take much part in the monthly board meetings or in the political decision making of the board. Pennsylvania, Massachusetts, and Illinois had the largest membership and these women exercised the greatest control. The New York branch, most active and radical during the war, gradually lost influence to the more moderate wing as WILPF tapped the hinterland to bring new members into the group. The U.S. section remained more conservative as a whole than the European section during the early twenties. It also remained more wealthy, financing the more radical international section during that time.[22]

One of the old suffrage tactics used by WILPF most effectively during the early 1920s was coalition work. Many members of WILPF also belonged to the new LWV of the United States (formed by NAWSA after passage of the Nineteenth Amendment) and worked actively to bring women into the peace movement. In New York, WILPF members worked through the LWV and were influential in the disarmament activity of that group in 1920. WILPF members also worked with the hastily assembled Women for World Disarmament, an emergency group formed primarily by members of the NWP who were concerned that no political pressure was being organized to influence Congress in favor of disarmament in early 1920. At the end of the war, despite the interest of a powerful minority of NWP members in taking up disarmament, the majority had voted to concentrate on passage of an equal rights amendment. Alice Paul kept her legions together, however, for the peace minority did not defect. Instead they worked independently in Women for World Disarmament; later some of Paul's most successful organizers joined WILPF but continued to work within the NWP as well. Members also worked through the General Federation of Women's Clubs (GFWC), the National Social Workers Association, the National Education Association (NEA), and the older National Congress of Women, established by Susan B. Anthony to draw women's clubs into coordinated efforts nationally and internationally. WILPF was not particular ly active in the National Congress of Women but it did keep in touch with various peace committees of clubs through this organization and most members belonged to one or more of its constituent organizations. WILPF did not belong to the Women's Joint Congressional Committee (WJCC) a coalition of women's groups which came together to discuss issues of public policy and to pressure Congress to implement selected legislation, but many of the other women's organizations did belong to the WJCC, where they worked together for legislation such as federal aid to reduce the high maternal and infant mortality rates in the United States. Women's patriotic groups, like the Daughters of the American Revolution (DAR) and the Daughters of the War of 1912, had been caught up in the women's movement preceding the war and had supported both federal welfare legislation and peace in the first years after the war. The DAR, for example, endorsed the goal of peace and joined the WJCC.[23]

During these first postwar years, regardless of their politics on other issues, women's groups tended to agree on peace and welfare legislation for women. Despite conflict during the war, certain assumptions were still held by the majority of organized middle-class women. They assumed that liberal reformists, moderate socialists, and moderate Republicans could work together on these bipartisan reforms. Women's issues were, in this sense, still beyond party politics.

In the first years of its organization, WILPF singled out what it called "militarism" as the chief cause of war. War was caused by men joined together in the military just as peace could be caused by women joined together in peace groups. Politics was the arena in which these two groups could struggle, for money fed militarism and money came from Congress. Thus, WILPF members needed to convince the public that appropriations to increase the military were unwise and that military structures already created should be modified or eliminated. Gradually, WILPF moved from general opposition to universal military training and increased armament to support for slashing military appropriations.

World War I was an overwhelming victory for the American military. Entering the war after the exhaustion and stalemate of the European belligerents, the American army had forced the Germans to ask for peace within a few months of their arrival in Europe in force. Mead had written to Balch in December 1918, "we did not expect our victory would be so overwhelming which makes the situation more strained in some ways."[24] For a part of the American public, that victory had confirmed a belief in the value of arms to settle international disputes and the importance of maintaining an increased military establishment. Warren G. Harding felt that way when he campaigned for president in 1920, and he appointed as his secretary of war John D. Weeks, an antisuffrage Republican stalwart who shared his views. With the support of Harding, Weeks presented to Congress a peacetime military program that included universal military training, an expanded peacetime army, and increased appropriations. Because of the opposition of peace groups and the disillusionment of the public engendered by the vast expense and civilian effort needed to achieve military victory, this program could not be enacted.[25]

Defeating universal military training proved relatively easy because wide opposition to conscription had developed in the war years. Sentiment on how best to maintain a voluntary army was more divided. Contemplating only a modest postwar cutback in 1920, the War Department asked for almost $1 million. Congress, responding to the mobilization by pacifists of sentiment for disarmament, cut the appropriation to less than $400,000. Harding and Weeks had settled for a National Defense Act in 1920 that provided for a regular army of 280,000 men, reinforced by a National Guard of 454,000 men and a large army reserve dependent for its officer recruits on the compulsory military training programs that most land-grant colleges had established for their male students during the early twentieth century. By 1922, Congress had halved the number of men in the regular army and cut back both guard and reserve. In September 1922, Secretary of War Weeks submitted a budget for the following year for 125,000 enlisted men but told President Harding that he needed at least 25,000 more men to implement the National Defense Act. Harding had warned Weeks that he would probably have to curtail the military program because they did not have the necessary financial resources.[26]

By this time WILPF was spearheading a drive to reduce the peacetime army by abolishing the National Defense Act of 1920 entirely. In Wisconsin, WILPF members went further. In league with other progressive groups, the Wisconsin WILPF lobbied to abolish compulsory military training at the University of Wisconsin and supported legislation abolishing the state National Guard. WILPF pointed to the Wisconsin success in abolishing military training as a possible project for other state groups. The focus on militarism and opposition to military spending brought a head-on confrontation with the War Department. Interpreting congressional limitations as both ungrateful and shortsighted, War Department officials — civilian and military — were already complaining about the inadequacies of the National Defense Act and the lack of money to maintain the army at the standards set by that act when appropriations time came around in fall 1922. WILPF members testified before the Senate Appropriations Committee and campaigned against candidates who supported increased appropriations.[27] The programs of WILPF and the War Department were on collision course by election time 1922.

In fall 1922, Secretary of War Weeks began a public campaign designed to increase the visibility of the army, convince the public of its importance, and counter the headway that peace groups were making in opposition to the War Department's national defense policy. He planned military exhibitions to illustrate the value of peacetime training in preparedness, a conference on "The Training of the Youth of Our Country" emphasizing the importance of military training, and began a speaking tour. In a speech before the Army Ordinance Association in New York in October, Weeks warned that he had no patience with "groups of silly pacifists who are seeking universal peace through undermining with their insidious propaganda the ability of their own country to protect itself." That same month Major General James G. Harbord, Deputy Chief of Staff, attacked those who "in the enthusiasm of newly conferred suffrage," were flooding the market with talk of disarmament as a substitute for military preparedness, "urging it with all that fascinating inconsistency of mingled charms and hysterics which so often characterizes lovely woman — without whose approval no war has ever been waged."[28]

WILPF continued their campaign against candidates who supported increased appropriations but waited until after the election to confront Weeks. Then, in November, Lucia Ames Mead as chairperson of the WILPF Committee on Education wrote to her old foe Weeks protesting that there was no national enemy against which the United States must be prepared and that instead the enemy lay within, in illiteracy, in the high numbers of deaths through homicide and industrial accidents, and in the social conditions that weakened the American people. Weeks immediately replied to Mead. He reminded her that the army was not only intended to meet foreign enemies but also that an effective system of national defense was needed for menaces from within. These menaces were, he wrote pointedly, "Strikes, which involve the discomfort and even the lives of our people . . . numerous organized groups in our body politic striving for class or sectional advantage; absurd political beliefs oftentimes striking at the very foundation of our form of government." When labor groups in the state of Washington discovered the next month that local intelligence officers had placed them under surveillance, saying that the army intelligence had as its primary purpose the "surveillance of all organizations or elements hostile or potentially hostile to the Government of this country" though Weeks had said that only in wartime was this the duty of the military, WILPF released the Weeks letter to the press. The press release asked: "Will Labor submit to arming against itself and pay for intelligence offices to keep their organizations under surveillance?"[29] The battle lines were now drawn.

In the following months a parade of army officers began to denounce WILPF with increasing rancor. Brigadier General Amos A. Fries, chief of the Chemical Warfare Service, began his speeches in December 1922 and in February 1923 singled out Harriet O'Connor Brown, executive board member of WILPF, as particularly dangerous. He denounced WILPF for circulating an oath composed by Brown that women would not support war efforts in any future war. Newspapers reported that Fries said members were swearing to an oath "nothing short of treason." WILPF sent protests to the War Department asking that Fries rectify his mistake — the group had not endorsed the oath — and then once more issued press releases criticizing the War Department. In reply, Secretary Weeks announced that groups being criticized by army officers included "some forces in America who are preaching revolution and the establishment of a communistic government," declared he would continue to support his officers because most of the organizations hurt by the charges were not very active in support of the government while men like Fries had been fighting the battles of the country, and in a May 1923 speech in San Diego promised to "rattle the sabre" as long as necessary to awaken the people of the United States to the need for adequate defense. That month the "spider web" chart began to be mailed out from Fries's Chemical Warfare Service office. The chart linked names of prominent female activists to supposed radical groups.[30]

It is not surprising that Fries lashed out at WILPF, since members had constantly attacked the Chemical Warfare Service since its establishment in 1920. What is surprising is how Fries became involved in the creation of the charts and that he knew they were being circulated from his office. The Negative Branch of the Military Intelligence Division, later renamed G-2, had charge of surveillance of civilians during the war and survived the retrenchment of 1919-1920 by actively engaging in investigations of radicals and participating in red raids. Public criticism of surveillance of civilians followed and the War Department in 1922 ordered G-2 to restrict its activities in peacetime primarily to liaison with other government agencies. At the same time, however, the War Department drew up War Plans White, contingency plans in case of a domestic revolution, and charged local intelligence officers with maintaining information on civilian groups. While intelligence officers were to engage in no investigations of their own, the War Department suggested that they could solicit information and cooperation from patriotic groups in their local areas. The American Legion became one of the primary groups charged with collecting this information for the War Department.[31]

During the war, the Military Intelligence Division had indexed material under the heading of "feminism" and had women undercover agents among women war workers, but not until 1922 did military intelligence officers begin to express concern about women's political activities. The concern was first evident when military intelligence agents discovered what they considered "socialist influence" in the Bryn Mawr College summer school for women workers and the unwillingness of the trustees to take action to "lessen the red influence there." In December 1922, intelligence chief General Marlborough Churchill requested a report from Major W. H. Cowles, head of the Negative Branch of G-2, on the activities of various pacifists and anti-military organizations in the country.[32]

The Chemical Warfare Service had meanwhile become a sort of collecting agency for G-2 with Cowles referring information to Fries and asking for his opinion on radical speakers. Fries was sending abstracts of information showing the political affiliations and "tendencies" of speakers and advising Cowles that most were either socialists or Bolsheviks or doing the work of the Bolsheviks. Cowles passed these reports on essentially unchanged to his chief. So when the December query came from Churchill, Cowles replied that pacifist and antimilitary organizations varied from "violent red to light pink" but that "the activities of all women's societies and many church societies may be regarded with suspicion." He attached a list of women's groups which included the WJCC and WILPF. Cowles explained to Churchill that the women's groups all interlocked with the Joint Amnesty Committee and the Labor Defense Council of the Communist Worker's party. In other words, as far as military intelligence agents were concerned, the women were all "pink sisters." The fear that generated this concept of women as all allied against the government was perhaps best summed up by an exchange between two military intelligence officers in 1923. One officer reported in alarm that speakers at Vassar, Wellesley, and Bryn Mawr were instilling pacifist views among women students so that in the future they would teach their children these ideas. The executive officer of G-2 replied: "All the work of industrial and physical preparation for defense will have been wasted if the younger generation are going to turn out to be pacifists and internationalists."[33]

Using the material collected by the War Department, the librarian of the Chemical Warfare Service, Lucia Maxwell, now began to compile a chart that would visually represent this interlocking directorate of women's organizations that threatened the government. The chart, as finally completed sometime in May 1923, was headed with a quote from the New York Lusk Committee warning that "the Socialist-Pacifist Movement in America is an absolutely fundamental and integral part of international socialism." At the bottom were quotes from Lenin and Alexandra Kollontai about the importance of women for communism and a poem by Maxwell which began: "Miss Bolsheviki has come to town, / With a Russian cap and a German Gown, / in *women's clubs* she's sure to be found, / For she's come to *disarm* AMERICA." The chart listed the names of twenty-one women and seventeen organizations to which they belonged. Fifteen of the organizations were listed as affiliates of the WJCC and the National Council for the Prevention of War. The original chart, though not later published versions, included the DAR. Maxwell sent some copies out under her name and home address; others she sent out in her official capacity. Copies of acknowledgements in G-2 files indicate that the American Defense Society received a copy, as did J. Edgar Hoover. Since copies of these acknowledgements were stamped received by G-2 in November 1923, G-2 as well as Fries knew that Maxwell was circulating this chart to patriotic groups before it was published in the March 1924 *Dearborn Independent* prefaced by a searing attack on women's organizations.[34]

Patriotic groups have played a role in maintaining political orthodoxy in ways still not adequately explained by historians. The patriotic groups formed a right counterpart to the reform groups on the left and worked as an interest group tugging political parties away from reform. Conservative politicians within parties used patriotic groups to mobilize public opposition to reform groups. This was probably the reason patriotic groups took up the condemnation of women's groups so actively in 1924, an election year when Progressives were beginning to gather around Robert La Follette in an attempt to launch a reform movement that might capture independent Republicans and move them into support for Democratic reform candidates or simply into a third-party movement drawing from both Democrats and Republicans. Patriotic groups had been active in the 1920 Red Scare, working with the military and local officials to publicize the dangers of allowing left political activity to continue unchecked and participating in raids and suppression of civil liberties. Once the alarm was raised, the public condoned these invasions of civil liberties. After 1920 patriotic groups became relatively quiet, but in 1924 they again revived, this time as opponents of liberal reformers rather than of radicals. Their usefulness for conservative politicians lay in their ability both to create enough fear in a normally conservative but lethargic public to rouse support for conservative candidates for office and to drive a wedge between independent Republicans and reformers. The campaign against women's groups that began in 1923 seemed to have both these functions. Women's politics for the first time were widely scrutinized and criticized. Criticism of women's reform groups became a way to separate an important source of support for the progressive Republicans in Congress who were looking to women's groups to deliver a large block of independent votes. Mead had argued in 1919 that women should remain independent and a balance of power, and that is exactly what they had become by 1924.[35]

The WJCC responded first to the publication of the spider web chart. It launched a special investigation to establish responsibility for the chart. In early April a delegation of five women from WJCC visited Secretary of War Weeks to deliver a letter charging the Chemical Warfare Service with a "contemptible attack on the women's organizations in the country." Maud Park, head of the WJCC, threatened political reprisals from 12 million women voters if Weeks did not withdraw the charts from circulation. Bowing to the organized power of women, Weeks immediately sent his regrets, ordered the charts destroyed, and carefully disassociated the War Department from the chart. He insisted that Maxwell had furnished the chart to patriotic groups in her capacity as chair of the Patriotic Committee of the League of American Penwomen and that the chart had been falsely represented as a product of the War Department.[36]

While the WJCC forced Weeks to back down, it also disassociated itself from WILPF and, as Catt noted in a letter to Addams, that furnished a precedent. In part because WILPF was in the midst of planning for an international meeting to be held in Washington in the spring of 1924, leaders at first were not inclined to publicly counterattack the patriotic groups who were now taking up the cry of disloyalty. Instead they countered the charges by investigating each attack and sending a letter explaining the position of WILPF on the issues raised by Fries and by the Maxwell chart, especially the oath supposedly taken by members to oppose all wars although the oath never became official policy of the league.

WILPF leaders were acting on the assumption that public opinion was formed by the free exchange of opinions in the marketplace. The side with the most truthful, accurate, and reasonable arguments would win. For example, the Washington headquarters contacted a man who had published a pamphlet called "Peace at Any Old Price," purporting to show how women had adopted the oath at their 1923 meeting, and offered him space in their *Bulletin* where he could make his charges and they could refute them one by one. Much time and effort went into these letters in the spring of 1924 and finally Emily Balch, who had recently returned from Europe, prepared a reply that could be circulated. Roger Baldwin and others suggested that WILPF bring lawsuits against the people who had charged them with being Bolsheviks; instead WILPF chose to rely upon the power of rational discourse in refuting the charges. Some patriotic groups charged Rosika Schwimmer — a founding member of the Woman's Peace Party but not involved in the reorganized WILPF — with being a German spy and a guiding influence in WILPF. Schwimmer would later successfully bring suit for libel against one of her detractors, but in 1924 most women seemed to respond with amazement that the peace movement had been able to generate such opposition rather than with fear of the attacks.[37]

Within WILPF, however, the attacks were cause for reconsideration of its activities. Mead wrote to Balch that they did have "loose joints in our armor," because many members, including their national executive secretary, had supported the oath. She also warned that continued opposition to state national guards was *"extremely dangerous."* Some members saw the attacks merely as a symptom of fear. Anna Garlin Spencer felt that "all women's organizations have been slandered" by the attacks. Nonetheless, she warned executive secretary Woods to "soft-pedal" their National Defense Act protests while they were soliciting funds for their international congress. The continued attacks by patriotic groups after the War Department had officially retracted the charts puzzled WILPF leaders. In November the American Legion and the Veterans of Foreign Wars (VFW) both passed resolutions at their annual meetings denouncing WILPF, and the DAR and two other women's groups threatened to withdraw from the Women's National Council if WILPF did not resign. That fall, Catt announced that she had called together representatives from women's groups to launch an independent peace movement not connected with any peace group. Thus the attacks on WILPF seemed to have the intended effect of moving more conservative and Republican women away from the coalition of women's groups and abandoning reform. The easy assumption that women's politics could take precedence over party politics disintegrated in the fall of 1924.[38]

The attacks that moved women further right did not, of course, affect the leaders in their willingness to work with each other, but it did put a strain on their ability to work out compromises that would calm their constituents while putting up a united front. The response of the Women's National Council (WNC) to the attack is perhaps most relevant for understanding these difficulties. The president of the WNC asked WILPF to resign in the summer of 1924 because their membership was affecting the council's ability to get appropriations from Congress for its coming international conference. The WNC president worked with the WILPF leadership to make the withdrawal an occasion for a public defense of its policies. Addams apparently had no objection to withdrawing, but Mead began to believe that withdrawal would be unprincipled and that WILPF should take a firm stand. The younger women on the board agreed with her, and at a September meeting WILPF refused to withdraw. Attacks on WILPF continued, threatening to lead to a split in the WNC with the more conservative Republican members withdrawing and the DAR breaking a contract with the WNC to use their Washington hall for the coming conference. The president of the WNC wrote in December pleading again for WILPF to withdraw. The board again refused, but then, during a conference and a subsequent board meeting, their sentiment gradually changed. Hull wrote to Addams and Balch that working with WNC seemed not worth the struggle to remain within the group. In January WILPF officially withdrew from the WNC. By this time Catt had also returned to the peace movement, intent on rescuing from the leadership of WILPF the more conservative women who still maintained an interest in peace.[39]

Catt returned to the peace movement gropingly in early 1924, unsure of how she could work with organized women. She had refused to join WILPF in 1919; nor had she responded to the urgings of old peace workers that she actively join the battle for United States entry into the League of Nations. "I am too tired to come into the fight," she had written in October 1920. During the next two years, Catt had only occasionally ventured forth from her farm, where she had gone to recuperate, but by fall 1922 she had recovered sufficient energy to tour Europe. In 1923 she committed herself to a three-week, fifteen-state lecture tour where she spoke on "Peace and War." Returning home late in 1923, she was convinced that there was "a real interest among women for peace but admitted to Mead of being "shaky" on her peace information because "it has not been my life work."[40]

In January 1924, Catt wrote to Mead that she was thinking about uniting women from mixed peace groups to work together. Although Catt did not go into detail, she apparently had in mind a sort of coalition that would draw together women who had complained to her that the men in their groups were formulating policy and leaving the work to the women. Such a women's group would have given women in the peace organizations, especially the church groups, an organization within which to achieve greater visibility and a greater role in formulating policy. It would also have taken considerable energy for Catt to organize such a group. In April, after the publication of the spider web chart and the denunciation of peace groups, however, Catt was approached by a group of representatives from nine national women's organizations who believed that their constituencies were interested in peace but were afraid now to continue working through WILPF. Catt met with 70 women at a Buffalo conference soon after and appeared before the national convention of the Federation of Women's Clubs in June to issue a call for a conference the following January in Washington, where they could begin to build a new women's peace movement that would be less militant and oriented more to the study of international relations rather than to political activism. Catt did talk to Addams when she was in Chicago, but she refused to ask peace groups to participate in the conference, refused to allow WILPF members to distribute their literature at the conference, and even refused a WILPF invitation to tea for the delegates. Still, WILPF members participated as individuals. Four of the speakers who addressed the conference were WILPF members, and the response of women to the conference showed great concern for peace. Women introduced many strong resolutions from the floor and prominent women made antiwar statements. Eleanor Roosevelt was reported as saying, "I don't see why there should be any such thing as a righteous war." Following the conference, Calvin and Grace Coolidge welcomed a large delegation at the White House. The 900 women at the conference represented almost 5 million women voters.[41]

Catt would later look back at the first conference as too emotional and too activist. Patriotic groups certainly recognized the potential of the new group, for they immediately attacked Catt as a pacifist. These attacks confused Catt. She did not consider herself a pacifist and had asked two military officers to speak at the conference to show her opposition to the antimilitarism of WILPF. Yet the American Legion Auxiliary convened a meeting before the peace conference had ended where militarists denounced the women as part of a plot to destroy the United States. When Catt asked WILPF members about the source of her opposition, one wrote gleefully that Catt was being treated as a "pacifist." Catt thawed a bit, writing that WILPF was "blazing a trail" for more conservative women, but when Hull asked for permission to publish her letter, she did not reply.[42]

The Conference on the Causes and Cures of War (CCCW), as the group mobilized by Catt was called, might have revitalized the women's movement in the same way that NAWSA had mobilized women for political activism. But CCCW came out of a period of criticism of political activism, and Catt guided the group into a form of political education that would discourage political activity. Catt took credit for toning down the women's enthusiasm at subsequent meetings. "At our first conference," Catt later recalled, "there were many emotional appeals made from the floor, much pouring forth of noble sentiments, pious hopes, fervent dismays over the futility of war. This year, not a single speech of that kind was made." Instead, delegates had looked on quietly while experts had exchanged questions and answers.[43]

Catt was not the only one who toned down her politics. WILPF leaders who had soft-pedaled their critique of the National Defense Act after the War Department's attacks in 1924 continued to mobilize opposition to military training in universities but never launched the type of aggressive antimilitarist campaigns that had so antagonized the army. While WILPF's pacifism continued to rouse military intelligence agents and their civilian cohorts to surveillance, WILPF methods shifted the locus of much political action from national defense policy to indirect and local policymaking.

An even more important result of the controversy over the spider web charts was that groups like the DAR actively moved to denounce the peace movement and to support military spending. These actions by women in patriotic groups made reformers much less willing to claim motherhood as a cause of pacifism. While WILPF remained an all-women group, it found itself increasingly involved in mixed groups with men who agreed with their political principles rather than with women who joined them in a special crusade against war. WILPF also gradually shifted its interest from the study of militarism as a cause of war to a study of the economic causes of war. The day after Catt's first peace conference, she had met several WILPF women at the University Women's Club and had asked them about the sources of opposition. One had flung out "economic imperialism." That came to be more of an answer to the causes of war for WILPF as the decade wore on. In part this shift was caused by the hostility to WILPF of various industrial associations; opposition that WILPF interpreted as a threat to their peace work. In part it resulted from a recognition that the army was moving more toward industrial preparedness as a substitute for military preparedness. WILPF's shift to economic causes both reflected and encouraged a new ideology that would see social issues as economic rather than feminine. WILPF was not alone in this. Other women reformers were moving in the same direction, toward a new interpretation of society that would see economic interests and classes instead of women and men as the primary basis for conflicts over power. Such an interpretation would lead many women reformers to join the reform wing of the Democratic party and leave the issues of militarism and relative power between men and women to a later generation.[44]

WILPF weathered the attacks from the right in the 1920s and by 1937 had over 13,000 members, a paid staff of 11, and 120 branches in the United States. After careful organizing on Capitol Hill, WILPF, through its executive secretary Dorothy Detzer, would spark the Nye investigation into the effect of the armaments trade as a cause of war. Detzer chose the chief investigator for the Nye committee, and, like most congressional committees, the choice of personnel shaped its conclusions. Not only hard-core pacifists joined WILPF, however, for once World War II began, two-thirds of its membership moved from pacifism to collective security and withdrew from the league.[45]

What then did WILPF accomplish and what did its experience mean in the context of the women's movement of the 1920s? Former anti-suffragists published the *Woman Patriot*, which attempted to influence women on the right, and continued to attack both Catt and Addams as the leaders of feminism and pacifism in the 1920s. Feminism and pacifism, according to the *Woman Patriot*, were doing the work of the Communists. "The Pinks are all Red Sisters under the skin," it insisted.[46] The conclusion of the right, that protection of women could best be attained by preservation of the military and political power of men, exempting women from "unnatural responsibilities" so that they could engage in "non-partisan moral and educational service to the state," did not die, but it did not gain ascendancy in the United States. The containment of this ideology of subservience must, in part, be credited to the work of women like those in WILPF, who may have refused the label "pink sisters," but who still subscribed to the "subversive" doctrine that regardless of assumptions about the family, men did not have the right to dominate women politically or militarily.

Notes

1. William L. O'Neill, *Everyone Was Brave: The Rise and Fall of Feminism in America* (Chicago: Quadrangle, 1969), ix, 264-294; William Chafe, *The American Woman: Her Changing Social, Economic, and Political Roles, 1920-1970* (New York: Oxford University Press, 1974 reprint of 1972 edition), 30, 46-47; and J. Stanley Lemons, *The Woman Citizen: Social Feminism in the 1920's* (Urbana, Ill.: University of Illinois Press, 1973). The importance of pressure group politics during the early 1920s is discussed in David P. Thelen, *Robert M. LaFollette and the Insurgent Spirit* (Boston and Toronto: Little, Brown, 1976), 155-178.

2. Chafe, *American Woman*, 29-30.

3. Lemons, *Woman Citizen*, 214-215. See also Clarke A. Chambers, *Seedtime of Reform: American Social Service and Social Action, 1918-1933* (Ann Arbor, Mich.: University of Michigan Press, 1967 reprint of 1963 edition), 78, 234; Allen F. Davis, *American Heroine: The Life and Legend of Jane Addams* (New York: Oxford University Press, 1973), 269; and Allan Davis, *Spearheads for Reform: The Social Settlements and the Progressive Movement, 1890-1914* (New York: Oxford University Press, 1967), 229-230.

4. There is no history of WILPF in the United States. For the international WILPF see Gertrude Bussey and Margaret Tims, *The Women's International League for Peace and Freedom* (London: Allen and Unwyn, 1956). See also Marie Louise Degen, *The History of the Woman's Peace Party* (Baltimore: Johns Hopkins, 1939); Dorothy Detzer, *Appointment on the Hill* (New York: Holt, 1948); and Regan Bresnahan,

"The Origins of the Woman's Peace Movement," Senior thesis, Swarthmore College, Swarthmore, Pa., 1981. Carrie Tropf has underway a study of the WILPF in the 1920s and 1930s, and I am indebted to her for answering questions about the later WILPF. Olga S. Opfell, *The Lady Laureates: Women Who Have Won the Nobel Prize* (Metuchen, N.J. and London: Scarecrow, 1978), 48, discusses prize money.

5. Carrie Chapman Catt to Jane Addams, December 14, 1914, Catt Papers, Box 4, Library of Congress, hereafter cited as LC.

6. Luther P. Gerlach and Virginia H. Hine, *People, Power, Change: Movements of Social Transformation* (Indianapolis: Bobbs-Merrill, 1970), 79-97, discusses the importance of personal contacts for recruitment.

7. This evaluation is based upon a reading of Catt letters in the LC; Mary Gray Peck, "Mrs. Catt at College: 1880-1930," *The Woman's Journal* (September 1930), 40-41; and David Howard Katz, "Carrie Chapman Catt and the Struggle for Peace (Ph.D. dissertation, Syracuse University, 1973). Jackie Van Voris has underway a long overdue biography on Catt.

8. Paul too is in the process of being reevaluated. Amelia R. Fry has underway a new biography. See her "Suffragist Alice Paul's Memoirs: Pros and Cons of Oral History," *Frontiers*, 2 (Summer 1977), 82-86. For a detailed account of a Congressional Union/National Woman's Party campaign in one state see Joan M. Jensen, "Disfranchisement is a Disgrace: Women and Politics in New Mexico, 1900-1940," *New Mexico Historical Review* 56 (January 1981): 5-35.

9. Catt's criticisms of the Congressional Union/National Woman's Party are in Catt to Jane Addams, January 5, 1915, Catt Papers, Box 4, LC, and Catt to Dr. Grace Raymond Hebard, December 30, 1918, National American Woman Suffrage Association, Container 76, LC.

10. There is no good biography of Mead. The Lucia Ames Mead Papers contain some revealing letters as do the Emily Greene Balch and WILPF papers which are all at Swarthmore College Peace Collection, hereafter cited as SCPC. See also *Lucia Ames Mead: Memorial Meeting, January 14, 1937* (Boston, 1937); and Lucia Ames Mead, *Law or War* (Garden City, N.Y.: Doubleday, Doran, 1928). The Mead-Eastman split is in Blanche Wiesen Cook, *Crystal Eastman on Women and Revolution* (New York: Oxford University Press, 1978), 19; and C. Roland Marchand, *The American Peace Movement and Social Reform, 1898-1918* (Princeton, N.J.: Princeton University Press, 1972), 218-220.

11. Davis, *American Heroine*, does not develop this aspect of Addams's leadership, but it is evident from reading the WILPF correspondence.

12. Crystal Eastman to Jane Addams, June 28, 1917, Woman's Peace Party Papers, DC 43, Correspondence Box 9, SCPC. Marchand, *American Peace Movement*, has a chapter entitled "The Maternal Instinct," but most of the ideology is from Charlotte Perkins Gilman, who was not a central leader in WILPF. Most of the chapter relates to political splits rather than ideology.

13. Jane Addams, "Women and War," in *The Overthrow of the War System*, edited by Lucia Ames Mead (Boston: Forum, 1915), 8.

14. Spencer's March 15, 1920 call to the Chicago meeting, WILPF, US Section, Series A,2, Box 1, SCPC; unidentified news clipping, September 9, 1923 quoted Wisconsin preamble, WILPF, US Section, Series C,1, Box 4, SCPC; Florence Allen, "Women and World Peace," Florence Allen Papers, Container 29, Folder 1, Western Reserve Historical Society.

15. For Catt defection see Marchand, *American Peace Movement*, 215-218; Cook, *Crystal Eastman*, 11-12; Addams to Hull, January 26, 1924, Hannah Clothier Hull to Catt, January 25, 1925, and Catt to Hull, January 30, 1925, Hull Papers, DG 16, Box 6, SCPC; and Katz, "Carrie Chapman Catt," 59, 107.

16. The importance of the Democratic split in 1920 and 1924 is discussed in Allan J. Lichtman, "Critical Election Theory and the Reality of American Presidential Politics, 1916-40," *American Historical Review*, 81 (April 1976), 333.

17. The executive board minutes from 1920-1922 contain numerous references to concern about civil liberties, including the release of political prisoners, repeal of wartime laws abrogating First and Fourth amendment rights, amnesty for political prisoners, as well as concern for the "dark peoples," an issue raised by board member Mary Church Terrell. See WILPF, US Section, Series A,2, Box 1, SCPC.

18. Mercedes M. Randall, *Beyond Nationalism: The Social Thought of Emily Greene Balch* (New York: Twayne, 1972), 50.

19. Subscriber list for 1918 "Special Fund for Congress After War," in WILPF, US Section, Series C, 1, Box 2, SCPC. Included on the list were Mrs. Charles Crane, Mrs. Jacob Schiff, and Mrs. Frank Vanderlip.

20. Charter members listed in Woman's Peace Party folder, WILPF, US Section, Series C,1, Box 4, SCPC. Reports on membership are in same collection.

21. Finances are discussed in various minutes of Executive Board, WILPF, US Section, Series A,2, Box 1, SCPC.

22. Copy of Balch to Mead, May 16, 1924, discussed left and right wings of WILPF in WILPF, US Section, Series C, 1, Box 2, SCPC. Brown asked Congress to eliminate the Chemical Warfare Service in U.S. House of Representatives, Committee on Military Affairs, *Hearings on World Disarmament* (Washington, D.C., 1921), 39.

23. For coalition work see Executive Board Minutes for April 11, 1921, June 27, 1921, and September 29, 1921, WILPF, US Section, Series A,2, Box 1, and Series C,1, Box 4, SCPC. See also Mead to Catt on the Massachusetts League of Women Voters, April 7, 1920, Mead Papers, DG 21, Box 6, SCPC.

24. Mead to Balch, December 9, 1918, Balch Papers, DG 6, Box 1a, SCPC.

25. For Harding and Congress see C. Leonard Hoag, *Preface to Preparedness: The Washington Disarmament Conference and Public Opinion* (Washington, D.C.: American Council on Public Affairs, 1941), 36, 51, 68-75.

26. Robert D. Ward, "Against the Tide: the Preparedness Movement of 1923-24," *Military History*, 38 (April 1974), 59. Even the business community supported disarmament in the early 1920s according to Joan Hoff Wilson, *American Business and Foreign Policy, 1920-1933* (Boston: Beacon, 1973 reprint of 1971 edition), 31-64.

27. The Executive Board had queried members about priorities in a questionnaire. Relations with Mexico and Japan were the least concern; military training was the most important according to members. See Minutes, December 2, 1920 and January 6, 1921, WILPF, US Section, Series A,2, Box 1, SCPC. The move to Washington, D.C., signalled the decision to increase political activity. During 1921 WILPF distributed 100,000 leaflets, including 27,000 on disarmament, 10,000 of Brown's testimony before the House Committee on Military Affairs opposing the Chemical Warfare Service, and 1,000 of her pamphlet *America Menaced*.

28. *New York Times*, October 24, 1923, 1:2; *New York Times*, October 5, 1922, 25:8. Belle C. LaFollette to Lucy Biddle Lewis, October 6, 1922, asking for protests against "sham battles" in Washington, and copy Weeks to Miss Caroline L. Hunt,

October 7, 1922, defending the exhibitions, WILPF, US Section, Series C,1, Box 3, SCPC.

29. Lucia Ames Mead to Weeks, November 13, 1922, and Weeks to Mead, November 16, 1922, WILPF, US Section, Series C,1, Box 3, and press releases November 14, 1922 and February 14, 1923, Series A,5, Box 1, SCPC.

30. *New York Times*, April 1, 1923, 1:2, May 21, 1923, 14:7. Other information on public speeches is in *New York World*, May 9, 1924, June 5, 1924, and June 10, 1924. Clippings in WILPF, US Section, Series C,1, Box 1, SCPC, and in MID 10314-556/63, National Archives, Record Group 165, hereafter cited as NA, RG.

31. For War Plans White see Joan M. Jensen, *The Price of Vigilance* (Chicago: Rand McNally, 1968), 270-291, and idem, *Military Surveillance of Civilians in America* (Morristown, N.J.: General Learning, 1975), 19-22.

32. Situation Survey, 6th Corps Area, February 16-28, 1922, MID 10110-246/1; P. Slaughter, Assistant G-2, 9th Corps Area, May 27, 1922, MID 10110-2473; W. H. Cowles to Marlborough Churchill, December 19, 1922, MID 10110-2491; James Justice, AC of S, G-2, 2d Corps Area to AC of S, G-2, October 26, 1923; M. E. Locke, Executive Officer, G-2 to AC of S, G-2, 2d Corps Area, October 30, 1923, MID 10110-2473/13-14.

33. Amos A. Fries, Chief, Chemical Warfare Service to Major W. H. Cowles, January 2, 1923, MID 10110-2423, NA, RG 165.

34. The fullest published description of the "spider web" controversy is in Lemons, *Woman Citizen*, 214-216. A copy of the original "spider web" chart is in MID 10110-1835/24, NA, RG 165. R. M. Whitney to Lucia R. Maxwell, June 14, 1923, J. Edgar Hoover to Lucia R. Maxwell, May 19, 1923, MID 10110-1935, NA, RG 165. When Maxwell later wrote an antiradical tract, "Red Wings," the War Department was more circumspect about its responsibility, Alfred T. Smith, AC of S, G-2 Memorandum for Chief, Chemical Warfare Service, October 22, 1931, Maxwell Memorandum to Executive Officer, Chemical Warfare Service, November 19, 1931, and other correspondence in MID 10110-2653, NA, RG 165.

35. On relations to the army of the American Legion see W. K. Naylor, Acting C of S, G-2, Memorandum August 4, 1923, MID 10110, NA, RG 165, and Jensen, *Military Surveillance*, 22.

36. Colonel Stanley H. Ford, AC of S, G-2 to Ida L. Jones, YMCA, Fort Wayne, Indiana, May 20, 1927, MID 10110-1935/74; Fries to Captain J. H. Bogard, April 23, 1924, MID 10110-1935, NA, RG 165. John D. Weeks to Maud Park, May 2, 1924 is reprinted in Mrs. Randolph Frothingham, "The War Department Letter That Pacifists Concealed," *The Woman Patriot*, 11 (June 1, 1927), 81. Frothingham presented the War Department version but said that the Maxwell chart did not go far enough in linking women's groups to communism and socialism.

37. The *Schwimmer* v. *Marium* trial is discussed in Bailie to Dorothy Detzer, November 11, 1929, and Bailie to Alger, June 30, 1928, WILPF, US Section, Series C,1, Box 8. For a typical reaction of amazement about the reaction to their work see Alice Lloyd to Addams, April 21, 1924, same series, Box 1, SCPC.

38. Unsigned copy of letter to Spencer, May 20, 1924, and Spencer to Balch, June 11, 1924, WILPF, US Section, Series C,1, Box 1, SCPC; Balch to Mead, May 16, 1924, and Mead to Balch, May 19 [1924], WILPF, US Section, Series C,1, Box 2; undated Spencer to Amy Woods [1924], WILPF, US Section, Series C,1, Box 3, SCPC.

39. Negotiations for WILPF withdrawal from NCW are in Eva Perry Moore to

Amy Woods, April 21, 1924, Woods to Moore, April 24, 1924, Woods to Moore, September 5, 1924, Moore to Woods, September 13, 1924, Woods to Moore, September 16, 1924, Woods to Moore, September 24, 1924, Moore to Lucy Biddle Lewis, October 3, 1924, WILPF, US Section, Series C,1, Box 3. See also Mead to Hull, September 16, 1924, Hull Papers, DG 16, Box 6, and Moore to Hull, December 6, 1924, and Hull to Moore, December 16, 1924, WILPF, US Section, Series C,1, Box 3. All in SCPC.

40. Catt to Mead, October 15, 1920, August 26, 1921, August 8, 1923, September 26, 1923, Mead Papers, DG 21, Box 6, SCPC.

41. Katz, "Carrie Chapman Catt," 121-123; Catt to Mead, January 9, 1924, Mead Papers, DG 21, Box 6, SCPC; Addams to Hull, December 10, 1924, December 31, 1924, Hull Papers, DG 16, Box 6, SCPC; and undated clipping, 1925, reporting Roosevelt's comments, CCCW Papers, Box 2, SCPC.

42. Alice Thatcher Post to Hull, Spencer, Mead, and Lewis, January 27, 1925, Mead Papers, DG 21, Box 6, SCPC; Catt to Hull, January 30, 1925, and Addams to Hull, January 31, 1925, Hull Papers, DG 16, Box 6, SCPC; unsigned copy letter to Balch, January 23, 1925, and various clippings in WILPF, US Section, Series C,1, Box 5, SCPC.

43. Catt's comments are in Isabel Malcolm, "Woman's War on War," and comments on 1927 meeting are in George Leonard, "Watch Out, Mars!" in CCCW Papers, Box 2, SCPC. Catt thought there was a "very intense militaristic group" within the government but did not want to confront them, Catt to Rosika Schwimmer, November 6, 1925, Box 8, Catt Papers, LC.

44. The shift in emphasis can be seen in Dorothy Detzer to Madeline Z. Doty, January 24, 1925, Box 8, and Spencer to Detzer, April 6, 1925, Box 4; also in Detzer to Miss Emily R. Kneubuhl, November 29, 1926, all in WILPF, US Section, Series C, 1, SCPC. The woman who retorted "economic imperialism" was Alice Thatcher Post, as recounted in her letter to Hull, Spencer, Mead, and Lewis, January 27, 1925, Mead Papers, DG 21, Box 6, SCPC.

45. John K. Nelson, *The Peace Prophets: American Pacifist Thought, 1919-1941* (Chapel Hill, N.C.: University of North Carolina Press, 1967), 36. Both Nelson and Lawrence S. Wittner, *Rebels Against War: The American Peace Movement, 1941-1960* (New York and London: Columbia University Press, 1969) manage to talk about the peace movement with almost no mention of individual or organized women. Charles Chatfield, *For Peace and Justice: Pacifism in America, 1914-1941* (Knoxville, Tenn.: University of Tennessee Press, 1971), 99-100, briefly mentions feminist pacifists in the 1920s. Charles DeBenedetti, "Alternative Strategies in the American Peace Movement in the 1920's," in Charles Chatfield, editor, *Peace Movements in America* (New York: Schocken, 1973), identifies the reformists as a group but does not discuss women's activism in that group.

46. The *Woman Patriot*, 11 (January 15, 1927), 15, and 1 (April 27, 1918), 4.

10

International Feminism between the Wars: The National Woman's Party versus the League of Women Voters

SUSAN BECKER

When the National Woman's Party (NWP) introduced the Equal Rights Amendment in 1923, social feminists, especially the League of Women Voters (LWV) of the United States, immediately opposed it — a schism that symbolized the failure of American feminists to reach consensus on the meaning of equality after suffrage was won. Although nearly all groups could support such specific issues as maternal health legislation, jury service, a married woman's right to her own citizenship, and her right to work outside her home for compensation, these shared concerns could not overcome the fundamental disagreement between the NWP and the social feminists concerning special labor legislation for women only. While the social feminists believed such legislation was protective of working women, the NWP insisted that these laws restricted opportunities. There is no doubt that personal antagonisms lingered long after suffrage was won, but protective legislation became the ideological rock upon which American feminism split during the 1920s. The international feminist movement, like the American movement, also divided over the issue of industrial equality.

Internationally, the NWP and its equal rights allies opposed further passage or ratification of International Labour Office (ILO) protective labor conventions for women employed at night or in such hazardous work as the mines and the lead paint industry, for they feared the precedent that would be set if women were excluded from any employment opportunities. The LWV and its social feminist supporters considered such international conventions a logical extension of American protective legislation for women, who were at a disadvantage because of their maternal functions and thus could not compete on the same basis as male workers. Moreover, American social feminists believed that any setbacks in the movement for international protective labor conventions would weaken similar hard-won legislation for women in the United States.

The postsuffrage leadership struggle between the NWP and the American social feminists had important ramifications for feminists and for all working women. The decade of the 1920s was characterized by economic

An earlier version of this paper was presented at the Organization of American Historians in New York, April 1978.

dislocations which greatly affected working women in the United States, Great Britain, and other industrialized European nations. By the early thirties, the worldwide depression and the rise of fascism made it increasingly clear that women, especially married women, employed in business and the professions were particularly vulnerable.[1]

Confrontations over how best to secure equality for working women occurred in both Europe and Latin America from the mid-twenties through the late thirties. In Europe the conflict took the form of a split in the International Alliance of Women for Suffrage and Equal Citizenship; this divided and diffused European feminist activities. The International Alliance of Women might have provided leadership against economic discriminations, but the application of the NWP for admission to this organization and the LWV's adamant opposition to the party's membership precipitated the schism. While equalitarian feminists then concentrated their efforts on supporting a revision of the night-work convention for women, opposing further ratification of protective labor conventions and lobbying for League of Nations approval of an Equal Rights Treaty modeled on the Equal Rights Amendment, social feminists combined to block these efforts. In Latin America, the social feminists were able both to undermine the NWP's leadership position and to halt the trend toward equalitarian feminism.

Early in 1926, Mary Anderson and the U.S. Women's Bureau had sponsored a Conference on Women in Industry, which the NWP had disrupted with its demands for a reconsideration of the impact of protective legislation on women. In a letter discussing what she considered a major setback for the NWP, Anderson wrote that "now most of them have left for Paris to do what they can in the meeting of the International Suffrage Alliance." Although J. Stanley Lemons in *The Woman Citizen* has also suggested that the NWP turned its attention to international treaties and conventions in the late twenties because the party was blocked in its American efforts, the NWP views on the Equal Rights Amendment and labor equality were gradually gaining support among uncommitted women's organizations. Furthermore, NWP members were always internationally minded, believing themselves to be part of a great historical movement toward equality. The party's underlying ideological framework was one of sisterhood which emphasized both the special characteristics of women and the common problems shared by women all over the world; these views were not unlike those of the social feminists.[2]

But just as the bitter conflict between the NWP and the social feminists led by the LWV was brought out into the open at the U.S. Conference for Women in Industry in 1926, so the international phase of the struggle between these two groups over protective legislation and leadership of the feminist movement erupted at the meeting of the International Alliance of Women later that year. In 1925, Alice Paul and Mrs. O.H.P. Belmont had recruited European feminists as members of the international advisory council of the NWP and had applied for membership in the International Alliance of Women. The alliance had referred the NWP application for admission to the LWV, which was the only American member of the alliance at that time. Ordinarily this procedure was merely a courteous formality and it was the alliance's committee on admission which decided whether the applicant organization met the requirements of the alliance constitution. But the executive board of the LWV voted unanimously against the admission, filing a formal protest which argued that the NWP did not educate women as citizens, was not organized into branches throughout the country, and was a "party" that engaged in partisan politics. The board also stressed the differences between the league and the party in both policies and tactics, although a similarity in techniques and ideology was not required by the alliance constitution. As Mrs. Carrie Chapman Catt wrote to LWV president Belle Sherwin, "the constitution, we must admit, is very loosely drawn and will admit a chicken yard if it applies."[3]

Mrs. Catt correctly concluded that since the admissions committee would not know what to do they would postpone action and refer the question to the 1926 Paris convention, where the LWV and the NWP would probably be expected to argue their cases before the delegates. "I do not recommend this plan," wrote Catt, and she then worked actively behind the scenes to prevent such a confrontation. The Leslie Commission, organized to distribute the remainder of the $1 million left to the suffrage cause, was dominated by Mrs. Catt. The commission sent a formal letter of protest to the board of the International Alliance of Women and to its admissions committee, charging that the NWP record was "one of continual prevarication with regard to organization, numbers and propaganda." Furthermore, warned the commission, "its presence in the Alliance may well lead to the withdrawal or alienation of other organizations."[4] This thinly veiled threat implied that the bulk of the financial support for the alliance would be removed if the LWV should withdraw.

The president of the International Alliance, Margery Corbett Ashby, was placed in a very difficult position. She explained that the English suffragists had experienced the same problem, but had given some representation within the alliance to the Women's Freedom League because "though we objected very strongly to their methods we realized that they did, as a matter of fact, represent a body of women who were working for our common object." But Mrs. Catt replied that the American situation was very different because the NWP had made little or no organizational efforts. "It has played the cuckoo," Catt wrote, "and laid its eggs in nests that had cost much to build." Catt also warned Sherwin that the British women had always resented the American control of the alliance. In fact, she maintained, things had run smoothly when she was president of the alliance only because "I held every rein in my own hands and raised the money for its maintenance." Yet Catt admitted that "behind this problem there is present the contention over the general question of equal rights." If the admission question were decided in favor of the NWP she believed the league should drop out of the International Alliance, because if the NWP were to be admitted as an equal with the league "it will surely bring contention back to this country and do the League much more mischief." Sherwin agreed, but expressed the hope that the party's application would be turned down.[5]

The executive board of the International Alliance of Women was the first to give in, and in November 1925 Mrs. Ashby wrote to Mrs. Catt giving her unofficial notice that the board had recommended against the NWP to the committee on admission. The following month, Ashby formally notified Alice Paul and the NWP that their application had been rejected, pointing out the objections of the LWV. Mrs. Ashby noted that under the alliance constitution the NWP could still take its membership application before the conference delegates, "but it may be that your executive will prefer to withdraw it in these circumstances." Perhaps Mrs. Ashby really expected the party to withdraw gracefully, but she was to be disappointed. *Equal Rights*, the NWP journal, published the correspondence between Ashby and the party, pointing out that the alliance had solicited financial support from the party and had suggested that it apply for admission. The NWP would never have applied for membership, Alice Paul insisted, if they had known that admission depended upon the approval of the LWV, "as their hostility to the Woman's Party campaign for equality between men and women in labor legislation is well known."[6] Thus the NWP decided to present its case for admission before the convention.

Unable to attend the Paris congress because of her health, Mrs. Catt sent Sherwin letters of opposition to be read to the delegates if necessary. "Do not be afraid of this rumpus," she wrote. "Remember that we are just washing our dirty linen in the International tub." Jane Norman Smith, Doris Stevens, and Burnita Shelton Matthews spoke for the NWP while other party members attended either as fraternal delegates authorized by ten governors or as part of the very active NWP press contingent. Well-known British feminists such as Chrystal MacMillan, Mrs. Pethick-Lawrence, and Lady Rhondda supported the NWP's case, but the congress upheld the board's decision by a vote of 123 to 48. Eleven members of the alliance executive board resigned over the issue and Lady Rhondda's Six Point Group withdrew its membership application. "The methods used in respect to the request for affiliation of the NWP, and with a view to preventing the affiliation," she wrote, "have been such that it would not be possible for the Six Point Group to associate itself with them."[7]

Alice Paul announced that the NWP would continue working for equality, and the alliance board asked the party to sign a statement to clear up any "false impressions" the public might have about the issues involved. This was designed to save face for all concerned and suggested that the

LWV and the NWP were "willing to work side by side, each according to its traditions and convictions, fully aware of the great aims that unite them." The NWP representatives, of course, refused to sign on the grounds that they had no authority to do so, that it did not coincide with their intentions, and that it in no way expressed the party's views or wishes. The damage was done, yet the NWP had not come to Paris with the intention of splitting the international feminist movement. When it became evident that those women's groups that favored labor equality might withdraw from the alliance if membership were withheld from the NWP, Stevens cabled Alice Paul for instructions. "I feel that unless we are ready to carry on [the] international movement ourselves," Paul replied, "we ought to support those doing it and not be responsible for split in their ranks."[8]

The LWV was forced on the defensive by the adverse publicity this whole affair engendered. In an effort to explain to its members "Why the League Objected," Gertrude Brown pointed out that the NWP often hindered the passage of the league's carefully selected bills because of the wide gap in their views about protective legislation. Concerning labor equality, Brown maintained that "the great mass of women are opposed to this viewpoint" and reiterated that because of their maternal functions women should be protected. The NWP also tried to clarify to its membership the differences between the league and the party. It was not just the issue of protective legislation that had kept the party out of the alliance, Jane Norman Smith declared, but also the NWP's uncompromising attitude on women's need for total equality, which was frightening to many women. The International Alliance, too, bore the scars of the conflict between the two groups of feminists. In its call for an eleventh congress to be held in Berlin in 1929, the alliance attempted to hold together its remaining members by an ideological statement encompassing both gradual citizenship education and future work for total equality, but the result was the defection of the immediatists.[9]

The underlying problem within the alliance in 1926 was its members' differing views about labor equality for women; this was also a major contributing factor in the LWV's opposition to the party's bid for membership. The league had managed to prevent the alliance from issuing any policy statement on the question of protective legislation during the twenties by insisting that the problem needed further study. In January 1926, however, the alliance committee on like conditions of work for men and women had issued a preliminary report advocating equal educational opportunities for women, equality in the civil service, and equal pay for equal work. With these aims the LWV was in full agreement, but the fourth resolution, dealing with the right of married women to work, contained the recommendation that future labor laws should tend toward equality between men and women. "The problem before us," the committee noted, "is whether restrictions embracing certain groups of workers only inside the same occupation will not restrain or ruin their chances of earning a living." In March the committee resolved that future protective legislation should not be framed in any way that might restrict women's job opportunities, and LWV officials prepared a substitute resolution which they hoped would replace the committee's at the congress. The LWV resolution argued that because of national differences, legislation must be drawn up specifically with regard to "the needs and wishes of working women of that country."[10]

The only real chance of diverting the congress from accepting the committee's report was based on the league's dominant position representing American women, which would be weakened if the NWP were allowed to present its arguments against special legislation. This confusing issue was not settled by the compromise resolution finally passed by the Paris congress, which recommended that "no obstacle should be placed in the way of married women who desire to enter or continue in paid work, and that the laws relative to women as mothers should not be framed as to handicap them in their economic position." A resolution condemning the ILO conventions on night work and hazardous employment for women was defeated. American journalists correctly identified the question of labor equality as the basis of the schisms that were occurring in European feminism, or as the *Survey* reported, "by that issue more than any other one's degree of feminism is measured."[11] Little effort was made, however, to put this European feminist concern with women's right to work into the context of economic dislocations so evident in countries like Great Britain or Germany.

The NWP also emphasized the connection between its rejection by the alliance and the controversy over labor equality. *Equal Rights* argued that labor equality, much like equal suffrage, could serve "to focus and vitalize the feminist movement." In Jane Norman Smith's notes on the Paris congress, she evaluated the schism in terms of a regrouping of feminists. The basis for this realignment, according to another NWP member, was evident. "They are reformers," she wrote, "we are Feminists."[12]

Feminists who, like the Six Point Group, favored industrial equality for women met to organize the Open Door Council in 1927. Although two NWP officers were present as fraternal delegates, the early membership was overwhelmingly British. The feminists announced that they hoped an international organization could be formed to work for women's labor equality and "to attack the anti-Feminist Labour Bureau of the League of Nations." By the summer of 1929, this hope had been transformed into reality by the organization of the Open Door International (ODI) in Berlin, which included men as well as women. The ODI manifesto, calling for equal economic freedom, opportunity, and status for women workers, expressed a fundamental belief "that a woman as well as a man is an end in herself." The ODI also issued an eleven-point "Woman Worker's Charter of Economic Rights" demanding that restrictive legislation be based on the job rather than on the sex of the worker and stressing the right of the married woman to engage in paid work of her choice, free from restrictions related to maternity, with complete control over her earnings. The ODI believed that supporters of protective legislation for women were living in the past. "We look to the future, realizing that this economic emancipation has hardly begun," declared their manifesto. "The struggle has become international."[13]

American feminists had always encouraged the growth of feminism in Latin America. The fifth Pan American Congress, held in Santiago, Chile, in 1923, passed a resolution to include a discussion of the rights of women at future conferences, and in 1926 an inter-American congress of women meeting in Panama City passed an equality resolution. As Mrs. Catt became more involved in her peace work during the mid-twenties, the LWV's overtures to Latin American women declined, and the stage was set for the NWP to assume a leadership position in the Latin American feminist movement. When the sixth Pan American Congress met at Havana, Cuba, in 1928, representatives of the party were present and succeeded in getting six countries to sponsor the inclusion of the Equal Rights Treaty, modeled on the Equal Rights Amendment, on the agenda of the seventh conference scheduled for Montevideo, Uruguay, in 1933. Even more significant was the congress's creation of an Inter-American Commission of Women to study women's status. The congress appointed NWP activist Doris Stevens as the chairperson of the commission.[14]

Party members, delighted with this assertive move into internationalism, compared the influence of the Pan American conferences in the Western hemisphere with the League of Nations' influence on European countries. Pan American states that approved the principle of equal rights would be much less likely to discriminate individually or through international conventions. Such Pan American action would lead the way for the rest of the world, but *Equal Rights* also warned that "if we fail now through carelessness or lack of determination, our grandchildren will then face the always difficult task of abolishing inequalities established now." Since the NWP consistently maintained that feminism should not be limited by national boundaries but rather should encompass the whole world, it immediately announced its intention to promulgate the Equal Rights Treaty at Geneva. The party believed that the success at Havana had provided a "conclusive demonstration" of "the proper method of procedure hereafter." As an *Equal Rights* editorial pointed out: "The few short weeks of intensive effort at Havana, the comparatively small sum of money invested in it, have already brought rewards greater a thousandfold than could have been realized through purely national activities."[15] Longtime NWP member Lavinia Dock termed the party's achievements "glorious" and "almost incredible." "I consider that Party members are classed with all the truly great crusaders," she wrote to Mabel Vernon, "and I don't understand why everyone doesn't see it." In Doris Stevens's analysis of the Havana accomplishments, she emphasized that women were finally to be treated as colleagues rather than auxiliaries at international conferences. Denying that the treaty method was revolutionary, she cited the ILO conventions that dealt with women's work.[16] In her speech to the Havana congress, she had insisted: "For you see, no man, no group of men, no government, no nation, no group of nations—ever had the right to withhold from us the rights we ask today. We ask to have restored rights which have been usurped. These are our human rights."[17]

The first question on which the Inter-American Commission of Women decided to research and to make recommendations was the problem of married women's nationality. This issue was on the agenda of both the Hague Codification Conference of 1930 and the League of Nations Assembly; the International Alliance of Women had also passed a resolution advocating complete independence of nationality. But this question too became a focus for controversy between the LWV and the NWP. The league had always supported the principle of independent nationality and had worked throughout the twenties and early thirties for congressional bills that gradually removed the discriminations against married women. But the LWV seemed to fear that the party would take credit for any advances toward equal nationality rights, and this was obvious by the hostility of the two groups at the Hague Codification Conference. The International Alliance, the LWV, and the NWP all lobbied the conference. At the first hearing league officials Maud Wood Park and Mrs. Pitman Potter spoke on behalf of all women, but, as LWV attorney Dorothy Strauss reported, "other women, less reasonable in method, appeared on the scene as spokesmen for less representative groups of women and these were permitted to join this second meeting."[18]

The LWV had always objected strongly to being put on a "parity" with the NWP, and the treaty method of obtaining nationality rights was just as objectionable to the league as was the amendment method of obtaining equality. When these were combined with the third NWP proposal, the Equal Rights Treaty, the league felt surrounded by the threat of the "blanket" legislation to which it had always been opposed and which it feared would destroy special labor laws for women. The Hague conference recommendation was that a woman's nationality should remain dependent on that of her husband, and the efforts of organized women shifted to the League of Nations, where they lobbied against ratification of the nationality convention.

In response to the Equal Rights Treaty, British feminists had created a new organization, Equal Rights International, and in 1930 formally extended an invitation to the NWP to join. But there was some resistance within the party itself to extensive international commitments which might take precedence over state and national work. When the question of affiliation with the ODI had arisen, there had been protests that efforts for international equality might spread the party's resources too thin, although most members agreed with Mrs. O.H.P. Belmont's often quoted statement that "no woman can be free anywhere until all women are free." *Equal Rights* stressed the similarities between the position of the Equal Rights Treaty before the League of Nations in 1930 and that of the federal suffrage amendment before the U.S. Congress in 1912. In both instances, the party journal pointed out, Alice Paul stood ready to assume the direction of an efficient and unified campaign. Internationalist members of the NWP believed that Equal Rights International could provide a catalyst for the approval of the Equal Rights Treaty, and that its Geneva headquarters could be immensely stimulating to European feminism. The NWP affiliated with both the ODI and Equal Rights International, and in 1931 the Women's International League for Peace and Freedom (WILPF) endorsed the equality treaty. A growing nucleus of feminist support for the party's position was being established in Europe.[19]

Most of the NWP's European activities during the remainder of the thirties were designed to advance its Equal Rights Treaty through the complicated machinery of the League of Nations. If it had been able to achieve this goal, the treaty would have become an international convention recommended to all member countries for ratification. When first faced with persistent feminist lobbying, the League of Nations' response had been to create a Women's Consultative Committee in 1931, charged with reporting on the status of women and making recommendations concerning equality. But this committee split over the question of protective legislation in 1932, and although as a whole it ceased to function, the subcommittee on propaganda continued its activities on behalf of total equality. Not surprisingly, this subcommittee included six NWP members as representatives of the various participating women's organizations.[20]

According to Alice Paul, their strategy was first to get the Equal Rights Treaty on the agenda of the League of Nations assembly, then to build up more support for the treaty by endorsements from international women's organizations, and finally to develop national support for ratification within individual countries. When the NWP did manage to get the Equal Rights Treaty on the agenda for the 1935 meeting, the LWV drew up a formal protest to be circulated among the League of Nations delegates, describing the treaty as unnecessary, impractical, and harmful, and suggesting that the status of women was a question which still needed intensive study.[21]

Only international organizations could circulate opinions in the League of Nations, but the International Alliance of Women would not annex the LWV statement. The league ultimately turned to the World YWCA to present the protest; the LWV strategy was carefully developed and made known to its officers in the form of a confidential paper. Its main effort would be to get the League of Nations to postpone the issue until further study was done. Other social feminist organizations would be approached for support on the basis that they could avoid expressing an opinion on protective conventions, "which statement they have been trying to avoid for years."[22] The strategy was successful and the League of Nations resolution recommended further study. The political status of women was assigned to individual governments for consideration while the question of protective legislation and its impact on women was assigned to the ILO for research.

It was Mary Anderson, the head of the U.S. Women's Bureau, who spearheaded the efforts of the social feminists to block the progress of the Equal Rights Treaty through the League of Nations. Although carefully instructed, American social feminists in international organizations had found themselves increasingly a distinct minority when advocating protective legislation in the 1930s. "There was practically no support to [the LWV] point of view outside the U.S. delegation," observed its representative to the 1935 alliance congress. Mary Anderson encouraged social feminists to write to the ILO stating their objections to the treaty and their support for protective legislation. Anderson also corresponded with Grace Abbott, American delegate to the ILO after the United States joined in 1934.[23]

In a private report to American social feminists in June 1935, Abbott observed that because of Hitler and Mussolini, European women were very much afraid of the closing of economic opportunities for women at all levels. "While we have felt some of the fear of these in the U.S.," Abbott wrote, "I was surprised to find how serious European women feel the situation to be." After consulting with social feminists in Geneva, she concluded that the Equal Rights Treaty had little chance of passage. However, she warned, the ODI had been actively urging the solidarity of women and "the effect of this situation on women, not all of them 'feminists,' has been . . . that some who favor industrial legislation have concluded that at this time they ought to stand for the 'Equal Rights' Treaty."[24]

Throughout 1935, the new LWV president Marguerite Wells kept Secretary of Labor Frances Perkins informed of the social feminists' concern about the Equal Rights Treaty. Perkins responded by instructing the U.S. delegates to the ILO to encourage a full study of protective legislation, to agree with the LWV position, and to oppose the treaty. Social feminists also kept pressure on Harold Butler and other ILO officials. "Miss Paul does not represent the working women of the U.S.," Mary Anderson wrote to Butler. "Her views are diametrically opposed to those of working women, who believe in special legislation for women and work for such legislation through their trade union organizations." The NWP insistently demanded that Perkins urge the ILO to deal with the question of women's right to work, and in a memo to the secretary of labor, Anderson argued that the party just wanted publicity. "It is for the purpose of showing the European women's organizations that they are all-powerful," Anderson wrote, "and for that reason they should support them in putting through the Treaty."[25] Both more accurate and more discouraging was the response of an ILO official to the LWV's Geneva lobbyist early in 1936. Governments were "nervous about taking a definite line," he wrote.

> The resolution of last year is, of course, only a compromise between reluctance to offend the women's organizations and inability to propose any rational form of action by the League; and it seems likely to give us an ill-digested encyclopaedic mass of information but very unlikely to provide us with anything approaching a policy. Being convinced as I am that the most that can emerge from the League's discussion is some form of pious resolution, . . . my fear is that the whole affair will slowly progress towards a fiasco which can only do the League harm.[26]

Anderson's most ambitious project was the development of the Woman's Charter, intended to serve as an alternative to both the Equal Rights Treaty and the Equal Rights Amendment. In the summer of 1936, a small group of representatives from social feminist organizations began meeting to formulate a charter safeguarding protective legislation for women. Also actively involved in the early planning stages were Mary Van Kleeck of the Russell Sage Foundation, Frieda Miller of the New York State Department of Labor, and historian Mary Beard. Anderson informed Mme. Marguerite Thibert of the ILO Women's Work division as well as Frances Perkins about the plan. "This is a good move," replied Perkins, "and I would suggest that you continue with the work of this Committee."[27] Although two NWP members had been appointed to the ILO's Correspondence Committee on Women's Work, the party was excluded from knowledge of and participation in these meetings.

The Woman's Charter group experienced difficulties from the beginning. Anderson, Van Kleeck, and a few others insisted upon a strong statement supporting protective legislation, but as one businesswoman noted, "there are hundreds and thousands of the group I represent who are muddled about this whole thing." Each attempt to broaden the unofficial committee to include other women's organizations, although still excluding the NWP, simply exacerbated the problems. The October meeting foundered over Mary Beard's suggestion that women should be trained to work and should expect to work, which won strong approval from some committee members and equally strong disapproval from others. Mary Anderson expressed the traditional view when she argued that a woman "must remember that when she marries and keeps house she also has a lifetime job." One representative voiced a hope that the charter "would not be a defense of position against the Woman's Party but would be something else which would include their general idea of wanting to get better status for women." When Van Kleeck argued that the charter was not merely defensive, another representative of professional women replied that "it was so interpreted by my group." There were heated discussions about whether to include a specific guarantee of the right of married women to work. "We cannot get together with the Woman's Party point of view unless they accept our point of view," insisted Mary Anderson, ". . . unless we sacrifice the working woman."[28]

Although the group managed to establish tentative procedures for publicity, promotion, and endorsement of the charter, the fundamental problems revealed by the attempt to formulate an alternative to the NWP's equality program were never resolved. Even the social feminists of the ILO Women's Work division had objections to the draft of the charter. It suggested "a demand for full responsibility and for special privileges at one and the same time," commented Alice Cheyney of the ILO staff in a letter to Anderson. Writing to a friend at the World YWCA six weeks later, Cheyney stated that she had rewritten parts of the charter but was still not completely satisfied. "It seems to me . . . ," she explained, "to bear too strongly for general appeal, the mark of its immediate origin in a desire to make a case for protective legislation."[29]

In her autobiography, Anderson described the committee as trying to produce a document that all women could endorse, and her hope that "perhaps we could, with this charter, bridge the gap between ourselves and the NWP." This statement is disingenuous at best. The charter specifically provided for protective legislation for women; when Van Kleeck sent it to Felix Frankfurter at the Harvard Law School for his legal opinion, she presented it as an alternative to equal rights. A suggested public presentation of the charter which stressed its protective aspects was vetoed by representatives of both the LWV and the Consumers' League as impolitic. News of the text was kept from the NWP until Anderson sent it simultaneously to newspapers and organizations in December 1936. Yet the charter was not a success, in spite of all the careful planning. "But nothing worked out the way we had wanted it to," Anderson wrote. "The movement was a complete flop."[30]

The Woman's Charter failed for a number of reasons. The NWP emphasized the secrecy of the planning committee and questioned whether the women involved in drafting the charter did so with the approval of the organizations that they were supposed to represent. Groups like the Business and Professional Women and the American Association of University Women were already badly split over the question of protective legislation. Mary Beard publicly repudiated the draft, while even the American Home Economics Association journal recognized that there were two schools of thought about labor equality. To complicate the situation further, the NWP circulated an amended version of the charter which substituted the concept of labor laws based only on the job and not on the sex of the worker. As one of the social feminists involved in planning the original charter replied, "it seems hardly necessary to say that I completely disagree with the changes made by you and your associates, and would under no circumstances support such a revision." Furthermore, large women's organizations like the LWV insisted that the charter go through their usual long and involved study procedure, and then often endorsed only the principles, not the actual document.[31]

By 1937, however, the social feminists had effectively blocked the progress of the Equal Rights Treaty through the ILO. At the labor conference that year, Grace Abbott successfully sponsored a resolution requesting further study of women's economic position, supporting the principle of equal pay, and calling for "legislative safeguards against physically harmful conditions of employment and economic exploitation, including the safeguarding of motherhood." The International Alliance of Women protested vigorously, but to no avail, that this action "could not be held to represent the views of women in general" and criticized Abbott for failing to consult with any international women's organizations. In America, Mary Van Kleeck announced the formation of a Joint Committee on Women's Work to implement the ILO resolution; this committee would be open to all women's organizations in sympathy with the Woman's Charter.[32] By the end of 1938, the movement for the charter had died.

The decade also ended badly for the NWP's leadership position in Latin America. The struggle between the social feminists led by the LWV and the NWP feminists was resumed at the Montevideo Pan American Congress in 1933. Sophonisba Breckinridge, a U.S. representative, wrote Belle Sherwin that the women's meeting was confused, disorderly, and poorly conducted. The Inter-American Commission of Women, led by Doris Stevens, had been able to present both the Equal Rights Treaty and the Equal Nationality Treaty to the conference. Breckinridge could only hope that the commission would be disbanded and that then those Latin American women "who do not share the characteristics of the leading members of the Woman's Party" could be reorganized. When the United States abstained from voting on the Equal Nationality Treaty, the publicity was very unfavorable and organized women other than the LWV expressed disapproval of the American action. As Stevens had cabled to the newspapers, "the attitude of the U.S. delegation was not only a matter of great regret and disappointment, but came as a profound shock and surprise."[33]

Belle Sherwin had informed Cordell Hull, Secretary of State, that although the LWV favored equal nationality, it opposed the treaty method for achieving this equality, and simultaneously the league had released its objections to the press. Writing later to a member about the unfavorable publicity that resulted, Sherwin admitted that the first league press release was hastily prepared, somewhat too grudging about the principle of equal nationality, and too flatly opposed to the treaty method in general. She explained that "the League of Women Voters is always on the defensive in respect to the action of the NWP," but went on to justify "the old policy of nonaggressive publicity in relation to points at issue with the NWP." Yet the league did feel compelled later to issue conciliatory press releases, and Dorothy Strauss wrote the *New York Times* to correct any misunderstanding of the league's attitude on equal nationality rights. Denying that Eleanor Roosevelt had intervened on behalf of the league with the State Department, Strauss stated that the league believed the treaty would not accomplish the desired goals and explained that the LWV's longtime interest in efficiency in government had led it to oppose "blanket" methods that might hinder more effective legislation. She also insisted that the league was not opposed to meaningful international agreements on nationality. Yet the underlying reasons for the league's opposition were its rivalry with the NWP and its fear of some future threat to protective laws in the United States. When league officials later testified against the ratification of the Equal Nationality Treaty at the Foreign Relations Committee hearing, it was on the basis that it would open all sorts of other areas to "blanket" legislation.[34]

The LWV also finally succeeded in ridding the InterAmerican Commission of Doris Stevens and the NWP influence. Instrumental in this accomplishment was Mary Winslow of the Women's Trade Union League, who began working behind the scenes a full year before the eighth Pan American Congress at Lima, Peru. Her first efforts utilized Mollie Dewson's influence in the State Department as a Democratic Party activist to get a reliable social feminist appointed to the delegation; this woman would be able to present a resolution safeguarding protective legislation yet speaking out for women's rights. Winslow and other social feminists drafted a resolution and circulated it quietly to selected women's groups. Two women went to Lima as technical advisors to the American delegation and Mary Anderson personally paid the expenses of a third woman, a journalist who would do publicity work. President Roosevelt had approved the resolution as modified by the State Department and had instructed the American delegates to support it. The LWV had arranged a communications system so that if further support were necessary, endorsements from women's organizations could be obtained and sent to Lima within twenty-four hours of notification.[35]

Social feminists also laid plans to have Stevens replaced as chair of the InterAmerican Commission by a State Department appointee. Mollie Dewson suggested Mary Winslow, while Elisabeth Christman of the Women's Trade Union League and Mary Anderson of the Women's Bureau quietly collected endorsements. Although the NWP leaders countered with a publicity campaign and by lobbying Congress, there is no doubt that they were taken by surprise, both by the Lima resolution and the move to replace Stevens. The State Department had announced Mary Winlow's appointment on 1 February 1939, and two weeks later Marguerite Wells sent her some observations from one of the technical advisors at the Lima conference. The latter believed that Stevens had somehow gained the loyalty of the *New York Times* and was therefore able to secure good publicity. Yet she also thought Stevens was "on the way out, both as a personality and the leader of her particular cause, but she may make quite a struggle getting out." Indeed, Stevens had earlier offered her resignation but the commission had refused to accept it, so her personal position was somewhat strengthened. However, since she had not been appointed by the United States, but rather by the Pan American Congress, her legal position was shaky.[36] The advisor suggested that the LWV make a concerted effort at lobbying, and concluded encouragingly: "Don't let the people in Washington get discouraged — we had Doris on the run once — we can get her there again. I don't see why the whole thing can't be handled by clever administrative rulings and appointments. You must get the Pan American Union to get over being intimidated by Doris. It's a bad habit people have. She is vulnerable in certain spots."[37]

The NWP counterattacked vigorously by lobbying U.S. senators and Pan American delegates. Although Stevens had considerable support among the delegates and senators, including some prominent Democrats, the InterAmerican Commission was reorganized completely in 1940, a Latin American woman appointed chair, and Winslow finally seated as U.S. representative. "We have deplored the agitation regarding feminist issues that have [sic] taken place in South America," Elisabeth Christman had announced to the press in the midst of the leadership struggle, "and feel they have been a great set back to the interests of women."[38] The NWP continued its battle with the social feminists over which group could best represent women's interests. "The situation is and has been for months," wrote Mary Murray of the NWP's industrial council, "[that] the Governing Board has before it the name of an appointee to a place not vacant, presented by a person having no jurisdiction in affairs of the Board, said person being the highest officer of one of the most powerful countries in the Pan American Union. Not a pleasant position for Board members from neighbor countries."[39]

The NWP's international activism during the twenties led it to assume a dominant position in the Latin American feminist movement and to precipitate, although not cause, a schism in the international movement. During the thirties it presented the Equal Rights Treaty and Equal Nationality Treaty for endorsement by women's organizations and passage by international conferences, but it was blocked by social feminists who favored the protective labor conventions of the ILO. By the end of the decade, Alice Paul's attempt to unite European feminists had been overwhelmed by the rise of fascism, while the NWP's leadership in Latin American feminism had been challenged successfully by American social feminists. Both groups of feminists were uncompromising, because at the heart of the matter lay an ideological disagreement over the meaning of economic equality for women.

The final result of more than a decade of international struggle between American social and equalitarian feminists was the development of a total impasse. The ILO study, *The Law and Women's Work* (1939), discussed the problem of women's right to employment, noted that women had historically formed a reserve labor pool, and maintained that there were "certain problems that are always with us, such as the fact of maternity, which underlies them all." The conclusion of the 1939 ILO study differed very little from that of the 1932 ILO report, neither condemning nor approving protective legislation for women.[40] And the outbreak of World War II made further debate on the question of women's right to work merely academic, at least for a few years.

Notes

1. Lois Scharf, *To Work and To Wed: Female Employment, Feminism, and the Great Depression* (Westport, Conn., Greenwood Press, 1980); for European economic dislocations, see Renata Bridenthal, "Something Old, Something New: Women Between the Two World Wars," in *Becoming Visible: Women In European History,* ed. by Renata Bridenthal and Claudia Koonz (Boston: Houghton Mifflin, 1977), 424-444.

2. Mary Anderson to Mrs. Raymond Robins, May 17, 1926, Mary Anderson Papers, Box 3, Schlesinger Library; J. Stanley Lemons, *The Woman Citizen* (Urbana, Ill.: University of Illinois, 1975), 196; Editorial, "An International Movement," *Equal Rights,* 11 (November 22, 1924), 324; "A Living Center of Union," *Equal Rights,* 12 (October 24, 1925), 291; "The International Movement," *Equal Rights,* 12 (April 4, 1925), 60; Susan Becker, "An Intellectual History of the National Woman's Party, 1920-1941," (Ph.D. dissertation, Case Western Reserve University, 1975).

3. Belle Sherwin to Anna Wicksell, April 6, 1925; Elizabeth J. Hauser to Anna Wicksell, May 2, 1925; Anna Wicksell to Elizabeth J. Hauser, May 25, 1925; Carrie Chapman Catt to Belle Sherwin, September 20, 1925; League of Women Voters Papers, series II, Box 51, Library of Congress.

4. Carrie Chapman Catt to Belle Sherwin, September 20, 1925; Harriet B. Wells to the Committee on Admissions and Board of the International Woman's Suffrage Association, September 22, 1925; League of Women Voters Papers, series II, Box 51, Library of Congress.

5. Margery Corbett Ashby to Belle Sherwin, October 10, 1925; Carrie Chapman Catt to Margery Corbett Ashby, October 20, 1925; League of Women Voters Papers, series II, Box 52, Library of Congress; Carrie Chapman Catt to Belle Sherwin, October 30, 1925, Belle Sherwin to Carrie Chapman Catt, November 25, 1925; League of Women Voters Papers, series II, Box 51, Library of Congress.

6. Margery Corbett Ashby to Alice Paul, December 15, 1925, League of Women Voters Papers, series II, Box 51, Library of Congress; Crystal Eastman, "The Great Rejection, Part I," *Equal Rights,* 13 (June 19, 1926), 149; "The International Suffrage Alliance," *Equal Rights,* 13 (February 27, 1926), 24; "The International Suffrage Alliance," *Equal Rights,* 13 (March 20, 1926), 48; Margery Corbett Ashby to Carrie Chapman Catt, (confidential letter), March 28, 1926, League of Women Voters Papers, series II, Box 52, Library of Congress.

7. Carrie Chapman Catt to Belle Sherwin, May 12, 1926, League of Women

Voters Papers, series II, Box 52, Library of Congress; "Equal Rights Before the World Congress," *Equal Rights*, 13 (June 5, 1926), 133-134; "Equal Rights Before the IWSA," *Equal Rights*, 13 (June 12, 1926), 141.

8. "Equal Rights Before the IWSA," *Equal Rights*, 13 (June 12, 1926), 141; Editorial, "A Gift of the Spirit," *Equal Rights*, 13 (June 19, 1926), 148; "The Suffragist Fight Over Industrial Equality," *Literary Digest*, 89 (June 12, 1926), 10; Crystal Eastman, "The Great Rejection, Part II," *Equal Rights*, 13 (June 19, 1926), 149-150; Cable, Alice Paul to Doris Stevens, May 30, 1926; Cable, Doris Stevens to Alice Paul, June 1, 1926; Cable, Alice Paul to Doris Stevens, June 1, 1926, Jane Norman Smith Papers, Box 5, Schlesinger Library.

9. Gertrude Fendall Brown, "Editorially Speaking — Why the League Objected," *Woman Citizen*, 11 (July 1926), 24; Jane Norman Smith, "The Different Purposes of the NWP and the League of Women Voters," *Equal Rights*, 13 (September 18, 1926), 254-255; Editorial, "The Significance of the Woman's Party," *Equal Rights*, 13 (September 18, 1926), 252; "Equal Rights the Ultimate Aim," *Equal Rights*, 14, bis (December 22, 1928), 367.

10. IWSA, Committee on Like Conditions of Work for Men and Women, "Appendix to the Preliminary Report, March 27, 1926," League of Women Voters Papers, series II, Box 51, Library of Congress; "Resolution on Legislation for Women in Industry to be Proposed by the LWV," n.d., League of Women Voters Papers, series II, Box 52, Library of Congress.

11. Edith Abbott to Belle Sherwin, April 13, 1926, League of Women Voters Papers, series II, Box 101, Library of Congress; "Equal Rights Before the World Congress of Women," *Equal Rights*, 13 (June 5, 1926), 133; "The Suffragists Fight Over Industrial Equality," *Literary Digest*, 89 (June 12, 1926), 10-11; Cornelia S. Parker, "feminists and Feminists," *Survey*, 56, (August 1926), 502-504.

12. Editorial, "Why the Emphasis?" *Equal Rights*, 13 (June 12, 1926), 140; Crystal Eastman, "The Great Rejection, Part I," *Equal Rights*, 13 (June 19, 1926), 150; "From Our Correspondents," *Equal Rights*, 13 (June 19, 1926), 224; "Notes from 10th Congress, IWSA," 1926, Jane Norman Smith Papers, Box 1, Schlesinger Library.

13. Editorial, "The Six Points," *Equal Rights*, 14 (June 25, 1927), 156; "The Open Door Council," *Equal Rights*, 14 (June 4, 1927), 131; "Press Comment," *Equal Rights*, 14 (July 20, 1929), 159; "Woman Worker's Charter of Economic Rights," *Equal Rights*, 15, (July 20, 1929), 187.

14. U.S. Department of Labor, Women's Bureau, "Summary of Pan American Conferences Concerning Status of Women, August 1938," Women's Trade Union League Papers, Box 8, Library of Congress; "Equal Rights in the Western Hemisphere," *Equal Rights*, 14 (January 21, 1928), 395; "Pan American Committee of Seven Completed," *Equal Rights*, 14 bis (November 10, 1928), 316.

15. Editorial, "Why We Are in Havana," *Equal Rights*, 14 (January 28, 1928), 402; Editorial, "Showing the Way," *Equal Rights*, 14 bis (February 25, 1928), 20.

16. Lavinia Dock to Mabel Vernon, May 7, 1928, in *Equal Rights*, 14 bis (May 19, 1928), 120; Doris Stevens, "Feminist History Was Made at Havana," *Equal Rights*, 14 bis (March 3, 1928), 29; "In Behalf of the Equal Rights Treaty; address by Doris Stevens," *Equal Rights*, 14 bis (March 10, 1928), 37-39.

17. "In Behalf of the Equal Rights Treaty; address by Doris Stevens," *Equal Rights*, 14 bis (March 10, 1928), 37-39.

18. "For Equality in Nationality," *Equal Rights*, 14 (July 13, 1929), 180-181; Idella Gwatkin Swisher, "Program of the National League of Women Voters," *Congressional Digest*, 9 (November 1930), 265-266, 288; IWSA, "Call for Demonstration at the Hague Codification Conference," March 14, 1930, League of Women Voters Papers, series II, Box 101, Library of Congress; Dorothy Strauss, "Independent Nationality Through National Laws," *Congressional Digest*, 9 (November 1930), 281-282.

19. Editorial, "Shall We Affiliate?" *Equal Rights*, 15 (September 28, 1929), 266; "Plans for Equal Rights Treaty," *Equal Rights*, 16 (August 2, 1930), 203; Editorial, "The Long Arm of the Lever," *Equal Rights*, 16 (September 27, 1930), 266; Editorial, "Equal Rights International," *Equal Rights*, 16 (October 11, 1930), 282; Elizabeth Rodgers, "The Open Door International at Geneva," *Equal Rights*, 16 (January 17, 1931), 397-398; "Open Door Council Meeting," *Equal Rights*, 16 (May 16, 1931), 117-118.

20. Memorandum, Miss Quinlan to League of Women Voters, October 4, 1933, League of Women Voters Papers, series II, Box 340, Library of Congress; Alice Paul, "Report to the Woman's Party Convention, Wilmington, Delaware, November 4 and 5, 1933, by the Committee on International Relations," *Equal Rights*, 19 (November 25, 1933), 331-332.

21. Lola Maverick Lloyd, "Feminist Attack," *Equal Rights*, 20 (November 17, 1934), 333; "Alice Paul Returns," *Equal Rights*, 21 (July 15, 1935), 1; Alice Paul to Alma Lutz, July 20, 1936, Alma Lutz Papers, Box 6, Schlesinger Library; "Statement Drawn Up by the National LWV of the U.S.A." [1935]; Memorandum, Mrs. Johnstone to Miss Wells, February 25, 1936, League of Women Voters Papers, series II, Box 340, Library of Congress.

22. Belle Sherwin to Marguerite M. Wells, August 20, 1935, League of Women Voters Papers, series II, Box 342, Library of Congress; "Some Confidential Information of Which Miss Wells has come into possession from an unofficial source," n.d. [1935], League of Women Voters Papers, series II, Box 340, Library of Congress.

23. Mollie Ray Carroll to Miss Marsh, February 10, 1935, League of Women Voters Papers, series II, Box 370, Library of Congress; Josephine Schain to Mrs. Anne Hartwell Johnstone, June 12, 1935, League of Women Voters Papers, series II, Box 340, Library of Congress; Lucy R. Mason to Harold Butler, May 18, 1935, Women's Bureau Papers, Box 843, National Archives.

24. Grace Abbott, "Women Delegates and the Subject of the Work of Women at the 19th Session of the ILO," typescript, June 1935, League of Women Voters Papers, series II, Box 342, Library of Congress.

25. Marguerite Wells to Frances Perkins, October 9, 1935, League of Women Voters Papers, series II, Box 340, Library of Congress; Marguerite Wells to Frances Perkins, October 14, 1935, Women's Rights Collection (WRC), Frances Perkins Papers, f. 875, Schlesinger Library; Memo, Frances Perkins to Mr. Wyzanski, October 30, 1935, WRC, Frances Perkins Papers, f. 875, Schlesinger Library; Memo, January 31, 1936, League of Women Voters Papers, series II, Box 340, Library of Congress; Memo, Mrs. Johnstone to Marguerite Wells, February 11, 1936, League of Women Voters Papers, series II, Box 340, Library of Congress; "Activities Related to International Alliance Since November Board Meeting," April 15, 1936, League of Women Voters Papers, series II, Box 369, Library of Congress; Mary Anderson to Harold B. Butler, February 14, 1936, League of Women Voters Papers, series II, Box

342, Library of Congress; Alice Paul to Frances Perkins, May 9, 1936, Women's Bureau Papers, Box 848, National Archives; Abby Scott Baker to Frances Perkins, May 18, 1936; Memo to the Secretary from Mary Anderson re: Miss Paul's letter, May 21, 1936, Women's Bureau Papers, Box 848, National Archives.

26. H. McKinnon Wood to Mrs. Pitman Potter, May 26, 1936, League of Women Voters Papers, series II, Box 369, Library of Congress.

27. Mary Beard to Mary Anderson, August 10, 1936; Mary Anderson to Mme. Marguerite Thibert, August 10, 1936; Memo to the Secretary from Mary Anderson, September 4, 1936; Memo from the Secretary to Mary Anderson, September 16, 1936, Women's Bureau Papers, Box 855, National Archives. The ILO Correspondence Committee on Women's Work included social feminists Mary Anderson, Elisabeth Christman, Mary Dingman, Elizabeth Morrisey, Mary Van Kleeck and Ethel Smith as well as NWP members Burnita Shelton Matthews and Lena Madesin Phillips.

28. Minutes, Conference, Women's Subcommittee on ILO, September 9, 1936; Minutes, Meeting of October 7, 1936, Rough Draft, Women's Bureau Papers, Box 855, National Archives.

29. Alice S. Cheyney to Mary Anderson, October 7, 1936; Alice S. Cheyney to Mrs. Beresford Fox, November 20, 1936 (copy), Women's Bureau Papers, Box 855, National Archives.

30. Mary Anderson, *Woman At Work* (Minneapolis, Minn.: University of Minnesota Press, 1951), 211; Mary Van Kleeck to Felix Frankfurter, October 16, 1936, National Consumers' League Papers, Box C-16, Library of Congress; "Memorandum Regarding Interpretation of Women's Charter," from Mary Van Kleeck to Dorothy Kenyon and Lucy R. Mason, January 13, 1937; Mary Anderson to Lucy Mason, December 10, 1936; National Consumers' League Papers, Box C-16, Library of Congress; Note, December 23, 1936, Women's Trade Union League Papers, Box 7, Library of Congress.

31. "A Dangerous Document," *Equal Rights Independent Feminist Weekly*, 2 (December 26, 1936), 341; "Beware of the 'Women's Charter'" *Equal Rights*, 23 (January 15, 1937), 4; "Equal Rights Treaty vs. the Women's Charter," *Equal Rights*, 13 (March 1, 1937), 27; Letters to members of BPW and AAUW, Alma Lutz Papers, Box 4, Schlesinger Library; "Proposal for a Women's Charter," *Independent Woman*, 16 (January 1937), 10; Elizabeth Baker et al., "About the Women's Charter," *Independent Woman*, 16 (March 1937), 72-74; *New York Times*, January 10, 1937, 6; Lucy R. Mason to Mary Anderson, May 20, 1937, National Consumers' League Papers, Box C-16, Library of Congress; "Women's Charter," *Journal of Home Economics*, 29 (March 1937), 180-182; Lucy R. Mason to Edith Houghton Hooker, March 1, 1937, National Consumers' League Papers, Box C-16, Library of Congress.

32. *Minutes of the 81st Session of the Governing Body of the ILO, Prague 6-9 October 1937* (Geneva, Switzerland: ILO, 1937), p. 112; Ethel M. Johnson, "Women and the International Labor Organization, 1919-1945," mimeograph, Women's Bureau Papers, Box 1698, National Archives; Katherine Bompas to Presidents of Alliance Auxiliaries, October 12, 1937, League of Women Voters Papers, series II, Box 369, Library of Congress; "Announcement of Organization of Joint Committee on Women's Work," March 10, 1938, mimeograph, Women's Bureau Papers, Box 855, National Archives.

33. Sophonisba Breckinridge to Belle Sherwin, December 8, 1933, League of

Women Voters Papers, series II, Box 340, Library of Congress; "First Equal Rights Convention to be Signed at Montevideo," *Equal Rights*, 19 (December 23, 1933), 363.

34. Cable, Bell Sherwin to Cordell Hull, December 14, 1933; Belle Sherwin to Mrs. Henry Goddard Leach, December 20, 1933; League of Women Voters press release, December 20, 1933; Dorothy Strauss to the Editor of the *New York Times*, December 19, 1933; League of Women Voters Papers, series II, Box 340, Library of Congress; LWV, "Statement to the Foreign Relations Committee Opposing Ratification of the Equal Nationality Treaty," n.d., League of Women Voters Papers, series II, Box 295, Library of Congress.

35. Mary Winslow, "The Story of the Lima Conference, Confidential, Not For Release," April 1939, Women's Trade Union League Papers, Box 8, Library of Congress.

36. Winslow, "Story of the Lima Conference"; Memorandum, Marguerite Wells to Mary Winslow, February 13, 1939, League of Women Voters Papers, series II, Box 418, Library of Congress.

37. Memorandum, Wells to Winslow, 1939, League of Women Voters Papers, series II, Box 418, Library of Congress.

38. *New York Times*, December 10, 1938, 8; December 19, 1938, 2; December 21, 1938, 12; January 8, 1939, II, 4; February 2, 1939, 21; February 3, 1939, 8; February 17, 1939, 3; March 3, 1939, 10; Press release, January 4, 1939, Women's Trade Union League Papers, Box 8, Library of Congress.

39. Mary Murray, "Muchas Gracias, Senator Burke," *Equal Rights*, 25 (September 1939), 111.

40. International Labour Office, Studies and Reports, Series I, *The Employment of Women and Children*, No. 4 *The Law and Women's Work* (Geneva, Switzerland: ILO, 1939), ix, xi, 347, xi, 565. See also No. 2 *Women's Work Under Labour Law* (Geneva, Switzerland: ILO, 1932).

11

"The Forgotten Woman": Working Women, the New Deal, and Women's Organizations

_____ LOIS SCHARF _____

The official papers of Secretary of Labor Frances Perkins contain a printed resolution of unknown origin. Its authors summarized and condemned what they considered the plight of women workers under the New Deal. "They have been thrown out of jobs as married women, refused relief as single women, discriminated against by the N.R.A. and ignored by the C.W.A."[1] These concerns were echoed at greater length by Genevieve Parkhurst, writer and former editor of _Pictorial Review_, in a 1935 article entitled "Is Feminism Dead?" Women, she contended, have suffered "in undue proportion by being deprived of their hard-won rights as human beings, discriminated against in matters of work and pay, and denied access to the same avenues of recovery as men." Furthermore, she held women's organizations largely responsible for this state of affairs. They lacked ideological consensus and inspiring leadership, were indifferent toward and inactive on behalf of working women. This judgment has persisted. According to William Chafe, by the 1930s the woman's movement was so entangled over the Equal Rights Amendment (ERA) that "instead of moving ahead together to attack the practical problems of discrimination, women's groups polarized over doctrinaire questions of ideology."[2]

Neither Parkhurst during the Depression nor Chafe since has underestimated the bitter rift among women's organizations (reform, feminist, and working women's groups including the Women's Bureau) over the potential threat to protective legislation for women posed by the ERA. Even the 1938 Fair Labor Standards Act (FLSA) did not alter entrenched positions. Amendment supporters had continuously advocated labor regulations if protective standards were based on the nature of the work and not on the sex of the worker. They hailed the new legislation as vindication of their position. Laura Berrien of the National Woman's Party (NWP) praised the FLSA because now "the only protection women have is to compete with men on terms of equality." Recognizing that significant numbers of workers were not covered by the federal act, the NWP called on all women's groups to eliminate protective legislation and to secure, instead, state laws that

This article is an excerpt from the author's monograph _To Work and To Wed: Female Employment, Feminism, and the Great Depression_ (Westport, Conn., Greenwood, 1980).

emulated the federal pattern of establishing regulations for workers regardless of sex.

The Women's Bureau replied on behalf of special legislation. The need for wage and hour guidelines for women not covered by the FLSA as well as other protective and prohibitive measures was unchanged because the assumptions that women were physically and emotionally different from men, rightfully filled different family roles, could not compete equally with men in the economic sphere, and therefore continued to require special legislation based on sex were unchanged.[3] Agreement over definitions of sexual and economic equality and, consequently, compromise among women's organizations remained as elusive as ever. Yet the inability of the groups to mend their ideological fences did not necessarily signify that they were incapable of unified action on behalf of embattled women workers in other areas.

Working conditions for men and women in industry had deteriorated rapidly and dramatically after 1929. In twelve months between 1929 and 1930 the average working woman in South Bend, Indiana, lost six hours and $4.45 per week. By the summer of 1931, 25 percent pay cuts were common among women in New England factories. Two months before Franklin Delano Roosevelt's inauguration, the YWCA described the plight of an experienced, skilled machine operator in a garment manufacturing plant whose wages were cut periodically until she earned $1.95 per 100 pairs of trousers, netting fifty-eight cents for nine hours work. Still, she stayed at work, "because I know that there are fifty girls waiting to take my job, and where would I find another now?"[4]

The resurgence of homework added to the difficulties of maintaining any semblance of industrial standards. Women, often with their children, worked on knit goods, earning five cents an hour for seventy hours of work a week. Desperate young girls took artificial flowers home to work on after their regular hours in the plant. Some woolen mills, circumventing supposedly mandatory minimum wages, sent mending to retired employees to do in their homes at lower rates.[5]

Workers, male and female, could hardly be blamed for grasping any job opportunity regardless of hours and pay. The insecurely employed and the underemployed never had to look far to find those who had no work at all. The extent of female unemployment during the Depression, like joblessness in general, was never accurately measured. Limited surveys at the beginning of the 1930s indicated that women fared reasonably well. Heavy industry bore the initial brunt of the economic downturn, and women in consumer goods industries and doing clerical work did not feel the impact of contraction until somewhat later. By 1932, however, the incidence of unemployment among women workers increased in all occupational categories. The New York Emergency Relief Committee reported that stenographers were hardest hit, with seamstresses and general clerical workers close behind. In industries employing large numbers of women, only shoe and candy manu-facturing escaped serious cutbacks. In 1930 the American Women's Associa-tion discovered that a small proportion of its New York City business and professionally employed members were out of work, but three years later the number had grown significantly. At that time the nationwide estimate of unemployed women was over two million.[6]

In these circumstances, women's organizations looked to the federal government to initiate programs that would protect work standards, pro-vide relief, and promote general economic recovery. Expecting men and women alike to benefit, the early New Deal legislation was greeted with hope and enthusiasm by the watchdogs of working women.

By summer 1933 it was already apparent that several industrial codes written under the provisions of Title I of the National Industrial Recovery Act (NIRA) contained wage provisions inimical to female workers. Women's organizations quickly discovered, publicized, and protested this development. The National Woman's Party (NWP) pointed out that twelve of the early, temporary codes listed wage differentials based on sex. Officers of the National Federation of Business and Professional Women's Clubs (BPW) immediately sent telegrams to Roosevelt and National Recovery Administration (NRA) administrator Hugh Johnson demanding that codes "assure equal pay for equal work and equal opportunity for equal ability regardless of sex." The League of Women Voters (LWV) of the United States joined the protest and complained directly to Johnson, who issued a policy statement: "Where women do men's work, they should get equal pay." Women found this guideline unsatisfactory and insisted that industrial operations be clearly described and defined with wage levels based upon the defined job and not on the sex of the employee.[7]

In spite of assurances by Eleanor Roosevelt and Frances Perkins that the wage differentials were temporary and would not survive the public hearings and final approval process, the discriminatory pay features remained. By October 1933, eight codes with sex-based wage differences had been signed by the president, including one in the coat and suit indus-try, which had earlier submitted its temporary code in which wage scales were based on the nature of work. A ten-cent differential between male and female operatives suddenly appeared in the permanent, approved code. Women's organizations expressed opposition for several reasons. As the first code to gain permanent status, it could establish a dangerous prece-dent. Disparity between the temporary and final agreements indicated that the public hearing process and the watchdog Labor Advisory Board were formalities easily circumvented. Finally, the code covered an industry with a large female work force.[8]

Dissatisfaction was compounded by the "July 1929 clause," a ruling by the NRA that stipulated persons paid below minimum NRA levels on that date could continue to be so paid. Thirty codes incorporated this feature. Six industries established wage minimums except for "employees engaged in light and repetitive work," a euphemism for "female."[9] The Women's Trade Union League (WTUL) protested to Johnson; the National Consumers League, the General Federation of Women's Clubs, and the YWCA also complained. The National Association of Women Lawyers suggested a selective boycott to force revisions, arguing that half the codes containing discriminatory features were written by industries dependent upon women as consumers. When the NRA was reorganized in fall 1934, Anita Pollitzer of the NWP wrote to the new chairman of the policy-making committee repeating earlier pleas that wages be based on the nature of work and not the sex of the worker. Armed with a comprehensive policy statement prepared by the WTUL and a study of the extent of discriminatory codes compiled by the Women's Bureau, organizations affiliated with the Women's Joint Congressional Committee (WJCC) subcommittee appeared before the NRA board.[10] Their efforts were futile. Customary industrial wage practices, an ineffectual Labor Advisory Board, and the Roosevelt administration's determination to certify codes with a minimum of delay all undermined attempts to delete wage differentials. Women's organizations, however, could not be accused of ignoring their presence or implications, and they united behind the principle of equal pay for equal work.

While the first section of the NIRA resulted in sex-based wage differentials in one-quarter of all approved codes, the second part of the legislation which created the Public Works Administration also had negative impact on women—it ignored them. Projects under the program resulted in carefully planned schools, hospitals, city halls, and bridges—boons to unemployed architects and construction workers. Women could not and did not qualify, since the female unemployed were primarily clerical workers, factory operatives in consumer goods industries, and domestic servants. The Federal Emergency Relief Administration (FERA) which used grants in aid to states but administered relief from Washington also depended heavily on construction projects. Eleanor Roosevelt's efforts to duplicate the popular Civilian Conservation Corps (CCC) for women eventually created eighty-six camps for 6,400 women. The number was insignificant in relation to the level of female unemployment (estimated at 3.5 million in 1937) or in proportion to the number of young men in CCC camps. And the financial compensation for the women was fifty cents per week compared to the one dollar per day received by men.[11]

The situation improved with the initiation of the Civilian Works Administration (CWA), a short-term program created to meet the unemployment crisis anticipated during the winter of 1933-1934. Women benefited after Eleanor Roosevelt convened a White House Conference on the Emergency Needs of Women because of her own genuine concern and the complaints of leaders of women's organizations. By the end of 1933, 100,000 women received work relief, but at no time did more than 7 percent of CWA jobs go to the female unemployed. In addition, the wage structure discriminated. Administrator Harry Hopkins established a one dollar per hour minimum for skilled labor, a forty-cent minimum for unskilled construction work, and a thirty-cent rate for persons on relief and educational projects — largely women.[12]

Government officials required constant prodding. The Los Angeles BPW had passed an early resolution which became the model for subsequent pressure on behalf of unemployed women: "...since the percentage of women employed in the United States is about 18% of the total of employed persons, that recommendations be sent to agencies handling funds for relief and employment stimulation asking that 18% of said funds be applied to women."[13] Ellen Woodward, director of women's projects under various federal programs, insisted that no conscious intentions to discriminate existed and that female heads of families and needy single women would receive increased consideration. Her assurances did not quell complaints. Helena Hill Weed of the NWP attacked the low proportion of women (8 percent) who received FERA aid, the wage differentials in CWA projects, and the practice of placing men in more highly paid supervisory positions on projects designed for women. Through fall 1934, groups ranging from the WTUL to the National Association of Women Lawyers protested, "urgently request[ing] the Federal Government to develop work relief projects for unemployed women."[14]

Significant change began under massive Works Progress Administration (WPA) programs. Proportions of women on work relief varied from 12 to 19 percent; in December 1938, over 400,000 women obtained relief (13.5 percent of the total at that time). But WPA applicants had to meet specific eligibility requirements which often hampered women, especially when administered at the local level where prevailing custom and prejudice also affected certification. No more than one member of a family could receive work relief and that individual had to demonstrate principal breadwinner status. Louisiana reinforced the concept of breadwinner as male by ruling "a woman with an employable husband is not eligible for referral, as her husband is the logical head of the family." WPA applicants also had to demonstrate that they were in the labor market. Michigan defined this requirement narrowly where women were concerned. Female heads of family were eligible only if they had been working or were seeking work outside the home and were registered at a public employment office. In Louisiana, women had to have previous work histories and prove they were actually seeking employment. In other states, lack of work experience often disqualified a woman forced into the labor force for the first time because of the exigencies of the Depression. Occasionally women were certified as breadwinners if programs for husbands did not exist, but when new projects were initiated, the women were removed and replaced by husbands as quickly as possible.[15] In the Southwest, citizenship laws were sometimes used by local officials to refuse certification to female applicants married to Mexicans. In the Southeast, white administrators and social welfare workers favored white women over black.[16]

Women who overcame these obstacles were still not guaranteed work relief. Approved projects had to be available, and availability depended on the size of annual congressional appropriations, the amount allocated to various states, and the degree to which local officials desired to match skills (or lack of skills) with available projects. While skills of male recipients were often downgraded in work relief, they were seldom dismissed outright, which often happened to women. Studies revealed that higher proportions of certified men than women actually received work assignments. And for the women who obtained relief over the lifetime of WPA, over half were engaged in the most traditional of female work—sewing. According to two observers, the sewing room became "a female ditch-digging project, a dumping ground for women for whom no other work can be found."[17]

Women's organizations were not oblivious to the difficulties involved in meeting eligibility requirements and in devising projects at the local level. The NWP warned members that honorable intentions of federal officials in Washington were not adequate protection for women. "Knowing also some state and local administrators, we fear that in some places, women will be given only such consideration as 'naggers' in Washington or elsewhere insist upon." The leadership encouraged all those concerned with the inability of needy women to receive an adequate share of work assignments to write to Ellen Woodward apprising her of inequities. And when WPA went into effect, the LWV warned "it will be necessary in the future as in the past for those concerned with unemployed women to exercise great ingenuity in devising projects and securing materials and facilities for them."[18] Spokespersons could not be accused of indifference toward unemployment relief for women. What they ignored was the nature of the projects. Along with placement in ubiquitous sewing rooms, eligible women were assigned to hot lunch programs for other relief workers and for school children or were placed in household training programs. Better-educated women with appropriate work experience obtained jobs as public health nurses, as librarians repairing books, and as adult education instructors. Relief programs duplicated and reinforced the sex-segregated structure of the labor force.[19]

As WPA expanded and articles by Woodward on female relief appeared in the journals of women's organizations, concern subsided.[20] When the NIRA was declared unconstitutional, furor over sex-based wage differentials in codes ended. The issue upon which organizational leadership focused was discrimination against married women workers, especially as exemplified by Section 213 of the 1932 Economy Act. This "married persons clause" was not part of New Deal legislation. The act of which it was part had been enacted during the Hoover administration. But whereas Hoover stated his opposition to the stipulation that a spouse of a federal employee was to be first fired in cases of personnel economies or not hired in instances of new civil service appointments, Roosevelt circumvented the issue. In May 1933, representatives of nine women's organizations met with the new president to ask that the clause be rescinded or allowed to expire. The Economy Act was the second part of an annual appropriation bill and could have quietly expired at the end of the fiscal year. Roosevelt, however, asked his attorney general for a ruling on its effective duration and received the opinion that its legislative history indicated that it was intended as general policy and therefore was permanent.[21]

For five years, women's organizations worked for the repeal of Section 213. In their publications, public pronouncements, and before a congressional committee hearing, women constantly attacked the clause in the face of a reticent administration and a recalcitrant Congress. The NWP and its Government Workers Council, the LWV, the WTUL, business and professional women's groups, and the Women's Bureau all reiterated their belief that dismissing a handful of government workers was a futile, though politically popular, gesture in the face of massive unemployment. Moreover, they believed and stated that discrimination against working wives represented an implicit threat to the economic status of all women. After repeal of Section 213 in 1937, half the states in the nation attempted similar legislative curbs, and the American Association of University Women (AAUW), the YWCA, and women's service organizations joined in opposition. Threats to married women workers created a unity among these diverse groups unmatched since the days of the suffrage campaigns.[22]

Elements of New Deal policies obviously discriminated against working women, but the charge that women's organizations were indifferent to the needs of female wage earners and were unable to unite on issues of importance to women workers was unfair and untrue. And to the extent that Parkhurst identified these concerns and action in these areas as a measure of feminist consciousness, feminism was alive and as well as could be expected in a hostile public setting. As the married woman worker issue eventually overshadowed other problems, leaders of the LWV were as concerned with the rights of all women to work, the occupational progress women had already achieved, and the incentive to continue the struggle for economic equality as were the self-proclaimed feminists of the National Woman's Party. In 1936, a league pamphlet on discrimination warned that "an attack of this sort at *married* women very soon becomes an attack on opportunities for employment of *all* women," and the Government Workers Council of the NWP agreed that such laws not only would affect all working women eventually and undermine the basic right of all adults to work but also would have extensive ramifications on the "social status of women—her education, her career." Without the right to employment and promotion opportunities regardless of marital status, "the incentive for preparation is gone . . . , [a woman] finds herself deprived of the priviledge of choice as to how she shall shape her life."[23] BPW reports stressed that "the strain of long-continued depression has raised in the minds of American women questions acute and arresting as to their place in the occupational world." Leaders warned of the necessity of women "to protect themselves from further loss of those opportunities which they have gained at such cost in the past." And the YWCA enrolled in efforts "to hold the gains in freedom of choice in work which women now have and allow no new laws and policies to be enacted to limit that freedom."[24]

As the attack on married women workers intensified after the mid-1930s and as the attention of women's organizations focused on this single issue, their arguments on behalf of embattled working wives became increasingly defensive. Earlier emphasis on the right to work, the desirability of productive work as a means of self-fulfillment, and the necessity of equality in economic opportunity became less prevalent. Instead the spokespersons of the women's organizations stressed the predominant role economic need of families played as the motivating factor in the gainful employment of married women. Through the 1920s, the Women's Bureau bulletins had demonstrated the important income contribution of working wives to family welfare, and the bureau continued to conduct similar surveys during the Depression in order to underscore the deleterious impact on families of efforts to proscribe the employment of married women. During the campaign against Section 213, the Government Workers Council collected the data that the bureau processed and that served to illustrate the unfortunate personal and ineffectual public ramifications of the "married persons clause." Later in the decade, the Utah BPW furnished material for a bureau bulletin used to combat discriminatory legislation introduced in that state. The BPW publications quoted widely from Women's Bureau reports insisting that "even before the Depression studies tended to show that as high as ninety percent of working women were doing so because of family necessity."[25] Early in 1937, however, the BPW could still reconcile the economic responsibilities of working wives with the feminist goal of autonomy and self-definition through gainful employment. "Revealed for the most part as a worker outside the home from family necessity," the married woman worker still symbolized "that freedom to seek self-realization that men and women should guard jealously."[26]

In response to intensified attacks by social critics who accused working wives of abdicating their traditional roles and responsibilities in the home, defenders increasingly depicted married working women as praiseworthy individuals who were meeting economic obligations to their families when, in fact, they would rather be at home. An intensive BPW study at the end of the decade concluded that constraints on the employment of married women were unconscionable, for these women worked "only because their families needed the money they earned. They preferred not to work outside the home." A syndicated columnist defended the right of wives to work because it was common knowledge that "90 percent of these women would rather be at home sewing on buttons, arranging flowers, and baking beans for their families." Furthermore, the willingness of young women to assume the burdens of work made marriage possible, given the economic uncertainties and inadequate wage scales of the period. Alma Lutz of the NWP attacked discriminatory practices because they penalized marriage, and those who believed "in high moral standards and the sanctity of the home may well be alarmed." Since few couples could marry on the salary of one, according to a NWP colleague of Lutz, the issue was not "can married women work?" but rather "can working women marry?" The right of a wife to work must be protected although her "place is in the home . . . she must have a home in which to stay, which her employment makes possible."[27] The traditional behavioral trait of self-sacrifice combined with the conventional social expectation of marriage to form the rationale protecting married women workers.

As the rhetoric of the leaders of women's organizations increasingly emphasized the self-denial and family-oriented values of working wives, they also insisted that these virtues precluded the personal desire to work and the satisfaction that one derived from employment. A BPW survey, published and circulated to blunt opposition to working wives, minimized the commitment of women to occupational continuity and success. "The number of married women who work simply for a career is negligible, despite the vast sums spent on specialized education for women. . . . These women are exceptions to the rule as to why married women work." The *Ladies Home Journal*, basing an editorial on behalf of working wives on the BPW study, popularized the argument that "no selfish desire for a career prompts [them] to work, simply the pressure of financial need."[28]

While interest in economic advancement was deprecated, the occupational structure itself was used to counter critics who stressed the threat that working women posed to "legitimate" breadwinners in a contracted labor market. Defenders emphasized the noncompetitive nature of female employment and the futility of solving male unemployment by dismissing women. According to Mary Anderson of the Women's Bureau, "the important fact is that women compete very little with men for jobs since all available data show that their occupations usually differ markedly from those of men." Low status, sex-stereotyped jobs were simply not "the kind men could or would take for their own employment."[29] Like the economic motivation that underlay the work roles of most wives and the anticipation of marriage of most young women, the description of female occupational distribution was well grounded in fact. But this argument made a virtue of occupational segregation by sex as well as serving as an implicit attack on those women in, or anticipating entrance into, nontraditional fields of employment.

Together with the denigration of careerism, it represented a self-defeating plea for the occupational status quo.

Over the course of the Depression decade, in order to mollify Americans overwhelmingly opposed to married women workers, their defenders adopted the least offensive, most expedient arguments which projected palatable feminine roles, images, and behavioral patterns. In so doing, they achieved modest success—the repeal of Section 213 and prevention of legislative imitations at the state level. However, widespread constraints in employment and retention policies affecting married women teachers and wives in clerical occupations, where the incidence of discrimination was greatest, remained unchanged.[30] In addition, by concentrating on overt but short-term manifestations of discrimination like Section 213, the defenders of married women workers overlooked more subtle, permanent New Deal social welfare policies that embodied features detrimental to working women. In 1939, while the president of the BPW announced that the legislative assault on working wives was "the most serious problem confronted since the organization formed in 1919,"[31] Congress was amending the Social Security Act in ways that discriminated against married women workers for decades afterwards.

As originally passed in 1935, the Social Security Act created old age insurance plans covering all workers under the age of sixty-five engaged in commerce and industry. Workers were fully insured if they had $2,000 of cumulative wage credits and had been employed at some time during each year for five years, although important groups of workers were exempted. Otherwise, old age insurance applied to all workers in concerns that employed at least ten persons for at least twenty weeks per year. The act also provided for unemployment insurance, but states were to receive grants-in-aid and determine coverage and benefits. Federal legislation did establish the guideline that firms employing at least eight workers must participate.[32]

The legislation marked an important turn in government assumption of responsibility for social welfare. The United States lagged behind other industrial nations in these types of programs. In spite of numerous shortcomings, which critics were quick to point out, especially in the tax structure of the insurance plans, most reformers who had long hoped for social and economic security legislation were reasonably pleased. The LWV and the YWCA recognized the need to extend protection to neglected workers, "yet many of us who have faith in social insurance believe that the principle is sound."[33] Only the NWP remarked on a little-noticed feature of the measure. The passage of the act coincided with the death of Charlotte Perkins Gilman. The NWP's feminist journal *Equal Rights* eulogized Gilman and acknowledged her ideological legacy to all women by stressing the importance of work and economic independence. According to *Equal Rights*, the Social Security Act reinforced the message. Under the terms of the legislation, adults who did not work for pay received no security. Women who chose marriage over employment or renounced careers upon marriage gave up government protection as well.[34]

The NWP analysis was correct, but it did not go far enough. There were a sizeable number of people who worked for pay and still did not qualify under the insurance plans. Women constituted almost all of the domestic workers exempted, as well as large proportions of farm laborers and educational, charitable, and hospital personnel. One critic suggested that business women demand to know why occupations of varying status, "so largely female employing," were excluded. In the case of domestic workers, a high proportion was married. In effect, that one area of exemption alone placed one-third of all married workers outside the protection of the social welfare program. Industries that engaged large numbers of married women participated in social security, with one important exception: the stipulation exempting firms that employed ten or less workers, for twenty or less weeks per year, was purposefully enacted to free canneries from covering their employees. Canneries had been in the past, and continued to be through the 1930s, large-scale, seasonal, and exploitative employers of married women.[35]

The 1939 revisions in social security legislation altered the focus of coverage from the individual worker to the worker's family. Widows' benefits were added and wives of insured workers were entitled to old age payments equal to one-half of their husbands' when both reached retirement age. The method of computing benefits and eligibility requirements was also changed. In the amended law, a working wife whose primary income benefit was less than 50 percent of her husband's still would receive the higher amount; the same amount she would have received if she had not worked at all. However, she paid taxes on those earnings. The legislation also established a family benefit limit: if her average earnings entitled her to a benefit that when combined with her husband's exceeded the limit, her benefit was reduced accordingly. Husbands and wives paid taxes at the same rates on their individual earnings, but they received benefits as a family. A working wife also purchased less insurance for the same tax paid. The act introduced survivor and dependents' benefits but only for widows and the children of widows, not for surviving husbands and their children. A working mother purchased protection for her children only if they were not living with their father or if their father was not paying some support. Inherent in the legislation were the assumptions that children were dependent upon the earnings of their fathers and that married women workers were secondary breadwinners. However true in terms of actual family structure and the economic status of family members, it was inequitable to tax wives at the same rate as husbands when they purchased no insurance protection for their husbands or children in case of death. In response to these massive changes and innovations in Social Security programs, the women's organizations were silent. The leaders who had displayed concern for women workers through the 1930s were oblivious to the discriminatory aspects and the concept of female dependency institutionalized in sweeping federal legislation and practice.[36]

The spokespersons of women's groups recognized overt threats to the economic status of working women, and they united to combat those threats. If they failed to distinguish the short-term but dramatic abuses experienced by married women workers from the lasting ramifications of Social Security legislation, the fault lay, in large measure, in the growing perception, shared by many of their contemporaries as the decade wore on, that economic downturn and stagnation might well be permanent. In addition, limited effectiveness in combating public policy discrimination stemmed from the incorporation of those features within New Deal measures that enjoyed great popular support — even among women covered by a wage differential who had never had the security of any established labor standard before. For desperate women on relief, the sewing room represented survival and not sex-typed work patterns. Within this context, the leadership of women's organizations shared the strengths, limited successes, shortcomings, and failures of their united efforts.

Consensus over an equal rights amendment as the most efficacious manner in which to combat the problems confronted by working women (Parkhurst's contention),[37] remained elusive, but the social class and occupational differences so often blamed for the split in feminist ranks were largely overcome. The NWP and business and professional women's groups vigorously opposed the NRA wage differentials that affected women in industry. Countering the judgment of one historian who believed that business and professional women identified with management and viewed industrial women as workers rather than as women,[38] the president of the National Association of Women Lawyers described the discriminatory aspects of the industrial codes as integral parts of widespread retrogression in women's economic rights generally.[39] And the LWV, the WTUL, and the Women's Bureau, whose principal focus remained in industry, played major roles in combating Section 213 and proposed state laws, the negative impact of which fell most heavily on professional and clerical workers.

Unity in concern and action on behalf of working women was achieved, but, by the end of the decade, with an unexpected development. Those women who opposed protective legislation because of their commitment to an uncomplicated concept of economic equality, and who presumedly could not work with women's organizations that supported such measures, increasingly confused rather than maintained the supposedly conflicting notions concerning the meaning of equality between men and women. The NWP, the BPW, and allied professional groups protested instances of economic discrimination, especially in relation to working wives, by increasingly depicting married working women as women rather than workers. They, too, projected an image of women workers within traditional familial and economic contexts that distinguished them from male workers. Their arguments were admittedly expedient—a special BPW group of committee chairpersons advised that "all plans to combat discrimination must be adopted to the atmospheric pressure of public opinion."[40] But in reinforcing the social assumptions upon which opponents of an equal rights amendment had based their position, feminist advocates of economic equality for women confused and compromised the feminist basis for their concerns and the most expeditious manner in which to achieve equality. Ideological cleavage did not divide and incapacitate the women's movement during the 1930s. At the level of public rhetoric, the women's movement achieved astonishing and ironic unity.

Notes

1. "Resolution on Unemployment and Working Women," Frances Perkins Papers, Box 82, Women-General folder, National Archives (NA).

2. Genevieve Parkhurst, "Is Feminism Dead?" *Harper's Magazine* 170 (May 1935): 735-45; William Chafe, *The American Woman: Her Changing Social, Economic, and Political Role, 1920-1970* (New York: Oxford University Press, 1974), p. 130.

3. *Equal Rights* 25 (January 1, 1939): 7; "I Appeal to Women for United Support," *ibid.* (February 1, 1939): 20; "Come Now, and Let Us Reason Together," *ibid.* 27 (April 1941): 1; "The Relation of the Fair Labor Standards Act to the Status of the Equal Rights Amendment," *ibid.* 27 (July 1941): 60; *Woman Worker* (July 1938): 3. Chafe surveys the basic ideological differences among women's groups in *The American Woman*, chapter 5.

4. U.S. Department of Labor, Women's Bureau, *Wage Earning Women and the Industrial Conditions of 1930*, Bulletin no. 92 (Washington, D.C.: Government Printing Office, (GPO), 1932), p. 5; William E. Leuchtenberg, *Franklin D. Roosevelt and the New Deal, 1932-1940* (New York: Harper and Row, 1963), p. 133; Helena Hill Weed, "The New Deal That Women Want," *Current History* 41 (November 1934): 183; Leuchtenberg, *FDR and the New Deal*, pp. 120-21.

5. Elsie D. Harper, "Back to the Sweatshops," *Woman's Press* 27 (February 1933): 89; Elsie D. Harper, "Labor Standards," *Woman's Press* 29 (February 1935): 78-79; "Homework Banned in Artificial Flowers," *Woman's Press* 32 (March 1938): 14-15.

6. *The Trained Woman and the Economic Crisis: Employment and Unemployment among a Selected Group of Business and Professional Women in New York City* (New York: American Woman's Association, 1931), pp. 11-22; Lorine Pruette, *Women Workers Through the Depression*, (New York: Macmillan, 1934), p. 197; U.S. Department of Labor, Women's Bureau, *Women in the Economy of the United States*, Bulletin no. 155 (Washington, D.C.: GPO, 1937), pp. 35-36.

7. Ruby Black, "Inequalities under the National Recovery Administration," *Equal Rights* 19 (August 12, 1933): 219-20; Anita Pollitzer, "Equal Pay and the N.R.A. Codes," *Equal Rights* 19 (September 2, 1933): 243; *New York Times*, 16 July 1933, p. 19; Summary of Biennial Report, April 1932-1934, Department of the Legal Status of

Women, National League of Women Voters Papers, Series 2, Box 323, Circular Letters, Government and Legal Status of Women Department folder, Library of Congress (LC); Geline Bowman to General Johnson, 10 August 1933, Frances Perkins Papers, Box 81, Women-General folder, NA; Maud Younger to Hugh Johnson, 5 August 1933, quoted in *Equal Rights* 19 (August 12, 1933): 219; *New York Times*, 9 August 1933, p. 2.

8. Lois MacDonald, Gladys L. Palmer, and Theresa Wolfson, *Labor and the N.R.A.* (New York: Affiliated Schools for Workers, 1934), pp. 10, 30.

9. Women's Joint Congressional Committee Report, 1933-1935, Selma Borchardt Papers, Box 158, folder 17, Archives of Labor History, Detroit; U.S. Department of Labor, Women's Bureau, *Employed Women Under N.R.A. Codes*, Bulletin No. 122 (Washington, D.C.: GPO, 1934), pp. 24-25; Elisabeth Christman to General Hugh S. Johnson, 28 February 1934, Women's Trade Union League Papers, Box 6, Headquarters Records, January to April 1934 folder, LC.

10. *Life and Labor Bulletin*, August 1933; Elisabeth Christman to Hugh Johnson, 21 February 1934, Women's Trade Union League Papers, Box 6, Headquarters Records, January to April 1934, LC; *New York Times*, 29 August 1934, p. 19; "Reorganized N.R.A. Asked to End Discrimination," *Equal Rights* 20 (October 23, 1934): 292-93; Weed, "The New Deal That Women Want," pp. 181-82; *Independent Woman* 13 (August 1934): 269; Women's Joint Congressional Committee Report, c. 1930-1935, Selma Borchardt Papers, Box 159, folder 8; Women's Bureau Memo to Eleanor Roosevelt, 19 February 1934, Marian Anderson Papers, Box 1, folder 14, Schlesinger Library (SL); unpublished history of the Labor Advisory Board, Rose Schneiderman Papers, Box 3, folder 2, Tamiment Library, New York University. The groups that joined with the WTUL included the LWV, BPW, YWCA, General Federation of Women's Clubs, National Education Association, and American Nurses Association.

11. Leuchtenberg, *Franklin D. Roosevelt*, p. 133; Weed, "The New Deal That Women Want," p. 183.

12. Leuchtenberg, *Franklin D. Roosevelt*, pp. 120-21; Paul A. Kurzman, *Harry Hopkins and the New Deal* (Fair Lawn, N.J.: R. E. Burdick, 1974), pp. 11-12; *New York Times*, 9 November 1933, p. 23, 26 December 1933, p. 17, 5 December 1933, p. 19; Ellen S. Woodward, "This Federal Relief," *Independent Woman* 13 (April 1934): 104; Tamara K. Hareven, *Eleanor Roosevelt: An American Conscience* (Chicago: Quadrangle Books, 1968), p. 64.

13. *Independent Woman* 10 (March 1931): 141.

14. Woodward, "This Federal Relief," pp. 126-27; Weed, "The New Deal That Woman Want," p. 183; *New York Times*, 28 August 1934, p. 23, 23 September 1934, 2:11.

15. Donald S. Howard, *The W.P.A. and Federal Relief Policy* (New York: Russell Sage Foundation, 1943), pp. 269, 278-82, 376, 481; Lewis Meriam, *Relief and Social Security* (Washington, D.C.: Brookings Institution, 1946), pp. 12-13; "Report of the Division of Women's and Professional Projects, July 1, 1935 to January 1, 1937," pt. 3, Works Progress Administration Collection, NA.

16. Howard, *The W.P.A.*, p. 279; Jeanne Westin, *Making Do: How Women Survived the '30s* (Chicago: Follette Publishing Co., 1976), p. 185; Gerda Lerner, ed. *Black Woman in White America: A Documentary History* (New York: Vintage Books, 1972), pp. 399, 404; Rosalyn Baxandall, Linda Gordon, and Susan Reverby,

eds., *America's Working Women: A Documentary History, 1600 to the Present* (New York: Vintage Books, 1976), pp. 249-51.

17. Howard, *The W.P.A.*, pp. 278, 281; *New York Times*, 12 August 1936, p. 8; "Assigned Occupations of Persons on W.P.A. Projects" November 1937 (Washington, D.C.: GPO, 1937), pp. 2, 4. Fifty-five percent of men on relief were classified as laborers, but work to which they were assigned was more varied. However, a lower proportion of men than women were engaged in professional technical, clerical, and supervisory relief work. See Ellen S. Woodward, "Women's and Professional Work in the W.P.A.," *Journal of Home Economics* 28 (November 1936): 617; Marie Dresden Lane and Frances Steegmuller, *Americans on Relief* (New York: Harcourt, Brace, 1938), p. 81.

18. "All Women, Here's Work," *Equal Rights Independent Feminist Weekly* 1 (July 20, 1935): 154; *National League of Women Voters Newsletter* 1 (May 23, 1935); *League News* 7 (October 1933): 3.

19. Ellen S. Woodward, "W.P.A. Puts Women to Work," *Labor Information Bulletin* 3 (July 1936): 3-5; Harry L. Hopkins, *Spending to Save: The Complete Story of Relief* (Seattle: University of Washington Press, 1936), p. 169; "Assigned Occupations of Persons on W.P.A. Projects," p. 4.

20. Woodward, "This Federal Relief," pp. 104, 126-27; "Jobs for Jobless Woman," *Equal Rights Independent Feminist Weekly*, 1 (July 20, 1935): 1, 5-6; Woodward, "Women's and Professional Work in the W.P.A.," p. 617; "Making Housework a Skilled Occupation," *Journal of the American Association of University Women* 30 (October 1936): 23-25.

21. "Congress Enacts 'Economy' Statute on Eve of New Fiscal Year," *Federal Employee* 17 (July 1932): 3; "The President and the Bill," *Equal Rights* 18 (August 13, 1932): 221-22; Louis McH. Howe to Mrs. Mae Wilson Camp, OF 252, 27 July 1933, Franklin D. Roosevelt Library; description of the meeting in OF, 8 May 1933, FDR Library. The organizations included the National Association of Women Lawyers, National Association of Woman Nurses, National Federation of Business and Professional Women's Clubs, Married Teachers Association of Philadelphia, and the National Woman's Party; Homer S. Cummings to the President, 24 June 1933, pp. 3-4, OF 95, FDR Library; "Attorney-General Opinion on 'Married Persons'," *Federal Employee* 18 (August 1933): 8, 27-29.

22. Minutes of the WJCC Subcommittee on the Dismissal of Married Women, Selma Borschardt Papers, Box 101, folder 16, Labor History Archives; Government Workers Council Progress Report Pamphlet, Alma Lutz Collection, Box 2, folder 27, SL; NWP Minutes, 1933-34, Lutz Collection, Box 1, folders 4, 5, 6, SL; U.S. Congress, House, *Hearings Before the Committee on the Civil Service on H.R. 5051*, "To Amend the Married Persons' Clause," 74th Congress, 1st session, 1935; "A Preliminary Study on the Application of Section 213 of the Economy Act of June 30, 1932," report of the U.S. Department of Labor, Women's Bureau, 1935 (mimeo); "History of Section 213," *Equal Rights Independent Feminist Weekly* 1 (March 30, 1935): 28; *Independent Woman* 14 (May 1935): 154; "On the Firing Line," *Independent Woman* 18 (April 1939): 114; *Journal of the AAUW* 30 (April 1939): 172; "Democracy – for Whom? – A Symposium," *Independent Woman* 18 (March 1939): 68-70, 88; Helena Robbins Bitterman, "It Has Happened Here!" *Equal Rights* 25 (May 1, 1939): 68, 70; *New York Times*, 26 February 1939, 2: 4; "Working Wives," *Woman's Home Companion* 66 (October 1939); "Should Wives Work?"

Ladies Home Journal 58 (January 1941): 4, 35; "Marriage — A Bar to Employment," *Journal of the AAUW* 32 (April 1939).

23. Edith Valet Cook, *The Married Woman and Her Job* (Washington, D.C.: NLWV, 1936), p. 4; Report of the Government Workers Council, "The Married Worker Ouster," Employment — Discrimination, Married Women folder, SL.

24. Iva Lowther Peters, *Occupational Discrimination Against Women: An Inquiry into the Economic Security of American Business and Professional Women* (New York: National Federation of Business and Professional Womens Clubs, 1935), p. 3; "Report on Committees," *Independent Woman* 14 (August 1935): 254; Henrietta Rollofs, "Women's Freedom of Choice," *Woman's Press* 30 (March 1936): 117.

25. Women's Bureau, *Married Women in Industry*, Bulletin No. 38 (1924); "Effects of Dismissing Married Persons from the Civil Service," March 1936 (mimeo); "Gainful Employment of Married Women," August 1936, (mimeo); *The Family Responsibilities of Employed Women in Three Cities*, Bulletin No. 168 (1939); *Female Workers in Their Family Environment*, Bulletin No. 183 (1941); *Wives Need Their Jobs* (New York: NFBPWC, 1939): 4.

26. "What Price the Career Mother?" *Independent Woman* 16 (February 1937): 42.

27. Ruth Shallcross, *Should Married Women Work?* Study by BPW published as Public Affairs Pamphlet No. 49 (New York, 1940), p. 12; *Cleveland Plain Dealer* 3 (March 1940); Helen Robbins Bitterman, "Can Working Women Marry?" *Equal Rights* 25 (March 15, 1939): 44; Clare Belle Thompson and Margaret Lukes Wise, "Shall We Fire the Married Women?" *Liberty* 16 (September 30, 1939): 14, 15.

28. Shallcross, *Should Married Women Work?*, p. 12; "Should Wives Work?" *Ladies Home Journal* 58 (January 1941): 4.

29. "Democracy — for Whom?" p. 68; Helen Pearce, "The Married Woman's Right to Work," *Zontian* (November 1938): 8. Among numerous references to noncompetitive job segregation see Anna Steese Richardson, "The Right of the Married Woman to Work for Wages," *Woman's Home Companion* 66 (October 1939): 8; "Should Wives Work?" p. 4; Kathleen McLaughlin, "Shall Wives Work?" *New York Times Sunday Magazine* 23 July 1939, p. 19; "Marriage — A Bar to Employment?" p. 172. The WTUL referred to the unlikelihood that men could fill jobs as domestic servants, dressmakers, secretaries, and typists in *Life and Labor Bulletin* 10 (January 1932), but the argument lay dormant until the end of the decade.

30. For discrimination against married women in teaching, offices, and stores, see "Teacher Personnel Procedures: Employment Conditions in Service," *NEA Research Bulletin* 20 (March 1942): 107; "Teacher Personnel: Selection and Appointment," ibid. (May 1942): 12; Women's Bureau, *The Employment of Women in Offices*, Bulletin No. 120 (1934); Doris Best, "Employed Wives Increasing," *Personnel Journal* 17 (December 1938): 212-19; "Employment of Women After Marriage," *Conference Board Management Record*, (October 1939), p. 151.

31. *New York Times*, 19 August 1939, p. 17.

32. *Statutes at Large of the United States of America from January, 1935 to June, 1936*, vol. 49, pt. 1 (Washington, D.C.: GPO, 1936), pp. 625-39; Joseph A. Peckman et al., *Social Security: Perspectives for Reform* (Washington, D.C.: Brookings Institution, 1968), p. 255.

33. *Woman's Press* 30 (November 1936): 504; *Woman's Press* 31 (January 1937): 38.

34. Editorial, *Equal Rights Independent Feminist Weekly* 1 (August 31, 1935): 202.

35. Evaline M. Burns, "Amending the Social Security Act," *Independent Woman* 16 (April 1937): 108; Robert B. Stevens, *Statutory History of the United States: Income Security* (New York: McGraw-Hill, 1970), pp. 117-19, 141, 144. The response of women's organizations to the new legislation appears limited to LWV and BPW approval of an administrative provision that placed state personnel handling the programs under the merit system. *New York Times* 1 January 1939, p. 3; "The Merit System in Social Security Agencies," *Independent Woman* 19 (February 1940): 46.

36. Joseph A. Peckman et al., *Social Security: Perspectives for Reform* (Washington, D.C.: Brookings Institution, 1968), p. 80; Meriam, *Relief and Social Security*, pp. 117, 123-25, 707-08; Arthur J. Altmeyer, *The Formative Years of Social Security* (Madison: University of Wisconsin Press, 1966), p. 102.

37. Parkhurst, "Is Feminism Dead?" p. 745.

38. J. Stanley Lemons, *The Woman Citizen: Social Feminism in the 1920s* (Urbana, Ill.: University of Illinois Press, 1975), p. 199.

39. *New York Times*, 28 August 1934.

40. *Independent Woman* 19 (August 1940): 265-66.

12

Discontented Black Feminists: Prelude and Postscript to the Passage of the Nineteenth Amendment

ROSALYN TERBORG-PENN

A significant number of black women and black women's organizations not only supported woman suffrage on the eve of the passage of the Nineteenth Amendment but attempted to exercise their rights to vote immediately after the amendment's passage in 1920. Unfortunately for them, black women confronted racial discrimination in their efforts to support the amendment and to win the vote. Consequently, discontented black feminists anticipated the disillusionment that their white counterparts encountered after 1920. An examination of the problems black women faced on the eve of the passage of the woman suffrage amendment and the hostility black women voters endured after the amendment passed serves as a preview of their political status from 1920 to 1945.

The way in which black women leaders dealt with these problems reveals the unique nature of feminism among Afro-American women. Black feminists could not overlook the reality of racism and class conflict as determining factors in the lives of women of their race. Hence, black feminists of the post-World War I era exhibited characteristics similar to those of black feminists of the woman suffrage era and of the late nineteenth-century black women's club movement. During each era, these feminists could not afford to dismiss class or race in favor of sex as the major cause of oppression among black women.

Prelude to Passage of the Nineteenth Amendment

On the eve of the passage of the Nineteenth Amendment, black women leaders could be counted among other groups of women who had worked diligently for woman suffrage. At least ninety black women leaders endorsed woman suffrage, with two-thirds of these women giving support during the decade immediately before passage of the amendment. Afro-American women organized suffrage clubs, participated in rallies and demonstrations, spoke on behalf of the amendment, and wrote essays in support of the cause. These things they had done since the inception of the nineteenth-century woman's rights movement. However, the largest woman suffrage effort among black women's groups occurred during the second decade of the twentieth century. Organizations such as the National Federation of Afro-American Women, the National Association of Colored

Women (NACW), the Northeastern Federation of Colored Women's Clubs, the Alpha Kappa Alpha Sorority, and the Delta Sigma Theta Sorority actively supported woman suffrage. These organizations were national or regional in scope and represented thousands of Afro-American women. Some of the women were from the working class, but most of them were of middle-class status. Across the nation, at least twenty black women suffrage organizations or groups that strongly endorsed woman suffrage existed during the period.[1]

Three examples provide an indication of the diversity in types of woman suffrage activities among black women's organizations. In 1915 the Poughkeepsie, New York, chapter of the Household of Ruth, a working-class, black women's group, endorsed woman suffrage by sending a resolution to the New York branch of the National Woman's Party (NWP) in support of the pending state referendum on woman suffrage. With the need for an intelligent female electorate in mind, black women of Texas organized voter leagues in 1917, the year Texas women won the right to vote. Among these was the Negro Women Voters' League of Galveston. Furthermore, in 1919, the Northeastern Federation of Colored Women's Clubs, representing thousands of women from Montreal to Baltimore, petitioned the National American Woman Suffrage Association (NAWSA) for membership.[2]

The enthusiastic responses of black women to woman suffrage may seem astonishing when one realizes that woman suffrage was a predominantly middle-class movement among native born white women and that the black middle class was very small during the early twentieth century. Furthermore, the heyday of the woman suffrage movement embraced an era that historian Rayford Logan called "the nadir" in Afro-American history, characterized by racial segregation, defamation of the character of black women, and lynching of black Americans, both men and women. It is a wonder that Afro-American women dared to dream a white man's dream — the right to enfranchisement — especially at a time when white women attempted to exclude them from that dream.[3]

The existence of a double standard for black and white women among white woman suffragists was apparent to black women on the eve of Nineteenth Amendment passage. Apprehensions from discontented black leaders about the inclusion of black women as voters, especially in the South, were evident throughout the second decade of the twentieth century. During the early years of the decade, black suffragists such as Adella Hunt Logan, a club leader and suffragist from Tuskegee, Alabama; Mary B. Talbert, president of the National Association of Colored Women; and Josephine St. Pierre Ruffin, a suffragist since the 1880s from Boston and the editor of the *Woman's Era*, a black women's newspaper, complained about the double standard in the woman suffrage movement and insisted that white suffragists set aside their prejudices to allow black women, burdened by both sexism and racism, to gain political equality.[4]

Unfortunately, with little influence among white women, the black suffragists were powerless and their words went unheeded. By 1916 Carrie Catt, president of the NAWSA, concluded that the South had to be conciliated if woman suffrage was to become a reality. Thus, in order to avoid antagonizing southern white women who resented participating in the association with black women, she urged southern white delegates not to attend the NAWSA convention in Chicago that year because the Chicago delegation would be mostly black.[5]

The trend to discriminate against black women as voters continued, and in 1917 the *Crisis*, the official organ of the National Association for the Advancement of Colored People (NAACP), noted that blacks feared white female voters because of their antiblack woman suffrage and antiblack male sentiments. Afro-American fears went beyond misgivings about white women. In 1918 the editors of the *Houston Observer* responded to black disillusionment when they called upon the men and women of the race to register to vote in spite of the poll tax, which was designed especially to exclude black voters.[6]

Skepticism about equality of woman suffrage among blacks continued. Mrs. A. W. Blackwell, an African Methodist Episcopal church leader in Atlanta, estimated that about 3 million black women were of voting age. She warned, however, that a "grandmother clause" would be introduced after passage of a suffrage amendment to prevent black women, 90 percent of whom lived in the South, from voting.[7]

Disillusionment among black suffragists became so apparent that several national suffrage leaders attempted to appease them with reassurances about their commitment to black woman suffrage. In 1917 Carrie Catt and Anna Shaw wooed black female support through the pages of the *Crisis*. In the District of Columbia, the same year, Congresswoman Jeanette Rankin of Montana addressed an enthusiastic group of Alpha Kappa Alpha Sorority women at Howard University. There she assured the group that she wanted all women to be given the ballot regardless of race.[8]

However, in 1917 while the New York state woman suffrage referendum was pending in the legislature, black suffragists in the state complained of discrimination against their organizations by white suffragists during the statewide woman suffrage convention at Saratoga. White leaders assured black women that they were welcomed in the movement. Although the majority of the black delegates were conciliated, a vocal minority remained disillusioned.[9]

By 1919, the year before the Nineteenth Amendment was adopted by Congress, antiblack woman suffrage sentiments continued to plague the movement. Shortly before the amendment was adopted, several incidents occurred to further disillusion black feminists. Mary Church Terrell, a Washington, D.C., educator and national leader among black club women, reported that white suffragists in Florida discriminated against black women in their attempts to recruit support for the campaign. In addition, the NAACP, whose policy officially endorsed woman suffrage, clashed with Alice Paul, president of the NWP because she allegedly said "that all this talk of Negro women voting in South Carolina was nonsense."[10] Later, Walter White, the NAACP's assistant to the executive secretary, complained to Mary Church Terrell about Alice Paul and agreed with Terrell that white suffrage leaders would be willing to accept the suffrage amendment even if it did not enfranchise black women.[11]

Within a week after receiving Walter White's letter, Mary Church Terrell received a letter from Ida Husted Harper, a leader in the suffrage movement and the editor of the last two volumes of the *History of Woman Suffrage*, asking Terrell to use her influence to persuade the Northeastern Federation of Colored Women's Clubs to withdraw their application seeking cooperative membership in the NAWSA. Echoing sentiments expressed earlier by NAWSA president Carrie Catt, Harper explained that accepting the membership of a black organization was inexpedient for NAWSA at a time when white suffragists sought the cooperation of white southern women. Harper noted that the major obstacle to the amendment in the South was fear among whites of the black woman's vote. She therefore asked federation president Elizabeth Carter to resubmit the membership application after the passage of the Nineteenth Amendment.[12]

At its Jubilee Convention in Saint Louis in March 1919, the NAWSA officially catered to the fears of their southern white members. In response to a proposal by Kentucky suffragist Laura Clay that sections of the so-called Susan B. Anthony amendment that would permit the enfranchisement of black women be changed, the convention delegates agreed that the amendment should be worded so as to allow the South to determine its own position on the black female vote.[13]

During the last months before the passage of the Susan B. Anthony amendment, black suffragists had been rebuffed by both the conservative wing of the suffrage movement, the NAWSA, and by the more radical wing, the NWP. Why then did Afro-American women continue to push for woman suffrage? Since the 1880s, most black women who supported woman suffrage did so because they believed that political equality among the races would raise the status of blacks, both male and female. Increasing the black electorate, they felt, would not only uplift the women of the race, but help the children and the men as well. The majority of the black suffragists were not radical feminists. They were reformers, or what William H. Chafe calls social feminists, who believed that the system could be amended to work for them. Like their white counterparts, these black suffragists assumed that the enfranchised held the key to ameliorating social ills. But unlike white social feminists, many black suffragists called for social and political measures that were specifically tied to race issues. Among these issues were antimiscegenation legislation, jim crow legislation, and "lynch law." Prominent black feminists combined the fight against sexism with the fight against racism by continuously calling the public's attention to these issues. Ida B. Wells-Barnett, Angelina Weld Grimke, and Mary Church Terrell spoke out against lynching. Josephine St. Pierre Ruffin and Lottie Wilson Jackson, as well as Terrell and Wells-Barnett took steps to challenge jim crow facilities in public accommodations, and antimiscegenation legislation was impugned by Terrell, Grimke, and Wells-Barnett.[14]

Blacks understood the potential political influence, if not political power, that they could harness with woman suffrage, especially in the South. White supremacists realized it too. Although there were several reasons for southern opposition to the Nineteenth Amendment, the one common to all states was fear of black female suffrage. This fear had been stimulated by the way in which Afro-American women responded to suffrage in states that had achieved woman suffrage before the passage of the federal amendment. In northern states with large black populations, such as Illinois and New York, the black female electorate was significant. Chicago elected its first black alderman, Oscar De Priest, in 1915, the year after women won the right to vote. In 1917, the year the woman suffrage referendum passed the New York state legislature, New York City elected its first black state assemblyperson, Edward A. Johnson. In both cities the black female vote was decisive in the election. In the South, Texas Afro-American women mobilized in 1918 to effectively educate the women of thei. race in order to combat white opposition to their voting.[15]

By 1920 white southern apprehensions of a viable black female electorate were not illusionary. "Colored women voter's leagues" were growing throughout the South, where the task of the leagues was to give black women seeking to qualify to vote instructions for countering white opposition. Leagues could be found in Alabama, Georgia, Tennessee, and Texas. These groups were feared also by white supremacists because the women sought to qualify black men as voters as well.[16]

Whites widely believed that black women wanted the ballot more than white women in the South. Black women were expected to register and to vote in larger numbers than white women. If this happened, the ballot would soon be returned to black men. Black suffrage, it was believed, would also result in the return of the two-party system in the South, because blacks would consistently vote Republican. These apprehensions were realized in Florida after the passage of the Nineteenth Amendment. Black women in Jacksonville registered in greater numbers than white women. In reaction, the Woman Suffrage League of Jacksonville was reorganized into the Duval County League of Democratic Women Voters. The members were dedicated to maintain white supremacy and pledged to register white women voters.[17]

In Texas, where women could vote before the passage of the Nineteenth

Amendment, black women, nevertheless, were discriminated against. In 1918 six black women had been refused the right to register at Forth Worth on the ground that the primaries were open to white Democrats only. Efforts to disfranchise black women in Houston failed, however, when the women took legal action against the registrars who attempted to apply the Texas woman suffrage law to white women only. A similar attempt to disqualify Afro-American women in Waxahachie, Texas, failed also.[18]

Subterfuge and trickery such as the kind used in Texas was being used throughout the South by 1920. In North Carolina, the predictions of Mrs. A. W. Blackwell came true when the state legislature introduced a bill known as the "grandmother clause" for women voters. The bill attempted to protect illiterate white women from disfranchisement, but the legislators had not taken into account that "grandfather clauses" had been nullified by the Supreme Court. Nonetheless, black leaders called to the women of the race to stand up and fight. This they did.[19]

In 1920 black women registered in large numbers throughout the South, especially in Georgia and Louisiana, despite major obstacles placed against them by the white supremacists. In defense, Afro-American women often turned to the NAACP for assistance. Field Secretary William Pickens was sent to investigate the numerous charges and recorded several incidents which he either witnessed personally or about which he received reports. In Columbia, South Carolina, during the first day of registration black women apparently took the registrars by surprise. No plan to disqualify them had been put into effect. Many black women reported to the office and had to wait for hours while the white women were registered first. Some women waited up to twelve hours to register. The next day, a $300 tax requirement was made mandatory for black women. If they passed that test, the women were required to read from and to interpret the state or the federal constitutions. No such tests were required of white women. In addition, white lawyers were on hand to quiz and harass black women. Although the *Columbia State*, a local newspaper, reported disinterest in registering among black women, Pickens testified to the contrary. By the end of the registration period, twenty Columbia black women had signed an affidavit against the registrars who had disqualified them. In the surrounding Richland County, Afro-American women were disqualified when they attempted to register to vote. As a result, several of them made plans to appeal the ruling.[20]

Similar reports came from Richmond, Virginia, where registrars attempted to deny or successfully denied black women the right to register. A black woman of Newburn, North Carolina, signed an affidavit testifying to the difficulty she had in attempting to register. First she was asked to read and to write the entire state constitution. After successfully reading the document, she was informed that no matter what else she did, the registrar would disqualify her because she was black. Many cases like this one were handled by the NAACP, and after the registration periods ended in the South, its board of directors presented the evidence to Congress. NAACP officials and others testified at a congressional hearing in support of the proposed enactment of the Tinkham Bill to reduce representation in Congress from states where there was restriction of woman suffrage. White supremacy prevailed, however, as southern congressmen successfully claimed that blacks were not disfranchised, just disinterested in voting. Hence, despite the massive evidence produced by the NAACP, the Tinkham Bill failed to pass.[21]

The inability of the NAACP to protect the rights of black women voters led the women to seek help from national woman suffrage leaders. However, these attempts failed also. The NWP leadership felt that since black women were discriminated against in the same ways as black men, their problems were not woman's rights issues, but race issues. Therefore, the woman's party felt no obligation to defend the rights of black women.[22]

That they would be abandoned by white female suffragists in 1920 came as no surprise to most black women leaders. The preceding decade of woman suffrage politics had reminded them of the assertions of black woman suffrage supporters of the past. Frederick Douglass declared in 1868 that black women were victimized mainly because they were blacks, not because they were women. Frances Ellen Watkins Harper answered in 1869 that for white women the priorities in the struggle for human rights were sex, not race. By 1920 the situation had changed very little, and many black suffragists had been thoroughly disillusioned by the machinations of the white feminists they had encountered.[23]

Postscript — Black Feminists, 1920-1945

Afro-American Women continued to be involved in local and national politics during the post-World War I years. However, few organized feminist activities were apparent among the disillusioned black feminists of the period. Afro-American women leaders and their organizations began to focus on issues that continued to plague both the men and the women of the race, rather than upon issues that concerned white feminists. The economic plight of black women kept most of them in poverty and among the lowest of the working classes. Middle-class black women were still relatively few in number. They were more concerned about uplifting the downtrodden of the race or in representing people of color throughout the world than in issues that were limited to middle-class feminists. Hence, during the 1920s there was little concern among black women over the Equal Rights Amendment debate between the more conservative League of Women Voters (LWV) and the more radical NWP. Although the economic roles of many white American women were expanding, the status of black women remained basically static between the wars. As a result, black feminists identified more with the plight of third world people who found themselves in similar oppressed situations. Former black suffragists were more likely to participate in the Women's International League for Peace and Freedom (WILPF) or the International Council of Women of the Darker Races than in the LWV or the NWP.

In 1920 Howard University professor Benjamin Brawley examined the economic status of black women. He found that there were over 1 million black females in the United States work force in 1910. Fifty-two percent of them worked as farmers or farm laborers, and 28 percent worked as cooks or washerwomen. In essence, 80 percent of black women workers were doing arduous, menial work. Brawley speculated that conditions had not changed much by 1920.[24] In 1922 black social worker Elizabeth Ross Haynes found that 2 million black women in the nation worked in three types of occupations: domestic and personal service, agriculture, and manufacturing and mechanical industries. Of the 2 million, 50 percent were found in domestic service. Only 20,000 were found in semiskilled jobs in manufacturing and mechanical industries. Haynes's findings in 1922 were in keeping with Brawley's speculations.[25] Unfortunately, by 1945 the position of black women in the work force had not changed significantly. Black women ranked lowest on the economic scale among men and women, black and white.

Geographically, during the period, the black population was shifting from the rural South to the urban North and West. Nearly 90 percent of the adult black female population lived in the South in 1920. By 1930 less than 80 percent of that population did. In 1940 the percentage had dropped to nearly 75 percent.[26] Even with this drop, however, three-fourths of the adult black women of the nation remained in the South, where they were virtually disfranchised. The black women who found their way north and west lacked the political influence necessary to change the status of black women because of their economic powerlessness. What temporary gains black women made in World War I industry quickly faded away during the postwar years.

In 1935 the average weekly wage for a black domestic worker was $3.00 and washerwomen received a mere 75¢ a week. Working conditions, as well as wages, were substandard, and black women were exploited by white women as well as by white men. In observing the working conditions of New York City domestic workers, Louise Mitchell found that standards had not changed much by 1940. Some women worked for as little as $2.00 a week and as long as 80 hours a week. Mitchell noted Women's Bureau findings that indicated that women took domestic work only as a last resort. She concluded that black women were the most oppressed of the working classes.[27]

As the United States entered World War II, black women found more opportunitites in industry. However, jobs available to black women were the ones for which white workers were not available. War industry jobs were often found in urban centers outside of the South. Consequently, the majority remained outside of the mainstream of feminist consciousness because feminist interests were not their interests, and those black feminists of the woman suffrage era found little comfort from white feminists. Several of the black feminists of the woman suffrage era remained in leadership positions during the 1920s and the 1930s, while others faded from the scene. In addition, new faces became associated with black female leadership. Among these were Amy Jacques Garvey and Mary McLeod Bethune. Although all of these women either identified themselves or have been identified as feminists, their major concerns between the world wars were racial issues, with the status of black women as a major priority.

A look at the 1920s reveals that most of the black women's organizations that were prominent during the woman suffrage era remained so. Nonetheless, new groups were organized as well. Elizabeth Carter remained president of the Northeastern Federation of Colored Women's Clubs, which celebrated its twenty-fifth anniversary in 1921. The leadership of the NACW was in transition during the 1920s. Mary B. Talbert retired as president and was succeeded by a former suffragist, Hallie Q. Brown, in 1922. In the middle of the decade Mary McLeod Bethune assumed the presidency. In 1922 several NACW leaders organized the International Council of Women of the Darker Races. Margaret Murray Washington, the wife of the late Booker T. Washington and the first president of the National Federation of Afro-American Women, was elected president.[28]

In addition to these established black women's organizations, there was the women's arm of Marcus Garvey's United Negro Improvement Association (UNIA). At its peak, in 1925, the UNIA had an estimated membership of 2 million and can be considered the first mass movement among working-class black people in the nation. Amy Jacques Garvey, Marcus Garvey's wife, was the articulate leader of the women's division and the editor of the women's department of the UNIA official newspaper, *Negro World*. A feminist in the international sense, Amy Jacques Garvey's feminist views embraced the class struggle as well as the problems of Third World women. A black nationalist, Garvey encouraged women of color throughout the world to organize for the benefit of themselves as well as their own people. Although she gave credit to the old-line black women's clubs, Garvey felt their approach to the problems of Third World women was limited. A Jamaican by birth, she called for revolutionary strategies that did not merely reflect the reform ideas of white middle-class women. Instead Garvey called upon the masses of black women in the United States to acknowledge that they were the "burden bearers of their race" and to take the lead in fighting for black independence from white oppression. Amy Jacques Garvey combined the UNIA belief in the power of the black urban working class with the feminist belief that women could think and do for themselves. The revolutionary implications of her ideas are reflected in the theme of the women's pages of *Negro World*—"Our Women and What They Think." Garvey called for black women's dedication to social justice and to national liberation, abroad as well as at home.[29]

Garvey was a radical who happened to be a feminist as well. Her views were ahead of her time; thus, she would have fit in well with the mid-twentieth century radical feminists. However, the demise of the UNIA and the deportation of Marcus Garvey in 1927 shattered much of Amy Jacques Garvey's influence in the United States and she returned to Jamaica. In the meantime, the majority of black feminists of the 1920s either joined the white social feminists, such as Jane Addams and the WILPF, or bypassed the feminists altogether to deal with race issues within black organizations.

The leadership of the WILPF was old-line and can be characterized as former progressives, woman suffragists, and social feminists. Jane Addams presided over the organization before U.S. entry into World War I and brought black women such as Mary Church Terrell, Mary B. Talbert, Charlotte Atwood, Mary F. Waring, and Addie W. Hunton into the fold. Terrell had been a member of the executive committee since 1915. As a league representative, she was elected a delegate to the International Congress of Women held in Paris in 1919. Upon her arrival, Terrell was impressed with the conference delegates but noticed that there were none from non-western countries and that she was the only delegate of color in the group. As a result, she felt obliged to represent the women of all the nonwhite countries in the world, and this she attempted to do. At the conference meeting in Zurich, Switzerland, Terrell agreed to represent the American delegation and did so by speaking in German before the largely German-speaking audience. In addition, she submitted her own personal resolution to the conference, despite attempts by American committee members to change her wording. "We believe no human being should be deprived of an education, prevented from earning a living, debarred from any legitimate pursuit in which he wishes to engage or be subjected to humiliations of various kinds on account of race, color or creed." Terrell's position and thinking were in keeping with the growing awareness among black women leaders in the United States that Third World people needed to fight oppression together.

Although Mary Church Terrell remained an active social feminist, her public as well as her private views reflected the disillusionment of black feminists of the woman suffrage era. In 1921 she was asked by members of the WILPF executive committee to sign a petition requesting the removal of black troops from occupied German territory, where they were alleged to be violating German women. Terrell refused to sign the petition because she felt the motives behind it were racist. In a long letter to Jane Addams, the executive committee chairman, Terrell explained why she would not sign the petition. She noted that Carrie Catt had investigated the charges against the black troops and found them to be unfounded. The troops, from French colonies in Africa, were victims, Terrell contended, of American propaganda against black people. Making a dramatic choice between the feminist organization position and her own loyalty to her race, Terrell offered to resign from the executive committee. Addams wrote her back, agreeing with Terrell's position and asking her not to resign.[31] In this case, when given the choice between the politics of feminism and race pride, Terrell felt that her energies were needed most to combat racism, and she chose to take a nationalist position in the controversy.

Several other attempts were made at interracial cooperation among women's groups during the early 1920s, but most of these efforts were white-dominated and short-lived. An exception was the Cooperative Women's League of Baltimore, founded in 1913 by Sarah C. Fernandis. This group maintained relations with white women's civic leagues in connection with local health and sanitation, home economics, art, and education projects. In 1925 the league initiated its twelfth annual program.[32] This organization was quite conventional, a far cry from feminist — black or white. However, the activities were, like most black women's group activities of the times, geared to strengthen local black communities.

Other black-white cooperative ventures on a grander scale included the Commission on Inter-Racial Cooperation of the Women's Council of the Methodist Episcopal Church South. In October 1920 the commission held a conference on race relations. Only four black women were invited and they were selected because of their husbands' prominence, rather than for their feminist views. The conference pledged a responsibility to uplift the status of black women in the South, calling for a reform of the conditions under which black domestics worked in white homes. The delegates passed resolutions supporting improved sanitation and housing for blacks, fair treatment of blacks in public accommodations, the prevention of lynching, and justice in the courts. Significantly, no mention of protecting black women's suffrage was made. Several months later, the National Federation of Colored Women's Clubs met at Tuskegee, Alabama, and issued a statement that seemed to remind the Methodist Episcopal women of their pledge and called for increased cooperation and understanding from southern white women. Interestingly, the black women included suffrage in their resolution.[33]

Nothing came of this attempt at interracial cooperation, for neither the social nor the economic status of black women improved in the South during the 1920s. The trend toward interracial cooperation continued nevertheless, and in 1922 the YWCA appointed a joint committee of black and white women to study race problems. Once, again, only four black women were invited to participate. Principles were declared, but little came of the gathering.[34]

In the meantime, most black women's organizations had turned from attempts to establish coalitions with white women's groups to concentrate upon pressing race problems. Lynching was one of the major American problems, and black women organized to fight it. On the national front, black women's groups used political strategies and concentrated their efforts toward passage of the Dyer Anti-Lynching Bill. In 1922 the Northeastern Federation of Colored Women's Clubs appointed a delegation to call on Senator Lodge of Massachusetts to urge passage of the Dyer bill. In addition, the Alpha Kappa Alpha Sorority held its national convention in Indianapolis and sent a telegram to President Warren Harding urging the support of his administration in the passage of the bill. Also that year, the NACW met in Richmond and appointed an antilynching delegation to make contact with key states needed for the passage of the Dyer bill in Congress. In addition, the delegation was authorized to meet with President Harding. Among the black women in the delegation were veteran antilynching crusader Ida B. Wells-Barnett, NACW president Hallie Q. Brown, and Rhode Island suffragist Mary B. Jackson.[35]

Perhaps the most renowned antilynching crusader of the 1920s was Spingarn Medal winner Mary B. Talbert. In 1922 she organized an executive committee of 15 black women, who supervised over 700 state workers across the nation in what Talbert called the Anti-Lynching Crusade. Her aim was to "unite a million women to stop lynching," by arousing the consciences of both black and white women. One of Talbert's strategies was to provide statistics that showed that victims of lynching were not what propagandists called sex-hungry black men who preyed upon innocent white women. The crusaders revealed that eighty-three women had been lynched in the United States since Ida B. Wells-Barnett had compiled the first comprehensive annual report in 1892. The Anti-Lynching Crusade was truly an example of woman power, for the crusaders believed that they could not wait for the men of America to stop the problem. It was perhaps the most influential link in the drive for interracial cooperation among women's groups. As a result of its efforts, the 1922 National Council of Women, representing 13 million American women, resolved to "endorse the Anti-Lynching Crusade recently launched by colored women of this country."[36]

Although the Dyer bill was defeated, it was revised by the NAACP and introduced again in the House of Representatives by Congressman Leonidas C. Dyer of Missouri and in the Senate by William B. McKinley of Illinois in 1926. That year the bill failed again, as did similar bills in 1935, 1940, and 1942. However, it was the effort of blacks and white women organized against lynching that pressed for legislation throughout the period. Without a doubt, it was the leadership of black women, many of whom had been active in the late nineteenth-century women's club movement and in the woman suffrage movement, who motivated white women in 1930 to organize the Association of Southern Women for the Prevention of

Lynching. Although a federal antilynching bill never passed the Congress, by the end of the 1940s public opinion had been sufficiently convinced by the efforts of various women's groups that lynching was barbarous and criminal. Recorded incidents of lynching ceased by 1950.

Even though interracial cooperation in the antilynching campaign was a positive factor among black and white women, discrimination against black women by white women continued to plague feminists. In 1925, for example, the Quinquennial of the International Council of Women met at the Washington Auditorium in the District of Columbia. The council sought the cooperation of NACW president Mary McLeod Bethune and arrangements were made to have a mass choir of black women perform. The night of the concert, black guests were placed in a segregated section of the auditorium. Mary Church Terrell reported that when the singers learned of what was happening, they refused to perform. Foreign women delegates were in the audience, as well as white women from throughout the nation. Many of them were angry because the concert had to be cancelled. Terrell felt that this was one of the most unfortunate incidents of discrimination against black women in the club movement. However, she agreed with the decision of her black sisters not to sing.[37]

National recognition of black women did not really come until 1936, when Mary McLeod Bethune was appointed director of the Division of Negro Affairs, National Youth Administration, under the Franklin D. Roosevelt administration. The founder of Bethune-Cookman Institute in Daytona, Florida, Bethune had been a leader in the black women's club movement since the early 1920s. NACW president from 1924 to 1928, she founded the National Council of Negro Women (NCNW) in 1935. What feminist consciousness Bethune acquired was thrust upon her in the mid-1930s because for the first time, a black woman had the ear of the president of the United States and the cooperation of the first lady, who was concerned not only about women's issues, but about black issues. In 1936 Bethune took advantage of her new status and presented the concerns of the NCNW to Eleanor Roosevelt. As a result, sixty-five black women leaders attended a meeting with Eleanor Roosevelt to argue the case for their greater representation and appointments to federal bureaus. They called for appointments of professional black women to the Children's Bureau, the Women's Bureau, and each department of the Bureau of Education that dealt with the welfare of women and children. The NCNW also wanted the appointment of black women to administrative positions in the Federal Housing Administration and Social Security Board. In addition, they called for enlarging the black staff of the Bureau of Public Health and for President Roosevelt to suggest to the American Red Cross that they hire a black administrator.[38]

The NCNW requests reflect two trends among middle-class women in the mid-1930s. First, they were calling for positions that black women had never held, nor would achieve until a generation later; consequently, their ideas were revolutionary ones in terms of federal policies. Second, they were calling for policies to benefit not only their sex, but their race; hence, the NCNW reflected the position established by black feminists a generation before.

Mary McLeod Bethune's leadership was acknowledged by black women's groups throughout the nation, and she accepted the responsibility by referring to herself as the representative of "Negro womanhood." In 1937 she visited the Flanner House, a black settlement house in Indianapolis whose black woman superintendent, Clio Blackburn, said the institution's aim was to help black people help themselves. If no other person represented this standard to black women at this time, Mary McLeod Bethune did. The following year she met with the Alpha Kappa Alpha Sorority in Boston to assist them in a benefit for the Mississippi Health Project, a project to help black people in that region which was sponsored by the national sorority.[39]

Middle-class black women clearly reflected their dedication to uplifting the race at a time when most Afro-Americans were thwarted not only by race prejudice but also by economic depression. Although activities that involved race uplift were not feminist in orientation, many black feminists took an active role in them. In an interview with Mary McLeod Bethune in 1939, Lillian B. Huff of the *New Jersey Herald News* asked her about the role of black women leaders and how Bethune related to her leadership position. Bethune, who had come from humble origins, felt that black women had room in their lives to be wives and mothers as well as to have careers. But most importantly, she thought, black women should think of their duty to the race.[40]

Bethune's feelings were not unique to black women, for most black feminists and leaders had been wives and mothers who worked yet found time not only to struggle for the good of their sex, but for their race. Until the 1970s, however, this threefold commitment – to family and to career and to one or more social movements – was not common among white women. The key to the uniqueness among black feminists of this period appears to be their link with the past. The generation of the woman suffrage era had learned from their late nineteenth-century foremothers in the black women's club movement, just as the generation of the post World War I era had learned and accepted the experiences of the preceding generation. Theirs was a sense of continuity, a sense of group consciousness that transcended class. Racial uplift, fighting segregation and mob violence, contending with poverty, as well as demanding rights for black women were longstanding issues of concern to black feminists.

The meeting of the National Conference on Problems of the Negro and Youth at Washington, D.C., in 1939 was a good example of this phenomenon among black women. Bethune called the meeting and invited a range of black leaders from Mary Church Terrell and feminist Nannie Burroughs,

who were both in their seventies, to Juanita Jackson Mitchell, the conference youth coordinator. The young Mitchell had been a leader among
black civil rights activists in the City-Wide Young People's Forum in Baltimore a few years before. Bethune noted the success of the meeting of young
and old, all of whom had a common interest in civil rights for Afro-
Americans.[41]

By 1940 Mary Church Terrell had written her autobiography. At the age
of seventy-seven, she was one of the few living links with three generations
of black feminists. In her introduction, Terrell established her own interpretation of her life story, which in many ways reflected the lives of other
black feminists. "This is the story of a colored woman living in a white
world. It cannot possibly be like a story written by a white woman. A white
woman has only one handicap to overcome – that of sex. I have two – both
sex and race. I belong to the only group in this country which has two such
huge obstacles to surmount. Colored men have only one – that of race"[42]

Terrell's reference to her status as an Afro-American woman applied
throughout United States history to most black women, regardless of class.
In view of this, it is not surprising that black women struggled, often in
vain, to keep the right to vote from 1920 to 1940. A brief reference to this
struggle, a story in itself, reveals that they fought to keep the little influence
they had although black feminists anticipated that many of them would
lose. Nonetheless, black female enthusiasm was great immediately following passage of the Nineteenth Amendment. In Baltimore alone, the black
electorate increased from 16,800 to over 37,400 in 1921, indicating that the
number of black women voters surpassed the number of black men registered to vote. By 1922, however, attempts to thwart the influence of black
women voters were spreading across the South. As a result, the NACW
recommended that all of its clubs lobby for the enforcement of the Nineteenth Amendment.[43]

By 1924 feminist Nannie Burroughs had assessed the status of black
women of voting age and their relationship to white feminists. Burroughs
noted that white women continued to overlook or to undervalue the worth
of black women as a political force in the nation. She warned white female
politicians to tap the potential black female electorate before white men
exploited it.[44] With the exception of Ruth Hanna McCormick, who recruited
Mary Church Terrell to head her 1929 Illinois campaign for the United
States Senate, warnings such as Burroughs's did not seem to influence white
female leaders. For example, disillusioned members of the Republican
Colored Women State Committee of Wilmington, Delaware, protested
unsuccessfully when they lost their representation on the state Republican
committee. A merger of the Women's Advisory Committee, a white group,
with the State Central Committee had caused the elimination of black
women representatives. The decline in black women's participation in
Republican party politics was evident by 1928, when only 8 out of 104 black

delegates to the Republican National Convention were women. The same year, the NACW program did not even bother to include suffrage among its priorities for women of the race.[45]

Although President Roosevelt made good his promise to Mary McLeod Bethune, so that by 1945 four black women had received outstanding federal appointments, the political viability of black women in the early 1940s was bleak. The list of black elected officials from 1940 to 1946 included no women.[46] Agents of white supremacy continued to subvert what vestiges of political influence blacks held. For example, in 1942 Congressman Martin Dies, chairman of the congressional committee investigating un-American activities, attempted to link several national black leaders to the Communist party. Among the group was Mary McLeod Bethune, who remained the only black woman prominent in national politics.[47]

Hence, over twenty years after the passage of the Nineteenth Amendment racial discrimination festered in most areas of American life, even among feminists and women in political life. Prejudice did not distinguish between middle-class and working-class black women, nor between feminists and nonfeminists who were black. Although black women continued to use what political rights they maintained, the small number of those politically viable made little impact upon public policies.

Notes

1. See Rosalyn Terborg-Penn, "Nineteenth Century Black Women and Woman Suffrage," *Potomac Review* 7 (Spring-Summer 1977): 13-24; and Rosalyn M. Terborg-Penn, "Afro-Americans in the Struggle for Woman Suffrage" (Ph.D. dissertation, Howard University, 1977), pp. 180-85.

2. *Indianapolis Freeman*, 28 August 1915; Monroe N. Work, ed., *The Negro Year Book, 1918-1919* (Tuskegee Institute, Ala.: The Negro Year Book Publishing Co., 1919), pp. 57-59 (hereafter cited as *Negro Year Book*, by year); Rosalyn Terborg-Penn, "Discrimination Against Afro-American Women in the Woman's Movement, 1830-1920," *The Afro-American Woman: Struggles and Images*, edited by Sharon Harley and Rosalyn Terborg-Penn (Port Washington, N.Y.: Kennikat Press, 1978), p. 26.

3. See Rayford W. Logan, *The Negro in the United States* (Princeton, N.J.: Van Nostrand, 1957); and Terborg-Penn, "Discrimination Against Afro-American Women," pp. 17-27.

4. Terborg-Penn, "Afro-Americans in the Struggle for Woman Suffrage," chapter 4.

5. David Morgan, *Suffragists and Democrats: The Politics of Woman Suffrage in America* (East Lansing, Mich.: Michigan State University Press, 1972), pp. 106-07.

6. *Crisis* 15 (November 1917): 18; *Negro Year Book, 1918-1919*, p. 60.

7. Mrs. A. W. Blackwell, *The Responsibility and Opportunity of the Twentieth Century Woman* (n.p., n.d.), pp. 1-5. This pamphlet is housed in the Trevor Arnett Library, Atlanta University.

8. *The Crisis* 15 (November 1917): 19-20; *New York Age,* 10 May 1917.

9. *New York Age,* September 20, 1917.

10. Walter White to Mary Church Terrell, 14 March 1919, Mary Church Terrell Papers, Box no. 3, Library of Congress, Washington, D.C. (hereafter cited as MCT Papers); Charles Flint Kellogg, *NAACP: A History of the National Association for the Advancement of Colored People, 1909-1920* (Baltimore: Johns Hopkins Press, 1967), p. 208.

11. Walter White to Mary Church Terrell, 14 March 1919, MCT Papers, Box no. 3.

12. Ida Husted Harper to Mary Church Terrell, 18 March 1919, and Ida Harper to Elizabeth Carter, 18 March 1919, MCT Papers, Box no. 3.

13. Aileen Kraditor, *The Ideas of the Woman Suffrage Movement, 1890-1920* (Garden City, N.Y.: Anchor Books, Doubleday and Co., 1971), pp. 168-69; *Crisis* 17 (June 1919): 103; Ida Husted Harper, ed., *The History of Woman Suffrage, 1900-1920* (New York: J. J. Little and Ives Co., 1922), pp. 580-81.

14. Terborg-Penn, "Afro-Americans in the Struggle for Woman Suffrage," chapters 4 and 5.

15. *Ibid.,* pp. 207, 217-18, 225.

16. *Crisis* 19 (November 1920): 23-25; *Negro Year Book, 1921,* p. 40.

17. Kenneth R. Johnson, "White Racial Attitudes as a Factor in the Arguments Against the Nineteenth Amendment," *Phylon* 31 (Spring 1970): 31-32, 35-37.

18. Terborg-Penn, "Afro-Americans in the Struggle for Woman Suffrage," pp. 301-02.

19. *Ibid.,* pp. 303-04.

20. William Pickens, "The Woman Voter Hits the Color Line," *Nation* 3 (October 6, 1920): 372-73.

21. *Ibid.,* p. 373; NAACP, *Eleventh Annual Report of the NAACP for the Year 1920* (New York: NAACP, 1921), pp. 15, 25-30.

22. William L. O'Neill, *Everybody Was Brave* (Chicago: Quadrangle Press, 1969), p. 275.

23. Terborg-Penn, "Afro-Americans in the Struggle for Woman Suffrage," p. 311.

24. Benjamin Brawley, *Women of Achievement: Written for the Fireside Schools* (Nashville, Tenn.: Woman's American Baptist Home Mission Society, 1919), pp. 14-17.

25. Elizabeth Ross Haynes, "Two Million Negro Women at Work," *Southern Workman* 15 (February 1922): 64-66.

26. United States Department of Commerce, Bureau of Census, *Population Trends in the United States, 1900-1960* (Washington, D.C.: U.S. Government Printing Office, 1964), pp. 231, 234.

27. Gerda Lerner, ed., *Black Women in White America: A Documentary History* (New York: Random House, Pantheon Books, 1972), pp. 226-27; Louise Mitchell, "Slave Markets Typify Exploitation of Domestics," *Daily Worker,* 5 May 1940.

28. *Negro Year Book, 1922-24,* p. 37.

29. *The Negro World,* 24 October 1925, 5 March 1927. See Mark D. Matthews, "'Our Women and What They Think,' Amy Jacques Garvey and *The Negro World,*" *Black Scholar* 10 (May-June 1979): 2-13.

30. Mary Church Terrell, *A Colored Woman in a White World* (Washington, D.C.: Randsdell, Inc., 1940), pp. 330-33.

31. *Ibid.*, pp. 360-64.

32. *Crisis* 30 (June 1925): 81.

33. *Negro Year Book, 1921-22*, pp. 6-9.

34. *Negro Year Book, 1922-24*, pp. 18-19.

35. *Ibid.*, pp. 37-38; *Crisis* 23 (March 1922): 218; *Crisis* 24 (October 1922): 260.

36. *Crisis* 24 (November 1922): 8.

37. Terrell, *A Colored Woman in a White World*, pp. 370-71.

38. Mary McLeod Bethune, Vertical File, Howard University, Washington, D.C., Clippings Folder, 1930, *Black Dispatch*, 16 April 1936 (hereafter cited as Bethune Vertical File and the source).

39. Bethune Vertical File, *Indianapolis Recorder*, 14 December 1937, *Boston Guardian*, 18 October 1938.

40. Bethune Vertical File, *New Jersey Herald News*, 14 October 1939.

41. Bethune Vertical File, *Black Dispatch*, 28 January 1939.

42. Terrell, *A Colored Woman in a White World*, first page of the introduction.

43. *Crisis* 23 (December 1921): 83; *Negro Year Book, 1922-24*, p. 37.

44. *Negro Year Book, 1922-24*, p. 70.

45. Terrell, *A Colored Woman in a White World*, pp. 355-56; *Negro Year Book, 1922-24*, p. 70; *Negro Year Book, 1931-32*, pp. 13, 92-93. Blacks did not vote the Democratic party on a large scale until the second Franklin D. Roosevelt administration.

46. *Negro Year Book, 1947*, pp. 286-87, 289-91.

47. Bethune Vertical File, *Black Dispatch*, 10 October 1942.

13

Socialist Feminism between the Two World Wars: Insights from Oral History
SHERNA BERGER GLUCK

Introduction

Women have been a visible presence among socialists since the development of an organized movement in Europe in the nineteenth century. They have been represented in all of the currents of socialism in the United States in the twentieth century. In fact, their importance far outweighs their numerical strength in socialist organizations (estimated to range from 10 percent of the membership of the Socialist party in the 1910s to over 30 percent of the membership of the Communist party in the 1930s), for the question of women's oppression poses a serious challenge to both the theory and practice of socialism. Women's emancipation was seriously addressed in socialist congresses, and socialist women, including North American women, participated in these discussions in the Second International, an organization composed primarily of European socialists. In the United States, in the early part of the century, these debates took place primarily within the framework of the Socialist party. Many of the women involved in these discussions formed semi-autonomous organizations, and their presence as socialist feminists was felt through the medium of their own publications.[1] No organized form of socialist feminism survived after World War I. Although Marxists continued to write about the "woman question," the basic feminist focus which had been evident earlier was absent.[2] It was not until the emergence and growth of the women's liberation movement in the United States in the late 1960s that the debates were rekindled and that an organized voice for socialist feminism reemerged. In its contemporary context, socialist feminist women, now organized into autonomous organizations and networks, have themselves defined the very terms of the debate and the framework for the discussions.

The reemergence of socialist feminism, like the "rebirth of feminism" generally in the second half of the twentieth century, has led to the search for an historical precedent. Though it can be found in the activities and publications of the early twentieth century socialist feminists, nagging questions about the intervening years between 1915 and the present persist.

This paper is a revised version of a paper delivered at the Fourth Berkshire Conference on Women's History, Mount Holyoke, 1978.

Does a consciousness which had taken root in organizational form in one period simply disappear, or does it find expression in a different form? If there is no organizational voice for that consciousness, as in the case of socialist feminism, what sources can be used in historical study?

Oral history, a valuable methodology for the development of new sources in women's history, becomes particularly important in the study of feminist consciousness and activity during periods when feminist organizations seemed to be in subsidence, like the period after the First World War. Changes in feminist expression can be traced in the lives of individual self-identified socialist women, as revealed through oral history. Cumulatively, these individual oral histories, when placed in their proper social and historical context, supplement and clarify the few existing written sources and point to a socialist feminist tradition kept alive by women workers and intellectuals.

The experiences of five such women illustrate how this tradition was expressed in the period between the two world wars. Ernestine Hara Kettler, Miriam Allen deFord, and Mary Inman all came out of the early Socialist party and all worked for woman's suffrage. Though their backgrounds were very different from one another, they were all intellectual women. Both their socialist and feminist consciousness were expressed in the realm of ideas—though all three were also active in the labor movement. Sarah Rozner and Rose Kaplan Himmelfarb were industrial workers whose socialism was rooted in their work experiences and whose feminism was expressed in their workplace activities.

To understand the course of socialist feminism it is necessary to distinguish between two different sets of attitudes toward women and their oppression. One set of attitudes, which came to be identified with the designation of the "woman question," reflects a focus on women's issues as part of a strategy for recruitment to revolutionary ideology and a revolutionary party. Women's issues became important as a means of attracting a large portion of the working class, a portion typically described as the most conservative. Party building was the major goal; the "woman question" existed primarily within that context. This is not to deny that there was a genuine recognition of and concern with women's oppression. The prevailing belief, however, was that women would be liberated under socialism and that, therefore, women's issues could be subsumed under these goals.

Socialist feminism, in contrast, espoused the belief that the fight had to be on two fronts simultaneously, for socialism and for women. Fighting for women's causes was a basic part of their revolutionary strategy *and* philosophy. This is not to imply that there was a uniform set of beliefs subscribed to by this second group of socialist feminists. Though they might have differed, for instance, in their specific attitudes on the family, woman's nature, and sexual freedom, they did believe that these were important political and social issues which had to be addressed. Though feminism and socialism were viewed as inseparable, the two were never fully integrated into a single, coherent ideology. This would have important implications for the historical development of socialist feminism, for the feminist principles were often lost or ignored during periods of political conservatism, when maintaining a socialist presence became the paramount task.

The differences between these two sets of attitudes about women are not always clear. Those whose primary concern was the winning of women to socialism also discussed issues like birth control, domestic relations, and child care. They even developed programs or supported legislation on these issues. Careful analysis of these discussions, however, reveals a different tone or emphasis than that found among socialist feminists. For instance, on birth control, it meant the difference between viewing birth control as an issue of woman's autonomy compared to birth control as "only one step in the big fight for the emancipation of the workers."[3]

Furthermore, the distinction between the two sets of attitudes is also obscured by the fact that, regardless of the intent of the writer or of the ideology reflected, the mere discussion of issues relating to the realities of women's everyday life often struck a responsive chord — and revealed what can be considered a basic feminist impulse. Even though birth control, for example, might be referred to as only a step in the fight for the emancipation of the workers, women readers would flood the magazines and papers with letters about their own desperate situations.

The Pre-World War I Socialist Feminist Legacy:

The scope of thought and activity of the earlier socialist feminist movement, which continued with vitality until almost 1915 and, indeed, of the Socialist party itself before World War I, is of major significance. First, as pointed out by historians of American socialism, to be a radical, let alone a socialist, in this period usually meant some sort of identification with the Socialist party.[4] The socialist ideology espoused varied: it might have been clearly defined as Marxist socialism, might have been a brand of Utopian socialism, or might even have been a vaguely defined anarchism. Despite the diversity of ideologies and the variety of class and ethnic backgrounds of Socialist party members, there was a spirit of unity. Members engaged in a range of activities including electoral politics and union organizing.

Since organizing the working class through the labor movement was not the *exclusive* or even major strategy during this period, a range of issues were considered as relevant and important to socialists. Issues relating to women which extended beyond the workplace were, therefore, legitimate. In some instances the party even developed platforms on these subjects, for example, mothers pensions.

The socialist feminists themselves displayed tremendous breadth in the women's issues that they addressed. These included the institution of marriage, sexual relations, woman's control over her body, woman's suffrage, and the work of women in the home.[5] However, they left no unified body of socialist feminist thought on which the women of the next decade could build.

Workplace Organizing:
Women and Socialist Politics, 1919-1929

Coming out of a period of heightened feminist consciousness, during which an active campaign for woman's suffrage was conducted by the Socialist party, the atmosphere immediately after World War I was still largely supportive of feminist strivings. Even the Communist party, as critical as it was of suffrage and bourgeois women, revealed its understanding of the depth of women's potential rage in an April 1919 *Daily Worker* editorial entitled "What is to Become of Women under Socialism?"[6] The editors speculated about the potential reprisals and revenge by women during the establishment of a socialist state—a danger that the editors accepted as an understandable reaction to ages of persecution. So in 1919, feminist was not yet a dirty word among socialists, though they might not use the term to describe their own thinking.

Before attempting to trace the course of socialist feminism during this period, it is necessary to understand the political context in which it was played out. Whereas during the 1910s workplace issues and union organizing were an important focus of activity for many socialists, including women, there were a multitude of other issues addressed and other activities in which they engaged. During the 1920s, however, workplace issues and union activity gained ascendancy. This change was probably a result of both external political repression and the growing importance of the Communist party during this period. First, the more covert political repression during the war dramatically culminated in the Palmer raids on suspected radicals throughout the country in 1919 and early 1920. These signalled the beginning of an all-out attack against radical activities, including union organizing. Whereas the 1910s had been a period of aggressive union expansion, by the mid-1920s the unions were barely holding their own. Furthermore, there was no longer a unified socialist movement. The Socialist party was all but moribund, having lost a large part of its membership in the 1919 split that led to the formation of the Communist Labor party (and, later, the Communist party). Both new parties joined the Third (Communist) International. The older Socialist party after bitter debate finally tried to join too, but was rejected. Even if it was no longer clear where to place political allegiances, most socialists realized that a labor movement now on the defensive needed their support.

For those who had joined the Communist party, the direction was even clearer. The Communist party, after functioning for two years as a secret organization, reemerged as the Workers party. Though eclectic, its focus was largely on the factories and in the unions. Initially the policy of the party was to work within the existing unions ("bore from within") and to build militant minorities within American Federation of Labor (AFL) unions. The Trade Union Educational League was to develop strategy and provide coordination for union activities. After the so-called turn to the left of the party in 1928, the policy was reversed and "dual unions" were formed. The Trade Union Educational League became the Trade Union Unity League and within the needle trades, where the majority of the workers were women, the Needle Trade Workers Industrial Union was founded.[7] Given this almost single-minded focus, any evidence of socialist feminism during this period would most likely be found within the context of the labor movement.

The Feminist Impulse: Case Studies of Two Union Women, 1919-1920

Among the women workers active in the labor movement a core were socialists: some remained in the Socialist party, others joined the Communist party. The experiences of two of these women, Sarah Rozner and Rose Kaplan Himmelfarb, can be used to illustrate the ways in which a feminist impulse was revealed or was tapped by the activities directed to women within their unions.[8]

Both Sarah Rozner and Rose Kaplan were East European Jewish women, typical in many ways of the idealistic and militant women who went to work in the needle trades in the 1910s. Both began their work in the garment industry and became involved in their respective unions in the 1910s, though it was not until 1919 that they each emerged as vocal activists and demonstrated a concern for women. It is hard to pinpoint precisely when they each first espoused socialism. Neither of them joined any party until the 1920s (Rozner didn't actually join the Socialist party until 1927; Kaplan joined the Communist party in 1921); but their awakening to a socialist consciousness probably dated back to about 1915-1916.

Sarah Rozner's feminist consciousness was first nudged when all seven women who ran as delegates to the 1920 Amalgamated Clothing Workers of America (ACWA) convention were defeated:

There were seven women from different locals running as delegates to the Convention, but every one of them was defeated. Every one! So it began to dawn on me what it was all about as far as the women workers were concerned. Up to that time I was mainly class conscious, but when I saw that they were so ruthless, so indifferent, to the biggest part of the organization, the women, I thought, how can we stand by and ignore it? I started hollering bloody murder: "What the hell is this? We are the majority! This will never do. If I can help it, there will never be another convention without women's delegates represented."[9]

With the help of one of the women organizers in the Chicago union office, Nettie Richardson — whom Rozner referred to as a *real* feminist — Rozner and several other women called a meeting:

We made a collection, we had leaflets printed. WOMEN COME TO A MEETING. LET'S PROTEST AGAINST THESE INJUSTICES. And I pointed out that every woman was defeated . . . about two hundred women came. So that's whan the local was born, in 1920. . . . See, every local has the prerogative of having their own convention delegates and of nominating a business agent, so if there was a woman's local, then there would *have* to be women's delegates, there would *have* to be a woman business agent.

Separate women's locals were eventually formed in five different cities. In 1920, the male leadership was responsive to this move by women to gain power in their unions, perhaps because they realized the recruitment potential of the women's locals. Feminist women saw these locals as a preliminary step toward power within the union. Sarah Rozner and women from the Chicago local, in concert with women in other cities, campaigned actively in the union for a national Women's Bureau of the ACWA. The general executive board had approved this bureau in 1924 and the union paper, *Advance*, set aside one page to be devoted exclusively to women. Although the union leaders may have considered the bureau primarily a means of more effectively organizing the women, it is clear from the later fights within the union about the bureau that the women's locals considered it a force for feminism. After a rather short-lived spurt of activity, the Women's Bureau of the ACWA slipped into obscurity, but in 1926 Mamie Santora, the only woman on the general executive board of the union, asked that the bureau be revitalized. Santora, Rozner, and the women of Local 275 committed themselves to not letting it fail a second time.

Following this 1926 convention, women from around the country joined a campaign in the pages of the *Advance* for the reestablishment of the bureau.[10] But the tide had already turned. When a formal resolution from the Chicago local was introduced by Rozner at the 1928 convention, even Mamie Santora, who two years earlier had committed herself to reestablishing the bureau, spoke against it. Sidney Hilman also spoke out against its formation, attacking a separate organization for women as tending to "separate our organization into two national offices, one for the women and one for the men."[11] He advocated forgetting about all group divisions. The time for recognition of separatism in the union, a separatism reflecting clear feminist intent, was over.

What had happened to defeat the women's drive for a separate bureau? The women may have been caught in a battle that had little to do with their goal of forming a special women's department in the union. Up to 1924, the ACWA had enjoyed a period of relative calm, but by 1926 several New York locals were plagued by internal dissension between the so-called left and right. In 1928 the Communist party formed a dual union called the Needle Trade Workers Industrial Union. It seems reasonable to speculate that the anti-separatist speech made by Hilman was directed not only to the women, but also to the left factions within the union.

The defeat of the bureau resolution seemed to break the spirit of organized feminist ACWA women. Though the woman's local in Chicago continued and, in fact, won a major battle in the 1930s over differential insurance benefits, and though Rozner remained active in the local until she moved away from Chicago in 1938, there was never another period in which Rozner became part of an *organized* feminist effort. She remained a socialist and still believes that through the evolutionary process a new day of democratic socialism will arrive. She remained a feminist—but rejected the label, never integrating her socialism and feminist consciousness. After this period of heightened feminist activity in the union, her feminism found expression only in an individual response to the mistreatment of women culminating, at the time of her retirement from the union in 1959, in the establishment of a scholarship for the training and education of women in her union.

Sarah Rozner's reluctance to be identified as a feminist had its roots in the battle over the Equal Rights Amendment (ERA). Rozner was at the 1926 Women in Industry Conference where a pitched battle occurred between the militant feminists of the National Woman's Party (NWP) and the women from the labor movement and the Women's Bureau of the U.S. Department of Labor. After this battle, socialist women, like most women loyal to the labor movement, identified feminism with the position of the NWP. Feminism came to be viewed as a middle-class ideology inimical to their commitment to destroy capitalism.

A period of heightened feminist consciousness and activity can thus be documented among the socialist women in the ACWA during the early 1920s, namely women organized primarily because of concern about issues directly affecting themselves. There is no evidence of such organized feminism within the International Ladies' Garment Workers' Union (ILGWU). *Justice*, the official organ of the ILGWU, devoted little attention to the special needs or interests of the women members; the *Proceedings* of the ILGWU conventions reveal even less. The only evidence of organized activity on behalf of the women seems to be the agitation which the left-wing faction in the union organized around the unequal status of the "Ladies Branches" of the locals.

Separate women's groups, or Ladies Branches, were formed in certain locals because, as Rose Kaplan Himmelfarb described their history, "the men wouldn't behave nicely or [they would] talk in a way that was insulting to the women." In this case separate groups were not a means to power as the ACWA women intended. The separate ILGWU groups relegated the women, who comprised over half the membership, to powerless sub-units. Although they did have representatives to the executive board of their local, the "Ladies Branches" did not have their own officers.

Rose Kaplan had joined the union when she arrived in the United States in 1911. It was not until 1919-1920, though, that she became involved politically, when she was "thrown into the left-wing group in the union." Significantly, she was at least partially motivated to join them by an appeal to a feminist consciousness:

"Of course I was impressed, I could see that they were taking the part of the women's interest, defending.

And then we started demanding the abolishment of the women branches, the ladies branches [laughter], they used to call it . . . from the branches themselves, it started putting on pressure that they should be abolished because our interests were not different from the men and they want to be together so we can discuss matters in the shop, the prices and all that. It was a struggle. We didn't get it very easy, but then the men realized that the women are just as capable and a few women came into the leadership, into the executives. They knew they don't have to have the branches."[12]

The Ladies Branches were discriminatory and not an effective means for ILGWU women to gain control of their union. The left-wing faction viewed the women's situation as part of the larger issue of union democracy. Once the branches were successfully abolished, the left faction displayed no further concern for the special interests of women.[13]

As should be clear from these two cases, there were socialist women within the labor movement who had a woman's consciousness which we can describe as feminist. Women like Sarah Rozner, who were loosely defined socialists not tied to a party, considered work on women's issues an important goal unto itself. Women like Rose Kaplan, who became involved in the Communist party, saw their work on women's issues only as part of their larger work in the party — though they themselves might have been individually motivated by a feminist consciousness.

For both Kaplan and Rozner, the labor movement was the major focus of their activity; their socialist consciousness and whatever feminist consciousness they had were expressed through their activities in their unions. Women's issues outside workplace problems were seldom discussed, especially among activists like Rozner and Kaplan who were unmarried and childless. If women's concerns were discussed, it was in private conversations, among friends. Rozner and Kaplan moved directly from their experiences in the workplace, through their unions, to socialism. They were not intellectuals who abstractly espoused socialism, but rather workers whose beliefs were rooted in their experience. Their feminism, to whatever extent it developed, would remain rooted in these experiences.

The Feminist Impulse: Case Studies of Two Intellectual Women, 1919-1929

Women whose feminism was not rooted exclusively in their experiences as workers, women who inherited the pre-World War I socialist feminist legacy, also devoted most of their political energies to the labor movement during the period 1919-1929. Ernestine Hara Kettler and Miriam Allen deFord both became involved in the Socialist party prior to the war.[14] Although neither was directly a part of the socialist-feminist movement or even recalled its publication, the *Progressive Woman* (earlier called the *Socialist Woman*), their attitudes toward women and their ideas about the nature of women's oppression reflected this earlier ideology. Both women explicitly identified themselves as feminist and socialist and maintained the inseparable relationship of the two ideologies.

Ernestine Hara Kettler, who came from a working-class immigrant background, began to identify with the intellectual/bohemian/radical circle as early as 1913, when she was a teenager hanging out at Socialist party headquarters on the Lower East Side of New York. For the next several years her total social environment was an intellectual one in which socialism, feminism, and anarchism merged and were part and parcel of daily life. Her feminism ran deep; female disfranchisement became an issue for her because it represented an insult to women. In 1917, following a Socialist party convention, she met a socialist woman from Montana who recruited her to join NWP members in picketing the White House. She went to Washington fully cognizant of the possibility of imprisonment; it was both an adventure and a political act. She was arrested and imprisoned and served thirty days in the Occoquan Workhouse. In fact, her group of prisoners instituted a work strike at Occoquan. Through she remained a feminist and a socialist, this was the last political act focused on women in which Ernestine Kettler participated until she joined the National Organization for Women (NOW) in 1968, when she was almost seventy years old.

After this suffrage activity, Kettler became increasingly involved with the Industrial Workers of the World (IWW). She worked as a secretary-stenographer for the Wobblies (as IWW members are known), in Butte, Montana, for a period of time and then moved to Seattle, where she became secretary of the local Young Peoples Socialist League and worked closely with the IWW. Her associates were, as she describes them, "dilettantes, as far as activity was concerned."

They were an interesting group and [it was] educational for me. . . . There were many women in this group of mine, and I'm sure that feminism was one of the issues we discussed. The men, though, found it either not practical to denigrate us or were in agreement. I cannot recall arguments, but then there were no very profound discussions. It was just taken for granted. Also, the issue then was suffrage, not full emancipation. I considered full emancipation as part of my entire philosophical struggle.[15]

In 1919 she married an IWW organizer. Because of her husband's IWW connections, Ernestine and he faced continuous police harassment following the 1919 government raids and prosecutions. Ultimately, she and her husband were forced to go into hiding for one year in the back-country of Washington.

During the 1920s, and continuing into the 1930s, Kettler's activities were almost exclusively tied to the labor movement. After her year in hiding with her husband, they separated, and in 1923 she went to work for the IWW in Chicago. Later, in New York she worked in various union offices and eventually became active in the Office and Professional Employees Union (OPEIU). In 1938 her loose political ties to first the Socialist party and later the IWW became more focused when she joined the Socialist Workers Party (SWP).

Within the SWP the issues were really political and on an extremely high level. . . . As for feminism, that wasn't really an issue. After all, Socialists were supposed to have a notion of equality between all people and naturally that equality would extend to women as well. . . . They claimed that so long as you live in a capitalist country you're not going to get that equality. Except that we couldn't turn the society overnight into a socialist one, so therefore you have to fight for individual, or piecemeal. Whenever I did have an argument it was short and not bitter. It was usually about whether or not women had the intellectual ability to absorb knowledge to the same degree as men.[16]

So Kettler chose to work in a political arena and with a group where feminism was not an issue. Basically, through the 1920s and 1930s, her feminism was expressed in individual defense of women and anger at their treatment by her male comrades in the union and the party. She remained childless, worked outside the home, and devoted her political energies to the labor movement. The only feminist issue that she continued openly to espouse was birth control. As late as 1974 Kettler firmly believed: "For as long as society exists, women are going to fight for their rights." Yet, like other radical women in the period between the two wars, there was no movement that could capture her imagination or that offered an ideology compatible with both socialism and feminism.

Miriam Allen de Ford came from a different background than Kettler. She was the daughter of a woman gynecologist. Too busy with her medical practice and with family responsibilities to work for suffrage herself, her mother sent Miriam, then fourteen, down to suffrage headquarters in 1902. A feminist since the age of six, when she witnessed the physical abuse of the family's household helper by the woman's new husband, deFord began campaigning atop soapboxes for woman's suffrage in Boston in 1912. She gradually became aligned with the radical groups in Boston and, like Kettler, married a man from these circles. He was a man like herself, an intellectual — and an anarchist. In 1915 they moved to San Diego, where she set up practice as a public stenographer. She supported the IWW, and was peripherally involved with the socialist and anarchist movements.

After separation from her husband, in the early 1920s she began to cohabit with Maynard Shipley, a longtime Socialist party organizer and former campaign manager for Eugene V. Debs. Both she and Shipley eventually left the Socialist party in 1922 "because [it was] going too far to the right." Neither of them were ever comfortable with the Communist party either, though she espoused "complete revolution, not reform" and considered herself a "good Marxist."

DeFord, more than any of the other socialist women interviewed, was quite explicit about the effect on feminism of the political repression during and following World War I. Not only was suffrage no longer an issue, but the political climate necessitated a concentration on sheer political survival. There was no room for organized feminism and there was no movement representing feminist interests *and* socialist interests. As deFord pointed out, until the women's liberation movement there was no movement for feminist women.

There were plenty of feminists and you knew who they were and they wrote individually, or spoke individually, but there was no organized movement outside of birth control. There was nothing for them, they had no organ, no avenue, to speak through. All they could do would be on their own and it was only writers you'd know about, because they could write. . . . I didn't change any of my own feelings but there wasn't anything, no movement, nothing to join. The only thing was that if, individually, anybody had anything to say, I told them what I thought. I wrote dozens of letters that were published in newspapers. Whenever anybody would make an anti-feminist remark, I'd call them on it. I had an article or two or three, mostly in Midwest farm women's magazines bearing more or less on the subject. . . . Some of my science fiction is oriented towards feminism.[17]

The only organizational voice deFord could find for a woman's issue was in the birth control movement, for which she regularly spoke. But, as Linda Gordon has shown, by the mid 1920s, the birth control movement had become far removed from its feminist, let alone its socialist and anarchist, roots.[18]

For both Kettler and deFord, feminism became an individual impulse; an individual philosophy and framework which could lead to criticism of male comrades but which no longer held the potential for promoting change. During a period of political repression like that ushered in after the war when energies were focused on defending radical organizations and unions, it was difficult for them to retain a feminism that could be translated into anything other than an individual response — particularly since their feminism and socialism had never really been integrated into a unified ideology.

Women in the Home and Community:
Socialist Feminism, 1929-1943

The heavy emphasis on workplace organizing, the absence of feminist organizations that were not anathema to women with a socialist consciousness, and the politically repressive climate of the 1920s all contributed to the continued quiescence of a socialist feminist movement.

Though work in the labor movement remained a major activity of the Communist party in the 1930s, particularly later in the decade during the organizing of the Congress of Industrial Organizations (CIO), the party paid increasing attention to women outside the paid labor force. In 1929 the Communist party formed the United Council of Working Women with the purpose of "uniting the men and women workers and the workers' wives . . . in the struggle for better conditions in the factory, shop and homes."[19] Shortly after this organization was founded, with its network of neighborhood councils, the party began to publish a tabloid called *Working Woman*, which was described on the masthead as the "Voice of Women Workers." Workers' wives and homes seldom appeared in its pages, however. The focus was still on workplace issues, including the problem of unemployment.

As unemployment spread, community work became more important within the Communist party and women were increasingly involved. Stories began to appear in the pages of the *Working Woman* about bread strikes and tenant action groups organized by women.[20] The party placed increasing emphasis on organizing working-class women into the United Council of Working Class Women, now described as an organization of working women and housewives united to fight in support of their men.[21]

Although *Working Woman* expanded coverage of non-workplace issues, it was not until March 1933 that an actual change in direction was made. *Working Woman* then became a magazine, complete with cover pictures, in an effort to "reach the broader masses of working women." Most significantly, the appeal was no longer primarily to wage-earning women. *Working Woman* now described itself as a "magazine for working women, farm women and working class housewives." More material relating to non-wage-earning issues was published, including articles on childbirth and birth control. The circulation climbed to almost 8,000. In a 1935 editorial, Margaret Cowl even advocated women getting together to discuss a program which called for free day nurseries, free birth control clinics, free hospitalization for pregnant mothers, free school lunches, and payment of benefits before and after childbirth.[22] This program, which she referred to as a "Mothers Bill of Rights" legitimized these women's issues as an important organizing principle. Women no longer had to wait for the socialist revolution for the "woman question" to be addressed.

However, the tone of the editorial revealed an attitude very similar to the previous concern expressed for women's issues. It was still mainly a means of organizing women. There was no real discussion of women's oppression or of the way in which these demands would help to change the lives of the women themselves. The focus was almost exclusively on the well-being of the babies and on the well-being of the family unit. Even in the blueprint for action designed to lead to legislation that would abolish anti-birth control laws, there was no appreciation of how these programs might help women to gain control over their own lives. The kind of personal female identification revealed in the work of the pre-World War I socialist-feminists was simply absent.

Despite the fact that these 1930 writings do not reveal a clear-cut socialist feminist consciousness, it is possible that the attention paid to these women's issues helped to legitimize feminist concerns. In other words, a climate might have been created that helped to foster a feminist consciousness and thereby contributed to the development of a socialist feminist ideology. Although it is difficult to assess this influence, it was in this period and context that Mary Inman developed her important socialist feminist theories.

"Premature Feminism": A Case Study of a Socialist-Feminist in the 1930s

Beginning in 1934, Mary Inman embarked on what was to become a forty-year project to develop a Marxist analysis and strategy for women.[23] Her work revealed a new socialist feminist consciousness even though she placed it squarely within the Marxist-Leninist tradition and rejected the socialist feminist label. (Her rejection of the label, like Rozner's, was a result of their identifying "feminism" with middle-class groups, like the NWP, who were fighting for the ERA in the 1920s and 1930s.)

Inman, like deFord and Kettler, had joined the Socialist party in the 1910s and, like them, she had not been directly affiliated with nor did she recall the socialist feminist movement. She did campaign for woman's suffrage in Oklahoma under the Socialist party platform, but denied any further involvement with women's issues. Yet, there are indications of what might be described as a feminist impulse. For instance, after her marriage in 1917 to an IWW organizer, she retained her name and, for political reasons, her husband adopted her name. Though ascribing this act to expediency—her work references were under her maiden name—she admitted that she and her husband would joke about being "Lucy Stoners." During the late 1910s and into the 1920s, Inman's work, like that of deFord and Kettler, was with the labor movement.

A dedicated Marxist, Inman was inspired by Clara Zetkin's 1920 conversations with V. I. Lenin, *Lenin on the Woman Question*, newly published in the United States. Particularly struck by Lenin's dictum to organize "not thousands, but millions," Inman began *her* work on the "woman question." She felt the compulsion to develop a theory and strategy that would address the reality of the lives of most women under capitalism who did not engage in wage-earning labor outside the home. She rented an office in the Bradbury Building in downtown Los Angeles and went there daily to work. One year later, in 1936, she had completed a five-hundred-page manuscript, *In Woman's Defense*.[24]

In this work Inman documented women's oppression. Believing in the class basis of women's subjection, she nevertheless was quite clear about the social and psychological ramifications as well:

The misnamed "war between the sexes" has many of the characteristics of race conflict between black and white. But the "war between the sexes" has invaded the home and for this reason there exists not only conflict between unrelated men and women, but the added complexities arising from intimate group relationships. The preparation of men and women for the respective roles they are to play in adult life, in this sham "war between the sexes," begins in early childhood. Thus there is laid a foundation in human behavior that is made the basis for a claim of "natural" antagonism between the sexes and of their complete and total unlikeness.[25]

The scope and breadth of Inman's analysis were revealed in the range of topics that she explored: the nature and effect of childhood socialization; the process of "manufacturing femininity"; the sex slave status of women; the culture of subjugation (the portrayal of women in the media); and the double standard, which she referred to as "fascism in the bedroom."[26] Examining marriage (which she thought promised women "*individual* escape from *organized* oppression") as a means of making a living, Inman was led, ultimately, to an examination of the role of the housewife in social production in much the same way the earlier socialist feminist movement examined the role of housework in relation to industrial work.

Over the years, beginning with the basis she laid in this initial writing, Inman developed an argument for two forms of production under capitalism: the production of life and the production of life's material requirements.[27] In the first form of production, Inman argued,

life is produced not merely by a biological process, but also by a social labor process and involves, among other things, the raising of children and the necessary tasks requisite to the day-to-day production of the energy of adults. . . . The production worker engaged in such tasks is usually the wife and mother of the household. In the second instance, production of life's material requirements takes place in the factories, fields, forests, mines and elsewhere, in general outside the home. . . . There is, generally speaking, a social division of labor along sex lines and the workers in this form of production are predominantly men.[28]

Proceeding from this premise, she argued that the wage of the production worker outside the home was a family wage.[29]

Perhaps most significant about *In Woman's Defense* was the clear stand taken by Inman on women's special oppression. In addition to class interests in common with men, she maintained that women "have general problems as women, such as the necessity to struggle against the ideology of female bondage; and against the subservient doctrines preached to them through most of the women's magazines and the general press".[30] As a result of her class and sex analysis on the nature of women's oppression, Inman concluded: "One thing that will aid in woman's struggles, is the growing unity between working and middle class women."³¹ *In Woman's Defense* laid the groundwork for a continuing analysis and for the development of a new socialist feminist ideology and movement. Instead, what followed after the completion of the book in 1936 was an escalating war with the Communist party — a war that Inman was still waging in the 1970s.

Although the party refused to publish her manuscript, Harrison George, editor of the *People's World*, began its publication in 1939 in installment form.³² Men and women alike praised it. Even Elizabeth Gurley Flynn, who was to later be "clarified" by the party on the woman question, praised it in the pages of the *Daily Worker* in New York.³³ Two years later, in 1941, the party launched an all-out attack, first, with the publication of articles by Ruth McKenney in the *New Masses* and, in 1943, by the publication of A. Landy's *Marxism and the Woman Question.*³⁴

As was obvious from the McKenney articles, part of the reaction to Inman's work was because of her clear feminist call for unity between middle-class and working-class women. Yet, at that very time, during the United Front period, the Communist party was encouraging work in bourgeois women's organizations; in fact, a great deal of energy was being devoted to building women's peace groups, groups which drew heavily from the ranks of middle-class women.

Inman considered the reaction to her as part of Browderism and what she called a turn to the right in the Communist party. In a forty-page indictment of "Thirteen Years of CPUSA Misleadership on the Woman Question," Inman cited the publication of the Landy book as one more example of what she referred to as Earl Browder's attempt to "liquidate" Communist work in general and the special forms of struggle and organization for women in particular.³⁵ She viewed her own work as correct, as an attempt to apply Marxist-Leninist theory to the problem of organizing women; she was attempting to follow Lenin's direction to "organize not thousands, but millions of women."

The fight within the Communist party over Inman's work raises complicated questions which can be answered only with more careful study of the Communist party. Inman's work represented a new expression of socialist feminism which was effectively smothered. For our purposes, what is crucial to understand is the extent and degree to which Inman's socialist feminist analysis, which *was* published in a popular party newspaper, reached and affected the women in Communist party circles.

According to Inman, immediately following the separate publication of *In Woman's Defense* and all during its publication in installments in the *People's World* in 1939-1940, women readers wrote scores of letters to her — letters on every conceivable issue relating to women's oppression. In one of his regular columns in the *People's World*, Mike Quinn even wrote humorously of the effect the articles were having in his own household. Following publication, Inman was teaching a class on women's status and condition at the Workers School in Los Angeles. On several occasions, the trade union class joined her class. A member of the trade union class, a teamster, reported to the group that his wife, after reading Inman, began to picket him outside their home. This incident revealed the degree to which Inman's work was affecting women. How she handled the discussion in this class reveals some of the contradictions in her own work — contradictions that have contributed largely to the problems of effectively integrating socialism and feminism. According to her, she helped the class to understand that the woman was mistaken; that her enemy was not the individual man in the home who was oppressing her, but rather that man's employer!

It appears that Inman tapped a source of socialist feminism that even she had difficulty in controlling. There were apparently other women in the party who were also socialist feminists, women who Dorothy Healey (a former Communist party functionary who now identifies herself as a socialist feminist) called "premature feminists." They were women who, like Inman, objected to all forms of women's oppression. But objections to sparsely clad entertainers and to cheesecake pictures in the *People's World* were considered irrelevant in those days, and so these isolated and unorganized manifestations of feminist attitudes among these socialist women never became a coherent program. Only in Mary Inman's work was a program developed that placed these "personal" reactions into a broader political context.

Conclusion

The course of socialist feminism in the United States has been an uneven one — a course marked by detours, blockades, and standstills. Before World War I there was a viable, organized socialist feminist movement; a group of women with a clear commitment to both a socialist and a feminist revolution. Despite this dual commitment, these early socialist feminists never developed an integrated socialist feminist theory. Without this legacy, socialist women with a feminist consciousness would have few outlets for the expression of this consciousness in the post World War I era — particularly in the context of a repressive political climate marked by a fractured socialist movement and an almost exclusive emphasis on workplace organizing.

Tracing the life experiences of socialist women in this period through the medium of the oral history interview, we do find a feminism that survives, though it is primarily an impulse which might find occasional individual expression. When supported, this feminism was translated into fighting for women's rights within the labor movement, as is demonstrated by Sarah Rozner and Rose Kaplan Himmelfarb. Without support and with no organizational base, women like Miriam Allen deFord and Ernestine Hara Kettler expressed their feminist impulses in individual writing, arguments with male comrades, and speaking on the one issue that still had resonance for feminists, birth control.

To nurture these feminist impulses and to sustain them, however, an organized socialist feminist analysis and program was essential. Mary Inman laid the groundwork for such a program beginning in 1936, but her work was ignored and systematically attacked. Many of Inman's ideas, especially on housework and child care, were the same as those espoused by Marxist feminists in the 1970s. Yet socialist feminists of the 1970s did not explicitly draw on her work. The lesson of the period from 1920 to 1945 seems to be that a fully integrated, unified, and coherent socialist feminist analysis is necessary. Otherwise, socialist or feminist goals can easily be lost in times of crises.

Notes

1. For a description of this movement, see Mari Jo Buhle, "Women and the Socialist Party, 1901-1914," *Radical America*, 4 (1970), pp. 36-58, and Bruce Dancis, "Socialism and Women in the United States, 1900-1917," *Socialist Revolution*, 27 (1976), pp. 81-144.

2. Robert Shaffer in "Women and the Communist Party, U.S.A., 1930-1940, *Socialist Review*, 9 (1979), pp. 73-118, discusses the Communist party's (CP) view of women's oppression in the period 1930-1940. Shaffer does not, however, present a convincing argument about the breadth of this analysis. The party's emphasis was usually on workplace issues and the need to organize women. When they dealt with nonworkplace issues, the purpose was primarily to recruit women into the party activity. The only exception to this was Mary Inman who, as will be discussed below, was totally repudiated by the party. Shaffer's use of Inman as an example of the CP's theoretical approach to the oppression of women completely distorts the handling of the woman question in the 1930s by the CP.

3. *Working Woman*, 5 (February 28, 1934), p. 15.

4. James Weinstein, *The Decline of Socialism in America, 1912-1925* (New York: Monthly Review Press, 1967); *Ambiguous Legacy: The Left in American Politics* (New York: New Viewpoints, 1975).

5. Dancis, "Socialism and Women." Also, in an excellent paper by Lynn Fonfa, which relies heavily on two socialist newspapers in Los Angeles, the range of these issues is revealed. (Graduate paper, U.C.L.A., 1976).

6. *Ohio Socialist* (later named the *Daily Worker*), April 30, 1919.

7. An excellent account of these changes in policy can be found in David Schneider, *The Workers' (Communist) Party and the American Trade Unions* (Baltimore: John Hopkins Press, 1928).

8. The material on Rozner and Kaplan is based on oral history interviews conducted by Sherna Gluck for the Feminist History Research Project. A series of nineteen interviews were conducted with Rozner between March 1973 and July 1974. One interview was conducted with Kaplan in March 1975. These are all on deposit with the Feminist History Research Project, Topanga, California.

9. The quote is edited from an interview with Sarah Rozner, Tape III, Side B, May 1, 1973.

10. *Advance*, September 3, October 8, October 29, and November 19, 1926; February 4 and April 8, 1927.

11. "Proceedings of the Cincinnati Convention," *Documentary History of the A.C.W.A.*, 1928, pp. 236-237.

12. Rose Kaplan Himmelfarb, Tape I, Side A (end), Side B (beginning), March 13, 1975.

13. Although no direct evidence has been found in either Communist party literature or in interviews of a new campaign to create women's branches, there is a letter in the union newspaper (*Justice*, January 21, 1927) that alludes to an effort by the Communists to create strife by promoting special sections for the women.

14. The material on deFord and Kettler is based on oral history interviews conducted by Sherna Gluck for the Feminist History Research Project. Three separate interviews were conducted with deFord between March 6 and August 23, 1973, and five interviews with Kettler between January 17 and March 23, 1973. Portions of these interviews are contained in transcript form in *From Tea Parties to Prison*, Regional Oral History Office, The Bancroft Library, University of California, Berkeley, 1975. The edited interviews can be found in *From Parlor to Prison* (New York: Vintage, 1976). Excerpts are used with the permission of Random House, Alfred A. Knopf, Inc.

15. Ernestine Hara Kettler, Tape III, Side B, February 7, 1973. Appears in edited form in *From Parlor to Prison*, p. 253.

16. Ernestine Hara Kettler, Tape IV, Side A, February 14, 1973. Appears in edited form in *From Parlor to Prison*, pp. 261-262.

17. Miriam Allen de Ford, Tape III, Sides A, B, August 23, 1973. Appears in edited form in *From Parlor to Prison*, pp. 176-177.

18. Linda Gordon, "The Politics of Population: Birth Control and the Eugenics Movement," *Radical America* 8 (1974), pp. 61-97.

19. "Declaration of Aims and Principles, Constitution and By-Laws of the United Council of Working Women, Adopted at the Conference June 22, 1929" (Tamiment Collection, New York University Library).

20. Beginning in *Working Woman*, 2, April 1931, these accounts began to appear fairly regularly.

21. *Working Woman*, 2 (April 1931), p. 3.

22. *Working Woman*, 6 (April 1935), p. 1.

23. A series of unrecorded "conversations" have been conducted with Mary Inman, beginning in March 1978. Because Inman will not agree to systematic oral history interviews, there are rather large gaps in the information on her and her activities, especially during the period from 1917 to 1934.

24. Mary Inman, *In Woman's Defense* (Los Angeles: Mercury Printing, 1940).

25. *Ibid.*, pp. 46-47.

26. *Ibid.*, p. 94.

27. Inman's argument was developed over the years, beginning in 1942 with *Woman Power* (Los Angeles: Committee to Organize The Advancement of Women, 1942) and refined further in 1964 in *Two Forms of Production Under Capitalism* (Los Angeles: Mary Inman, 1964).

28. Inman, *Two Forms of Production under Capitalism*, pp. 9-10.

29. Later, in 1946, Inman designed a program for women which included an organization of housewives, the Union of Labor Power Production Workers; a minimum of four-hour daily free child care for the children of *all* women; a municipal diaper service; a rationalized system of housework; and an equal rights amendment. See *Facts for Women*, 4 (April-May 1946), pp. 1-4.

30. Inman, *In Woman's Defense*, p. 170.

31. *Ibid.*, p. 171.

32. *People's World*, October 19, 1939, to March 20, 1940.

33. *Sunday Worker*, February 9, 1941, p. 6.

34. Ruth McKenney, "Women are Human Beings," *New Masses*, Part I (December 10, 1940), Part II (December 17, 1940), pp. 9-10; Exchange between Harrison George and Ruth McKenney, *New Masses* (February 11, 1941), pp. 10-11; A. Landy, *Marxism and the Woman Question* (New York: Workers Library, 1943).

35. Mary Inman, "Thirteen Years of CPUSA Misleadership on the Woman Question," mimeographed pamphlet, (Los Angeles: Mary Inman, 1949).

For Further Reading

Many recent articles and monographs that focus on women in the 1920s and 1930s are cited in the notes to the introduction and chapters. In many cases, topical concerns of this period are part of broader chronological surveys. The best remains William Chafe's *The American Woman: Her Changing Social, Economic, and Political Roles, 1920-1970* (New York: Oxford University Press, 1972), parts one and two. *Women in Modern America: A Brief History* by Lois Banner (New York: Harcourt Brace Jovanovich, 1974) begins in 1890 and ranges widely over women's varied activities with attention to class and ethnicity, organizational activities, and popular culture. William L. O'Neill's *Everyone Was Brave: The Rise and Fall of Feminism in America* (Chicago: Quadrangle Books, 1969) concentrates on women's reform activities from the turn of century and stresses the decline of feminism after 1920 because of feminists' ideological shortcomings and their internal conflicts. Like Banner, Peter Filene identifies modern America with post 1890 developments but concentrates on the pre-1920 period. Still Filene's *Him/Her Self: Sex Roles in Modern America* (New York: Harcourt Brace, 1974) describes career and marriage feminism and reality in the twenties and the discrimination experienced by working women during the Depression.

O'Neill distinguishes between social and hard-core feminism in "Feminism As a Radical Ideology" in *Dissent: Explorations in the History of American Radicalism*, edited by Alfred F. Young (DeKalb, Ill.: Northern Illinois University Press, 1968) and expands upon the conflicts between the two groups after the suffrage victory. J. Stanley Lemons concentrates on the social feminists' continuing reform activities through the mid-twenties in *The Woman Citizen: Social Feminism in the 1920s* (Urbana, Ill.: University of Illinois Press, 1972). Like O'Neill, he describes the internecine disputes between reformers and National Woman's Party feminists and finds the latter wanting. Chafe presents a more evenhanded analysis of the conflicts over the Equal Rights Amendment. In *Seedtime of Reform: American Social Service and Social Action, 1918-1933* (Minneapolis, Minn.: University of Minnesota Press, 1963), Clarke A. Chambers describes social reform and settlement house activities (largely women's efforts) that bridge the gap between the Progressive and New Deal eras, explicitly denying the "twenties as dark ages" historical conceptualization and implicitly designating women as the bridge. In a few brief comments, Otis L. Graham, Jr., concurs that women with social consciences were links of continuity in *An Encore for Reform: The Old Progressives and the New Deal* (New York: Oxford University Press, 1967).

In *Another Part of the Twenties* (New York: Columbia University Press, 1977), Paul Carter describes isolated political and athletic achievements of women during the twenties as well as the split in Women's Christian Temperance Union ranks over prohibition that parallels the split among former suffrage allies over female equality. Anne Firor Scott concludes the *Southern Lady: From Pedestal to Politics,* (Chicago: University of Chicago Press, 1970) with political activity in the 1920s. Mary J. Oates's "Organized Volunteerism: The Catholic Sisters in Massachusetts, 1870-1940," and Norma Pratt's "Transitions in Judaism: The Jewish American Woman through the 1930s," in *American Quarterly* 30 (Winter 1978) are two of the few assessments of women in religious contexts and organizations during this period, a serious historiographic gap.

These monographs and references which concentrate on white, middle-class public roles, activities, and ideologies should be supplemented with insightful contemporary surveys and series. Sophonisba P. Breckenridge wrote a scholarly overview, *Women in the Twentieth Century: A Study of their Political, Social and Economic Activities* (New York: McGraw-Hill, 1933) and much of the material was summarized in her chapter, "The Activities of Women Outside the Home," in *Recent Social Trends in the United States: Reports of the President's Research Committee on Social Trends* (New York: McGraw-Hill, 1933). The latter contains a number of articles on related subjects like the family, consumerism, and education. Mary Ross edited a special *Survey* issue (December 1926) on women, work, and the family containing numerous articles by noted contributors.

In 1926 and 1927, *Nation* ran a series of articles reflecting the gamut of feminist sensibilities and personal experience. Elaine Showalter has edited and introduced the anonymous articles in *These Modern Women: Autobiographical Essays from the Twenties* (Old Westbury, N.Y.: Feminist Press, 1978). The May 1929 volume of the *Annals of the AAPSS (American Academy of Political and Social Sciences)* was devoted to *Women in the Modern World* and contained articles on topics ranging from discrimination against professional women, to women in industry, to upgrading homemaking. *Woman's Coming of Age*, edited by Samuel D. Schmalhauser and V. F. Calverton (New York: Horace Livright, 1931), contains some contributions that belie the optimism of the title. In addition to an incisive analysis, "Why Women Fail," by Lorine Pruette, several articles reveal the growing preoccupation with female sexuality and sexual compatibility in marriage.

Presumed changes in sexual behavior and possible connections with feminist aspirations are revealed in another *Nation* series collected by Freda Kirchwey and published in 1924 as *Our Changing Morality: A Symposium* (reissued, New York: Arno Press, 1972). Though primarily a survey of nineteenth-century ideas, Sidney Ditzion describes "radical" ideologies of sex in the 1920s in *Marriage, Morals and Sex in America: A History of Ideas* (New York: Bookman Associates, 1953). Reality, not ideology, is illustrated in the letters received by Margaret Sanger from desperate women which she published in *Motherhood in Bondage* (New York: Brentano's, 1928). Although her essay purposefully avoids autobiographical and biographical references, it is difficult to divorce the birth control movement from the life of Sanger. For a less than sympathetic treatment of the connection between the two, see David M. Kennedy's *Birth Control in America: The Career of Margaret Sanger* (New Haven: Yale University Press, 1970) which uses and critiques, among other sources, Sanger's *Margaret Sanger: An Autobiography* (New York: W. W. Norton, 1938). More recently, chapters 10, 11, and 12 of Linda Gordon's *Woman's Body, Woman's Right: A Social History of Birth Control in America* (New York: Viking Press, 1976) deal specifically with the 1920-1945 period. Discussion of birth control is one of the social policies Sheila M. Rothman relates to altering concepts of womanhood in *Woman's Proper Place: A History of Changing Ideals and Practices, 1870 to the Present* (New York: Basic Book, 1978). Lesbianism during these years, as well as generally, is just beginning to surface. Blanche Wiesen Cook discusses literary works as well as political feminist implications in "'Women Alone Stir My Imagination': Lesbianism and the Cultural Tradition," *Signs* 4 (Summer 1979): 718-39. Arno Press has recently reprinted a series on homosexuality in which many selections by and about lesbians stem from this period. A bibliographic guide, *The Lesbian in Literature* (Reno, Nev.: The Ladder, 1975), is a good resource.

Heterosexuality, marriage, family life, and work patterns were and are still the major focus of historians, and no student of the period can overlook the works of the sociologists Robert and Helen Lynd. *Middletown* and *Middletown in Transition* (New York: Harcourt Brace, 1929, and 1937) are classics on midwestern urban middle-class and working-class life style and attitudes during the 1920s and 1930s. Sociologists also provided the studies of the impact of the Depression on family life and despite a number of methodological shortcomings, they should still be consulted. Robert Angell in *The Family Encounters the Depression* (New York: Charles Scribner's Sons, 1936) samples middle-class families' responses to economic deprivation. Working-class families are examined by Ruth Shoule Cavan and Katherine Howland Ranch in *The Family and the Depression: A Study of One Hundred Chicago Families* (Chicago: University of Chicago Press, 1938); by Mirra Komarovsky in *The Unemployed Man and His Family: The Effect of Unemployment upon the Status of the Man in Fifty-Nine Families* (New York: Dryden Press, 1949); and by E. Wright Bakke in *The Unem-*

ployed Worker: A Study of the Task of Making a Living Without a Job and *Citizens Without Work: A Study of the Effects of Unemployment upon the Workers and Social Relations and Practices* (New Haven: Yale University Press, 1940). The studies focus on male responses to economic dislocation, but close reading reveals much about women's roles as well. Two surveys of the impact of the Depression on working woman are *The Trained Women and the Economic Crisis: Employment and Unemployment Among a Selected Group of Business and Professional Women in New York City* (New York: American Woman's Association, 1931), and *Women Workers through the Depression: A Study of White Collar Employment Made by the American Woman's Association* by Lorine Pruette (New York: Macmillan, 1934). A mimeographed Works Progress Administration study of families in Dubuque, Iowa, "The Personal Side," presents the family (and female) response to deprivation in a smaller, midwestern city. A close look at these studies supports the notion of female labor intensification in the home of Ruth Milkman, "Women's Work and Economic Crisis: Some Lessons of the Great Depression," *Review of Radical Political Economics* 8 (Spring 1976). Glen Elder agreed and speculated on the generational impact of the Depression on young Oakland, California, men and women in *Children of the Great Depression: Social Change in Life Experience* (Chicago: University of Chicago Press, 1974). The white, urban focus of these studies is unmistakable.

A number of books published during the 1920s and 1930s and of more recent vintage span the female occupational spectrum, covering all or part of the period in broader chronological contexts. David M. Katzman's *Seven Days a Week: Women and Domestic Service in Industrializing America* (New York: Oxford University Press, 1978) traces household employment to the eve of the Depression. The interaction of cultural and demographic focus on work roles of ethnic women on the lower rungs of the economic ladder is the subject of "Why Women Work: A Comparison of Various Groups—Philadelphia, 1910-1930" by Barbara Klaczynska in *Labor History* 17 (Winter 1976). Julia Kirk Blackwilder describes the Depression experiences of black, white, and Chicana women in three urban areas in "Women in the Work Force: Atlanta, New Orleans, and San Antonio, 1930-1940," *Journal of Urban History* 4 (May 1978). The role of women in union organizing activities in the southern textile industry is graphically pictured in Vera Bush Weisbord's *A Rebel Life* (Bloomington, Ind.: University of Indiana Press, 1977). Philip Foner, *Women and the American Labor Movement after 1914* (New York: Free Press, 1980) gives a fine union overview of the subject during the 1920s and 1930s.

Waitresses and sales clerks are vividly described by Frances Donovan in *The Woman Who Waits* (Boston: Richard G. Badger, 1920) and *The Saleslady* (Chicago: University of Chicago Press, 1929). Her book *The Schoolma'am* (New York: Frederick A. Slokes, 1938) is less insightful and can be supplemented with appropriate sections from *The American Teacher: Evolution of a Professional in a Democracy* (New York: American Book Co., 1939). See chapter 4 of Lois Scharf's *To Work and To Wed: Female Employment, Feminism, and the Great Depression* (Westport, Conn.: Greenwood Press, 1980) on teachers during the twenties and thirties as well as other aspects of working women during the 1930s.

For a feminist analysis of nursing which includes trends during the twenties and thirties see *Hospitals, Paternalism, and the Role of the Nurse* (New York: Columbia University Press, 1976). Ray Lubove's *The Professional Altruist: The Emergence of Social Work As a Career, 1880-1930* (Cambridge, Mass.: Harvard University Press, 1965) is implicitly concerned with a feminized profession but ends before social work becomes a "growth industry." The retreat of women from medicine is recounted by Mary Roth Walsh in *Doctors Wanted: No Women Need Apply* (New Haven: Yale University Press, 1977). Scharf suggests that the career impulse suffered as a result of the Depression experience; Margaret Rossiter describes the efforts of female scientists to attain and maintain status in "Sexual Segregation in the Sciences: Some Data and a Model," *Signs* 4 (Spring 1978). In "Cookbooks and Law Books: The Hidden History of Career Women in Twentieth Century America," *Journal of Social History* 10 (Fall 1976), Frank Stricher argues that the career impulse did not dissipate after 1920.

More general studies of working women, descriptive and statistical, include Elizabeth Faulkner Baker's *Technology and Women's Work* (New York: Columbia University Press, 1965); Robert Smuts's *Women and Work in America* (New York: Columbia University Press, 1959); Valerie Kincard Oppenheimer's *The Female Labor Force in the United States: Demographic and Economic Factors Governing Its Growth and Changing Composition* (Berkeley: Institute of International Studies, 1970). A number of excellent collections of documents with useful introductions containing selections from this period include: *America's Working Women: A Documentary History, 1600 to the Present*, edited by Rosalyn Baxandall, Linda Gordon, and Susan Reverby (New York: Vintage Books, 1976); *Women in the American Economy: A Documentary History, 1615-1929*, edited by W. Elliott Brownlee and Mary M. Brownlee (New Haven: Yale University Press, 1976); *Black Women in White America: A Documentary History*, edited by Gerda Lerner (New York: Vintage Press, 1972). Recently published oral histories convey moving testimony from the 1930. Studs Terkel's *Hard Times* (New York: Pantheon Books, 1970); Alice Lynd's and Staughton Lynd's *Rank and File: Personal Histories by Working-Class Organizers* (Boston: Beacon Press, 1973); and Vivian Gornick's *The Romance of American Communism* (New York: Basic Books, 1977) contain the reminiscences of men and women. Jeanne Westin focuses solely on the female experience in *Making Do: How Women Survived the Depression* (Chicago: Follette, 1976).

Two recent documentary movies provide fine records of women's labor organizing activities in urban areas. *Union Maids* and *With Babies and Banners* do for activist women in Chicago and Flint, Michigan, forty years later what Farm Security Administration photographers did for rural women during the thirties. The former can be supplemented with the contemporary written accounts of activist women in industry in *I Am a Woman Worker*, edited by Andrea Taylor Horwich and Gladys L. Palmer (New York: Affiliated Schools for Workers, 1936); the latter, with Margaret Hagood's *Mothers of the South: Portraiture of the White Tenant Farm Woman* (Chapel Hill, N.C.: University of North Carolina Press, 1939). Women in town and country are sprinkled through the Federal Writers' Project's *These Are Our Lives* (Chapel Hill, N.C.: University of North Carolina Press, 1939). Women are represented more fully in a sequel, *Such As Us: Southern Voices of the Thirties* (New York: W. W. Norton, 1978).

Recent studies of popular culture, especially the movies, provide insights into the portrayal of women. Andrew Bergman took a quick look at prostitutes on film in the early thirties in *We're in the Money: Depression America and Its Films* (New York: New York University Press, 1971). Marjorie Rosen in *Popcorn Venus: Women, Movies and the American Dream* (New York: Avon Books, 1973), and Molly Haskell in *From Reverence to Rape: The Treatment of Women in the Movies* (New York: Penguin Books, 1974) span wider chronological periods and more varied, changing imagery before and after sound; before and after the Production Code. Both look at that special genre of the late thirties and forties, the woman's film. Just as so much research remains to be done on women, work, and the family in different class, ethnic, and geographic contexts, the portrayal of women in many areas of popular culture is yet to be examined—women as radio comediennes, women in soap operas, women in "best sellers," as well as the lives of the performers and creators themselves. For a start see Jacqueline D. St. John, "Sex Role Stereotyping in Early Broadcast History: The Career of Mary Margaret McBride," *Frontiers* 3 (Fall 1978): 31-38 and Marion J. Morton, "'My Dear, I Don't Give a Damn': Scarlet O'Hara and the Great Depression," *Frontiers* 5 (Fall 1980): 52-56.

Finally, bibliographic guides can be helpful in beginning investigation. See Marcella Cordova's and Rose Marie Raybal's compilation, *Bibliography on the Chicana* (Lakewood, Colo.: by the authors, 1973); Lenwood G. Davis, *The Black Woman in American Society: A Selected Annotated Bibliography* (Boston: G. K. Hall, 1975); Beatrice Medicine, "Bibliography on Native American Women," *The Indian Historian*, 8; Jayne Loader, "Women on the Left, 1906-1941: A Bibliography of Primary Resources," *University of Michigan Papers in Women's Studies* 11 (September 1975).

For Further Reading—An Update

One contribution to this anthology has since been published in monograph form: *Sisterhood Denied: Race, Gender, and Class in a New South Community* (Philadelphia: Temple University Press, 1985) by Dolores Janiewski. Julia Kirk Blackwilder also examines the crosscurrents of class and race in *Women of the Depression: Caste and Culture in San Antonio* (College Station: Texas A & M University Press, 1984). The complexities of labor organizing are evaluated by Sharon Hartman Strom in "Challenging Woman's Peace: Feminism, the Left, and Industrial Unionism in the 1930s," *Feminist Studies* (Summer 1983), and by Nina Asher's "Dorothy Jacobs Bellanca: Women Clothing Workers in the Runaway Shops," in *A Needle, A Bobbin, a Strike: Women Needleworkers in America,* Joan M. Jensen and Sue Davidson, eds. (Philadelphia: Temple University Press, 1984).

The economic condition of women has attracted only slight attention. Joan M. Jensen examines both the economic hardship and personal satisfaction of women in agriculture in "'I've Worked, I'm Not Afraid of Work': Farm Women in New Mexico, 1920–1940," in *New Mexico Historical Review* (January 1986). The experience of Native American women moving from self-sufficient agriculture to dependent commercial society is explored by Terry R. Reynolds in "Women, Pottery, and Economics at Acoma Pueblo" in Joan M. Jensen and Darlis A. Miller, eds., *New Mexico Women: Intercultural Perspectives* (Albuquerque: University of New Mexico Press, 1986).

Women's political activism during the interwar years has recently been more widely explored. Susan Ware examines a network of female social reformers and Democrats in the nation's capital in *Beyond Suffrage: Women in the New Deal* (Cambridge: Harvard University Press, 1981). Dorothy Johnson, "Organized Women as Lobbyists in the 1920s," *Capitol Studies* (Spring 1972), Virginia Sapiro, "Women, Citizenship and Nationality: Immigration Politics in the U.S.," *Politics and Society* (1984), and Paul Kleppur, "Were Women to Blame? Female Suffrage and Voter Turnout," *Journal of Interdisciplinary History* (Spring 1982), all discuss various aspects of women's political history. For studies on the state level, see Carole Nichols, *Votes and More for Women: Suffrage and After in Connecticut* (New York, 1983); Felice D.Gordon, *After Winning: The Legacy of the New Jersey Suffragists 1920–1947* (New Brunswick, N.J.: Rutgers University Press, 1986); Joan D. Carver, "First League of Women Voters in Florida: Its Troubled History" and Allen Morris, "Florida's First Women Candidates," both in *Florida Historical Quarterly* (April 1985); Joan M. Jensen, "'Disfranchisement is a Disgrace': Women and Politics in New Mexico, 1900–1940," in *New Mexico Historical Review* (January 1981); and Vinton M. Price, Jr., "Will Women Turn the Tide? Mississippi Women and the U.S. Senate Race," *Journal of Mississippi History* (August 1980).

Although obviously biographical, several contributors to *Without Precedent: The Life and Career of Eleanor Roosevelt*, edited by Joan Hoff Wilson and Marjorie Lightman (Bloomington: Indiana University Press, 1984), deal with women's political organizations and schisms. See especially "Training for Public Life: Eleanor Roosevelt and Women's Political Networks in the 1920s" by Elizabeth Israels Perry, "Eleanor Roosevelt and Democratic Politics: Women in the Post-Suffrage Era" by Susan Ware, and "Eleanor Roosevelt and Feminism" by Lois Scharf.

Index

About the Contributors

Susan Becker received her Ph.D. from Case Western Reserve University, where her research and writing focused on the National Woman's Party 1920-1940. She is associate professor of history at the University of Tennessee at Knoxville. Her study of the National Woman's Party and the Equal Rights Amendment was published by Greenwood Press in December 1981.

Julie Boddy received her Ph.D. from the State University of New York at Buffalo, where she has taught courses in photography and culture. She served as still photography consultant on the film *With Babies and Banners* and also served on the editorial board of the *Review of Radical Political Economy*. At present, she teaches at the University of the District of Columbia.

Estelle B. Freedman teaches history at Stanford University. She received her Ph.D. from Columbia University and is currently working on a collection of documents on Victorian women. She is the author of *Their Sisters Keepers: Women's Prison Reform in America, 1830-1930* (University of Michigan Press, 1981) and is a consulting editor for *Feminist Studies*.

Sherna Gluck teaches in the Women's Studies program at California State University, Long Beach, directs the Feminist History Research Project in Los Angeles, and is a consultant on oral history. She received a master's degree in Sociology from the University of California, Los Angeles. She has published a book of oral history interviews, *From Parlor to Prison* (New York: Vintage, 1976) and coedited with Joan M. Jensen a special issue of women's oral history for *Frontiers* 2 (1977). She is an active member of the West Coast Association of Women Historians.

Rosalinda González completed her dissertation on Chicanas in the labor force in the Comparative Cultures program at the University of California, Irvine. She is Assistant Professor at the University.

Dolores Janiewski recently completed her dissertation in history at Duke University on working women in Durham between 1880 and 1940. She is the author of "Making Common Cause: The Needlewomen of New York, 1831-69," *Signs* 1 (Spring 1976).

Joan M. Jensen teaches in the History department at New Mexico State University. She received her Ph.D. from the University of California, Los Angeles. In addition to coediting a special issue on Women's Oral History for *Frontiers* with Sherna Gluck, she is the author of "Native American Women and Agriculture: A Seneca Case Study," *Sex Roles: A Journal of Research* 3 (1977), and *With These Hands: Women Working on the Land* (Old Westbury, N.Y.: Feminist Press, 1981).

Norma Fain Pratt teaches history at Mount San Antonio College, Walnut, California, and at California State University, Los Angeles. She received her Ph.D. from the University of California, Los Angeles, in American Labor History. She is the author of *Morris Hillquit: A Political History of an American Jewish Socialist* (Westport, Conn.: Greenwood Press, 1979) and "Transitions in Judaism: Jewish American Women through the 1930s," *American Quarterly* 30 (Winter 1978): 681-702. She has been active in the Southwest Labor Studies Conference.

Mary P. Ryan is the author of the award-winning *Cradle of the Middle Class: The Family in Oneida County, New York, 1790-1865.* (New York: Cambridge University Press, 1981). Her articles on female reform and revivalist activities in antebellum America have appeared in scholarly journals. She teaches at the University of California, Irvine.

Lois Scharf teaches history at Case Western Reserve University where she received her Ph.D. She is the author of *To Work and To Wed: Female Employment, Feminism, and the Great Depression* (Westport, Conn.: Greenwood Press, 1980). She has been active in the Ohio Academy of History and Women Historians of Greater Cleveland and is presently executive director of National History Day.

Ruth Schwartz Cowan teaches history at the State University of New York at Stony Brook. She received her Ph.D. from Johns Hopkins University. She is the author of "The 'Industrial Revolution' in the Home: Household Technology and Social Change in the 1920s," *Technology and Culture* 17 (January 1976) and "The Washing Machine and the Working Wife: A Case Study of Technology and Social Change," in *Clio's Consciousness Raised: New Perspectives on the History of Women,* edited by Mary Hartman and Lois Banner (New York: Harper and Row, 1974). She has been active in the History of Science Society.

Rosalyn Terborg-Penn received her Ph.D. from Howard University for her dissertation, "Afro-Americans in the Struggle for Woman Suffrage." She has written several articles on black women and family history, and she coauthored *A Special Mission: The Story of Freedmen's Hospital.* She is associate professor of history at Morgan State University and active in the Association of Black Women Historians.

Winifred D. Wandersee teaches history at Hartwick College in New York. She received her Ph.D. from the University of Minnesota and is currently researching American women, children, and work. She has been active in Women Historians of the Midwest. Her doctoral dissertation, "Women, Work and Family Values, 1920-40," was published by Harvard University Press in Spring 1981.